Sociology Matters

Also available from McGraw-Hill
by Richard T. Schaefer
Sociology: A Brief Introduction, 13th edition (2018)
Sociology in Modules, 4th edition (2018)
Sociology and Your Life with P.O.W.E.R. Learning (2016),
co-authored with Robert Feldman

Sociology Matters

Seventh Edition

Richard T. Schaefer

DePaul University

SOCIOLOGY MATTERS, SEVENTH EDITION

Published by McGraw-Hill Education, 2 Penn Plaza, New York, NY 10121. Copyright © 2019 by McGraw-Hill Education. All rights reserved. Printed in the United States of America. Previous editions © 2014, 2012, and 2009. No part of this publication may be reproduced or distributed in any form or by any means, or stored in a database or retrieval system, without the prior written consent of McGraw-Hill Education, including, but not limited to, in any network or other electronic storage or transmission, or broadcast for distance learning.

Some ancillaries, including electronic and print components, may not be available to customers outside the United States.

This book is printed on acid-free paper.

2 3 4 5 6 7 8 9 LCR 21 20 19 18

ISBN 978-0-07-782327-6
MHID 0-07-782327-3

Portfolio Manager: *Jamie Laferrera*
Product Developer: *Alexander Preiss*
Marketing Manager: *Kaitlyn Lombardo*
Content Project Manager: *Maria McGreal*
Buyer: *Susan K. Culbertson*
Design: *MPS Limited*
Content Licensing Specialist: *Ann Marie Jannette*
Cover Image: *©Arthimedes/Shutterstock*
Compositor: *MPS Limited*

All credits appearing on page or at the end of the book are considered to be an extension of the copyright page.

Library of Congress Cataloging-in-Publication Data

Schaefer, Richard T., author.
    Sociology matters / Richard T. Schaefer, DePaul University.
    Seventh edition. | New York, NY : McGraw-Hill Education, [2019]
    LCCN 2017050812 | ISBN 9780077823276 (alk. paper)
    LCSH: Sociology. | Cultural relations. | Social stratification.
    LCC HM447 .S33 2019 | DDC 301–dc23 LC record available at https://lccn.loc.gov/2017050812

The Internet addresses listed in the text were accurate at the time of publication. The inclusion of a website does not indicate an endorsement by the authors or McGraw-Hill Education, and McGraw-Hill Education does not guarantee the accuracy of the information presented at these sites.

mheducation.com/highered

To my readers, may they benefit from learning that sociology does matter.

About the Author

Richard T. Schaefer: Professor, DePaul University
BA Northwestern University
MA, PhD University of Chicago

Growing up in Chicago at a time when neighborhoods were going through transitions in ethnic and racial composition, Richard T. Schaefer found himself increasingly intrigued by what was happening, how people were reacting, and how these changes were affecting neighborhoods and people's jobs. His interest in social issues caused him to gravitate to sociology courses at Northwestern University, where he eventually received a BA in sociology.

"Originally as an undergraduate I thought I would go on to law school and become a lawyer. But after taking a few sociology courses, I found myself wanting to learn more about what sociologists studied, and fascinated by the kinds of questions they raised." This fascination led him to obtain his MA and PhD in sociology from the University of Chicago. Dr. Schaefer's continuing interest in race relations led him to write his master's thesis on the membership of the Ku Klux Klan and his doctoral thesis on racial prejudice and race relations in Great Britain.

Dr. Schaefer went on to become a professor of sociology at DePaul University in Chicago. In 2004 he was named to the Vincent DePaul professorship in recognition of his undergraduate teaching and scholarship. He has taught introductory sociology for over 35 years to students in colleges, adult education programs, nursing programs, and even a maximum-security prison. Dr. Schaefer's love of teaching is apparent in his interaction with his students. "I find myself constantly learning from the students who are in my classes and from reading what they write. Their insights into the material we read or current events that we discuss often become part of future course material and sometimes even find their way into my writing."

Dr. Schaefer is the author of *Sociology in Modules*, fourth edition (McGraw-Hill, 2018), the thirteenth edition of *Sociology: A Brief Introduction* (McGraw-Hill, 2018), the thirteenth edition of *Sociology* (McGraw-Hill, 2012), and, with Robert Feldman, *Sociology and Your Life with P.O.W.E.R. Learning* (2016). He is also the author of *Racial and Ethnic Groups,* now in its fifteenth edition (2018), *Racial and Ethnic Diversity in the USA* (first edition, 2014), and *Race and Ethnicity in the United States* (ninth edition, 2018), all published by Pearson. Together with William Zellner, he coauthored the ninth edition of *Extraordinary Groups,* published by Waveland Press in 2015.

Dr. Schaefer served as the general editor of the three-volume *Encyclopedia of Race, Ethnicity, and Society,* published by Sage in 2008. These books have been translated into Chinese, Japanese, Portuguese, and Spanish, as well as adapted for use in Canadian colleges.

Dr. Schaefer's articles and book reviews have appeared in many journals, including *American Journal of Sociology; Phylon: A Review of Race and Culture; Contemporary Sociology; Sociology and Social Research; Sociological Quarterly;* and *Teaching Sociology.* He served as president of the Midwest Sociological Society in 1994–1995.

Dr. Schaefer's advice to students is to "look at the material and make connections to your own life and experiences. Sociology will make you a more attentive observer of how people in groups interact and function. It will also make you more aware of people's different needs and interests—and perhaps more ready to work for the common good, while still recognizing the individuality of each person."

Preface

Sociology has been my life's work for several decades. In the classroom and in the pages of my textbooks, I have tried to spark students' interest in the discipline by showing them its real-life implications. My aim has been to convince students that sociology is more than just another academic pursuit, an exercise in scholarship for the sake of scholarship. Sociology illuminates the world around us—our families, schools, neighborhoods, and other familiar institutions we have lived with all our lives. It puts into larger perspective our culture and our socialization—the way we come to be the way we are. Sociology makes us think deeply about the divide between ourselves and those of different races, classes, and ethnicities. It forces us to recognize the effects of power, technological advances, electronic media, and the increasingly rapid process of social change on our own lives. Sociology matters—to you, me, and everyone with a stake in the society we live in.

This concise volume stresses the same theme, in fewer pages and with fewer illustrations and study aids. *Sociology Matters* is intended for instructors who desire an especially short, relatively inexpensive introductory text. This text covers the essential content in *Sociology: A Brief Introduction,* twelfth edition, in much the same depth. Its 11 chapters can be covered easily in a quarter- or semester-long course, together with other materials instructors might wish to add.

Major Emphases

Like the brief twelfth edition of *Sociology,* this volume includes comprehensive, balanced coverage of the major theoretical perspectives. Chapter 1 introduces, defines, and contrasts the functionalist, conflict, and interactionist perspectives, as well as the increasingly important feminist perspective. Later chapters use these distinctive viewpoints to explore topics such as deviance (Chapter 4); social stratification (Chapter 5); race and ethnicity (Chapter 6); gender (Chapter 7); social institutions (Chapters 8 and 9); population, community, health, and the environment (Chapter 10); and social movements, social change, and technology (Chapter 11).

This volume also includes strong coverage of gender, race, ethnicity, and social class. Three entire chapters are devoted to these topics: Chapter 5, on stratification in the United States and global inequality; Chapter 6, on race and ethnicity; and Chapter 7, on gender. Related discussions appear throughout the book. For instance, Chapter 3 examines race and gender as ascribed statuses; Chapter 4, racial profiling and the perceived seriousness of white-collar crime; Chapter 10, the connection between health and a person's social class, race, ethnicity, and gender; and Chapter 11, the role of gender in social movements.

Finally, this volume includes considerable cross-cultural coverage. Chapter 2 covers the development of culture around the world. Chapter 4 covers international crime rates. Chapter 5 treats social stratification from a global perspective, including coverage of world systems analysis, dependency theory, modernization theory, the development of multinational corporations, and the global economy. Chapter 7 covers cross-cultural differences in gender roles. Chapter 8 takes a global view of the family. Chapter 10, which opens with a vignette on the Gulf Coast oil spill, treats global environmental issues. And Chapter 11 covers global social change.

Special Features

This volume offers a variety of learning aids designed to help students understand and review basic concepts, including:

- Chapter outline
- Chapter-opening vignette with chapter overview
- Use Your Sociological Imagination exercises, which prompt students to apply their knowledge of sociology to the world around them
- Tables and figures, some with sticker-style captions and Think About It questions
- Two series of tables, Tracking Sociological Perspectives and Summing Up, which aid students in their review of chapter content
- Photographs and cartoons
- Online Learning Center icons, which alert students to relevant material on the book's companion website
- Boldfaced key terms
- *Sociology Matters* sections at the end of each chapter, which point out the relevance of a chapter's content to students' lives
- Numbered 10-point chapter summary
- End-of-chapter key terms list with page references
- End-of-book Appendix, "Careers in Sociology"
- End-of-book glossary with page references

What's New in the Seventh Edition?

The most important changes in this edition include the following:

CHAPTER 1   THE SOCIOLOGICAL VIEW

- Chapter-opening example about fake news
- Example of different sports around the world to introduce term "sociological imagination"
- Example of minimum wage to demonstrate difference between social sciences
- Subsection on Queer Theory in section on the conflict perspective
- "Use Your Sociological Imagination" questions about suicide and social and cultural capital
- Expanded table, "Comparing Theoretical Perspectives"

CHAPTER 2   CULTURE AND SOCIALIZATION

- Expanded definition and discussion of the term "ethnocentrism"
- Expanded discussion of the concept of subcultures
- "Use Your Sociological Imagination" question about the influence of gender on research results
- Example of importance of peer groups to adolescent Syrian refugees
- Figure 2-3, Media Profiles of 8- to 12-Year-Olds: Daily Time Spent with Each Type of Media
- Updated discussion of workplace socialization

CHAPTER 3   SOCIAL INTERACTION, GROUPS, AND SOCIAL STRUCTURE

- Chapter-opening photo showing Stanford Prison Experiment
- Additional details in Figure 3-1, Social Statuses, and Figure 3-2, Social Structure: An Overview
- Enhanced coverage of role exit, with Key Term treatment
- Enhanced coverage of social networks
- Cartoon about Gemeinschaft vs. Gesellschaft
- "Use Your Sociological Imagination" question about bureaucracy
- Enhanced coverage of the importance of ascribed statuses in formal organizations

CHAPTER 4   DEVIANCE AND SOCIAL CONTROL

- "Think About It" question for Table 4-2, Sociological Approaches to Deviance
- Enhanced coverage of white-collar crime
- Enhanced coverage of hate crime
- Enhanced discussion of cybercrime, including Key Term treatment

CHAPTER 5   STRATIFICATION IN THE UNITED STATES AND GLOBAL INEQUALITY

- Enhanced coverage of human trafficking, including Table 5-1, Human Trafficking Report
- Enhanced discussion of conspicuous consumption
- "Think About It" question for Table 5-2, Perspectives on Social Stratification
- Updated and enhanced discussion of income and wealth
  - Updated and enhanced discussion of poverty
- Enhanced discussion of the impact of ethnicity and race on social mobility

CHAPTER 6   INEQUALITY BY RACE AND ETHNICITY

- Chapter-opening photo showing middle-school-age children
- "Use Your Sociological Imagination" question about the effects of social networking on prejudice and discrimination
- Enhanced coverage of immigration to the United States and of functions of immigration
- Expanded coverage of refugees, including Table 6-2, Sources of Refugees, 2005 and 2015
- Expanded coverage of the labeling perspective, including discussion of stop and frisk
- Key Term treatment of "refugee" and "remittances"

CHAPTER 7   INEQUALITY BY GENDER

- Updated discussion of men's gender roles
- "Think About It" question for Table 7-1, An Experiment in Gender Norm Violation by College Students
- Figure 7-2, Weekly Time (in Hours) Spent on Primary Activities, by Gender
- Subsection "Intersectionality" in main section on sociological perspectives on gender
- Enhanced detail and "Think About It" question for Figure 7-1, Matrix of Domination
- Research projections on when White, Black, and Latino women will reach salary parity with White men
- Key Term treatment of "intersectionality," "matrix of domination"

CHAPTER 8   SOCIAL INSTITUTIONS: FAMILY AND RELIGION

- Entirely revamped material on human sexuality, now titled Labeling and Human Sexuality
- "Use Your Sociological Imagination" questions about sociological perspectives on education institutions, viewing sexual identity as a continuum
- Figure 8-1, Living Arrangements of Adults Age 18 and Over, 2014
- Key Term treatment of "gender identity" and "sexual identity"

CHAPTER 9   SOCIAL INSTITUTIONS: EDUCATION, GOVERNMENT, AND THE ECONOMY

- "Use Your Sociological Imagination" questions about sociological functions of education, effects of tracking, schools as bureaucracies, rational-legal authority
- Enhanced information in Figure 9-1, Annual Median Earnings by Educational Level, Workers Aged 25-34
- "Think About It" question for Table 9-1, Sociological Perspectives on Education
- Figure 9-3, The World's Largest Economies
- Discussion of the informal economy
- Main section, "Sharing Economies," with Figure 9-4, Foreign-Born Workers in the United States, by Region, 2012
- Key Term treatment of "informal economy," "precarious work," "sharing economy"

CHAPTER 10   POPULATION, COMMUNITY, HEALTH, AND THE ENVIRONMENT

- "Think About It" question for Figure 10-1, Infant Mortality Rate in Selected Countries
- Enhanced discussion of labeling perspective on health and illness
- Discussion of Flint, Michigan, water crisis as an example of the need for environmental justice
- "Use Your Sociological Imagination" questions about pollution, as well as the connection between human and physical environments

CHAPTER 11   SOCIAL MOVEMENTS, SOCIAL CHANGE, AND TECHNOLOGY

- Figure 11-1, Declining Drive-Ins; Figure 11-2, Walking to Work; Figure 11-3, The Changing U.S. Economy, 1999-2012
- Enhanced discussion of technology and social change

Teaching and Learning with Sociology Matters

A wealth of complimentary teaching and learning resources is available to students and instructors who use *Sociology Matters.* Students will benefit from the free study aids accessible to them through McGraw-Hill Connect, including an online glossary and self-quizzes containing multiple-choice and true-false questions.

connect The seventh edition of *Sociology Matters* is now available online with Connect, McGraw-Hill Education's integrated assignment and assessment platform. Connect also offers SmartBook for the new edition, which is the first adaptive reading experience proven to improve grades and help students study more effectively. All of the title's website and ancillary content is also available through Connect, including:

- A full Test Bank of multiple-choice questions that test students on central concepts and ideas in each chapter.
- An Instructor's Manual for each chapter with full chapter outlines, sample test questions, and discussion topics.
- Lecture Slides for instructor use in class

Instructors may also take advantage of two new offerings, McGraw-Hill's Create™, a custom publishing system, and CourseSmart, an adaptive learning system available through McGraw-Hill Connect.

create Design your own ideal course materials with McGraw-Hill's **Create™, http://www .mcgrawhillcreate.com.** Rearrange or omit chapters, combine material from other sources, upload your syllabus or any other content you have written to make the perfect resource for your students. Search thousands of leading McGraw-Hill textbooks to find the best content for your students; then arrange it to fit your teaching style. You can even personalize your book's appearance by selecting the cover and adding your name, school, and course information. When you order a Create book, you receive a complimentary review copy. Get a printed copy in 3 to 5 business days or an electronic copy (e-Comp) via e-mail in about an hour. Register today at **http://www.mcgrawhillcreate.com** and craft your course resources to match the way you teach.

CourseSmart offers thousands of the most commonly adopted textbooks across hundreds of courses from a wide variety of higher education publishers. It is the only place for faculty to review and compare the full text of a textbook online, providing immediate access without the environmental impact of requesting a printed exam copy. At CourseSmart, students can save up to 50 percent off the cost of a printed

book, reduce their impact on the environment, and gain access to power-ful Web tools for learning, including full text search, notes and highlight-ing, and e-mail tools for sharing notes among classmates. Learn more at **www.coursesmart.com.**

As a full-service publisher of quality educational products, McGraw-Hill does much more than just sell textbooks to your students. We create and publish an extensive array of supplements to support instruction on your campus. Orders of new (versus used) textbooks help us to defray the cost of developing such supplements, which is substantial. Please consult your local McGraw-Hill representative to learn about the availability of the supplements that accompany Sociology Matters. *If you are not sure who your representative is, you can find him or her by using the Rep Locator at www.mhhe.com.*

Acknowledgments

Elaine Silverstein, who collaborated with me on several editions of my longer introductory textbooks for undergraduates, brought her experi-ence and knowledge to the seventh edition of *Sociology Matters.*

I deeply appreciate the contributions my editors made to this book. Art Pomponio and Erin Melloy helped to shape this fresh approach to sociology for undergraduates. This edition also benefits from the continu-ing contributions made by Gina Boedeker, Managing Director, Products and Markets for Sociology, Alexander Preiss, Product Developer, and Rhona Robbin, Director of Development for Sociology, who have lent their expertise and experience to this book for several editions.

As is evident from these acknowledgments, the preparation of a text-book is truly a team effort. The most valuable member of this effort con-tinues to be my wife, Sandy, who provides the support so necessary to my creative and scholarly activities.

I have had the good fortune to be able to introduce students to soci-ology for many years. Those students have been enormously helpful in spurring my own sociological imagination. In ways I can fully appreciate but cannot fully acknowledge, their questions in class and queries in the hallway have found their way into this textbook.

Richard T. Schaefer
schaeferrt@aol.com

Academic Reviewers

Many sociologists reviewed this book and offered constructive and thorough evaluations of its content. I would like to thank the following reviewers for their thoughtful comments on the sixth edition manuscript and its features:

Krisler Bailey
Tarrant County College

Carolyn Benson
Tarrant County College

Marketa Cawood
Hopkinsville Community College

Jill K. Doerner
University of Rhode Island

Dr. Mark Eldridge
*Neosho County Community
College*

Colette G. Ellinghouse
*Ivy Tech Community College,
South Bend*

Gina Finelli
Anne Arundel Community College

Mehdi Haghshenas
University of Texas at Austin

Dr. Gretchen Hester
Houston Community College

Bonniejean Alford Hinde
College of DuPage

Myron Syvelle Hopes
Houston Community College

Matthew Howell
Ivy Tech Community College

Patricia R. Johnson
Houston Community College

Tina Yarbrough Jones
San Antonio College

Arnold Korotkin
Montclair State University

Dr. Alison M. Lacny
*Moraine Valley Community
College*

Janet Lanci
Charter Oak College

Phil Lewis
University at Albany SUNY

William H Lockhart
McLennan Community College

Maryhelen MacInnes
*Community College of Rhode
Island*

Dr. Debra Marshall
Eastern Florida State College

Jon McCarthy
SUNY Adirondack

Rodney A. McDanel
Ivy Tech Community College

Donna Williams Miller
University of Texas at San Antonio

Dr. Michael Ostrowsky
Southern Utah University

Barbara Katz Rothman
Baruch College CUNY

Theresa Lee Schrantz
Tarrant County College

Leonard A. Steverson
Flagler College

Jolene Sundlie
Saint Paul College

Linda Tobin
Austin Community College

Nicole Tortoris
College of the Desert

Niki Weller
Indiana University Kokomo

Erica Yeager
Anne Arundel Community College

McGraw-Hill Connect® is a highly reliable, easy-to-use homework and learning management solution that utilizes learning science and award-winning adaptive tools to improve student results.

Homework and Adaptive Learning

- Connect's assignments help students contextualize what they've learned through application, so they can better understand the material and think critically.

- Connect will create a personalized study path customized to individual student needs through SmartBook®.

- SmartBook helps students study more efficiently by delivering an interactive reading experience through adaptive highlighting and review.

Connect's Impact on Retention Rates, Pass Rates, and Average Exam Scores

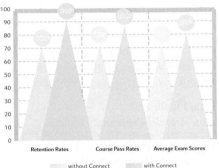

without Connect   with Connect

Over **7 billion questions** have been answered, making McGraw-Hill Education products more intelligent, reliable, and precise.

Using **Connect** improves retention rates by **19.8** percentage points, passing rates by **12.7** percentage points, and exam scores by **9.1** percentage points.

73% of instructors who use **Connect** require it; instructor satisfaction increases by 28% when **Connect** is required.

Quality Content and Learning Resources

- Connect content is authored by the world's best subject matter experts, and is available to your class through a simple and intuitive interface.

- The Connect eBook makes it easy for students to access their reading material on smartphones and tablets. They can study on the go and don't need Internet access to use the eBook as a reference, with full functionality.

- Multimedia content such as videos, simulations, and games drive student engagement and critical thinking skills.

Robust Analytics and Reporting

©Hero Images/Getty Images

- Connect Insight® generates easy-to-read reports on individual students, the class as a whole, and on specific assignments.

- The Connect Insight dashboard delivers data on performance, study behavior, and effort. Instructors can quickly identify students who struggle and focus on material that the class has yet to master.

- Connect automatically grades assignments and quizzes, providing easy-to-read reports on individual and class performance.

Impact on Final Course Grade Distribution

	without Connect	with Connect
A	22.9%	31.0%
B	27.4%	34.3%
C	22.9%	18.7%
D	12.4%	6.1%
F	14.2%	9.9%

More students earn **As** and **Bs** when they use **Connect**.

Trusted Service and Support

- Connect integrates with your LMS to provide single sign-on and automatic syncing of grades. Integration with Blackboard®, D2L®, and Canvas also provides automatic syncing of the course calendar and assignment-level linking.

- Connect offers comprehensive service, support, and training throughout every phase of your implementation.

- If you're looking for some guidance on how to use Connect, or want to learn tips and tricks from super users, you can find tutorials as you work. Our Digital Faculty Consultants and Student Ambassadors offer insight into how to achieve the results you want with Connect.

www.mheducation.com/connect

Brief Contents

Contents

The Sociological View

©Hill Street Studios/Blend Images

One presidential candidate operated a child sex ring located over Comet Ping Pong, a pizzeria in Washington, D.C. Another received the endorsement of Pope Francis. NASA confirms that the world will experience six days of total darkness. A women wearing heavy makeup was mistaken for a clown and attacked by an angry mob.

All these accounts are false, circulated online to ridicule a public figure or just to profit from web advertisements. Yet stories like these are part of our social world today, and people often act on them as if they were true. They stop their friends and family members and say, "Have you heard . . . ?" or occasionally respond in potentially dangerous ways. For example, in 2016, a 28-year-old man marched into the pizza restaurant named above armed with an assault rifle to "investigate" the phony story about a sex ring.

Sociologists might view this development in many different ways. First, they might look at what groups tend to accept or share dubious online "news" accounts. Does the content of a story—either liberal or conservative—relate to other social characteristics of a group? Second, sociologists might try to identify the characteristics of people who consume little news at all or who have redefined news in a very limited way. For example, what groups think of news only as the events in their own lives and the lives of favorite celebrities? And third, what is the significance of this social phenomenon of "fake news" for people whose limited online access does not allow them to select what they follow? In other words, how do limits on Internet access affect people?

Whatever the subject, sociologists study social patterns that are shared by many people. This focus on the group rather than on the individual is a distinguishing feature of sociology. As the sociologist C. Wright Mills wrote more than half a century ago, if one person is unemployed, his difficulty is a personal problem, but if thousands of people are unemployed, their difficulty is a social problem. Sociologists look for the root causes of such social patterns in the way society is organized and governed (Mills [1959] 2000a).

As a field of study, sociology is extremely broad in scope. You'll see throughout this book the tremendous range of topics sociologists investigate—from tattooing to tweeting, from neighborhood groups to global economic patterns, from peer pressure to class consciousness. Sociologists look at how other people influence your behavior; how the government, religion, and the economy affect you; and how you yourself affect others. These aren't just academic questions. Sociology matters because it illuminates your life and your world, whether you are going to school, working for pay, or raising a family.

This first chapter introduces sociology as a social science, one that is characterized by a special skill called the *sociological imagination*. We'll meet four pioneering thinkers—Émile Durkheim, Max Weber, Karl Marx, and W. E. B. DuBois—and discuss the concepts and theoretical perspectives that grew out of their work. We'll see how sociologists use the scientific method to investigate the many questions they pose. Sociologists use surveys, ethnographic studies, experiments, and existing sources in their research; they often wrestle with ethical issues that arise during their studies. We'll examine some practical uses for their research at the end of the chapter.

What Is Sociology?

Sociology is the scientific study of social behavior and human groups. It focuses primarily on the influence of social relationships on people's attitudes and behavior and on how societies are established and change. This textbook deals with such varied topics as families, the workplace, street gangs, business firms, political parties, genetic engineering, schools, religions, and labor unions. It is concerned with love, poverty, conformity, discrimination, illness, technology, and community.

THE SOCIOLOGICAL IMAGINATION

In attempting to understand social behavior, sociologists rely on a unique type of creative thinking. C. Wright Mills described such thinking as the *sociological imagination*—an awareness of the relationship between an individual and the wider society, both today and in the past. This awareness allows all of us (not just sociologists) to comprehend the links between our immediate, personal social settings and the remote, impersonal social world that surrounds us and helps to shape us (Mills [1959] 2000a).

A key element in the sociological imagination is the ability to view one's own society as an outsider would, rather than only from the perspective of personal experiences and cultural biases. Consider something as simple as sporting events. On college campuses in the United States, thousands of students cheer well-trained football players. In parts of South America and the Caribbean, spectators gather around two cages, each holding a finch. The covers are lifted, and the owner of the first bird to sing 50 songs wins a trophy, a cash prize, and great prestige. In speed singing as in football, eager spectators debate the merits of their favorites and bet on the outcome of the events. Yet what is considered a normal sporting event in one part of the world is considered unusual in another part (Rueb 2015).

The sociological imagination allows us to go beyond personal experiences and observations to understand broader public issues. Divorce, for example, is unquestionably a personal hardship for the partners who split apart. However, C. Wright Mills advocated using the sociological imagination to view divorce not as simply an individual's personal problem but rather as a societal concern. Using this perspective, we can see that an increase in the divorce rate actually redefines a major social institution—the family. Today's households frequently include stepparents and half-siblings whose parents have divorced and remarried. Through the complexities of the blended family, this private concern becomes a public issue that affects schools, government agencies, businesses, and religious institutions.

The sociological imagination is an empowering tool. It allows us to look beyond a limited understanding of things to see the world and its people in a new way and through a broader lens than we might otherwise use. It may be as simple as understanding why a roommate prefers country music to hip-hop, or it may open up a whole different way of understanding whole populations. For example, in the aftermath of the terrorist attacks on the United States on September 11, 2001, many citizens wanted to understand how Muslims throughout the world perceived their country, and why. From time to time this textbook will offer you the chance to exercise your own sociological imagination in a variety of situations. We'll begin with one that may be close to home for you.

You are walking down the street in your city or hometown. Looking around, you can't help noticing that half or more of the people you see are overweight. How do you explain your observation? If you were C. Wright Mills, how do you think you would explain it?

SOCIOLOGY AND THE SOCIAL SCIENCES

Is sociology a science? The term *science* refers to the body of knowledge obtained by methods based on systematic observation. Like researchers in other scientific disciplines, sociologists engage in organized, systematic study of phenomena (in this case, human behavior) in order to enhance understanding. All scientists, whether studying mushrooms or murderers, attempt to collect precise information through methods of study that are as objective as possible. They rely on careful recording of observations and accumulation of data.

Of course, there is a great difference between sociology and physics, between psychology and astronomy. For this reason, the sciences are commonly divided into natural and social sciences. *Natural science* is the study of the physical features of nature and the ways in which they interact and change. Astronomy, biology, chemistry, geology, and physics are all natural sciences. *Social science* is the study of various aspects of human society. The social sciences include sociology, anthropology, economics, history, psychology, and political science.

These social science disciplines have a common focus on the social behavior of people, yet each has a particular orientation. Anthropologists usually study past cultures and preindustrial societies that continue today, as well as the origins of men and women. Economists explore the ways in which people produce and exchange goods and services, along with money and other resources. Historians are concerned with the peoples and events of the past and their significance for us today. Political scientists study international relations, the workings of government, and the exercise of power and authority. Psychologists investigate personality and individual behavior. So what does *sociology* focus on? It emphasizes the influence that society has on people's attitudes and behavior and the ways in which people shape society. Humans are social animals; therefore, sociologists examine our social relationships scientifically.

Let's consider how different social scientists might consider the minimum wage and efforts to raise it. Historians would stress that the contemporary effort is the latest in a long list of labor reforms dating back to the 1800s. These include restrictions on child labor as well as health and safety regulations.

Economists would use quantitative methods to evaluate whether a rise in the minimum wage would help or hurt workers overall. In contrast, anthropologists would examine how minimum wage laws work in different types of societies. For example, Bangladesh, one of the world's largest apparel exporters, raised its minimum wage for garment workers to about $68 per month in 2013. Combined with the rise in wages, what was the impact of the increase in the number of women workers? Further, in a country where labor laws are weakly enforced, what were the effects on young workers age 10 to 17 (Asadullah and Wahhaj 2016)?

Psychologists would be interested in how increased income, especially among low-income workers, affects emotional and behavioral disorders. Would self-esteem improve as wages grew? And political scientists, aware of the strong support for an increase in the minimum wage among the general public, would focus on how policy makers frame the issue. Would there be efforts to make legislation bipartisan? Would it be accompanied by protections for small businesses, which often feel they can least afford wage hikes? Would lobbyists from certain groups, such as restaurant franchise operations, try to protect their special interests?

What approach might sociologists take? Many aspects of the issue would be of interest. Is it possible for a family to live on the current minimum wage, and if not, what wage is practical? How is the Fight for 15 movement (as in a $15 per hour minimum wage) organized? What are the long-term effects on the education opportunities for the children of low-income workers? Would low-paying jobs be less stigmatized if people earned closer to a living wage?

Sociologists put their sociological imaginations to work on a variety of subjects—including gender, the family, human ecology, and religion. Throughout this textbook, you will see how sociologists develop theories and conduct research to study and better understand societies. And you will be encouraged to use your own sociological imagination to examine the United States (and other societies) from the viewpoint of a respectful but questioning outsider.

SOCIOLOGY AND COMMON SENSE

Sociology focuses on the study of human behavior. Yet we all have experience with human behavior and at least some knowledge of it. All of us might well have theories about why people buy lottery tickets, for example, or why people become homeless. Our theories and opinions typically come from "common sense"—that is, from our experiences and conversations, from what we read, from what we see on television, and so forth.

In our daily lives, we rely on common sense to get us through many unfamiliar situations. However, this commonsense knowledge, while sometimes accurate, is not always reliable, because it rests on commonly held beliefs rather than on systematic analysis of facts. It was once considered "common sense" to accept the idea that the earth was flat—a view rightly questioned by Pythagoras and Aristotle. Incorrect commonsense notions are not just a part of the distant past; they remain with us today.

Contrary to the common notion that women tend to be chatty compared to men, researchers have found little difference between the sexes in terms of their talkativeness. Over a five-year period they placed unobtrusive microphones on 396 college students in various fields, at campuses in Mexico as well as the United States. They found that both men and women spoke about 16,000 words per day (Mehl et al. 2007).

Similarly, common sense tells us that today, violent crime holds communities on the border between the United States and Mexico in a kind of death grip, creating an atmosphere of lawlessness reminiscent of the old Wild West. Based on news accounts of political candidates and elected officials calling for massive deportations and efforts to secure the border, this assertion may sound reasonable; however, it is not true. Although some communities in Mexico have fallen under the control of drug cartels, the story is different on the U.S. side of the border. All available crime data—including murder, extortion, robbery, and kidnapping rates, whether reported or documented in victim surveys—show that in the hundred-mile-deep border area stretching from San Diego to Brownsville, Texas, crime rates are significantly lower than in similar U.S. cities outside the area. Furthermore, the crime rate has been dropping faster near the border than in other similar-size U.S. communities for at least the last 15 years (Aguillar 2016; Johnson and Gomez 2012).

Like other social scientists, sociologists do not accept something as a fact because "everyone knows it." Instead, each piece of information must be tested and recorded, then analyzed in relation to other data. Sociologists rely on scientific studies in order to describe and understand a social environment. At times, the findings of sociologists may seem like common sense, because they deal with familiar facets of everyday life. The difference is that such findings have been *tested* by researchers. Common sense now tells us that the earth is round. However, that particular commonsense notion is based on centuries of scientific work that began with the breakthroughs made by Pythagoras and Aristotle.

What Is Sociological Theory?

Why do people die by suicide? One traditional commonsense answer is that people inherit the desire to kill themselves. Another view is that sunspots drive people to take their own lives. These explanations may not seem especially convincing to contemporary researchers, but they represent beliefs widely held as recently as 1900.

Sociologists are not particularly interested in why any one individual completes suicide; they are more concerned with identifying the social forces that systematically cause some people to take their own lives. In order to undertake this research, sociologists develop a theory that offers a general explanation of suicidal behavior.

We can think of theories as attempts to explain events, forces, materials, ideas, or behavior in a comprehensive manner. Within sociology, a *theory* is a set of statements that seeks to explain problems, actions, or behavior. An effective theory may have both explanatory and predictive power. That is, it can help us to see the relationships among seemingly isolated phenomena, as well as to understand how one type of change in an environment leads to other changes.

The World Health Organization (2010) estimates that nearly 1 million people die by suicide each year. More than a hundred years ago, a sociologist tried to look at suicide data scientifically. Émile Durkheim ([1897] 1951) developed a highly original theory about the relationship between suicide and social factors. He was primarily concerned not with the personalities of individual suicide victims but rather with suicide *rates* and how they varied from country to country. As a result, when he looked at the number of reported suicides in France, England, and Denmark in 1869, he noted the total population of each country so that he could determine the rate of suicide in each. He found that whereas England had only 67 reported suicides per million inhabitants, France had 135 per million and Denmark had 277 per million. The question then became: "Why did Denmark have a comparatively high rate of reported suicides?"

Durkheim went much deeper into his investigation of suicide rates; the result was his landmark work *Suicide,* published in 1897. He refused to automatically accept unproven explanations regarding suicide, including the beliefs that cosmic forces or inherited tendencies caused such deaths. Instead, he focused on such problems as the cohesiveness or lack of cohesiveness of religious, social, and occupational groups.

Durkheim's research suggested that suicide, while a solitary act, is related to group life. Protestants had much higher suicide rates than Catholics; the unmarried had much higher rates than married people; soldiers were more likely to take their lives than civilians. In addition, there seemed to be higher rates of suicide in times of peace than in times of war and revolution, and in times of economic instability and recession rather than in times of prosperity. Durkheim concluded that the suicide rate of a society reflected the extent to which people were or were not integrated into the group life of the society.

Émile Durkheim, like many other social scientists, developed a theory to explain how individual behavior can be understood within a social context. He pointed out the influence of groups and societal forces on what had always been viewed as a highly personal act. Clearly, Durkheim offered a more *scientific* explanation for the causes of suicide than that of sunspots or inherited tendencies. His theory has predictive power, since it suggests that suicide rates will rise or fall in conjunction with certain social and economic changes.

Of course, a theory—even the best of theories—is not a final statement about human behavior. Durkheim's theory of suicide is no exception. Sociologists continue to examine factors that contribute to differences in suicide rates around the world and to a particular society's rate of suicide. In Las Vegas, for example, sociologists have observed that the chances of dying by suicide are strikingly high—twice as high as in the United States as a whole. Noting Durkheim's emphasis on the relationship between suicide and social isolation, researchers have suggested that Las Vegas's rapid growth and constant influx of tourists have undermined the community's sense of permanence, even among longtime residents. Although gambling—or more accurately, losing while gambling—may seem a likely precipitating factor in suicides there, careful study of the data has allowed researchers to dismiss that explanation. What happens in Vegas may stay in Vegas, but the sense of community cohesiveness that the rest of the country enjoys may be lacking (Wray et al. 2008, 2011).

The Development of Sociology

Use Your Sociological Imagination

If you were Durkheim's successor in his research on suicide, how would you investigate the factors that may explain the increase in suicide rates among young people in the United States today?

People have always been curious about sociological matters—such as how we get along with others, what we do for a living, and whom we select as our leaders. Philosophers and religious authorities of ancient and medieval societies made countless observations about human behavior. They did not test or verify their observations scientifically; nevertheless, those observations often became the foundation for moral codes. Several of the early social philosophers predicted that a systematic study of human behavior would one day emerge. Beginning in the 19th century, European theorists made pioneering contributions to the development of a science of human behavior.

EARLY THINKERS: COMTE, MARTINEAU, AND SPENCER

The 19th century was an unsettled time in France. The French monarchy had been deposed in the revolution of 1789, and Napoleon had subsequently suffered defeat in his effort to conquer Europe. Amid this chaos, philosophers considered how society might be improved. Auguste Comte (1798–1857), credited with being the most influential of the philosophers of the early 1800s, believed that a theoretical science of society and a systematic investigation of behavior were needed to improve French society. He coined the term *sociology* to apply to the science of human behavior.

Writing in the 1800s, Comte feared that the excesses of the French Revolution had permanently impaired France's stability. Yet he hoped that the systematic study of social behavior would eventually lead to more rational human interactions. In Comte's hierarchy of sciences, sociology was at the top. He called it the "queen," and its practitioners "scientist-priests." This French theorist did not simply give sociology its name; he also presented a rather ambitious challenge to the fledgling discipline.

Scholars learned of Comte's works largely through translations by the English sociologist Harriet Martineau (1802–1876). As a sociologist, Martineau was a pathbreaker in her own right. She offered insightful observations of the customs and social practices of both her native Britain and the United States. Martineau's book *Society in America* ([1837] 1962) examines religion, politics, child rearing, and immigration in the young nation. This groundbreaking book gives special attention to social class distinctions and to such factors as gender and race. Martineau ([1838] 1989) also wrote the first book on sociological methods.

Martineau's writings emphasized the impact that the economy, law, trade, health, and population could have on social problems. She spoke out in favor of the rights of women, the emancipation of slaves, and religious tolerance. Later in life, deafness did not keep her from being an activist. In Martineau's ([1837] 1962) view, intellectuals and scholars should not simply offer observations of social conditions; they should *act* on their convictions in a manner that will benefit society. That is why Martineau conducted research on the nature of female employment and pointed to the need for further investigation of the issue (Deegan 2003; Hill and Hoecker-Drysdale 2001).

Another important contributor to the discipline of sociology is Herbert Spencer (1820–1903). A relatively prosperous Victorian Englishman, Spencer (unlike Martineau) did not feel compelled to correct or improve society; instead, he merely hoped to understand it better. Drawing on Charles Darwin's study *On the Origin of Species,* Spencer applied the concept of evolution of the species to societies in order to explain how they change, or evolve, over time. Similarly, he adapted Darwin's evolutionary view of the "survival of the fittest" by arguing that it is "natural" that some people are rich while others are poor.

Spencer's approach to societal change was extremely popular in his own lifetime. Unlike Comte, Spencer suggested that since societies are bound to change eventually, one need not be highly critical of present social arrangements or work actively for social change. This viewpoint appealed to many influential people in England and the United States who had a vested interest in the status quo and were suspicious of social thinkers who endorsed change.

ÉMILE DURKHEIM

As discussed earlier, Émile Durkheim made many pioneering contributions to sociology, including his important theoretical work on suicide. The son of a rabbi, Durkheim (1858–1917) was educated in both France and Germany. He established an impressive academic reputation and was appointed one of the first professors of sociology in France. Above all, Durkheim will be remembered for his insistence that behavior must be understood within a larger social context, not just in individualistic terms.

To give one example of this emphasis, Durkheim ([1912] 2001) developed a fundamental thesis to help understand all forms of society. Through intensive study of the Arunta, an Australian tribe, he focused on the functions that religion performs and underscored the role that group life plays in defining what we consider to be religious. Durkheim concluded that like other forms of group behavior, religion reinforces a group's solidarity.

Like many other sociologists, Durkheim did not limit his interests to one aspect of social behavior. Later in this book, we will consider his thinking on crime and punishment, religion, and the workplace. Few sociologists have had such a dramatic impact on so many different areas within the discipline.

MAX WEBER

Another important early theorist is Max Weber (pronounced VAY-ber). Born in Germany in 1864, Weber studied legal and economic history, but he gradually developed an interest in sociology. Eventually, he became a professor at various German universities. Weber taught his students that they should employ *Verstehen* (pronounced fair-SHTAY-en), the German word for "understanding" or "insight," in their intellectual work. He pointed out that we cannot analyze much of our social behavior by the same criteria we use to measure weight or temperature. To fully comprehend behavior, we must learn the subjective meanings people attach to their actions—how they themselves view and explain their behavior.

We also owe credit to Weber for a key conceptual tool: the ideal type. An *ideal type* is a construct, a made-up model that serves as a measuring rod against which actual cases can be evaluated. In his own works, Weber identified various characteristics of bureaucracy as an ideal type (discussed in detail in Chapter 3). In presenting this model of bureaucracy, Weber was not describing any particular organization, nor was he using the term *ideal* in a way that suggested a positive evaluation. Instead, his purpose was to provide a useful standard for measuring how bureaucratic an actual organization is (Gerth and Mills 1958). Later in this textbook, we will use the concept of an ideal type to study the family, religion, authority, and economic systems and to analyze bureaucracy.

KARL MARX

Karl Marx (1818–1883) shared with Durkheim and Weber a dual interest in abstract philosophical issues and the concrete reality of everyday life. Unlike them, Marx was so critical of existing institutions that a conventional academic career was impossible for him. He spent most of his life in exile from his native Germany.

Marx's personal life was a difficult struggle. When a paper that he had written was suppressed, he fled to France. In Paris, he met Friedrich Engels (1820–1895), with whom he formed a lifelong friendship. The two lived at a time when European and North American economic life was increasingly dominated by the factory rather than the farm.

In 1847, in London, Marx and Engels attended secret meetings of an illegal coalition of labor unions known as the Communist League. The following year, they prepared a platform called *The Communist Manifesto,* in which they argued that the masses of people who have no resources other than their labor (whom they referred to as the *proletariat*) should unite to fight for the overthrow of capitalist societies.

In Marx's analysis, society was fundamentally divided between classes that clash in pursuit of their own class interests. When he examined the industrial societies of his time, such as Germany, England, and the United States, he saw the factory as the center of conflict between the exploiters (the owners of the means of production) and the exploited (the workers). Marx viewed these relationships in systematic terms; that is, he believed that an entire system of economic, social, and political relationships maintained the power and dominance of the owners over the workers. Consequently, Marx and Engels argued, the working class needed to *overthrow* the existing class system. Marx's influence on contemporary thinking has been dramatic. His writings inspired those who were later to lead communist revolutions in Russia, China, Cuba, Vietnam, and elsewhere.

Even apart from the political revolutions that his work fostered, Marx's significance is profound. Marx emphasized the *group* identifications and associations that influence an individual's place in society. This area of study is the major focus of contemporary sociology. Throughout this textbook, we will consider how membership in a particular gender classification, age group, racial group, or economic class affects a person's attitudes and behavior. In an important sense, we can trace this way of understanding society back to the pioneering work of Karl Marx.

W. E. B. DUBOIS

Marx's work encouraged sociologists to view society through the eyes of those segments of the population that rarely influence decision making. In the United States, some early Black sociologists, including W. E. B. DuBois (1868–1963), conducted research that they hoped would assist in the struggle for a racially egalitarian society. DuBois (pronounced doo-BOYSS) believed that knowledge was essential in combating prejudice and achieving tolerance and justice. Sociologists, he contended, needed to draw on scientific principles to study social problems such as those experienced by Blacks in the United States. To separate opinion from fact, he advocated basic research on the lives of Blacks. Through his in-depth studies of urban life, both White and Black, in cities such as Philadelphia and Atlanta, DuBois ([1899] 1995) made a major contribution to sociology.

Like Durkheim and Weber, DuBois saw the importance of religion to society. However, he tended to focus on religion at the community level and the role of the church in the lives of its members ([1903] 2003). DuBois had little patience with theorists such as Herbert Spencer, who seemed content with the status quo. He believed that the granting of full political rights to Blacks was essential to their social and economic progress.

Because many of his ideas challenged the status quo, DuBois did not find a receptive audience within either the government or the academic world. As a result, he became increasingly involved with organizations whose members questioned the established social order. In 1909 he helped to found the National Association for the Advancement of Colored People, better known today as the NAACP (Wortham 2008).

DuBois's insights have been lasting. In 1897 he coined the term **double consciousness** to refer to the division of an individual's identity into two or more social realities. He used the term to describe the experience of being Black in White America. Today, African American parents can tell their children with credibility that they may grow up to become president of the United States, the most powerful person in the nation. Yet for millions of African Americans, the reality of being Black in the United States typically is not one of power ([1903] 1961).

MODERN DEVELOPMENTS

Sociology today builds on the firm foundation developed by Émile Durkheim, Max Weber, Karl Marx, and W. E. B. DuBois. However, the discipline has certainly not remained stagnant over the last 100 years. While Europeans have continued to make contributions, sociologists from throughout the world, and especially the United States, have advanced sociological theory and research. Their new insights have helped us to better understand the workings of society.

Charles Horton Cooley   Charles Horton Cooley (1864–1929) is typical of the sociologists who came to prominence in the early 1900s. Born in Ann Arbor, Michigan, Cooley received his graduate training in economics but later became a sociology professor at the University of Michigan. Like other early sociologists, he had become interested in this "new" discipline while pursuing a related area of study.

Cooley shared the desire of Durkheim, Weber, W. E. B. DuBois, and Marx to learn more about society. But to do so effectively, he preferred to use the sociological perspective to look first at smaller units—intimate, face-to-face groups such as families, gangs, and friendship networks. He saw these groups as the seedbeds of society, in the sense that they shape people's ideals, beliefs, values, and social nature. Cooley's work increased our understanding of groups of relatively small size.

Jane Addams   In the early 1900s, many leading sociologists in the United States saw themselves as social reformers dedicated to systematically studying and then improving a corrupt society. They were genuinely concerned about the lives of immigrants in the nation's growing cities, whether those immigrants came from Europe or from the rural American south. Early female sociologists, in particular, often took active roles in poor urban areas as leaders of community centers known as *settlement houses.* For example, Jane Addams (1860–1935), a member of the American Sociological Society, cofounded the famous Chicago settlement, Hull House.

Addams and other pioneering female sociologists commonly combined intellectual inquiry, social service work, and political activism—all with the goal of assisting the underprivileged and creating a more egalitarian society. For example, working with the Black journalist and educator Ida Wells-Barnett, Addams successfully prevented racial segregation in the Chicago public schools. Addams's efforts to establish a juvenile court system and a women's trade union also reveal the practical focus of her work (Addams 1910, 1930; Deegan 1991; Lengermann and Niebrugge-Brantley 1998).

By the middle of the 20th century, however, the focus of the discipline had shifted. Sociologists for the most part restricted themselves to theorizing and gathering information; the aim of transforming society was left to social workers and others. This shift away from social reform was accompanied by a growing commitment to scientific methods of research and to value-free interpretation of data. Not all sociologists were happy with this emphasis. A new organization, the Society for the Study of Social Problems, was created in 1950 to deal more directly with social inequality and other social ills.

Robert Merton   Sociologist Robert Merton (1910–2003) made an important contribution to the field by successfully combining theory and research. Born in 1910 to Slavic immigrant parents in Philadelphia, Merton subsequently won a scholarship to Temple University. He continued his studies at Harvard, where he acquired his lifelong interest in sociology. Merton's teaching career was based at Columbia University.

Merton produced a theory that is one of the most frequently cited explanations of deviant behavior. He noted different ways in which people attempt to achieve success in life. In his view, some may deviate from the socially agreed-upon goal of accumulating material goods or the socially accepted means of achieving that goal. For example, in Merton's classification scheme, "innovators" are people who accept the goal of pursuing material wealth but use illegal means to do so, including robbery, burglary, and extortion. Merton based his explanation of crime on individual behavior—influenced by society's approved goals and means—yet it has wider applications. It helps to account for the high crime rates among the nation's poor, who may see no hope of advancing themselves through traditional roads to success. Chapter 4 discusses Merton's theory in greater detail.

Merton also emphasized that sociologists should strive to bring together the "macro-level" and "micro-level" approaches to studying society. *Macrosociology* concentrates on large-scale phenomena or entire civilizations. For example, Émile Durkheim's cross-cultural study of suicide was a macro-level analysis. In contrast, *microsociology* concentrates on small groups, often through experimental means. Micro-level investigations are particularly useful to sociologists who study everyday forms of social interaction, such as routine encounters on the job and in public places.

Pierre Bourdieu   Increasingly, scholars in the United States have been drawing on the insights of sociologists in other countries. The ideas of the late French sociologist Pierre Bourdieu (1930–2002) have found a broad following both in North America and elsewhere. As a young man, Bourdieu did fieldwork in Algeria during its struggle for independence from France. Today, scholars study Bourdieu's research techniques as well as his conclusions.

Bourdieu wrote about how capital in its many forms sustains individuals and families from one generation to the next. To Bourdieu, *capital* included not just material goods, but cultural and social assets. *Cultural capital* refers to noneconomic goods such as family background and education, which are reflected in a knowledge of language and the arts. Not necessarily book knowledge, cultural capital refers to the kind of education that is valued by the socially elite. Though a knowledge of Chinese cuisine is culture, for example, it is not the prestigious kind of culture that is valued by the elite. In the United States, immigrants—especially those who arrived in large numbers and settled in ethnic enclaves—have generally taken two or three generations to develop the same level of cultural capital enjoyed by more established groups. In comparison, *social capital* refers to the collective benefit of social networks, which are built on reciprocal trust. Much has been written about the importance of family and friendship networks in providing people with an opportunity to advance. In his emphasis on cultural and social capital, Bourdieu's work extends the insights of early social thinkers such as Marx and Weber (Bourdieu and Passerson 1990; Poder 2011; Putnam 2015:207).

Today sociology reflects the diverse contributions of earlier theorists. As sociologists approach such topics as divorce, drug addiction, and religious cults, they can draw on the theoretical insights of the discipline's pioneers. A careful reader can hear Comte, Durkheim, Weber, Marx, DuBois, Cooley, Addams, and many others speaking through the pages of current research. Sociology has also broadened beyond the intellectual confines of North America and Europe. Contributions to the discipline now come from sociologists studying and researching human behavior in other parts of the world. In describing the work of today's sociologists, it is helpful to examine a number of influential theoretical approaches (also known as *perspectives*).

Major Theoretical Perspectives

Sociologists view society in different ways. Some see the social world basically as a stable, ongoing entity. They are impressed with the endurance of the family, organized religion, and other social institutions. Some see society in terms of many conflicting groups, competing for scarce resources. To other sociologists, the most fascinating aspects of the social world are the everyday, routine interactions among individuals, which we often take for granted. These three views, the ones most widely used by sociologists, are the functionalist, conflict, and interactionist perspectives. Together, they will provide an introductory look at the discipline.

FUNCTIONALIST PERSPECTIVE

Think of society as a living organism in which each part of the organism contributes to its survival. This view is the *functionalist perspective* (also referred to as the *structural functionalist approach*). The functionalist perspective emphasizes the way that the parts of a society are structured to maintain its stability. In examining any aspect of society, then, functionalists emphasize the contribution that it makes to overall social stability.

Let's look at how functionalists would evaluate the effects of an environmental catastrophe like the Gulf Coast oil spill. The disaster began in April 2010 with a spectacular explosion on a BP drilling platform, followed quickly by a devastating fire. Eleven workers died in the blast. Residents along the southern coast of the United States watched helplessly as BP made one unsuccessful attempt after another to cap the damaged well. Although the platform was located far off the coast in extremely deep water, oil slicks soon began to wash up on the shores of Alabama, Louisiana, Mississippi, Florida, and Texas. As photos of oil-soaked birds and dirty beaches filled the news, the shellfish and tourism industries shut down, throwing thousands of people out of work. Not since the *Exxon Valdez* ran aground off the coast of Alaska two decades earlier had the United States seen such a destructive oil spill.

In evaluating the effects of the spill, functionalists would stress society's supportive function. They would observe that churches and charities provided spiritual and material support to those affected by the disaster. They might also note full employment in selected occupations, such as the manufacture of containment booms, even when jobs in other industries were scarce. They would not be surprised that because offshore oil drilling is an integral part of the Gulf Coast economy, the governor of Louisiana strongly opposed a moratorium on deep-sea drilling, despite concerns about its safety. And they might predict a revitalization of the environmental movement, as happened in the 1990s after wildfires swept through the Everglades.

Talcott Parsons (1902–1979), a Harvard University sociologist, was a key figure in the development of functionalist theory. Parsons had been greatly influenced by the work of Émile Durkheim, Max Weber, and other European sociologists. For over four decades, Parsons dominated sociology in the United States with his advocacy of functionalism. He saw any society as a vast network of connected parts, each of which helps to maintain the system as a whole. According to the functionalist approach, if an aspect of social life does not contribute to a society's stability or survival—if it does not serve some identifiably useful function or promote value consensus among members of a society—it will not be passed on from one generation to the next (Joas and Knobl 2009; Knudsen 2010).

Manifest and Latent Functions   A college catalog typically states various functions of the institution. It may inform you, for example, that the university intends to "offer each student a broad education in classical and contemporary thought, in the humanities, in the sciences, and in the arts." However, it would be quite a surprise to find a catalog that declared, "This university was founded in 1895 to assist people in finding a marriage partner." No college catalog will declare this as the purpose of the university. Yet societal institutions serve many functions, some of them quite subtle. The university, in fact, *does* facilitate mate selection.

Robert Merton (1968) made an important distinction between manifest and latent functions. **Manifest functions** of institutions are open, stated, conscious functions. They involve the intended, recognized consequences of an aspect of society, such as the university's role in certifying academic competence and excellence. By contrast, **latent functions** are unconscious or unintended functions that may reflect hidden purposes of an institution. One latent function of universities is to serve as a meeting ground for people seeking marital partners.

Dysfunctions   Functionalists acknowledge that not all parts of a society contribute to its stability all the time. A **dysfunction** refers to an element or process of a society that may actually disrupt the social system or reduce its stability.

We view many dysfunctional behavior patterns, such as homicide, as undesirable. Yet we should not automatically interpret them in this way. The evaluation of a dysfunction depends on one's own values, or as the saying goes, on "where you sit." For example, the official view in prisons in the United States is that inmate gangs should be eradicated because they are dysfunctional to smooth operations. Yet some guards have actually come to view prison gangs as a functional part of their jobs. The danger posed by gangs creates a "threat to security," requiring increased surveillance and more overtime work for guards, as well as requests for special staffing to address gang problems (G. Scott 2001).

CONFLICT PERSPECTIVE

In contrast to the functionalists' emphasis on stability and consensus, conflict sociologists see the social world in continual struggle. Proponents of the **conflict perspective** assume that social behavior is best understood in terms of tension between groups over power or the allocation of resources, including housing, money, access to services, and political representation. Such conflict need not be violent; it can take the form of labor negotiations, party politics, competition between religious groups for members, or disputes over the federal budget.

Because conflict theorists see the social order in this way, they would approach the Gulf Coast oil spill by emphasizing the coercion and exploitation that underlies relations between the oil industry and Gulf Coast communities. The oil industry, they would note, is a form of big business, in which profits are considered more important than the health and safety of workers. Conflict theorists would also emphasize the often-overlooked effect of the Gulf Coast oil spill on minority groups living in inland communities, including Vietnamese Americans, American Indian tribal groups, and African Americans. These groups, which were living a marginal existence before the spill, endured particularly significant economic setbacks after the spill. Finally, conflict theorists would note that although news outlets tend to focus on oil spills that affect wealthy industrial countries, often the worst spills afflict communities in less well-off developing nations, such as Nigeria.

Throughout most of the 1900s, advocates of the functionalist perspective had the upper hand among sociologists in the United States. However, proponents of the conflict approach have become increasingly persuasive since the late 1960s. The widespread social unrest resulting from battles over civil rights, bitter divisions over the war in Vietnam, the rise of the feminist and gay liberation movements, the Watergate scandal, urban riots, confrontations at abortion clinics, and shrinking economic prospects for the middle class have offered support for the conflict approach—the view that our social world is characterized by continual struggle between competing groups. Currently, sociologists accept conflict theory as one valid way to gain insight into a society.

The Marxist View   As we saw earlier, Karl Marx viewed the struggle between social classes as inevitable, given the exploitation of workers under capitalism. Expanding on Marx's work, sociologists and other social scientists have come to see conflict not merely as a class phenomenon but as a part of everyday life in all societies. In studying any culture, organization, or social group, sociologists want to know who benefits, who suffers, and who dominates at the expense of others. They are concerned with the conflicts between women and men, parents and children, cities and suburbs, and Whites and Blacks, to name only a few. Conflict theorists are interested in how society's institutions—including the family, government, religion, education, and the media—may help to maintain the privileges of some groups and keep others in a subservient position. Their emphasis on social change and the redistribution of resources makes conflict theorists more "radical" and "activist" than functionalists (Dahrendorf 1959).

Feminist Perspective   Sociologists began embracing the feminist perspective in the 1970s, although it has a long tradition in many other disciplines. Proponents of the *feminist perspective* view inequity based on gender as central to all behavior and organization. Because this perspective clearly focuses on one aspect of inequality, it is often allied with the conflict perspective. But unlike conflict theorists, those who hold to the feminist perspective tend to focus on the relationships of everyday life, just as interactionists would. Drawing on the work of Marx and Engels, many contemporary feminist theorists view women's subordination as inherent in capitalist societies. Some radical feminist theorists, however, view the oppression of women as inevitable in *all* male-dominated societies, whether capitalist, socialist, or communist.

An early example of this perspective (long before the label came into use by sociologists) can be seen in the life and writings of Ida Wells-Barnett (1862–1931). Following her groundbreaking publications in the

1890s on the practice of lynching Black Americans, she became an advocate in the women's rights campaign, especially the struggle to win the vote for women. Like feminist theorists who succeeded her, Wells-Barnett used her analysis of society as a means of resisting oppression. In her case, she researched what it meant to be African American, a woman in the United States, and a Black woman in the United States (Giddings 2008; Wells-Barnett 1970).

Feminist scholarship has broadened our understanding of social behavior by extending the analysis beyond the male point of view. Consider sports, for example. Feminist theorists study how watching or participating in sports reinforces the roles that men and women play in the larger society:

- Although sports generally promote fitness and health, they may also have an adverse effect on participants' health. Men are more likely to resort to illegal steroid use (among bodybuilders and baseball players, for example); women, to excessive dieting (among gymnasts and figure skaters, for example).

- Gender expectations encourage female athletes to be passive and gentle, qualities that do not support the emphasis on competitiveness in sports. As a result, women find it difficult to enter sports traditionally dominated by men, such as Indy or NASCAR.

- Although professional women athletes' earnings are increasing, they typically trail those of male athletes.

Queer Theory   Traditionally, sociologists and other researchers have assumed that men and women are heterosexual. They either ignored other sexual identifications or treated them as abnormal. Yet as French social theorist Michel Foucault (1978) has pointed out, what is regarded as normal or even acceptable human sexuality varies dramatically from one culture to another, as well as from one time period to another.

Today, in *queer theory,* sociologists have moved beyond narrow assumptions to study sexuality in all its forms. Historically, the word *queer* was used in a derogatory manner, to stigmatize a person or behavior. Beginning in the early 1970s, however, gay and lesbian activists began to use the word as a term of empowerment. They dismissed the notion of heterosexuality as the only normal form of sexuality, along with the belief that people must be either heterosexual or homosexual. Instead, they recognized multiple sexual identities, including bisexuality. ***Queer theory*** is the study of society from the perspective of a broad spectrum of sexual identities, including heterosexuality, homosexuality, and bisexuality.

Queer theorist Eve Sedgwick (1990) argues that any analysis of society is incomplete if it does not include the spectrum of sexual identities that people embrace. Consider, for example, the reelection of President Obama in 2012. Political scientists have often noted the overwhelming support the president received from African Americans, Latinos, and women voters.

Yet most have ignored the huge support—76 percent—that the president enjoyed among gay, lesbian, and bisexual voters. In comparison, heterosexual voters split evenly (49 percent to 49 percent nationwide) between Obama and his opponent, Mitt Romney. In the three battleground states of Florida, Ohio, and Virginia, support from gay, lesbian, and bisexual voters alone was enough to put Obama over the top. If Romney had carried just 51 percent of the gay, lesbian, and bisexual vote nationwide, he would have become the next president of the United States (Gates 2012).

INTERACTIONIST PERSPECTIVE

Workers interacting on the job, encounters in public places like bus stops and parks, behavior in small groups—these are all aspects of microsociology that catch the attention of interactionists. Whereas functionalist and conflict theorists both analyze large-scale, societywide patterns of behavior, proponents of the *interactionist perspective* generalize about everyday forms of social interaction in order to understand society as a whole. Today, given rising concern over the cost and availability of gas, interactionists have begun to study a form of commuter behavior called "slugging." To avoid driving to work, commuters gather at certain preappointed places to seek rides from complete strangers. When a driver pulls into the parking area or vacant lot and announces his destination, the first slug in line who is headed for that destination jumps in. Rules of etiquette have emerged to smooth the social interaction between driver and passenger: neither the driver nor the passenger may eat or smoke; the slug may not adjust the windows or radio or talk on a cell phone. The presence of the slugs, who get a free ride, may allow the driver to use special lanes reserved for high-occupancy vehicles (Slug-Lines.com 2011).

You are a sociologist who uses the conflict perspective to study various aspects of our society. How do you think you would interpret the practice of prostitution? Contrast this view with the functionalist perspective. Do you think your comments would differ if you took the feminist view? The perspective of queer theory?

In studying the social order, interactionists are especially interested in shared understandings of everyday behavior. They would examine the Gulf Coast oil spill on a micro level, by focusing on how it shaped personal relations and day-to-day social behavior. Difficult times, for example, often strengthen ties among neighbors and family members, who depend on one another for help. At the same time, stressful events can contribute to social breakdowns, from divorce to suicide. Observations like these were made two decades ago in the aftermath of the *Exxon Valdez* oil spill.

Though the functionalist and conflict approaches were initiated in Europe, interactionism developed first in the United States. George Herbert Mead (1863–1931) is widely regarded as the founder of the interactionist perspective. Mead taught at the University of Chicago from 1893 until his death. His sociological analysis, like that of Charles Horton Cooley, often focused on human interactions within one-to-one situations and small groups. Mead was interested in observing the most minute forms of communication—smiles, frowns, the nodding of one's head—and in understanding how such individual behavior was influenced by the larger context of a group or society. Despite his innovative views, Mead only occasionally wrote articles, and never a book. He was an extremely popular teacher; in fact, most of his insights have come to us through edited volumes of lectures that his students published after his death.

Interactionism is a sociological framework in which human beings are seen to be living in a world of meaningful objects. These "objects" may include material things, actions, other people, relationships, and even symbols. The interactionist perspective is sometimes referred to as the *symbolic interactionist perspective,* because interactionists see symbols as an especially important part of human communication. Symbols carry shared social meanings that are generally recognized by all members of a society. For example, a salute symbolizes respect, while a clenched fist signifies defiance.

Different cultures may use different symbols to convey the same idea. For example, consider the different ways various societies portray suicide without the use of words. People in the United States point a finger at the head (shooting); urban Japanese bring a fist against the stomach (stabbing); and the South Fore of Papua, New Guinea, clench a hand at the throat (hanging). These symbolic interactions are classified as a form of *nonverbal communication,* which can include many other gestures, facial expressions, and postures (Masuda et al. 2008).

What symbols at your college or university have special meaning for students?

THE SOCIOLOGICAL APPROACH

Which perspective should a sociologist use in studying human behavior—functionalist, conflict, interactionist, feminist? Despite their differences, proponents of these viewpoints have much in common. All would agree, for example, that disasters are worthy subjects of investigation. All would admit that there is much more to be learned about the Gulf Coast oil spill than can be addressed from a single theoretical perspective. In fact, sociologists make use of all the perspectives summarized in Table 1-1, since each offers unique insights into the same issue. We can gain the broadest understanding of our society, then, by drawing on all the major perspectives, noting where they overlap and where they diverge.

Although no one approach is "correct," and sociologists draw on all of them for various purposes, many sociologists tend to favor one particular perspective over others. A sociologist's theoretical orientation influences his or her approach to a research problem in important ways. The choice of what to study, how to study it, and what questions to pose (or not to pose) can all be influenced by a researcher's theoretical orientation. In the next part of this chapter, we will see how sociologists have adapted the scientific method to their discipline and how they apply that method in surveys, case studies, and experiments. Bear in mind, though, that even with meticulous attention to all the steps in the scientific method, a researcher's work will always be guided by his or her theoretical viewpoint. Research results, like theories, shine a spotlight on one part of the stage, leaving other parts in relative darkness.

Table 1–1 Comparing Major Theoretical Approaches

Tracking Perspectives

	Functionalist	Conflict	Interactionist
View of Society	Stable, well integrated	Characterized by tension and struggle between groups	Active in influencing and affecting everyday social interaction
Level of Analysis Emphasized	Macro Meso Global	Macro Meso Global	Micro, as a way of understanding the larger social phenomena
Key Concepts	Manifest functions Latent functions Dysfunctions	Inequality Capitalism Stratification	Symbols Nonverbal communication Face-to-face interaction
View of the Individual	People are socialized to perform societal functions	People are shaped by power coercion and authority	People manipulate symbols and create their social worlds through interaction
View of the Social Order	Maintained through cooperation and consensus	Maintained through force and coercion	Maintained by shared understanding of everyday behavior
View of Social Change	Predictable, reinforcing	Change takes place all the time and may have positive consequences	Reflected in people's social positions and their communications with others
Example	Public punishments reinforce the social order	Laws reinforce the positions of those in power	People respect laws or disobey them based on their own past experience
Proponents	Emile Durkheim Talcott Parsons Robert Merton	Karl Marx W. E. B. DuBois Ida Wells-Barnett	George Herbert Mead Charles Horton Cooley Erving Goffman

What Is the Scientific Method?

Like all of us, sociologists are interested in the central questions of our time. Is the family falling apart? Why is there so much crime in the United States? Can the world feed a growing population? Such issues concern most people, whether or not they have academic training. However, unlike the typical citizen, the sociologist is committed to using the scientific method in studying society. The *scientific method* is a systematic, organized series of steps that ensures maximum objectivity and consistency in researching a problem.

Many of us will never actually conduct scientific research. Why, then, is it important that we understand the scientific method? Because it plays a major role in the workings of our society. Residents of the United States are constantly being bombarded with "facts" or "data." A television reporter informs us that "one in every two marriages in this country now ends in divorce." An advertiser cites supposedly scientific studies to prove that a particular product is superior. Such claims may be accurate or exaggerated. We can better evaluate such information—and will not be fooled so easily—if we are familiar with the standards of scientific research.

These standards are quite stringent and demand as strict adherence as possible. The scientific method requires precise preparation in developing research. Otherwise, the research data collected may not prove accurate. Sociologists and other researchers follow five basic steps in the scientific method: (1) defining the problem, (2) reviewing the literature, (3) formulating the hypothesis, (4) selecting the research design and then collecting and analyzing data, and (5) developing the conclusion (see Figure 1-1). We'll use an actual example to illustrate the workings of the scientific method.

DEFINING THE PROBLEM

Does it "pay" to go to college? Some people make great sacrifices and work hard to get a college education. Parents borrow money for their children's tuition. Students work part-time jobs or even take full-time positions while attending evening or weekend classes. Does it pay off? Are there monetary returns for getting that degree?

The first step in any research project is to state as clearly as possible what you hope to investigate—that is, *define the problem*. In this instance, we are interested in knowing how schooling relates to income. We want to find out the earnings of people with different levels of formal schooling.

Early on, any social science researcher must develop an operational definition of each concept being studied. An ***operational definition*** is an explanation of an abstract concept that is specific enough to allow a researcher to assess the concept. For example, a sociologist interested in status might use membership in exclusive social clubs as an operational definition of status. Someone studying prejudice might consider a person's unwillingness to hire or work with members of minority groups as an operational definition of prejudice. In our example, we need to develop two operational definitions—one for education and the other for earnings—in order to study whether it pays to get an advanced educational degree.

Figure 1–1
The Scientific Method

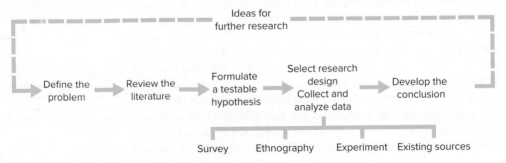

Initially, we will take a functionalist perspective (although we may end up incorporating other approaches). We will argue that opportunities for more earning power are related to level of schooling and that schools prepare students for employment.

REVIEWING THE LITERATURE

By conducting a *review of the literature*—the relevant scholarly studies and information—researchers refine the problem under study, clarify possible techniques to be used in collecting data, and eliminate or reduce avoidable mistakes. In our example, we would examine information about the salaries for different occupations. We would see if jobs that require more academic training are better rewarded. It would also be appropriate to review other studies on the relationship between education and income.

The review of the literature would soon tell us that many other factors besides years of schooling influence earning potential. For example, we would learn that the children of richer parents are more likely to go to college than are those from modest backgrounds. As a result, we might consider the possibility that the richer parents may also help their children to secure better-paying jobs after graduation.

FORMULATING THE HYPOTHESIS

After reviewing earlier research and drawing on the contributions of sociological theorists, the researchers may then *formulate the hypothesis*. A **hypothesis** is a speculative statement about the relationship between two or more factors known as *variables*. Income, religion, occupation, and gender can all serve as variables in a study. We can define a **variable** as a measurable trait or characteristic that is subject to change under different conditions.

Researchers who formulate a hypothesis generally must suggest how one aspect of human behavior influences or affects another. The variable hypothesized to cause or influence another is called the **independent variable.** The second variable is termed the **dependent variable** because its action "depends" on the influence of the independent variable.

Our hypothesis is that the higher one's educational degree, the more money a person will earn. The independent variable that is to be measured is the level of educational degree. The variable that is thought to "depend" on it—income—must also be measured.

Identifying independent and dependent variables is a critical step in clarifying cause-and-effect relationships. **Causal logic** involves the relationship between a condition or variable and a particular consequence, with one event leading to the other. Under causal logic, being less integrated into society (the independent variable) may be directly related to or produce a greater likelihood of suicide (the dependent variable). Similarly, parents' income levels (an independent variable) may affect the likelihood that their children will enroll in college (a dependent variable).

Later in life, the level of education their children achieve (independent variable) may be directly related to their children's income levels (dependent variable). Note that income level can be either an independent or a dependent variable, depending on the causal relationship.

A *correlation* exists when a change in one variable coincides with a change in the other. Correlations are an indication that causality *may* be present; they do not necessarily indicate causation. For example, data showed that at-risk children in a mentoring program were more likely to get in to trouble than those who were not being served by a social agency. This is a correlation, but it does not necessarily mean causation. The young people who were in the special program tended to be older and were much more likely to have had ongoing delinquent experiences. So being in assistance programs may be *correlated* with bad behavior, but it does not represent a *causal* link. Sociologists seek to identify the *causal* link between variables; the suspected causal link is generally described in the hypothesis (Morris 2017).

COLLECTING AND ANALYZING DATA

How do you test a hypothesis to determine if it is supported or refuted? You need to collect information, using one of the research designs described later in the chapter. The research design guides the researcher in collecting and analyzing data.

Selecting the Sample   In most studies, social scientists must carefully select what is known as a *sample*. A *sample* is a selection from a larger population that is statistically representative of that population. There are many kinds of samples, but the one social scientists use most frequently is the random sample. In a ***random sample,*** every member of an entire population being studied has the same chance of being selected. Thus, if researchers want to examine the opinions of people listed in a city directory (a book that, unlike the telephone directory, lists all households), they might use a computer to randomly select names from the directory. This selection would constitute a random sample. The advantage of using specialized sampling techniques is that sociologists do not need to question everyone in a population (Igo 2007).

For example, while reading online, users are often encouraged to give their opinions or offer preferences between different consumer products. Then they are immediately given the results of what the "public thinks." Even when these techniques include answers from tens of thousands of people, they will be far less accurate than a carefully selected representative sample of 1,500 respondents.

For the purposes of our research example, we will use information collected in the Current Population Survey conducted by the Bureau of the Census. Each year the Census Bureau surveys approximately 77,000 households across the United States. Technicians at the bureau then use the data to estimate the nation's entire population.

Ensuring Validity and Reliability   The scientific method requires that research results be both valid and reliable. *Validity* refers to the degree to which a measure or scale truly reflects the phenomenon under study. A valid measure of income depends on the gathering of accurate data. Various studies show that people are reasonably accurate in reporting how much money they earned in the most recent year. If a question is written unclearly, however, the resulting data might not be accurate. For example, respondents to an unclear question about income might report their parents' or spouse's income instead of their own. *Reliability* refers to the extent to which a measure produces consistent results. One problem of reliability is that some people may not *disclose* accurate information, but most do.

DEVELOPING THE CONCLUSION

Scientific studies, including those conducted by sociologists, do not aim to answer all the questions that can be raised about a particular subject. Therefore, the conclusion of a research study represents both an end and a beginning. Although it terminates a specific phase of the investigation, it should also generate ideas for future study.

Supporting Hypotheses   In our example, we find that the data support our hypothesis: People with more formal schooling *do* earn more money. As Figure 1-2 shows, as a group, those with a high school diploma earn

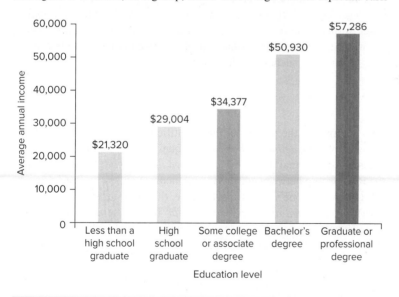

Figure 1–2

Effect of a College Education on Income

Higher degrees bring significantly higher annual income, a benefit that adds up over a worker's lifetime.

NOTE: *For population age 25 and over with earnings in 2015. High school graduate includes equivalencies.*

SOURCE: American Community Survey 2016: Table B20004.

Think About It
What kinds of knowledge and skills do people with an associate's degree or higher possess, compared to those with a high school education or less? Why would employers value those kinds of knowledge and skills?

more than those who failed to complete high school, but those with an associate's degree earn more than high school graduates. The relationship continues through more advanced levels of schooling; those with graduate degrees earn the most.

Sociological studies do not always generate data that support the original hypothesis. In many instances, a hypothesis is refuted, and researchers must reformulate their conclusions. Unexpected results may also lead sociologists to reexamine their methodology and make changes in the research design.

Controlling for Other Factors   A *control variable* is a factor held constant to test the relative impact of the independent variable. For example, if researchers wanted to know how adults in the United States feel about restrictions on smoking in public places, they would probably attempt to use a respondent's smoking behavior as a control variable. That is, how do smokers versus nonsmokers feel about smoking in public places? The researchers would compile separate statistics on how smokers and nonsmokers feel about antismoking regulations.

Our study of the influence of education on income suggests that not everyone enjoys equal educational opportunities, a disparity that is one of the causes of social inequality. Since education affects a person's income, we may wish to call on the conflict perspective to explore this topic further. What impact does a person's race or gender have? Is a woman with a college degree likely to earn as much as a man with similar schooling? Later in this textbook we will consider these other factors and variables. We will examine the impact that education has on income, while controlling for variables such as gender and race.

IN SUMMARY: THE SCIENTIFIC METHOD

Let's summarize the process of the scientific method through a review of our example. We *defined a problem* (the question of whether it pays to get a higher educational degree). We *reviewed the literature* (other studies of the relationship between education and income) and *formulated a hypothesis* (the higher one's educational degree, the more money a person will earn). We *collected and analyzed the data,* making sure the sample was representative and the data were valid and reliable. Finally, we *developed the conclusion:* The data do support our hypothesis about the influence of education on income.

Major Research Designs

An important aspect of sociological research is deciding how to collect the data. A *research design* is a detailed plan or method for obtaining data scientifically. Selection of a research design requires creativity and ingenuity. This choice will directly influence both the cost of the project and the amount of time needed to collect the results of the research. Research designs that sociologists use regularly to generate data include surveys, ethnographic studies, experiments, and existing sources.

What might be the effects of a college education on society as a whole? Think of some potential effects on the family, government, and the economy.

SURVEYS

Almost all of us have responded to surveys of one kind or another. We may have been asked what kind of detergent we use, which presidential candidate we intend to vote for, or what our favorite television program is. A *survey* is a study, generally in the form of an interview or question-naire, that provides researchers with information about how people think and act. Among the United States' best-known surveys of opinion are the Gallup poll and the Harris poll. As anyone who watches the news knows, these polls have become a staple of political life.

In preparing to conduct a survey, sociologists must not only develop a representative sample; they must exercise great care in the wording of questions. An effective survey question must be simple and clear enough for people to understand it. It must also be specific enough so that there are no problems in interpreting the results. Open-ended questions ("What do you think of the programming on educational television?") must be carefully phrased to solicit the type of information that is desired. Surveys can be indispensable sources of information, but only if the sampling is done properly and the questions are worded accurately and without bias.

There are two main forms of the survey: the *interview,* in which a researcher obtains information through face-to-face or telephone questioning, and the *questionnaire,* a printed or written form used to obtain information from a respondent. Each of these has its own advantages. An interviewer can obtain a high response rate, because people find it more difficult to turn down a personal request for an interview than to throw away a written questionnaire. In addition, a skillful interviewer can go beyond written questions and probe for a subject's underlying feelings and reasons. On the other hand, questionnaires have the advantage of being cheaper, especially in large samples.

Surveys are an example of *quantitative research,* in which scientists collect and report data primarily in numerical form. Most of the survey research discussed so far in this book has been quantitative. While this type of research is appropriate for large samples, it doesn't offer great depth and detail on a topic. That is why researchers also make use of *qualitative research,* which relies on what scientists see in field and naturalistic settings. Qualitative research often focuses on small groups and communities rather than on large groups or whole nations. The most common form of qualitative research is ethnography.

ETHNOGRAPHY

Investigators often collect information or test hypotheses through first-hand studies. *Ethnography* is the study of an entire social setting through extended systematic fieldwork. *Observation,* or direct participation in closely watching a group or organization, is the basic technique of ethnography. However, ethnographic research also includes the collection of historical information and the conduct of in-person interviews. Although ethnography may seem a relatively informal method compared to surveys or experiments, ethnographic researchers are careful to take detailed notes while observing their subjects.

In some cases, the sociologist actually joins a group for a period, to get an accurate sense of how it operates. This approach is called *participant observation.* In Barbara Ehrenreich's widely read book, *Nickel and Dimed: On (Not) Getting By in America,* the author was a participant observer. Disguising herself as a divorced, middle-aged housewife without a college degree, Ehrenreich set out to see what life was like for low-wage workers. Her book chronicles her own and others' experiences trying to make ends meet on a minimum wage (Ehrenreich 2001).

During the late 1930s, in a classic example of participant-observation research, William F. Whyte moved into a low-income Italian neighborhood in Boston. For nearly four years he was a member of the social circle of "corner boys" that he describes in *Street Corner Society.* Whyte revealed his identity to these men and joined in their conversations, bowling, and other leisure-time activities. His goal was to gain greater insight into the community that these men had established. As Whyte (1981:303) listened to Doc, the leader of the group, he "learned the answers to questions I would not even have had the sense to ask if I had been getting my information solely on an interviewing basis." Whyte's work was especially valuable, since at the time, the academic world had little direct knowledge of the poor, and tended to rely on the records of social service agencies, hospitals, and courts for information (P. Adler et al. 1992).

The initial challenge that Whyte faced—and that every participant observer encounters—was to gain acceptance into an unfamiliar group. It is no simple matter for a college-trained sociologist to win the trust of a religious cult, a youth gang, a poor Appalachian community, or a circle of skid row residents. Doing so requires a great deal of patience and an accepting, nonthreatening personality on the part of the observer.

Ethnographic research poses other complex challenges for the investigator. Sociologists must be able to fully understand what they are observing. In a sense, then, researchers must learn to see the world as the group sees it in order to fully comprehend the events taking place around them.

EXPERIMENTS

When sociologists want to study a possible cause-and-effect relationship, they may conduct experiments. An *experiment* is an artificially created situation that allows the researcher to manipulate variables.

In the classic method of conducting an experiment, two groups of people are selected and matched for similar characteristics, such as age or education. The researchers then assign one of the groups to be the experimental group and the other to be the control group. The *experimental group* is exposed to an independent variable; the *control group* is not. Thus, if scientists were testing a new type of antibiotic drug, they would administer that drug to an experimental group but not to a control group.

In some experiments, just as in ethnographic research, the presence of a social scientist or other observer may affect the behavior of the people being studied. The recognition of this phenomenon grew out of an experiment conducted during the 1920s and 1930s at the Hawthorne plant of the Western Electric Company. A group of researchers set out to determine how to improve the productivity of workers at the plant. The investigators manipulated such variables as the lighting and working hours to see what impact the changes would have on productivity. To their surprise, they found that *every* step they took seemed to increase productivity. Even measures that seemed likely to have the opposite effect, such as reducing the amount of lighting in the plant, led to higher productivity.

Why did the plant's employees work harder even under less favorable conditions? Their behavior apparently was influenced by the greater attention being paid to them in the course of the research and by the novelty of being subjects in an experiment. Since that time sociologists have used the term *Hawthorne effect* to refer to the unintended influence of observers or experiments on subjects of research, who deviate from their typical behavior because they realize that they are under observation (Franke and Kaul 1978).

You are a researcher interested in the effect of social media use on schoolchildren's grades. How would you go about setting up an experiment to measure the effect?

USE OF EXISTING SOURCES

Sociologists do not necessarily need to collect new data in order to conduct research and test hypotheses. The term *secondary analysis* refers to a variety of research techniques that make use of previously collected and publicly accessible information and data. Generally, in conducting secondary analysis, researchers utilize data in ways unintended by the initial collectors of information. For example, census data that were compiled for specific uses by the federal government are also valuable to marketing specialists in locating everything from bicycle stores to nursing homes.

Sociologists consider secondary analysis to be *nonreactive,* since it does not influence people's behavior. For example, Émile Durkheim's statistical analysis of suicide neither increased nor decreased human self-destruction. Researchers, then, can avoid the Hawthorne effect by using secondary analysis.

Many social scientists find it useful to study cultural, economic, and political documents, including newspapers, periodicals, radio and television tapes, the Internet, scripts, diaries, songs, folklore, and legal papers, to name some examples (see Table 1–2). In examining these sources, researchers employ a technique known as *content analysis,* which is the systematic coding and objective recording of data, guided by some rationale.

Content analysis can be revealing. We might think that in the 21st century, blatant favoritism in media representations of men versus women is a thing of the past. However, research suggests otherwise. An analysis of hundreds of characters in children's coloring books shows that males are more likely than females to be shown taking an active role. Gender-stereotyped behavior dominates, with only 3 percent of males engaged in stereotypically female behavior, and only 6 percent of females engaged in stereotypically male behavior (Fitzpatrick and McPherson 2010).

Table 1–2 Existing Sources Used in Sociological Research

Most Frequently Used Sources

Census data

Crime statistics

Birth, death, marriage, divorce, and health statistics

Other Sources

Newspapers and periodicals

Personal journals, diaries, e-mail, and letters

Records and archival material of corporations, religious denominations, and other organizations

Transcripts of radio programs

Motion pictures and television programs

Web pages, blogs, and chat rooms

Song lyrics

Scientific records (such as patent applications)

Speeches of public figures (such as politicians)

Votes cast in elections or by elected officials on specific legislative proposals

Attendance records for public events

Videos of social protests and rallies

Literature, including folklore

Table 1–3 Major Research Designs

Method	Examples	Advantages	Limitations
Survey	Questionnaires Interviews	Yields information about specific issues	Can be expensive and time-consuming
Ethnography	Observation	Yields detailed information about specific groups or organizations	Involves months if not years of labor-intensive data
Experiment	Deliberate manipulation of people's social behavior	Yields direct measures of people's behavior	Ethical limitations on the degree to which subjects' behavior can be manipulated
Existing sources/ Secondary analysis	Analysis of census or health data	Cost-efficiency	Limited to data collected for some other purpose

Content analysis can also document what we suspect is happening as well as reveal surprising trends. A 2015 study analyzed coverage of women's sports on the Los Angeles local television market as well as on ESPN over 25 years. Despite the tremendous increase in women's participation in sports over the last quarter century, content analysis revealed that only 3.2 percent of airtime was devoted to women's sports; further, this represented a decline from the levels back in 1989. ESPN's heavily watched SportsCenter consistently devotes 2 percent of airtime to women; of this, 82 percent represents coverage of basketball (Cooky et al. 2015).

Table 1–3 summarizes the advantages and limitations of the four major research designs.

Ethics of Research

A biochemist cannot inject a drug into a human being unless the drug has been thoroughly tested and the subject agrees to the shot. To do otherwise would be both unethical and illegal. Sociologists must also abide by certain specific standards in conducting research, called a *code of ethics.* The professional society of the discipline, the American Sociological Association (ASA), first published its *Code of Ethics* in 1971. The code puts forth the following basic principles:

1. Maintain objectivity and integrity in research.
2. Respect the subject's right to privacy and dignity.
3. Protect subjects from personal harm.

4. Preserve confidentiality.

5. Seek informed consent when data are collected from research partici-
    pants or when behavior occurs in a private context.

6. Acknowledge research collaboration and assistance.

7. Disclose all sources of financial support (American Sociological
    Association 1999).

You are a sociological researcher who is having difficulty maintaining a neutral attitude toward your research topic. Your topic isn't racism or sexism. What is it?

Most sociological research uses *people* as sources of information—as respondents to survey questions, subjects of observation, or participants in experiments. In all cases, sociologists need to be certain that they are not invading the privacy of their subjects. Generally, they handle this responsibility by assuring them anonymity and by guaranteeing the confidentiality of personal information.

We have examined the process of sociological research, including related ethical considerations, in detail. But not all sociologists are researchers. Some practice what is known as *applied sociology,* or the application of sociological knowledge to real-world social problems.

Applied and Clinical Sociology

Sociology matters because it addresses real issues that affect people's lives. Many early sociologists—notably, Jane Addams and George Herbert Mead—were strong advocates for social reform. They wanted their theories and findings to be relevant to policy makers and to people's lives in general. For instance, Mead was the treasurer of Hull House, where for many years he used his theory to improve the lives of those who were powerless (especially immigrants). He also served on committees dealing with Chicago's labor problems and with public education.

Today, ***applied sociology*** is defined as the use of the discipline of sociology with the specific intent of yielding practical applications for human behavior and organizations. By extension, Michael Burawoy (2005), in his presidential address to the American Sociological Association, endorsed what he called *public sociology,* encouraging scholars to engage a broader audience in bringing about positive outcomes. In effect, the applied sociologist reaches out to others and joins them in their efforts to better society.

Often, the goal of such work is to assist in resolving a social problem. For example, in the past 50 years, eight presidents of the United States have established commissions to delve into major societal concerns facing our nation. Sociologists are often asked to apply their expertise to studying such issues as violence, pornography, crime, immigration, and population. In Europe, both academic and government research departments are offering increasing financial support for applied studies.

One example of applied sociology is the growing interest in learning more about local communities. Since its founding in 1994, the Northeast Florida Center for Community Initiatives (CCI), based at the University of North Florida in Jacksonville, has conducted several community studies, including a homeless census and survey, an analysis of the economic impact of the arts in Jacksonville, and a long-term survey of the effects of Hurricane Katrina. Typical of applied sociology, these outreach efforts are collaborative, involving faculty, undergraduate and graduate students, volunteers, and community residents (Center for Community Initiatives 2011).

Another of CCI's applications of sociology, the Magnolia Project, is based in a storefront clinic in an underprivileged area of Jacksonville. Part of the federal Healthy Start initiative, which aims to decrease high infant mortality rates, the project serves women of childbearing age who have little or no regular access to health care. CCI's responsibilities include (1) interviewing and surveying key community participants, (2) coordinating data collection by the project's staff, (3) analyzing data, and (4) preparing progress reports for funding agencies and community partners. Through August 2011, not a single infant death had occurred among the 117 participants in the program (Center for Community Initiatives 2012).

The growing popularity of applied sociology has led to the rise of the specialty of clinical sociology. Louis Wirth (1931) wrote about clinical sociology more than 70 years ago, but the term itself has become popular only in recent years. While applied sociologists may simply evaluate social issues, *clinical sociology* is dedicated to altering social relationships (as in family therapy) or to restructuring social institutions (as in the reorganization of a medical center).

Applied sociologists generally leave it to others to act on their evaluations. By contrast, clinical sociologists take direct responsibility for implementation and view those with whom they work as their clients. This specialty has become increasingly attractive to graduate students in sociology because it offers an opportunity to apply intellectual learning in a practical way. Up to now, a shrinking job market in the academic world has made such alternative career routes appealing.

Applied and clinical sociology can be contrasted with *basic sociology* (also called *pure sociology*), which seeks a more profound knowledge of the fundamental aspects of social phenomena. This type of research is not necessarily meant to generate specific applications, although such ideas may result once findings are analyzed. When Durkheim studied suicide rates, he was not primarily interested in discovering a way to eliminate suicide. In this sense, his research is an example of basic rather than applied sociology.

What issues facing your local community would you like to address with applied sociological research?

Sociology Matters

Sociology matters because it offers new insights into what is going on around you, in your own life as well as in the larger society. Consider the purpose of a college education:

- What are your own reasons for going to college? Are you interested only in academics, or did you enroll for the social life as well? Does your college encourage you to pursue both, and if so, why?

- How does your pursuit of a college education impact society as a whole? What are the social effects of your decision to become a student, both now and later in life, after you receive your degree?

Sociology also matters because sociologists follow a scientific research design to reach their conclusions. Consider the importance of careful research:

- Have you ever acted on incomplete information, or even misinformation? What were the results?

- What might be the result if legislators or government policy makers were to base their actions on faulty research?

CHAPTER RESOURCES

Summary

Sociology is the scientific study of social behavior and human groups. This chapter presented a brief history of the discipline and introduced the concept of the **sociological imagination.** It surveyed sociological **theory,** including contemporary perspectives, and suggested some practical uses for theory. This chapter also presented the principles of the **scientific method** and showed how sociologists use them in their research.

1. The **sociological imagination** is an awareness of the relationship between an individual and the wider society. It is based on an ability to view society as an outsider might, rather than from the perspective of an insider.

2. Sociologists employ **theory** to explain problems, actions, or behavior. Nineteenth-century thinkers who contributed to the development of sociological theory include Émile Durkheim, who pioneered work on suicide; Max Weber, a German thinker who taught the need for *Verstehen,* or "insight," in intellectual work; Karl Marx, a German intellectual who emphasized the importance of class conflict; and W. E. B. DuBois, who emphasized the importance of race.

3. Today, several theoretical perspectives guide sociological research. The **functionalist perspective** holds that society is structured in ways that maintain social stability, so that social change tends to be slow and evolutionary.

4. The **conflict perspective,** on the other hand, emphasizes the importance of conflict between competing social groups, so that social change tends to be swift and revolutionary. A related perspective, the *feminist perspective,* stresses conflict based on gender inequality.

5. The **feminist perspective** stresses gender as the key to understanding social interactions. Feminist sociologists charge that too often, scholars concentrate on male social roles, ignoring male–female differences in behavior.

6. **Queer theory** is the study of society from the perspective of a broad spectrum of sex identities, including heterosexuality, homosexuality, and bisexuality.

7. The **interactionist perspective** is concerned primarily with the everyday ways in which individuals shape their society and are shaped by it. Interactionists see social change as an ongoing and very personal process.

8. The **scientific method** includes five steps: defining the problem; reviewing the literature; formulating the *hypothesis;* selecting the **research design** and collecting and analyzing data; and developing the conclusion. The **hypothesis** states a possible relationship between two or more variables, usually one **independent variable** and a **dependent variable** that is thought to be related to it.

9. To avoid having to test everyone in a population, sociologists use a **sample** that is representative of the general population. Using a representative sample lends **validity** and **reliability** to the results of scientific research.

10. Sociologists use four major research designs in their work: **surveys** of the population; ethnographic studies of behaviors and communities; **experiments** that test hypothetical cause-and-effect relationships; and analysis of existing sources.

11. **Applied sociology**—the practical application of the discipline to problems in human behavior and organizations—is a growing field that includes community research and **clinical sociology.**

Key Terms

applied sociology, 32

basic sociology, 33

causal logic, 23

clinical sociology, 33

code of ethics, 31

conflict
    perspective, 16

content analysis, 30

control group, 29

control variable, 26

correlation, 24

cultural capital, 14

dependent
    variable, 23

double
    consciousness, 11

dysfunction, 16

ethnography, 28

experiment, 29

experimental
    group, 29

feminist
    perspective, 17

functionalist
    perspective, 14

Hawthorne
    effect, 29

hypothesis, 23

ideal type, 10

independent
    variable, 23

interactionist
    perspective, 19

interview, 27

latent function, 16

macrosociology, 13

manifest function, 16

microsociology, 13

natural science, 4

nonverbal
    communication, 20

observation, 28

operational
    definition, 22

qualitative
    research, 27

quantitative
    research, 27

queer theory, 18

questionnaire, 27

random sample, 24

reliability, 25

research design, 26

sample, 24

science, 4

scientific
    method, 21

secondary
    analysis, 29

social capital, 14

social science, 4

sociological
    imagination, 3

sociology, 2

survey, 27

theory, 6

validity, 25

variable, 23

Verstehen, 10

Culture and Socialization

©Ingram Publishing

In May 2012, Facebook founder and CEO Mark Zuckerberg flew to Manhattan to promote his company's initial stock offering. A celebrity before he turned 30, Zuckerberg had already been named *Time magazine*'s Person of the Year. Instead of dressing to impress Wall Street bankers, however, Zuckerberg wore his familiar hooded sweatshirt and a dark T-shirt. To the casual observer, he looked more like a computer hacker than the owner of a multibillion-dollar company. When questioned, Zuckerberg responded, "I feel like I'm not doing my job if I spend my energy on things that are silly or frivolous about my life" (Stone 2016).

Just three months earlier, wearing a dark hoodie and carrying a bag of Skittles and an Arizona iced tea, 17-year-old Trayvon Martin headed back to the townhouse where his father was staying in a gated community in Central Florida. A neighborhood watch coordinator, the same age as Zuckerberg, spotted the boy and thought he looked "suspicious," "up to no good." A few moments later, George Zimmerman shot Trayvon Martin dead. Clearly there was nothing frivolous about Trayvon's choice of attire. Within a few days of his death, the social movement of #BlackLivesMatter emerged.

A national debate ensued. Had being Black and wearing a hoodie contributed to Martin's death? Had being White allowed Zimmerman to avoid a homicide charge? A lot of people, both Black and White, thought so. In cities across the United States, demonstrators wearing hoodies protested the handling of the case. For many people, the story hit close to home. As President Barack Obama observed, "If I had a son, he'd look like Trayvon" (White House 2012). Many parents of teenagers, especially African American teens, cautioned their children to leave their hoodies in the closet.

What cultural meaning do we attach to a hoodie? Like many other symbols, the hoodie has multiple meanings. Depending on the context and the person, it can represent defiance or youthful indifference, casual comfort or sinister intentions. Through nationwide publicity, it can even become a symbol of protest against racism. Ultimately, the particular meanings that we attach to the clothing we and others wear reflect our culture and our upbringing.

Although most of us go about our daily lives unaware of culture and its importance to us, it is fundamental to any society. Culture includes the meanings we attach not just to clothes, but to all aspects of the world around us. Culture also affects the basic attitudes, values, and behaviors that we learn as children through a process called **socialization.** It can even affect a child's **personality**—the individual characteristics, attitudes, needs, and behaviors that set one person apart from another. Throughout the life course, culture prescribes the roles people take and the ceremonies they participate in as they pass from one life stage to another. It molds the most fundamental institutions of society, from the family, schools, and peer groups to the mass media, the workplace, and the state. Culture, in other words, is all-encompassing (Burch 2012; Contee 2012).

What Is Culture?

Culture is the totality of learned, socially transmitted customs, knowledge, material objects, and behavior. It includes the ideas, values, customs, and artifacts (for example, iPods, comic books, and birth control devices) of groups of people. Patriotic attachment to the flag of the United States is an aspect of culture, as is a national passion for the tango in Argentina.

Sometimes people refer to a particular person as "very cultured" or to a city as having "lots of culture." That use of the term *culture* is different from our use in this textbook. In sociological terms, *culture* does not refer solely to the fine arts and refined intellectual taste. It consists of *all* objects and ideas within a society, including ice cream cones, rock music, and slang words. Sociologists consider both a portrait by Rembrandt and a portrait by a billboard painter to be aspects of a culture. A tribe that cultivates soil by hand has just as much culture as a people that relies on computer-operated machinery. Each people has a distinctive culture with its own characteristic ways of gathering and preparing food, constructing homes, structuring the family, and promoting standards of right and wrong.

The fact that you share a similar culture with others helps to define the group or society to which you belong. A fairly large number of people are said to constitute a *society* when they live in the same territory, are relatively independent of people outside it, and participate in a common culture. The city of Los Angeles is more populous than many nations of the world, yet sociologists do not consider it a society in its own right. Rather, it is part of—and dependent on—the larger society of the United States.

A society is the largest form of human group. It consists of people who share a common heritage and culture. Members of the society learn this culture and transmit it from one generation to the next. They even preserve their distinctive culture through literature, art, video recordings, and other means of expression.

Sociologists have long recognized the many ways in which culture influences human behavior. Through what has been termed a toolkit of habits, skills, and styles, people of a common culture construct their acquisition of knowledge, their interactions with kinfolk, their entrance into the job market—in short, the way in which they live. If not for the social transmission of culture, each generation would have to reinvent television, not to mention the wheel (Swidler 1986).

Having a common culture also simplifies many day-to-day interactions. For example, when you buy an airline ticket, you know you don't need to bring along hundreds of dollars in cash. You can pay with a credit card or smartphone. When you are part of a society, you can take many small (as well as more important) cultural patterns for granted. You assume that theaters will provide seats for the audience, that physicians will not disclose confidential information, and that parents will be careful when crossing the street with young children. All these assumptions reflect basic values, beliefs, and customs of the culture of the United States.

Today, when text, sound, and video can be transmitted around the world instantaneously, some aspects of culture transcend national borders. The German philosopher Theodor Adorno and others have spoken of the worldwide *culture industry* that standardizes the goods and services demanded by consumers. Adorno contends that globally, the primary effect of popular culture is to limit people's choices. Yet others have shown that the culture industry's influence does not always permeate international borders. Sometimes it is embraced; at other times, soundly rejected (Adorno [1971] 1991:98–106; Horkheimer and Adorno [1944] 2002).

CULTURAL UNIVERSALS

All societies, despite their differences, have developed certain general practices known as *cultural universals.* Many cultural universals are, in fact, adaptations to meet essential human needs, such as people's need for food, shelter, and clothing. Anthropologist George Murdock (1945:124) compiled a list of cultural universals that includes athletic sports, cooking, dancing, visiting, personal names, marriage, medicine, religious ritual, funeral ceremonies, sexual restrictions, and trade.

The cultural practices listed by Murdock may be universal, but the manner in which they are expressed varies from culture to culture. For example, one society may let its members choose their own marriage partners. Another may encourage marriages arranged by the parents.

Not only does the expression of cultural universals vary from one society to another; it may also change dramatically over time within a society. Each generation, and each year for that matter, most human cultures change and expand through the processes of *innovation* and *diffusion.*

ETHNOCENTRISM

Many everyday statements reflect our attitude that our culture is best. We use terms such as *underdeveloped, backward,* and *primitive* to refer to other societies. What "we" believe is a religion; what "they" believe is superstition and mythology.

It is tempting to evaluate the practices of other cultures on the basis of our perspectives. Sociologist William Graham Sumner (1906) coined the term *ethnocentrism* to refer to the tendency to assume that one's own culture and way of life represent the norm or are superior to all others. The ethnocentric person sees his or her group as the center or defining point of culture and views all other cultures as deviations from what is "normal." Westerners who think cattle are to be used for food might look down on India's Hindu religion and culture, which view the cow as sacred. Or people in one culture may dismiss as unthinkable the mate selection or child-rearing practices of another culture. In sum, our view of the world is dramatically influenced by the society in which we were raised.

Ethnocentrism is hardly limited to citizens of the United States. Visitors from many African cultures are surprised at the disrespect that children in the United States show their parents. People from India may be repelled by our practice of living in the same household with dogs and cats. Many Islamic fundamentalists in the Arab world and Asia view the United States as corrupt, decadent, and doomed to destruction. All these people may feel comforted by membership in cultures that in their view are superior to ours.

While ethnocentrism is the evaluation of foreign cultures using the familiar culture of the observer as a standard of correct behavior, *cultural relativism* is the evaluation of a people's behavior from the perspective of their own culture. Medical practitioners who seek to adapt to their patients' cultural expectations are exhibiting this approach. Cultural relativism places a priority on understanding other cultures rather than dismissing them as "strange" or "exotic." Unlike ethnocentrism, cultural relativism employs a kind of *value neutrality* in scientific study, which Max Weber saw as being extremely important.

Cultural relativism stresses that different social contexts give rise to different norms and values. Thus, we must examine practices such as polygamy, bullfighting, and monarchy within the particular contexts of the cultures in which they are found. While cultural relativism does not suggest that we must unquestionably *accept* every cultural variation, it does require a serious and unbiased effort to evaluate norms, values, and customs in light of their distinctive culture.

How one views a culture—whether from an ethnocentric point of view or through the lens of cultural relativism—has important consequences for social policy. Consider the practice of children marrying adults. Most people in North America cannot fathom the idea of a 12-year-old girl marrying. The custom, which is illegal in the United States, is common in West Africa and South Asia. Should the United States respect such marriages? The apparent answer is no. In 2006 the U.S. government spent $623 million to discourage the practice in many of the countries with the highest child-marriage rates.

From the perspective of cultural relativism, we might ask whether one society should spend its resources to dictate the norms of another. However, federal officials have defended the government's actions. They contend that child marriage deprives girls of education, threatens their health, and weakens public health efforts to combat HIV/AIDS (Jain and Kurz 2007; Slavin 2007).

Development of Culture around the World

We've come a long way from our prehistoric heritage. The human species has produced such achievements as the novels of Leo Tolstoy, the art of Pablo Picasso, and the films of Ang Lee. As we begin a new millennium, we can transmit an entire book around the world via the Internet, clone cells, and prolong lives through organ transplants. We can peer into the outermost reaches of the universe or analyze our innermost feelings. In all these ways, we are remarkably different from other species of the animal kingdom. Though cultures differ in their customs, artifacts, and languages, they all share certain basic characteristics. In this section we will see how those characteristics change as cultures develop and how cultures influence one another through their technological, commercial, and artistic achievements.

Name one culturally significant discovery and one culturally significant invention that occurred in your lifetime. Explain how these innovations have affected the culture to which you belong.

INNOVATION

The process of introducing a new idea or object to a culture is known as *innovation.* Innovation interests sociologists because of the potential social consequences of introducing something new. There are two forms of innovation: discovery and invention. A *discovery* involves making known or sharing the existence of some aspect of reality. The finding of the DNA molecule and the identification of a new moon of Saturn are both acts of discovery. A significant factor in the process of discovery is the sharing of newfound knowledge with others. By contrast, an *invention* results when existing cultural items are combined into a form that did not exist before. The bow and arrow, the automobile, and the Internet are all examples of inventions, as are Protestantism and democracy.

GLOBALIZATION, DIFFUSION, AND TECHNOLOGY

The familiar green Starbucks logo beckons you into a comfortable coffee shop where you can order decaf latte and a cinnamon ring. What's unusual about that? This Starbucks happens to be located in the heart of Beijing's Forbidden City, just outside the Palace of Heavenly Purity, former residence of Chinese emperors. In 2002 it was one of 25 Starbucks stores in China; eight years later there were more than 375. The success of Starbucks in a country in which coffee drinking is still a novelty (most Chinese are tea drinkers) has been striking (Sanchanta 2010).

The emergence of Starbucks in China illustrates a rapidly escalating trend called *globalization.* **Globalization** may be defined as the worldwide integration of government policies, cultures, social movements, and financial markets through trade and the exchange of ideas. While public discussion of globalization is relatively recent, intellectuals have been pondering its social consequences for a long time. Karl Marx and Friedrich Engels warned in *The Communist Manifesto* (written in 1848) of a world market that would lead to production in distant lands, sweeping away existing working relationships. Today, more and more cultural expressions and practices are crossing national borders, transforming the traditions and customs of the societies exposed to them. Sociologists use the term *diffusion* to refer to the process by which a cultural item spreads from group to group or society to society. Diffusion can occur through a variety of means, among them exploration, military conquest, missionary work, the influence of the mass media, tourism, and the Internet.

Sociologist George Ritzer (2015) coined the term **McDonaldization** to describe the process through which the principles of the fast-food restaurant have come to dominate certain sectors of society, both in the United States and throughout the world. For example, hair salons and medical clinics now take walk-in appointments. In Hong Kong, sex selection clinics offer a menu of items, from fertility enhancement to methods of increasing the likelihood of producing a child of the desired sex.

Religious groups—from evangelical preachers on local stations or websites to priests at the Vatican Television Center—use marketing techniques similar to those that are used to sell Happy Meals.

McDonaldization is associated with the melding of cultures, through which we see more and more similarities in cultural expression. In Japan, for example, African entrepreneurs have found a thriving market for hip-hop fashions popularized by teens in the United States. Similarly, the familiar Golden Arches of McDonald's can be seen around the world. Yet corporations like McDonald's have had to make some adjustments of their own. Until 2001, McDonald's ran its overseas operations from corporate headquarters in suburban Chicago. After a few false starts, executives recognized the need to develop the restaurant's menus and marketing strategies overseas, relying on advice from local people. Now in Japan, customers can enjoy the Mega Tamago Burger—beef, bacon, and fried egg with special sauces. In India, patrons who don't eat beef can order a double chicken-patty sandwich known as the Maharaja Mac. And in Austria, the locals' love of coffee, cake, and conversation has inspired the McCafe (Hughlett 2008; Ritzer 2002, 2015).

Technology in its many forms has increased the speed of cultural diffusion and broadened the distribution of cultural elements. Sociologist Gerhard Lenski has defined *technology* as "cultural information about the ways in which the material resources of the environment may be used to satisfy human needs and desires" (Nolan and Lenski 2015:357). Today's technological developments no longer need await publication in journals with limited circulation. Press conferences, often carried simultaneously on the Internet, now trumpet new developments.

Sociologist William F. Ogburn (1922) made a useful distinction between the elements of material and nonmaterial culture. *Material culture* refers to the physical or technological aspects of our daily lives, including food items, houses, factories, and raw materials. *Nonmaterial culture* refers to ways of using material objects and to customs, beliefs, philosophies, governments, and patterns of communication. Generally, the nonmaterial culture is more resistant to change than the material culture. Ogburn introduced the term *culture lag* to refer to the period of maladjustment when the nonmaterial culture is still struggling to adapt to new material conditions. For example, the ethics of using the Internet, particularly issues concerning privacy and censorship, have not yet caught up with the explosion in Internet use and technology.

Cultural Variation

Each culture has a unique character. Inuit tribes in northern Canada—wrapped in furs and dining on whale blubber—have little in common with farmers in Southeast Asia, who dress for the heat and subsist mainly on the rice they grow in their paddies. Cultures adapt to meet specific sets of circumstances, such as climate, level of technology, population, and geography. Thus, despite the presence of cultural universals such as courtship and religion, great diversity exists among the world's many cultures. Moreover, even *within* a single nation, certain segments of the populace develop cultural patterns that differ from the patterns of the dominant society.

SUBCULTURES

Rodeo riders, residents of a retirement community, workers on an offshore oil rig—all are examples of what sociologists refer to as *subcultures.* A *subculture* is a segment of society that shares a distinctive pattern of customs, rules, and traditions that differs from the pattern of the larger society. In a sense, a subculture can be thought of as a culture existing within a larger, dominant culture. The existence of many subcultures is characteristic of complex societies such as the United States.

Members of a subculture participate in the dominant culture while at the same time engaging in unique and distinctive forms of behavior. Frequently, a subculture will develop an ***argot,*** or specialized language, that distinguishes it from the wider society. Athletes who play *parkour,* an extreme sport that combines forward running with fence leaping and the vaulting of walls, water barriers, and even moving cars, speak an argot they devised especially to describe their feats. Parkour runners talk about doing *King Kong vaults*—diving arms first over a wall or grocery cart and landing in a standing position. They may follow this maneuver with a *tic tac*—kicking off a wall to overcome some kind of obstacle (Kidder 2012).

Argot allows "insiders," the members of the subculture, to understand words with special meanings. It also establishes patterns of communication that "outsiders" can't understand. Sociologists associated with the interactionist perspective emphasize that language and symbols offer a powerful way for a subculture to feel cohesive and maintain its identity.

In India, a new subculture has developed among employees at the international call centers established by multinational corporations. To serve customers in the United States and Europe, the young men and women who work there must be fluent speakers of English. But the corporations that employ them demand more than proficiency in a foreign language; they expect their Indian employees to adopt Western values and work habits, including the grueling pace U.S. workers take for granted.

In effect, workers at these call centers live in a state of virtual migration—not quite in India, but not in the United States, either. Significantly, call centers allow employees to take the day off only on U.S. holidays, like Labor Day and Thanksgiving—not on Indian holidays like Diwali, the Hindu festival of lights. While most Indian families are home celebrating, call center employees see only each other; when they have the day off, no one else is free to socialize with them. As a result, these employees have formed a tight-knit subculture based on hard work and a taste for Western luxury goods and leisure-time pursuits (Rowe et al. 2013).

Another shared characteristic among some employees at Indian call centers is their contempt for the callers they serve. In performing their monotonous, repetitive job day after day, hundreds of thousands of these workers have come to see the faceless Americans they deal with as slow, often rude customers. Such shared understandings underpin this emerging subculture (Bhagat 2007; Gentleman 2006; Patel 2010).

COUNTERCULTURES

By the end of the 1960s, an extensive subculture had emerged in the United States, composed of young people turned off by a society they believed was too materialistic and technological. This group included primarily political radicals and "hippies" who had "dropped out" of mainstream social institutions. These young men and women rejected the pressure to accumulate more and more cars, larger and larger homes, and an endless array of material goods. Instead, they expressed a desire to live in a culture based on more humanistic values, such as sharing, love, and coexistence with the environment. As a political force, this subculture opposed the United States' involvement in the war in Vietnam and encouraged draft resistance (Flacks 1971; Roszak 1969).

When a subculture conspicuously and deliberately *opposes* certain aspects of the larger culture, it is known as a ***counterculture.*** Countercultures typically thrive among the young, who have the least investment in the existing culture. In most cases, a 20-year-old can adjust to new cultural standards more easily than someone who has spent 60 years following the patterns of the dominant culture (Zellner 1995).

In the last decade, counterterrorism experts have become concerned about the growth of ultraconservative militia groups in the United States. Secretive and well armed, members of these countercultural groups tend to be antigovernment, and they often tolerate racism in their midst. Watchdogs estimate that 1,274 antigovernment groups are operating in the United States today (Southern Poverty Law Center 2015).

CULTURE SHOCK

Anyone who feels disoriented, uncertain, out of place, even fearful when immersed in an unfamiliar culture may be experiencing ***culture shock.*** For example, a resident of the United States who visits certain areas in China and wants local meat for dinner may be stunned to learn that the specialty is dog meat. Similarly, someone from a strict Islamic culture may be shocked upon first seeing the comparatively provocative dress styles and open displays of affection common in the United States and Europe.

All of us, to some extent, take for granted the cultural practices of our society. As a result, it can be surprising and even disturbing to realize that other cultures do not follow our "way of life." The fact is, customs that seem strange to us are considered normal and proper in other cultures, which may see *our* customs as odd.

You arrive in a developing African country as a Peace Corps volunteer. What aspects of this very different culture do you think will be the hardest to adjust to? What might the citizens of that country find shocking about your culture?

Language and Culture

The English language makes extensive use of words dealing with war. We speak of "conquering" space, "fighting the battle" of the budget, "waging war" on drugs, making a "killing" on the stock market, and "bombing" an examination; something monumental or great is "the bomb." An observer from an entirely different and warless culture could gauge the importance of war and the military in our lives simply by recognizing the prominence that militaristic terms have in our language. Similarly, cattle are so important to the Nuer of southern Sudan that they have more than 400 words to describe the animals (Haviland et al. 2008).

Language is, in fact, the foundation of every culture. *Language* is an abstract system of word meanings and symbols for all aspects of culture. It includes speech, written characters, numerals, symbols, and gestures and expressions of nonverbal communication.

Because of the long history of immigration to North America, the United States has a rich diversity of languages. Indeed, each of 29 other languages is spoken by at least 200,000 U.S. residents. According to the Bureau of the Census, in 2015 over one in five U.S. residents over the age of five spoke a language other than English at home, as their primary language (Figure 2-1; American Community Survey 2016r; C. Ryan 2013).

Though language is a cultural universal, striking differences are evident in its use. For decades, the Navajo have referred to cancer as *lood doo na'dziihii*. Now, through a project funded by the National Cancer

Figure 2–1

Percentage of People Who Speak a Language Other Than English at Home, by State

NOTE: *Data drawn from the 2015 American Community Survey of people five years and over. National average was 21.5 percent.*

SOURCE: American Community Survey 2016b: Table R1601.

Percentage of People

- 25.0 or more
- 15.0–24.9
- 10.0–14.9
- Under 10

Institute, the tribal college is seeking to change the phrase. Why? Literally, the word means "the sore that does not heal," and health educators are concerned that tribal members who have been diagnosed with cancer view it as a death sentence. Their effort to change the Navajo language, not easy in itself, is complicated by the Navajo belief that to talk about the disease is to bring it on one's people (Fonseca 2008).

The thumbs-up gesture is an example of *nonverbal communication,* or the use of gestures, facial expressions, and other visual images to communicate. If you are in the midst of a friendly meeting and one member suddenly sits back, folds his arms, and turns down the corners of his mouth, you know at once that trouble has arrived. When you see a friend in tears, you may give her a quick hug. After winning a big game, you probably high-five your teammates. These are all examples of nonverbal communication.

We are not born with these expressions. We learn them, just as we learn other forms of language, from people who share our culture. That is as true for the basic expressions of happiness and sadness as it is for more complex emotions, such as shame or distress (Fridlund et al. 1987).

Like other forms of language, nonverbal communication is not the same in all cultures. For example, sociological research done at the micro level documents that people from various cultures differ in the degree to which they touch others during the course of normal social interactions. Even experienced travelers are sometimes caught off guard by these differences. In Saudi Arabia, a middle-aged man may want to hold hands with a partner after closing a business deal. The gesture, which would shock an American businessman, is considered a compliment in that culture. The meaning of hand signals is another form of nonverbal communication that can differ from one culture to the next. In Australia, the thumbs-up sign is considered rude (Passero 2002; Vaughan 2007).

Norms and Values

"Wash your hands before dinner." "Thou shalt not kill." "Respect your elders." All societies have ways of encouraging and enforcing what they view as appropriate behavior while discouraging and punishing what they consider to be improper behavior. They also have a collective idea of what is good and desirable in life—or not. In this section we will learn to distinguish between the closely related concepts of norms and values.

NORMS

Norms are the established standards of behavior maintained by a society. For a norm to become significant, it must be widely shared and understood. For example, in movie theaters in the United States, we typically expect that people will be quiet while the film is shown. Of course, the application of this norm can vary, depending on the particular film and type of audience. People who are viewing a serious artistic film will be more likely to insist on the norm of silence than those who are watching a slapstick comedy or horror movie.

One persistent social norm in contemporary society is that of heterosexuality. Children are socialized to accept this norm from a very young age. Overwhelmingly, parents describe adult romantic relationships to their children exclusively as heterosexual relationships. That is not necessarily because they consider same-sex relationships unacceptable, but more likely because they see heterosexuality as the norm in marital partnerships. According to a national survey of mothers of three- to six-year-olds, one in five mothers teaches her young children that homosexuality is wrong. The same survey showed that parenting reflects the dominant ideology, in which homosexuality is treated as a rare exception. Most parents assume that their children are heterosexual; only one in four had even considered whether his or her child might grow up to be gay or lesbian (K. Martin 2009).

Types of Norms   Sociologists distinguish between norms in two ways. First, norms are classified as either formal or informal. *Formal norms* generally have been written down and specify strict punishment of violators. In the United States, we often formalize norms into laws, which must be very precise in defining proper and improper behavior. Sociologist Donald Black (1995) has termed *law* "governmental social control," meaning formal norms that are enforced by the state. Laws are just one example of formal norms. The requirements for a college major and the rules of a card game are also considered formal norms.

By contrast, *informal norms* are generally understood but are not precisely recorded. Standards of proper dress are a common example of informal norms. Our society has no specific punishment or sanction for a person who comes to school, say, wearing a monkey suit. Making fun of the nonconforming student is usually the most likely response.

Norms are also classified by their relative importance to society. When classified in this way, they are known as *mores* and *folkways*. *Mores* (pronounced MOR-ays) are norms deemed highly necessary to the welfare of a society, often because they embody the most cherished principles of a people. Each society demands obedience to its mores; violations can lead to severe penalties. Thus, the United States has strong mores against murder, treason, and child abuse, which have been institutionalized into formal norms.

Folkways are norms governing everyday behavior. Folkways play an important role in shaping the daily behavior of members of a culture. Still, society is less likely to formalize folkways than mores, and their violation raises comparatively little concern. For example, walking up a "down" escalator in a department store challenges our standards of appropriate behavior, but it will not result in a fine or a jail sentence.

Acceptance of Norms   People do not follow norms, whether mores or folkways, in all situations. In some cases, they can evade a norm because they know it is weakly enforced. It is illegal for U.S. teenagers to drink

Use Your Sociological Imagination

You are a high school principal. What norms would you want to govern students' behavior? How might those norms differ from those typical of college students?

alcoholic beverages, yet drinking by minors is common throughout the nation. In fact, teenage alcoholism is a serious social problem.

Norms are violated in some instances because one norm conflicts with another. For example, suppose one night you hear the screams of the woman next door, who is being beaten by her husband. If you decide to intervene by ringing their doorbell or calling the police, you are violating the norm of "minding your own business," while at the same time following the norm of assisting a victim of violence.

Acceptance of norms is subject to change as the political, economic, and social conditions of a culture are transformed. Until the 1960s, for example, formal norms throughout much of the United States prohibited the marriage of people from different racial groups. Over the last half century, however, such legal prohibitions were cast aside. The process of change can be seen today in the increasing acceptance of single parents and growing support for the legalization of marriage between same-sex couples (see Chapter 8).

SANCTIONS

Suppose a football coach sends a 12th player onto the field. Or imagine a college graduate showing up in shorts for a job interview at an accounting firm. Consider a driver who neglects to put any money into a parking meter. These people have violated widely shared and understood norms. So what happens? In each of these situations, the person will receive sanctions if his or her behavior is detected.

Sanctions are penalties and rewards for conduct concerning a social norm. Note that the concept of *reward* is included in this definition. Conformity to a norm can lead to positive sanctions such as a pay raise, a medal, a word of gratitude, or a pat on the back. Negative sanctions include fines, threats, imprisonment, and stares of contempt.

Table 2-1 summarizes the relationship between norms and sanctions. As you can see, the sanctions associated with formal norms (those that are written down and codified) tend to be formal as well. If a coach sends

Table 2-1 Norms and Sanctions

| Norms | Sanctions | |
	Positive	Negative
Formal	Salary bonus	Demotion
	Testimonial dinner	Firing from a job
	Medal	Jail sentence
	Diploma	Expulsion
Informal	Smile	Frown
	Compliment	Humiliation
	Cheers	Bullying

too many players onto the field, the team will be penalized 15 yards. The driver who fails to put money in the parking meter will be ticketed and expected to pay a fine. But sanctions for violations of informal norms can vary. The college graduate who comes to the job interview in shorts will probably lose any chance of getting the job; on the other hand, he or she might be so brilliant, the interviewer will overlook the unconventional attire. Obviously only the Mark Zuckerbergs of the world can get away wearing a hoodie to formal business occasions.

The entire fabric of norms and sanctions in a culture reflects that culture's values and priorities. The most cherished values will be most heavily sanctioned; matters regarded as less critical will carry light and informal sanctions.

VALUES

Though we all have our own personal sets of standards—which may include caring, fitness, or success in business—we also share a general set of objectives as members of a society. Cultural *values* are collective conceptions of what is considered good, desirable, and proper—or bad, undesirable, and improper. They indicate what people in a given culture prefer, as well as what they find important and morally right or wrong. Values may be specific, such as honoring one's parents and owning a home, or they may be more general, such as health, love, and democracy. Of course, the members of a society do not uniformly share its values. Angry political debates and billboards promoting conflicting causes tell us that much.

Values influence people's behavior and serve as criteria for evaluating the actions of others. There is often a direct relationship among a culture's values, norms, and sanctions. For example, if a culture highly values the institution of marriage, it may have norms (and strict sanctions) that prohibit the act of adultery. If a culture views private property as a basic value, it will probably have stiff laws against theft and vandalism.

Socially shared, intensely felt values are a fundamental part of life in the United States. Even so, our values can and do change.

Each year nearly 142,000 full-time, newly entering students at nearly 200 of the nation's four-year colleges fill out a questionnaire about their values. Because this survey focuses on an array of issues, beliefs, and life goals, it is commonly cited as a barometer of the nation's values. The respondents are asked what values are personally important to them. Over the past half century, the value of "being very well-off financially" has shown the strongest gain in popularity; the proportion of first-year college students who endorse this value as "essential" or "very important" rose from 42 percent in 1966 to 82 percent in 2015 (Figure 2–2).

During the 1980s and 1990s, support for values having to do with money, power, and status grew. At the same time, support for certain values having to do with social awareness and altruism, such as "helping others," declined. According to the 2015 nationwide survey, only 44 percent

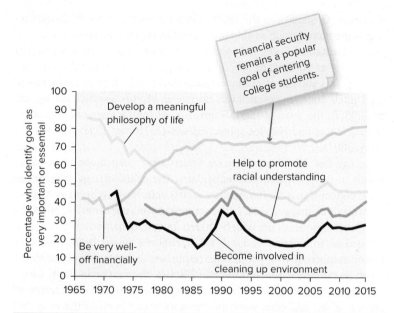

Figure 2–2

Life Goals of First-Year College Students in the United States, 1966–2015

Sources: Eagan et al. 2016; Pryor et al. 2007.

Think About It

Why do you think values have shifted among college students in the past few decades? Which of these values is important to you?

of first-year college students stated that "influencing social values" was an "essential" or "very important" goal. The proportion of students for whom "helping to promote racial understanding" was an essential or very important goal reached a record high of 46 percent in 1992, then leveled off at 41.2 percent in 2015. Like other aspects of culture, such as language and norms, a nation's values are not necessarily fixed.

Whether the slogan is "Think Green" or "Reduce Your Carbon Footprint," students have been exposed to values associated with environmentalism. How many of them accept those values? Poll results over the past 50 years show fluctuations, with a high of nearly 46 percent of students in the early 1970s indicating a desire to become involved in cleaning up the environment. By the 1980s, however, student support for embracing this objective had dropped to around 20 percent or even lower (see Figure 2–2). Even with recent attention to climate change, the proportion remains level at only 28.8 percent of first-year students in 2015.

Global Culture War

When people's cultural values clash, social conflict may follow. For almost a generation, public attention in the United States has focused on *culture war,* or the polarization of society over controversial elements of culture. Originally, in the 1990s, the term referred to political debates over heated issues such as abortion, religious expression, gun control, and sexual orientation. Soon, however, it took on a global meaning—especially after 9/11, as Americans wondered, "Why do they hate us?" Through 2000, global studies of public opinion had reported favorable views of the United States in countries as diverse as Morocco and Germany. But by 2003, in the wake of the U.S. invasion of Iraq, foreign opinion of the United States had become quite negative (J. Hunter 1991; Kohut et al. 2005, 2007).

In the last 30 years, extensive efforts have been made to compare values in different nations, recognizing the challenges in interpreting value concepts in a similar manner across cultures. Psychologist Shalom Schwartz has measured values in more than 60 countries. Around the world, certain values are widely shared, including benevolence, which is defined as "forgiveness and loyalty." In contrast, power, defined as "control or dominance over people and resources," is a value that is endorsed much less often (Hitlin and Piliavin 2004; S. Schwartz and Bardi 2001).

Despite this evidence of shared values, some scholars have interpreted the terrorism, genocide, wars, and military occupations of the early 21st century as a "clash of civilizations." According to this thesis, cultural and religious identities, rather than national or political loyalties, are becoming the prime source of international conflict. Critics of this thesis point out that conflict over values is nothing new; only our ability to create havoc and violence has grown. Furthermore, speaking of a clash of "civilizations" disguises the sharp divisions that exist within large groups. Christianity, for example, runs the gamut from Quaker-style pacifism to certain elements of the Ku Klux Klan's ideology (Berman 2003; Huntington 1993; Said 2001; Schrad 2014).

Culture and the Dominant Ideology

Functionalist and conflict theorists agree that culture and society are mutually supportive, but for different reasons. Functionalists maintain that social stability requires a consensus and the support of society's members; strong central values and common norms provide that support. This view of culture became popular in sociology beginning in the 1950s. It was borrowed from British anthropologists who saw cultural traits as a stabilizing element in a culture. From a functionalist perspective, a cultural trait or practice will persist if it performs functions that society seems to need or contributes to overall social stability and consensus.

Conflict theorists agree that a common culture may exist, but they argue that it serves to maintain the privileges of certain groups. Moreover, in protecting their own self-interest, powerful groups may keep others in a subservient position. The term *dominant ideology* describes the set of

Look around your campus. Do the people you see suggest that the United States has a core culture with a dominant ideology, or a diverse culture with differing values and ideologies? What about the city or town where your college or university is located—does it suggest the same conclusion?

cultural beliefs and practices that help to maintain powerful social, economic, and political interests. This concept was first used by Hungarian Marxist Georg Lukacs (1923) and Italian Marxist Antonio Gramsci (1929); it did not gain an audience in the United States until the early 1970s. In Karl Marx's view, a capitalist society has a dominant ideology that serves the interests of the ruling class.

From a conflict perspective, the dominant ideology has major social significance. Not only do a society's most powerful groups and institutions control wealth and property; even more important, they control the means of producing beliefs about reality through religion, education, and the media. From a feminist perspective, if all the most important social institutions tell women they should be subservient to men, that dominant ideology will help to control women and keep them in a subordinate position.

A growing number of social scientists believe it is not easy to identify a "core culture" in the United States. For support, they point to the lack of consensus on national values, the diffusion of cultural traits, the diversity within our culture, and the changing views of young people. Instead, they suggest that the core culture provides the tools that people of all persuasions need to develop strategies for social change. Yet there is no way of denying that certain expressions of values have greater influence than others, even in so complex a society as the United States (Swidler 1986).

Table 2-2 summarizes the major theoretical perspectives on culture.

Table 2–2 Sociological Perspectives on Culture

	Functionalist Perspective	Conflict Perspective	Feminist Perspective	Interactionist Perspective
Cultural Variation	Ethnocentrism reinforces group solidarity; subcultures serve the interests of subgroups	Ethnocentrism devalues groups; countercultures question the dominant social order	Cultural relativism respects variations in the way men and women are viewed in different societies	Customs and traditions are transmitted through intergroup contact and through the media
Norms	Reinforce societal standards	Reinforce patterns of dominance	Reinforce roles of men and women	Are maintained through face-to-face interaction
Values	Are collective conceptions of what is good	May perpetuate social inequality	May perpetuate men's dominance	Are defined and redefined through social interaction
Culture and Society	Culture reflects a society's strong central values	Culture reflects a society's dominant ideology	Culture reflects society's view of men and women	A society's core culture is perpetuated through daily social interactions

Tracking Perspectives

Culture and Socialization

What makes us who we are? Is it the genes we are born with, or the environment we grow up in? Researchers have traditionally clashed over the relative importance of biological and environmental factors in human development, a conflict called the *nature versus nurture* (or *heredity versus environment*) debate. Today, most social scientists have moved beyond this debate, acknowledging instead the *interaction* of the two variables in shaping human development. However, we can better appreciate how heredity and environment interact to influence the socialization process if we first examine situations in which one factor operates almost entirely without the other (Homans 1979).

SOCIOBIOLOGY: THE IMPACT OF HEREDITY

While sociology emphasizes diversity and change in the expression of culture, another school of thought, sociobiology, stresses the universal aspects of culture. *Sociobiology* is the systematic study of how biology affects human social behavior. Sociobiologists assert that many of the cultural traits humans display, such as the almost universal expectation that women will be nurturers and men will be providers, are not learned but are rooted in our genetic makeup.

Sociobiology is founded on the naturalist Charles Darwin's (1859) theory of evolution. In traveling the world, Darwin had noted small variations in species from one location to another. He theorized that over hundreds of generations, random variations in genetic makeup had helped certain members of a species to survive in a particular environment. The species was slowly adapting to its environment. Darwin called this process of adaptation to the environment through random genetic variation *natural selection*.

Sociobiologists apply Darwin's principle of natural selection to the study of social behavior. They assume that particular forms of behavior become genetically linked to a species if they contribute to its fitness to survive (van den Berghe 1978). In its extreme form, sociobiology suggests that *all* behavior is the result of genetic or biological factors and that social interactions play no role in shaping people's conduct.

Sociobiologists do not seek to describe individual behavior on the level of "Why is Fred more aggressive than Jim?" Rather, they focus on how human nature is affected by the genetic composition of a *group* of people who share certain characteristics (such as men or women, or members of isolated tribal bands). In general, sociobiologists have stressed the basic genetic heritage that *all* humans share and have shown little interest in speculating about alleged differences between racial groups or nationalities. A few researchers have tried to trace specific behaviors, like criminal activity, to certain genetic markers, but those markers are not deterministic. Family cohesiveness, peer group behavior, and other social factors can override genetic influences on behavior (Guo et al. 2008; E. Wilson 1975, 1978).

Certainly most social scientists would agree that there is a biological basis for social behavior. But there is less support for the extreme positions taken by certain advocates of sociobiology. Like interactionists, conflict theorists and functionalists believe that people's behavior rather than their genetic structure defines social reality. Conflict theorists fear that the socio-biological approach could be used as an argument against efforts to assist disadvantaged people, such as schoolchildren who are not competing successfully (Freese 2008; Machalek and Martin 2010; E. Wilson 2000).

SOCIAL ENVIRONMENT: THE IMPACT OF ISOLATION

In the 1994 movie *Nell*, Jodie Foster played a young woman hidden from birth by her mother in a backwoods cabin. Raised without normal human contact, Nell crouches like an animal, screams wildly, and speaks or sings in a language all her own. The movie was drawn from the actual account of an emaciated 16-year-old boy who appeared mysteriously in 1828 in the town square of Nuremberg, Germany (Lipson 1994).

Some viewers may have found the story of Nell difficult to believe, but the painful childhood of a girl called Isabelle was all too real. For the first six years of her life, Isabelle lived in almost total seclusion in a darkened room. She had little contact with other people, with the exception of her mother, who could neither speak nor hear. Isabelle's grandparents had been so deeply ashamed of her illegitimate birth that they kept her hidden away from the world. Ohio authorities finally discovered the child in 1938, when Isabelle's mother escaped from her parents' home, taking her daughter with her.

When Isabelle was discovered at age six, she could not speak; she could merely make various croaking sounds. Her only communications with her mother were simple gestures. Isabelle had been largely deprived of the typical interactions and socialization experiences of childhood. Since she had seen few people, she initially showed a strong fear of strangers and reacted almost like a wild animal when confronted with an unfamiliar person. As she became accustomed to seeing certain individuals, her reaction changed to one of extreme apathy. At first, observers believed that Isabelle was deaf, but she soon began to react to nearby sounds. On tests of maturity, she scored at the level of an infant rather than a six-year-old.

What events in your life have had a strong influence on who you are?

Specialists developed a systematic training program to help Isabelle adapt to human relationships and socialization. After a few days of training, she made her first attempt to verbalize. Although she started slowly, Isabelle passed quickly through six years of development. In a little over two months, she was speaking in complete sentences. Nine months later she could identify both words and sentences. Before Isabelle reached the age of nine, she was ready to attend school with other children. By her 14th year she was in 6th grade, doing well in school, and was emotionally well-adjusted (K. Davis 1947:435–437).

Isabelle's experience is important to researchers because there are only a few cases of children reared in total isolation. Unfortunately, however, there are many cases of children raised in extremely neglect-ful social circumstances. Recently, attention has focused on infants and young children from orphanages in the formerly communist countries of Eastern Europe. In Romanian orphanages, babies once lay in their cribs for 18 to 20 hours a day, curled against their feeding bottles and receiving little adult care. Such minimal attention continued for the first five years of their lives. Many of them were fearful of human contact and prone to unpredictable antisocial behavior.

This situation came to light as families in North America and Europe began adopting thousands of the children. The adjustment problems for about 20 percent of them were often so dramatic that the adopting fami-lies suffered guilty fears of being ill-fit adoptive parents. Many of them have asked for assistance in dealing with the children. Slowly, efforts are being made to introduce the deprived youngsters to feelings of attachment that they have never experienced before (Groza et al. 1999; C. Smith 2006).

Increasingly, researchers are emphasizing the importance of early socialization experiences for children who grow up in more normal environments. We know now that it is not enough to care for an infant's physical needs; parents must also concern themselves with children's social development. If, for example, children are discouraged from hav-ing friends, they will miss out on social interactions that are critical for emotional growth.

How do you view yourself as you interact with others around you? How do you think you formed this view of yourself?

The Self and Socialization

We all have various perceptions, feelings, and beliefs about who we are and what we are like. How do we come to develop these ideas? Do they change as we age?

We were not born with these understandings. Building on the work of George Herbert Mead (1964b), sociologists recognize that we create our own designation: the *self.* The *self* is a distinct identity that sets one apart from others. It is not a static phenomenon, but continues to develop and change throughout our lives.

Sociologists and psychologists alike have expressed interest in how the individual develops and modifies the sense of self as a result of social interaction. The work of sociologists Charles Horton Cooley and George Herbert Mead, pioneers of the interactionist approach, has been espe-cially useful in furthering our understanding of these important issues.

COOLEY: LOOKING-GLASS SELF

In the early 1900s, Charles Horton Cooley advanced the belief that we learn who we are by interacting with others. Our view of ourselves, then, comes not only from direct contemplation of our personal qualities but also from our impressions of how others perceive us. Cooley used the phrase *looking-glass self* to emphasize that the self is the product of our social interactions with other people.

The process of developing a self-identity or self-concept has three phases. First, we imagine how we present ourselves to others—to relatives, friends, even strangers on the street. Then we imagine how others evaluate us (attractive, intelligent, shy, or strange). Finally, we develop some sort of feeling about ourselves, such as respect or shame, as a result of these impressions (Cooley 1902; M. Howard 1989).

A subtle but critical aspect of Cooley's looking-glass self is that it results from an individual's "imagination" of how others view him or her. As a result, we can develop self-identities based on *incorrect* perceptions of how others see us. A student may react strongly to a teacher's criticism and decide (wrongly) that the instructor views him or her as stupid. This misperception can easily be converted into a negative self-identity through the following process: (1) The teacher criticized me, (2) the teacher must think that I'm stupid, (3) I *am* stupid. Yet self-identities are also subject to change. If the student receives an A at the end of the course, he or she will probably no longer feel stupid.

MEAD: STAGES OF THE SELF

George Herbert Mead continued Cooley's exploration of interactionist theory. Mead (1934, 1964a) developed a useful model of the process by which the self emerges, defined by three distinct stages: the preparatory stage, the play stage, and the game stage.

The Preparatory Stage   During the *preparatory stage,* children imitate the people around them, especially family members with whom they continually interact. Thus, a small child will bang on a piece of wood while a parent is engaged in carpentry work, or will try to throw a ball if an older sibling is doing so nearby.

As they grow older, children become more adept at using symbols to communicate with others. *Symbols* are the gestures, objects, and language that form the basis of human communication. By interacting with relatives and friends, as well as by watching cartoons on television and looking at picture books, children in the preparatory stage begin to understand the use of symbols.

The Play Stage   Mead was among the first to analyze the relationship of symbols to socialization. As children develop skill in communicating through symbols, they gradually become more aware of social relationships. As a result, during the *play stage,* the child begins to pretend to be other people. Just as an actor "becomes" a character, a child becomes a doctor, parent, superhero, or ship captain.

In fact, Mead noted that an important aspect of the play stage is role playing. *Role taking* is the process of mentally assuming the perspective of another in order to respond from that imagined viewpoint. Through this process, a young child will gradually learn when it is best to ask a parent for favors. If the parent usually comes home from work in a bad mood, the child will wait until after dinner, when the parent is more relaxed and approachable.

The Game Stage   In Mead's third stage, the *game stage,* the child of about eight or nine years old no longer just plays roles but begins to consider several tasks and relationships simultaneously. At this point in development, children grasp not only their own social positions but also those of others around them—just as in a football game the players must understand their own and everyone else's positions. Consider a girl or boy who is part of a scout troop out on a weekend hike in the mountains. The child must understand what he or she is expected to do but must also recognize the responsibilities of other scouts and of the leaders. This is the final stage of development in Mead's model; the child can now respond to numerous members of the social environment.

Mead uses the term **generalized other** to refer to the attitudes, viewpoints, and expectations of society as a whole that a child takes into account in his or her behavior. Simply put, this concept suggests that when an individual acts, he or she takes into account an entire group of people. For example, a child will not act courteously merely to please a particular parent. Rather, the child comes to understand that courtesy is a widespread social value endorsed by parents, teachers, and religious leaders. Table 2–3 summarizes the three stages of the self outlined by George Herbert Mead.

MEAD: THEORY OF THE SELF

Mead is best known for his theory of the self. According to Mead (1964b), the self begins as the privileged center of a person's world. Young children picture themselves as the focus of everything around them and find

Table 2–3 Mead's Stages of the Self

Stage	Self Present?	Definition	Example
Preparation	No	Child imitates the actions of others	When adults laugh and smile, child laughs and smiles
Play	Developing	Child takes the role of a single other, as if he or she were the other	Child first takes the role of doctor, then the role of patient
Game	Yes	Child considers the roles of two or more others simultaneously	In game of hide-and-seek, child takes into account the roles of both hider and seeker

it difficult to consider the perspectives of others. When shown a mountain scene and asked to describe what an observer on the opposite side of the mountain sees (such as a lake or hikers), they describe only objects visible from their own vantage point. This childhood tendency to place ourselves at the center of events never entirely disappears. Many people with a fear of flying automatically assume that if any plane goes down, it will be the one they are on. And who reads the horoscope section in the paper without looking at their own horoscope first? Why else do we buy lottery tickets, if we don't imagine ourselves winning?

Nonetheless, as people mature, the self changes and begins to reflect greater concern for the reactions of others. Mead used the term *significant others* to refer to those individuals who are most important in the development of the self. Parents, friends, coworkers, coaches, and teachers are often among those who play a major role in shaping a person's self. Many young people, for example, find themselves drawn to the same kind of work their parents engage in (H. Sullivan [1953] 1968).

Who have been your significant others? Are you someone else's significant other?

GOFFMAN: PRESENTATION OF THE SELF

How do we manage our "self"? How do we display to others who we are? Erving Goffman, a sociologist associated with the interactionist perspective, suggested that many of our daily activities involve attempts to convey impressions of who we are.

Early in life, the individual learns to slant his or her presentation of the self in order to create distinctive appearances and satisfy particular audiences. Goffman (1959) refers to this altering of the presentation of the self as *impression management.* In analyzing such everyday social interactions, Goffman makes so many explicit parallels to the theater that his view has been termed the *dramaturgical approach.* According to this perspective, people resemble performers in action. For example, a clerk may try to appear busier than he or she actually is if a supervisor happens

People judge us by our appearance, attire, body language, demeanor, and mannerisms. Knowing that they do, most of us alter the way we present ourselves to others, a strategy that Goffman called impression management.

Cartoonstock.com

to be watching. A customer in a singles' bar may try to look as if he or she is waiting for a particular person to arrive.

Goffman's work on the self represents a logical progression of the sociological work begun by Cooley and Mead on how personality is acquired through socialization and how we manage the presentation of the self to others. Cooley stressed the process by which we come to create a self; Mead focused on how the self develops as we learn to interact with others; Goffman emphasized the ways in which we consciously create images of ourselves for others.

PSYCHOLOGICAL APPROACHES TO THE SELF

Psychologists have shared the interest of Cooley, Mead, and other sociologists in the development of the self. Early work in psychology, such as that of Sigmund Freud (1856-1939), stressed the role of inborn drives—among them the drive for sexual gratification—in channeling human behavior. More recently, psychologists such as Jean Piaget have emphasized the stages through which human beings progress as the self develops.

Like Charles Horton Cooley and George Herbert Mead, Freud believed that the self is a social product and that aspects of one's personality are influenced by other people (especially one's parents). However, unlike Cooley and Mead, he suggested that the self has components that work in opposition to each other. According to Freud, our natural impulsive instincts are in constant conflict with societal constraints. Part of us seeks limitless pleasure, while another part favors rational behavior. By interacting with others, we learn the expectations of society and then select behavior most appropriate to our own culture. (Of course, as Freud was well aware, we sometimes distort reality and behave irrationally.)

Research on newborn babies by the Swiss child psychologist Jean Piaget (1896-1980) has underscored the importance of social interactions in developing a sense of self. Piaget found that newborns have no self in the sense of a looking-glass image. Ironically, though, they are quite self-centered; they demand that all attention be directed toward them. Newborns have not yet separated themselves from the universe of which they are a part. For these babies, the phrase "you and me" has no meaning: They understand only "me." However, as they mature, children are gradually socialized into social relationships, even within their rather self-centered world.

In his well-known *cognitive theory of development,* Piaget (1954) identified four stages in the development of children's thought processes. In the first, or *sensorimotor,* stage, young children use their senses to make discoveries. For example, through touching they discover that their hands are actually a part of themselves. During the second, or *preoperational,* stage, children begin to use words and symbols to distinguish objects and ideas. The milestone in the third, or *concrete operational,* stage is that children engage in more logical thinking. They learn that even when a formless lump of clay is shaped into a snake, it is still the same clay. Finally, in the fourth, or *formal operational,* stage, adolescents become capable of sophisticated abstract thought and can deal with ideas and values in a logical manner.

Piaget suggested that moral development becomes an important part of socialization as children develop the ability to think more abstractly. When children learn the rules of a game such as checkers or jacks, they are learning to obey societal norms. Those under eight years old display a rather basic level of morality: Rules are rules, and there is no concept of "extenuating circumstances." As they mature, children become capable of greater autonomy and begin to experience moral dilemmas and doubts as to what constitutes proper behavior.

According to Jean Piaget, social interaction is the key to development. As children grow older, they pay increasing attention to how other people think and why they act in particular ways. In order to develop a distinct personality, each of us needs opportunities to interact with others. As we saw earlier, Isabelle was deprived of the chance for normal social interactions, and the consequences were severe (Kitchener 1991).

We have seen that a number of thinkers considered social interaction the key to the development of an individual's sense of self. As is generally true, we can best understand this topic by drawing on a variety of theory and research. Table 2–4 summarizes the rich literature, both sociological and psychological, on the development of the self.

Table 2–4 Theoretical Approaches to Development of the Self

Scholar	Key Concepts and Contributions	Major Points of Theory
Charles Horton Cooley 1864–1929 sociologist (USA)	Looking-glass self	Stages of development not distinct; feelings toward ourselves developed through interaction with others
George Herbert Mead 1863–1931 sociologist (USA)	The self Generalized other	Three distinct stages of development; self develops as children grasp the roles of others in their lives
Erving Goffman 1922–1982 sociologist (USA)	Impression management Dramaturgical approach	Self developed through the impressions we convey to others and to groups
Sigmund Freud 1856–1939 psychotherapist (Austria)	Psychoanalysis	Self influenced by parents and by inborn drives, such as the drive for sexual gratification
Jean Piaget 1896–1980 child psychologist (Switzerland)	Cognitive theory of development	Four stages of cognitive development; moral development linked to socialization

summing UP

Agents of Socialization

We have seen that each culture considers its own distinctive ways of handling basic societal tasks to be "natural." Yet methods of education, marital ceremonies, religious doctrines, and other aspects of culture differ markedly from one society to another. Parents in India are accustomed to arranging marriages for their children; parents in the United States leave marital decisions up to their offspring. Lifelong residents of Naples consider it natural to speak Italian; lifelong residents of Buenos Aires feel the same way about Spanish. These cultural preferences are learned and transmitted through the process of socialization.

The continuing and lifelong socialization process involves many different social forces that influence our lives and alter our self-images. The family is the most important agent of socialization in the United States, especially for children. We'll also give particular attention in this section to six other agents of socialization: the school, the peer group, the mass media, the workplace, religion, and the state.

FAMILY

Children in Amish communities are raised in a highly structured and disciplined manner. But they are not immune to the temptations posed by their peers in the non-Amish world—"rebellious" acts such as dancing, drinking, and riding in cars. Still, Amish families don't get too concerned; they know the strong influence they ultimately exert over their offspring. The same is true for the family in general. It is tempting to say that the "peer group" or even the "media" really raise children these days, especially when the spotlight falls on young people involved in shooting sprees and hate crimes. Almost all available research, however, shows that the role of the family in socializing a child cannot be overestimated (Schaefer and Zellner 2011).

The lifelong process of learning begins shortly after birth. Since newborns can hear, see, smell, taste, and feel heat, cold, and pain, they are constantly orienting themselves to the surrounding world. Human beings, especially family members, constitute an important part of their social environment. People minister to the baby's needs by feeding, cleansing, carrying, and comforting the baby.

Families also communicate cultural assumptions regarding gender and race to children. In the case of Black parents, they must strive to counteract negative cultural messages about Blacks that children as young as age two can absorb from children's books, toys, and television shows—all of which are designed primarily for White children. At the same time, they must deal with the fact that Black children are exposed more often than others to the inner-city youth gang culture. Because most Blacks, even those who are middle class, live near very poor neighborhoods, Black children are susceptible to these influences, despite their parents' strong family values (Linn and Poussaint 1999; Pattillo-McCoy 1999).

Parents deal with cultural expectations regarding gender through *gender roles*. The term **gender role** refers to expectations regarding the proper behavior, attitudes, and activities of males or females. For example, we traditionally think of "toughness" as masculine—and desirable in men but not women—while we view "tenderness" as feminine. Yet other cultures do not necessarily assign these qualities to each gender in the way that our culture does.

The existence of gender roles does not imply that inevitably, males and females will assume certain roles, nor does it imply that those roles are quite distinct from each other. Rather, gender roles emphasize the fact that males and females are not genetically predetermined to occupy certain roles.

As the primary agents of childhood socialization, parents play a critical role in guiding children into those gender roles deemed appropriate in a society. Other adults, older siblings, the mass media, and religious and educational institutions also have a noticeable impact on a child's socialization into feminine and masculine norms. A culture or subculture may require that one sex or the other take primary responsibility for the socialization of children, economic support of the family, or religious or intellectual leadership.

Interactionists remind us that socialization concerning not only masculinity and femininity but also marriage and parenthood begins in childhood as a part of family life. Children observe their parents as they express affection, deal with finances, quarrel, complain about in-laws, and so forth. These experiences represent an informal process of anticipatory socialization. The child develops a tentative model of what being married and being a parent are like.

SCHOOL

Where did you learn the national anthem? Who taught you about the heroes of the American Revolution? Where were you first tested on your knowledge of your culture? Like the family, schools have an explicit mandate to socialize people in the United States—and especially children—into the norms and values of our culture.

As conflict theorists Samuel Bowles and Herbert Gintis (1976) have observed, schools in this country foster competition through built-in systems of reward and punishment, such as grades and evaluations by teachers. Consequently, a child who is working intently to learn a new skill can sometimes come to feel stupid and unsuccessful. However, as the self matures, children become capable of increasingly realistic assessments of their intellectual, physical, and social abilities.

Functionalists point out that as agents of socialization, schools fulfill the function of teaching children the values and customs of the larger society. Conflict theorists agree but add that schools can reinforce the divisive aspects of society, especially those of social class. For example, higher education in the United States is costly despite the existence of financial aid programs. Students from affluent backgrounds have an advantage in gaining access to universities and professional training. At the same time, less affluent young people may never receive the preparation that would qualify them for the best-paying and most prestigious jobs.

PEER GROUP

As a child grows older, the family becomes somewhat less important in social development. Instead, peer groups increasingly assume the role of Mead's significant others. Within the peer group, young people associate with others who are approximately their age, and who often enjoy a similar social status (Giordano 2003).

We can see how important peer groups are to young people when their social lives are strained by war or disaster. In Syria, social groupings have been torn apart by civil war, invasion, and bombings. In 2012, Fatmeh described her life as that of a typical teenager whose daily routine was all about school, classes, friends, and homework. Three years later, at age 15, she was living in a makeshift shelter in Lebanon. When she left Syria, she still hoped to continue her studies in Lebanon and become a language teacher, but that is unlikely to happen, because her whole family must do farm work seven days a week to maintain their meager life. Her only connection beyond her immediate family is her cell phone, which allows her to keep up with news about Syria and to hear songs about her homeland. Fatmeh says she still has "very small hope" that someday she will be able to return to school and eventually go to college. "Very small, small hope," she says (Beaubien and Davis 2015).

Peers can be the source of harassment as well as support, as news stories around the world have shown. This problem has received considerable attention in Japan, where bullying in school is a constant fact of life. Groups of students act together to humiliate, disgrace, or torment a specific student, a practice known in Japan as *ijime*. Most students go along with the bullying out of fear that they themselves might become the target. In some cases the *ijime* has led to a child's suicide. In 1998 the situation became so desperate that a volunteer association set up a 24-hour telephone hotline in Tokyo just for children. The success of the effort convinced the government to sponsor a nationwide hotline system (Matsushita 1999; Sugimoto 1997).

MASS MEDIA AND TECHNOLOGY

Over the past three generations, media innovations—radio, motion pictures, recorded music, and television—have become important agents of socialization. Now in the last 20 years, the Internet, including social media, has emerged as a critical force in the socialization of even relatively young children (see Figure 2-3). The majority of children age 8 to 12 spend on average over six hours *every day* on some form of

©Universal Uclick

electronic media. Children in that age group access social media less than an hour a day—usually through a smartphone. But by their teen years, their consumption increases dramatically. These sites usually echo and amplify much of the young person's socialization.

These media, however, are not always a negative socializing influence. Television programs and even commercials can introduce young people to unfamiliar lifestyles and cultures. Not only do children in the United

Figure 2–3
Media Profiles of 8- to 12-Year-Olds: Daily Time Spent with Each Type of Media

SOURCE: Common Sense Media 2015:17. (Figure 3)

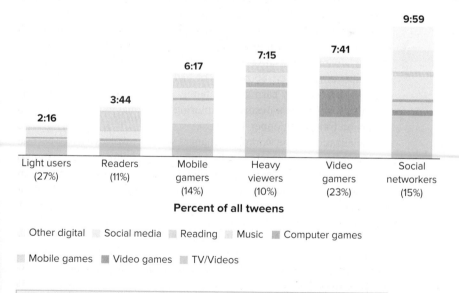

Think About It
How do these data compare to your social media use when you were 12 years old?

States learn about life in "faraway lands," but inner-city children learn about the lives of farm children, and vice versa. The same thing happens in other countries.

Sociologists and other social scientists have begun to consider the impact of technology on socialization. They are particularly interested in the online social media networks, like Facebook. Does this way of communicating resemble face-to-face interaction, or does it represent a new form of social interaction?

Not just in industrial nations, but in Africa and other developing areas, people have been socialized into relying on new communications technologies. Not long ago, if Zadhe Iyombe wanted to talk to his mother, he had to make an eight-day trip from the capital city of Kinshasa up the Congo River by boat to the rural town where he was born. Now both he and his mother have access to a cell phone, and they send text messages to each other daily. Iyombe and his mother are not atypical. Although cell phones aren't cheap, 1.4 billion owners in developing countries have come to consider them a necessity. Today, there are more cell phones in developing nations than in industrial nations—the first time in history that developing nations have outpaced the developed world in the adoption of a telecommunications technology (K. Sullivan 2006).

WORKPLACE

Learning to behave appropriately in the workplace is a fundamental aspect of human socialization. Once, "going to work" began with the end of one's formal schooling, but that is no longer the case, at least not in the United States. More and more young people work today, and not just for a parent or relative. Adolescents generally seek jobs in order to make spending money; 80 percent of high school seniors say that little or none of what they earn goes to family expenses. They rarely look on their employment as a means of exploring vocational interests or getting on-the-job training (Cooper 1998).

Socialization in the workplace changes when it involves a more permanent shift from an after-school job to full-time employment. Occupational socialization can be most intense during the transition from school to job, but it continues throughout one's work history. Technological advances may alter the requirements of the position and necessitate some degree of resocialization. Today, men and women change occupations, employers, or places of work many times during their adult years. For example, the typical worker spends about four years with an employer. Occupational socialization continues, then, throughout a person's years in the labor market (Bialik 2010).

College students today recognize that occupational socialization is not socialization into one lifetime occupation. They anticipate going through a number of jobs. The Bureau of Labor Statistics (2015a) has found that from ages 18 to 48, the typical person has held 12 jobs, but nearly half of these jobs are held between ages 18 and 24. This high rate of turnover in employment applies to both men and women, and to those with a college degree as well as those with a high school diploma.

RELIGION AND THE STATE

Increasingly, social scientists are recognizing the importance of both government ("the state") and religion as agents of socialization, because of their impact on the life course. Traditionally, family members have served as the primary caregivers in our culture, but in the 20th century, the family's protective function was steadily transferred to outside agencies such as hospitals, mental health clinics, and child care centers. Many of these agencies are run by the state or by groups affiliated with certain religions.

Both government and organized religion have impacted the life course by reinstituting some of the rites of passage once observed in agricultural communities and early industrial societies. For example, religious organizations stipulate certain traditional rites that may bring together all the members of an extended family, even if they never meet for any other reason. And government regulations stipulate the ages at which a person may drive a car, drink alcohol, vote in elections, marry without parental permission, work overtime, and retire. These regulations do not constitute strict rites of passage: Most 18-year-olds choose not to vote, and most people choose their age of retirement without reference to government dictates.

Socialization Throughout the Life Course

THE LIFE COURSE

Among the Kota people of the Congo, adolescents paint themselves blue. Mexican American girls go on a daylong religious retreat before dancing the night away. Egyptian mothers step over their newborn infants seven times, and students at the U.S. Naval Academy throw their hats in the air. These are all ways of celebrating *rites of passage,* a means of dramatizing and validating changes in a person's status. The Kota rite marks the passage to adulthood. The color blue, viewed as the color of death, symbolizes the death of childhood. Hispanic girls celebrate reaching womanhood at age 15 with a *quinceañera* ceremony. In many Latino communities in the United States, the popularity of the *quinceañera* supports a network of party planners, caterers, dress designers, and the Miss Quinceañera Latina pageant (Van Gennep [1909] 1960).

These specific ceremonies mark stages of development in the life course. They indicate that the process of socialization continues through

What was the last rite of passage you participated in? Was it formal or informal?

all stages of the life cycle. In fact, some researchers have chosen to concentrate on socialization as a lifelong process. Sociologists and other social scientists who take such a *life-course approach* look closely at the social factors that influence people throughout their lives, from birth to death. They recognize that biological changes mold but do not dictate human behavior.

ANTICIPATORY SOCIALIZATION AND RESOCIALIZATION

The development of a social self is literally a lifelong transformation that begins in the crib and continues even as one prepares for death. Two types of socialization occur at many points throughout the life course: anticipatory socialization and resocialization.

Anticipatory socialization refers to the processes of socialization in which a person "rehearses" for future positions, occupations, and social relationships. A culture can function more efficiently and smoothly if members become acquainted with the norms, values, and behavior associated with a social position before actually assuming that status. Preparation for many aspects of adult life begins with anticipatory socialization during childhood and adolescence and continues throughout our lives as we prepare for new responsibilities.

You can see the process of anticipatory socialization take place when high school students start to consider what colleges they may attend. Traditionally, this task meant looking at publications received in the mail or making campus visits. However, with new technology, more and more students are using the Web to begin their college experience. Colleges are investing more time and money in developing attractive websites through which students can take virtual campus tours and hear audio clips of everything from the college anthem to a sample zoology lecture.

Occasionally, assuming new social and occupational positions requires us to *unlearn* an established orientation. *Resocialization* refers to the process of discarding former behavior patterns and accepting new ones as part of a transition in one's life. Often resocialization occurs when there is an explicit effort to transform an individual, as happens in reform schools, therapy groups, prisons, religious conversion settings, and political indoctrination camps. The process of resocialization typically involves considerable stress for the individual, much more so than socialization in general or even anticipatory socialization (Gecas 2004).

Resocialization is particularly effective when it occurs within a total institution. Erving Goffman (1961) coined the term *total institution* to refer to institutions such as prisons, the military, mental hospitals, and convents, which regulate all aspects of a person's life under a single authority. Because the total institution is generally cut off from the rest of society, it provides for all the needs of its members. Quite literally, the crew of a merchant vessel at sea becomes part of a total institution. So elaborate are its requirements, so all-encompassing its activities, a total institution often represents a miniature society.

Goffman (1961) identified four common traits of total institutions, as follows:

1. All aspects of life are conducted in the same place under the control of a single authority.

2. Any activities within the institution are conducted in the company of others in the same circumstances—for example, army recruits or novices in a convent.

3. The authorities devise rules and schedule activities without consulting the participants.

4. All aspects of life within a total institution are designed to fulfill the purpose of the organization. Thus, all activities in a monastery might be centered on prayer and communion with God (Davies 1989; P. Rose et al. 1979).

People often lose their individuality within total institutions. For example, a person entering prison may experience the humiliation of a *degradation ceremony* as he or she is stripped of clothing, jewelry, and other personal possessions. From this point onward, scheduled daily routines allow for little or no personal initiative. The individual becomes secondary and rather invisible in the overbearing social environment (Garfinkel 1956).

Sociology Matters

Sociology matters because it raises your awareness of cultural patterns you would otherwise take for granted.

- What culture and/or subcultures do you belong to? Have you ever questioned your culture's norms and values?

- How does your culture relate to cultures in other societies? Do you feel comfortable in mainstream society?

Sociology matters, too, because it shows you how you became who you are.

- How do you view yourself as you interact with others around you? How do you think you formed this view of yourself?

- What people, groups, or social institutions have been particularly important in helping you to define who you are?

Summary

Culture is the totality of learned, socially transmitted customs, knowledge, material objects, and behavior that defines the group or **society** to which we belong. People learn these elements of culture through the life-long process of **socialization.** This chapter presented the basic elements that are common to all cultures, as well as variations that distinguish one culture from another. It examined the role of socialization in human development, including the way in which people develop their concept of the **self.** It closed with a description of the major agents of socialization and the **life-course approach** to socialization.

1. **Cultural universals** are general practices that are found in every **culture,** including sports, cooking, dancing, medicine, religious ritual, and sexual restrictions. The manner in which these universal practices are expressed varies from one culture to the next, however.

2. Most people use their own culture as the standard for evaluating other cultures, a perspective that is called **ethnocentrism.** Some sociologists attempt to see other cultures as members of those cultures see them, a perspective called **cultural relativism.**

3. In recent decades, international trade and the exchange of ideas have accelerated cultural change. Sociologists use the term **globalization** to refer to the resulting worldwide integration of government policies, cultures, social movements, and financial markets.

4. **Language,** an important element of culture, includes speech, writing, and **symbols** as well as gestures and other forms of **nonverbal communication.** Language both describes and shapes culture.

5. **Norms** are the standards of behavior members of a society are expected to uphold. Norms may be **formal**—written down—or **informal**—generally understood. **Sanctions** are the rewards and punishments meted out to those who comply with or violate social norms.

6. Every culture has a **dominant ideology**—a set of beliefs and practices that reinforce powerful social, economic, and political interests. Large cultures may include **subcultures**—groups of people who share norms and **values** that differ from those of the larger society and may contradict the dominant ideology.

7. The process of **socialization** to a society's cultural values is influenced both by the environment and by heredity. The study of the biological bases of social behavior is called **sociobiology.**

8. Charles Horton Cooley asserted that we learn who we are by interacting with others, a phenomenon he called the **looking-glass self.** Another interactionist, George Herbert Mead, proposed a three-stage theory of the development of the **self.**

9. Erving Goffman showed that many of our daily activities involve attempts to convey distinct impressions of who we are, a process he called **impression management.**

10. Sociologists who take a **life-course approach** to the study of socialization are interested in the social factors that influence people throughout their lives, from birth to death. The primary agents in this process are the family, schools, peer groups, the mass media and technology, the workplace, religion, and the state.

Key Terms

anticipatory socialization, 68

argot, 44

cognitive theory of development, 60

counterculture, 45

cultural relativism, 41

cultural universal, 40

culture, 38

culture industry, 39

culture lag, 43

culture shock, 45

culture war, 51

degradation ceremony, 69

diffusion, 42

discovery, 42

dominant ideology, 52

dramaturgical approach, 59

ethnocentrism, 40

folkway, 48

formal norm, 48

gender role, 63

generalized other, 58

globalization, 42

impression management, 59

informal norm, 48

innovation, 42

invention, 42

language, 46

law, 48

life-course approach, 68

looking-glass self, 57

material culture, 43

McDonaldization, 42

mores, 48

nonmaterial culture, 43

norm, 47

personality, 38

resocialization, 68

rite of passage, 67

role taking, 57

sanction, 49

self, 56

significant other, 59

socialization, 38

society, 39

sociobiology, 54

subculture, 44

symbol, 57

technology, 43

total institution, 68

value, 50

Social Interaction, Groups, and Social Structure

©Design Pics/Don Hammond

Social Interaction and Reality

Elements of Social Structure

Social Structure in Global Perspective

Understanding Organizations

In the early 1970s, social psychologist Philip Zimbardo asked 70 male students at Stanford University to participate in an unorthodox experiment: a mock prison he had set up in the basement of a campus building. Using a coin toss, Zimbardo assigned half the subjects to play the role of prisoner and half to act as prison guards, as the photo shows. He told the "guards" to make up their own rules for running the prison, then waited to see what would happen.

The results both astonished and frightened Zimbardo. Virtually overnight, the guards became tough enforcers of the rules, shouting curt commands at the prisoners. Some became cruel and abusive; one even forced a prisoner into "solitary confinement" in a closet. The prisoners reacted just as swiftly: some became depressed, apathetic, and helpless; others, rebellious and angry. In just six days, the situation became so intolerable that Zimbardo was forced to abandon the study. Given the anxiety and distress he had observed in the student prisoners, continuing the experiment would have been unethical (Zimbardo 2007).

In this study, college students adopted predictable patterns of behavior (those expected of guards and prisoners) when they were placed together in a mock prison. Sociologists use the term **social interaction** to refer to the ways in which people respond to one another. Social interaction need not be face-to-face; talking over the telephone and communicating via e-mail are also forms of social interaction. In Zimbardo's mock prison experiment, the social interactions between guards and prisoners were highly impersonal. Guards wore reflective sunglasses that made eye contact impossible and addressed prisoners by number rather than by name.

As in many real-life prisons, the simulated prison at Stanford had a social structure in which guards held virtually total control over prisoners. Formally defined, **social structure** is the way in which a society is organized into predictable relationships. Clearly, the prison's social structure influenced how the guards and prisoners interacted. As Zimbardo et al. (2009:516) noted, it was a real prison "in the minds of the jailers and their captives." The experiment, conducted 40 years ago, has since been repeated—with similar findings—both in the United States and in other countries.

Zimbardo's experiment took on new relevance in 2004, in the wake of shocking revelations of prisoner abuse at the U.S.-run Abu Ghraib military facility in Iraq. Graphic photos showed U.S. soldiers humiliating naked Iraqi prisoners and threatening to attack them with police dogs. The structure of the wartime prison, coupled with intense pressure on military intelligence officers to secure information regarding terrorist plots, contributed to the breakdown in the guards' behavior. But Zimbardo himself noted that the guards' depraved conduct could have been predicted simply on the basis of his research. So strong was public reaction to the Abu Ghraib scandal that in 2009, during his first week in office, President Barack Obama declared that henceforth interrogators will use only noncoercive methods for questioning suspected terrorists (Ratnesar 2011; Zimbardo 2015).

The two concepts of social interaction and social structure are closely linked to groups and organizations. Often, social interactions take place in groups of friends, relatives, or coworkers or in formal organizations such as universities and prisons. Whatever the setting, an underlying social structure dictates the relationships among members of the group or organization and the ways in which they respond to one another. In this chapter we will study the five basic elements of social structure: statuses, social roles, groups, social networks, and social institutions such as the family, religion, and government. We'll see that functionalists, conflict theorists, and interactionists approach these institutions quite differently. Next, we'll compare our modern social structure with simpler forms, using typologies developed by Émile Durkheim, Ferdinand Tönnies, and Gerhard Lenski. And we'll examine how and why formal organizations, such as a corporation or the college you attend, came into existence, touching on Max Weber's model of the modern bureaucracy in the process.

Social Interaction and Reality

How do we define our social reality? As an example, let's consider something as simple as how we regard tattoos. Not too long ago, most people in the United States considered tattoos to be "weird" or "kooky." Tattoos were associated with fringe countercultural groups, such as punk rockers, biker gangs, and skinheads. Among many people, a tattoo elicited an automatic negative response. Now, however, there are so many tattooed people, including society's trendsetters and major sports figures, and the ritual of getting a tattoo has become so legitimized that people regard tattoos differently. At this point, as a result of increased social interactions with tattooed people, tattoos look perfectly at home to us in a number of settings.

The nature of social interaction and what constitutes reality varies across cultures. In Western societies, with their emphasis on romantic love, couples see marriage as a relationship as well as a social status. From Valentine's Day flowers to more informal, everyday gestures, professions of love are an expected part of marriage. In Japan, however, marriage is considered more a social status than a relationship. Although many or most Japanese couples undoubtedly do love each other, saying "I love you" does not come easily to them, especially not to husbands. Nor do most husbands call their wives by name (they prefer "Mother") or look them in the eyes. In 2006, in an effort to change these restrictive customs, some Japanese men formed the Devoted Husband Organization, which has been sponsoring a new holiday, Beloved Wives Day. Recently, the group organized an event called Shout Your Love from the Middle of a Cabbage Patch Day. Dozens of men stood in a cabbage patch north of Tokyo and shouted, "I love you!" to their wives, some of whom had never heard their husbands say those words. In another rare gesture, husbands pledged to be home by 8 P.M. that day (Japan Aisaika Organization 2012; Kambayashi 2008).

The ability to define social reality reflects a group's power within a society. In fact, one of the most crucial aspects of the relationship between dominant and subordinate groups is the ability of the dominant or majority group to define a society's values. Sociologist William I. Thomas (1923), an early critic of theories of racial and gender differences, recognized that the "definition of the situation" could mold the thinking and personality of the individual. Writing from an interactionist perspective, Thomas observed that people respond not only to the objective features of a person or situation but also to the *meaning* the person or situation has for them. For example, in Philip Zimbardo's mock prison experiment, student "guards" and "prisoners" accepted the definition of the situation (including the traditional roles and behavior associated with being a guard or prisoner) and acted accordingly.

Let's take a closer look at the elements of social structure that help to define social reality.

Elements of Social Structure

We can examine predictable social relationships in terms of five elements: statuses, social roles, groups, social networks, and social institutions. These elements make up a social structure just as a foundation, walls, and ceilings make up a building's structure. The elements of social structure are developed through the lifelong process of socialization, described in Chapter 2.

STATUSES

We normally think of a person's "status" as having to do with influence, wealth, and fame. However, sociologists use the term *status* to refer to any of the full range of socially defined positions within a large group or society, from the lowest to the highest position. Within our society, a person can occupy the status of president of the United States, fruit picker, son or daughter, violinist, teenager, resident of Minneapolis, dental technician, or neighbor. A person can hold several statuses at the same time.

Ascribed and Achieved Status   Sociologists view some statuses as *ascribed* and others as *achieved* (see Figure 3–1). An *ascribed status* is "assigned"

Figure 3–1
Social Statuses

Ascribed statuses   Achieved statuses

Think About It
The person in this figure—"me"—occupies many positions in society, each of which involves distinct statuses. How would you define *your* statuses? Which have the most influence in your life?

to a person by society without regard for the person's unique talents or characteristics. Generally, this assignment takes place at birth; thus, a person's racial background, gender, and age are all considered ascribed statuses. Though these characteristics are biological in origin, they are significant mainly because of the *social* meanings they have in our culture. Conflict theorists are especially interested in ascribed statuses, since they often confer privileges or reflect a person's membership in a subordinate group. The social meanings of race, ethnicity, and gender will be analyzed more fully in Chapters 6 and 7.

In most cases, we can do little to change an ascribed status. However, we can attempt to change the traditional constraints associated with such statuses. For example, the Gray Panthers—an activist political group founded in 1971 to work for the rights of older people—have tried to modify society's negative and confining stereotypes of elderly individuals. As a result of their work and that of other groups supporting older citizens, the ascribed status of "senior citizen" is no longer as difficult for millions of older people.

Unlike ascribed statuses, an ***achieved status*** comes to us largely through our own efforts. Both "bank president" and "prison guard" are achieved statuses, as are "lawyer," "pianist," "sorority member," "convict," and "social worker." You must do something to acquire an achieved status—go to school, learn a skill, establish a friendship, or invent a new product. As we will see in the next section, our ascribed status heavily influences our achieved status. Being male, for example, decreases the likelihood that a person will consider becoming a child care worker.

Master Status   Each person holds many different and sometimes conflicting statuses; some may connote higher social positions and some, lower positions. How, then, do others view one's overall social position? According to sociologist Everett Hughes (1945), societies deal with such inconsistencies by agreeing that certain statuses are more important than others. A *master status* is a status that dominates others and thereby determines a person's general position within society. For example, Arthur Ashe, who died of AIDS in 1993, had a remarkable career as a tennis star, but at the end of his life, his status as a well-known personality with AIDS may have outweighed his statuses as a retired athlete, an author, and a political activist. Throughout the world, many people with disabilities find that their status as "disabled" receives undue weight and overshadows their actual ability to perform successfully in meaningful employment.

Our society gives so much importance to race and gender that they often dominate our lives. These ascribed statuses frequently influence achieved status. The African American activist Malcolm X (1925–1965), an eloquent and controversial advocate of Black power and Black pride in the early 1960s, recalled that his feelings and perspectives changed dramatically when he was in middle school. Elected class president and finishing near the top of his class academically, he had developed a positive outlook. However, his teachers, all of them White, discouraged him from taking more challenging courses, which they felt were not appropriate for Black students. When his eighth-grade English teacher, a White man, advised him that his goal of becoming a lawyer was not realistic, and encouraged him instead to become a carpenter, Malcolm X concluded that his being a Black man (ascribed status) was an obstacle to his dream of becoming a lawyer (achieved status). In the United States, the ascribed statuses of race and gender can function as master statuses that impact one's potential to achieve a desired professional and social status (Malcolm X [1964] 1999:37; Marable 2011:36–38).

SOCIAL ROLES

What Are Social Roles?   Throughout our lives, we acquire what sociologists call *social roles.* A *social role* is a set of expectations for people who occupy a given social position or status. Thus, in the United States, we expect that cab drivers will know how to get around a city, that receptionists will be reliable in handling phone messages, and that police officers will take action if they see a citizen being threatened. With each distinctive social status—whether ascribed or achieved—come particular role expectations. However, actual performance varies from individual to individual. One secretary may assume extensive administrative responsibilities, while another may focus on clerical duties. Similarly, in Philip Zimbardo's mock prison experiment, some students were brutal and sadistic guards, but others were not.

Roles are a significant component of social structure. Viewed from a functionalist perspective, roles contribute to a society's stability by enabling members to anticipate the behavior of others and to pattern their own actions accordingly. Yet social roles can also be dysfunctional, by restricting people's interactions and relationships. If we view a person only as a "police officer" or a "supervisor," it will be difficult to relate to the person as a friend or neighbor.

Role Conflict   Imagine the delicate situation of a woman who has worked for a decade on an assembly line in an electrical plant, and has recently been named supervisor of her unit. How is this woman expected to relate to her longtime friends and coworkers? Should she still go out to lunch with them, as she has done almost daily for years? Is it her responsibility to recommend the firing of an old friend who cannot keep up with the demands of the assembly line?

Role conflict occurs when incompatible expectations arise from two or more social positions held by the same person. Fulfillment of the roles associated with one status may directly violate the roles linked to a second status. In the example just given, the newly promoted supervisor will most likely experience a sharp conflict between her social and occupational roles. Role conflicts call for important ethical choices. The new

If you were a male nurse, what aspects of role conflict would you need to consider? Now imagine you are a professional boxer and a woman. What conflicting role expectations might that involve? In both cases, how well do you think you would handle role conflict?

supervisor will have to make a difficult decision about how much allegiance she owes her friend and how much she owes her employers, who have given her supervisory responsibilities.

Another type of role conflict occurs when individuals move into occupations that are not common among people with their ascribed status. Male preschool teachers and female police officers experience this type of role conflict. In the latter case, female officers must strive to reconcile their workplace role in law enforcement with the societal view of a woman's role, which does not embrace many skills needed in police work. And while female police officers encounter sexual harassment, as women do throughout the labor force, they must also deal with the "code of silence," an informal norm that precludes their implicating fellow officers in wrongdoing (Fletcher 1995; S. Martin 1994).

Role Strain   Role conflict describes the situation of a person dealing with the challenge of occupying two social positions simultaneously. However, even a single position can cause problems. Sociologists use the term *role strain* to describe the situation that occurs when the same social position imposes conflicting demands and expectations.

People who belong to minority cultures may experience role strain while working in the mainstream culture. Criminologist Larry Gould (2002) interviewed officers of the Navajo Nation Police Department about their relations with conventional law enforcement officials, such as sheriffs and FBI agents. Besides enforcing the law, Navajo Nation officers practice an alternative form of justice known as Peacemaking, in which they seek reconciliation between the parties to a crime. The officers expressed great confidence in Peacemaking, but worried that if they did not make arrests, other law enforcement officials would think they were too soft, or "just taking care of their own." Regardless of the strength of their ties to traditional Navajo ways, all felt the strain of being considered "too Navajo" or "not Navajo enough."

Role Exit   Often, when we think of assuming a social role, we focus on the preparation and anticipatory socialization a person undergoes for that role. Such is true if a person is about to become an attorney, a chef, a spouse, or a parent. Yet until recently, social scientists have given little attention to the adjustments involved in *leaving* social roles.

Sociologist Helen Rose Fuchs Ebaugh (1988) developed the term *role exit* to describe the process of disengagement from a role that is central to one's self-identity in order to establish a new role and identity. Drawing on interviews with 185 people—among them ex-convicts, divorced men and women, recovering alcoholics, ex-nuns, former doctors, retirees, and transsexuals—Ebaugh (herself an ex-nun) studied the process of voluntarily exiting from significant social roles.

Ebaugh has offered a four-stage model of role exit. The first stage begins with *doubt*. The person experiences frustration, burnout, or simply unhappiness with an accustomed status and the roles associated with the social position. The second stage involves a *search for alternatives*. A person who is unhappy with his or her career may take a leave of absence; an unhappily married couple may begin what they see as a temporary separation. The third stage of role exit is the action stage or *departure*. Ebaugh found that the vast majority of her respondents could identify a clear turning point that made them feel it was essential to take final action and leave their jobs, end their marriages, or engage in another type of role exit. The fourth stage of role exit involves the *creation of a new identity*. Many people participate in a role exit when they get married. They assume a new role that further redefines the old role of son or daughter.

GROUPS

In sociological terms, a *group* is any number of people with similar norms, values, and expectations who interact with one another on a regular basis. The members of a women's basketball team, of a hospital's business office, or of a symphony orchestra constitute a group. However, the residents of a suburb would not be considered a group, since they rarely interact with one another at one time.

Every society is composed of many groups in which daily social interaction takes place. People seek out groups to establish friendships, to accomplish certain goals, and to fulfill the social roles they have acquired. Groups, then, play a vital part in a society's social structure. Much of our social interaction takes place within groups and is influenced by their norms and sanctions. Being a teenager or a retired person takes on special meaning when you interact within a group designed for people with that particular status. The expectations associated with many social roles, including those accompanying the statuses of brother, sister, and student, become more clearly defined in the context of a group.

Primary and Secondary Groups Charles Horton Cooley (1902) coined the term *primary group* to refer to a small group characterized by intimate, face-to-face association and cooperation. The members of a street gang constitute a primary group; so do members of a family living in the same household, as well as a group of "sisters" in a college sorority.

Primary groups play a pivotal role both in the socialization process (see Chapter 2) and in the development of roles and statuses. Indeed, primary groups can be instrumental in a person's day-to-day existence. When we find ourselves identifying closely with a group, it is probably a primary group.

We also participate in many groups that are not characterized by close bonds of friendship, such as large college classes and business associations. The term *secondary group* refers to a formal, impersonal group in which there is little social intimacy or mutual understanding (see Table 3–1). The distinction between primary and secondary groups is not always clear-cut. Some social clubs may become so large and impersonal that they no longer function as primary groups.

In-Groups and Out-Groups A group can hold special meaning for members because of its relationship to other groups. People in one group sometimes feel antagonistic to or threatened by another group, especially if that group is perceived as being different culturally or racially. Sociologists explain these "we" and "they" feelings using two terms first employed by William Graham Sumner (1906): *in-group* and *out-group.*

An *in-group* can be defined as any group or category to which people feel they belong. Simply put, it comprises everyone who is regarded as "we" or "us." The in-group may be as narrow as a teenage clique or as broad as an entire society. The very existence of an in-group implies that there is an out-group viewed as "they" or "them." An *out-group* is a group or category to which people feel they do *not* belong.

Conflict between in-groups and out-groups can turn violent. In 1999 two disaffected students at Columbine High School in Littleton, Colorado, launched an attack on the school that left 15 students and teachers dead, including themselves. The gunmen, members of an out-group that other students referred to as the Trenchcoat Mafia, apparently resented the taunting of an in-group referred to as the Jocks. Similar episodes have occurred in schools across the nation, where rejected adolescents, overwhelmed by personal and family problems, peer group pressure, academic responsibilities, or media images of violence, have struck out against more popular classmates.

Reference Groups Both in-groups and primary groups can dramatically influence the way an individual thinks and behaves. Sociologists call any group that individuals use as a standard in evaluating themselves and their own behavior a *reference group.* For example, a high school student who aspires to join a social circle of hip-hop music devotees will pattern

Use Your Sociological Imagination

Try putting yourself in the shoes of an out-group member. What does your in-group look like from that perspective?

Table 3–1 Comparison of Primary and Secondary Groups

Primary Group	Secondary Group
Generally small	Usually large
Relatively long period of interaction	Relatively short duration, often temporary
Intimate, face-to-face association	Little social intimacy or mutual understanding
Some emotional depth in relationships	Relationships generally superficial
Cooperative, friendly	Formal and impersonal

summing UP

his or her behavior after that of the group. The student will begin dressing like these peers, downloading the same music, and hanging out at the same stores and clubs.

Reference groups have two basic purposes. First, they serve a normative function by setting and enforcing standards of conduct and belief. The high school student who wants the approval of the hip-hop crowd will have to follow the group's dictates, at least to some extent. Second, reference groups perform a comparison function by serving as a standard against which people can measure themselves and others. An actor will evaluate himself or herself against a reference group composed of others in the acting profession (Merton and Kitt 1950).

Reference groups may help the process of anticipatory socialization. For example, a college student majoring in finance may read the *Wall Street Journal,* study the annual reports of corporations, and listen to midday stock market news on the radio. Such a student is using financial experts as a reference group to which he or she aspires.

SOCIAL NETWORKS

Groups do not merely serve to define other elements of the social structure, such as roles and statuses; they also link the individual with the larger society. We all belong to a number of different groups, and through our acquaintances we make connections with people in different social circles. These connections are known as a *social network*—a series of social relationships that links a person directly to others, and through them, indirectly to still more people. Some networks may constrain people by limiting the range of their interactions, yet networks can also empower people by making vast resources available to them (Christakis and Fowler 2009).

Involvement in social networks—commonly known as *networking*—is especially valuable in finding employment. Albert Einstein was successful in finding a job only when a classmate's father put him in touch with his future employer. These kinds of contacts—even those that are weak and distant—can be crucial in establishing social networks and facilitating the transmission of information.

In the mid-1990s, sociologists studied romantic relationships at a high school with about 1,000 students. They found that about 61 percent of the girls had been sexually active over the past 18 months. Among the sexually active respondents, the researchers counted only 63 steady couples, or pairs with no other partners. A much larger group of 288 students— almost a third of the sample—was involved in a free-flowing network of relationships (Bearman et al. 2004).

Research indicates, however, that both in person and online, not everyone participates equally in social networks. Women and racial and ethnic minorities are at a disadvantage when seeking new and better job opportunities or social contacts (Trimble and Kmec 2011).

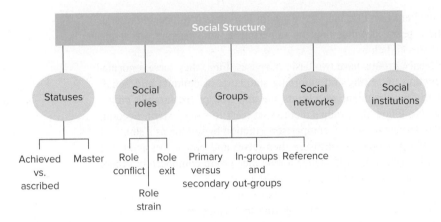

Figure 3–2
Social Structure:
An Overview

SOCIAL INSTITUTIONS

The mass media, the government, the economy, the family, and the health care system are all examples of social institutions found in our society. *Social institutions* are organized patterns of beliefs and behavior centered on basic social needs, such as replacing personnel (the family) and preserving order (the government).

A close look at social institutions gives sociologists insight into the structure of a society. Consider religion, for example. The institution of religion adapts to the segment of society that it serves. Church work has very different meanings for ministers who serve a skid row area or a middle-class suburban community. Religious leaders assigned to a skid row mission will focus on tending to the ill and providing food and shelter. Clergy in the suburbs will focus on counseling those considering marriage and divorce, arranging youth activities, and overseeing cultural events (Schaefer 2008b).

We will examine social institutions in more detail in Chapters 8 and 9. Figure 3–2 summarizes the major elements of social structure.

Social Structure in Global Perspective

Modern societies are complex, especially when compared with earlier social arrangements. Sociologists Émile Durkheim, Ferdinand Tönnies, and Gerhard Lenski have offered three ways to contrast modern societies with simpler forms of social structure.

DURKHEIM'S MECHANICAL AND ORGANIC SOLIDARITY

In his *Division of Labor* ([1893] 1933), Durkheim argued that social structure depends on the division of labor in a society—in other words, on the manner in which tasks are performed. Thus, a task such as providing food can be carried out almost totally by one individual, or it can be divided among many people. The latter pattern is typical of modern societies, in which the cultivation, processing, distribution, and retailing of a single food item are performed by literally hundreds of people.

In societies in which there is minimal division of labor, a collective consciousness develops that emphasizes group solidarity. Durkheim termed this collective frame of mind *mechanical solidarity,* implying that all individuals perform the same tasks. In this type of society, no one needs to ask, "What do your parents do?" since all are engaged in similar work. Each person prepares food, hunts, makes clothing, builds homes, and so forth. Because people have few options regarding what to do with their lives, there is little concern for individual needs. Instead, the group is the dominating force in society. Both social interaction and negotiation are based on close, intimate, face-to-face social contacts. Since there is little specialization, there are few social roles.

As societies become more advanced technologically, they rely on greater division of labor. The person who cuts down timber is not the same person who puts up your roof. With increasing specialization, many different tasks must be performed by many different individuals—even in manufacturing a single item, such as a radio or stove. In general, social interactions become less personal than in societies characterized by mechanical solidarity. People begin relating to others on the basis of their social positions ("butcher," "nurse") rather than their distinctive human qualities. Because the overall social structure of the society continues to change, statuses and social roles are in perpetual flux.

Once society has become more complex and division of labor is greater, no individual can go it alone. Dependence on others becomes essential for group survival. In Durkheim's terms, mechanical solidarity is replaced by *organic solidarity,* a collective consciousness resting on the need a society's members have for one another. Durkheim chose the term *organic solidarity* because in his view, individuals become interdependent in much the same way as organs of the human body.

TÖNNIES'S *GEMEINSCHAFT* AND *GESELLSCHAFT*

Ferdinand Tönnies (1855–1936) was appalled by the rise of an industrial city in his native Germany during the late 1800s. In his view, the city marked a dramatic change from the ideal type of a close-knit community, which Tönnies termed *Gemeinschaft,* to that of an impersonal mass society, or *Gesellschaft* (Tönnies [1887] 1988).

The *Gemeinschaft* (pronounced guh-MINE-shoft) community is typical of rural life. It is a small community in which people have similar backgrounds and life experiences. Virtually everyone knows one another, so that social interactions are intimate and familiar, almost as one might find among kinfolk. A commitment to the larger social group and a sense of togetherness characterize the community. People relate to others in a personal way, not just as "clerk" or "manager." With this personal interaction, however, comes little privacy.

Social control in the *Gemeinschaft* community is maintained through informal means, such as moral persuasion, gossip, and even gestures. These techniques work effectively because people genuinely care about how others feel toward them. Social change is relatively limited in the *Gemeinschaft;* the lives of members of one generation may be quite similar to those of their grandparents.

By contrast, the **Gesellschaft** (pronounced guh-ZELL-shoft) is an ideal type characteristic of modern urban life. Most people are strangers and feel little in common with other community residents. Relationships are governed by social roles that grow out of immediate tasks, such as purchasing a product or arranging a business meeting. Self-interest dominates, and little consensus exists concerning values or commitment to the group. As a result, social control must rely on more formal techniques, such as laws and legally defined punishments. Social change is an important aspect of life in the *Gesellschaft;* it can be strikingly evident, even within a single generation.

Table 3-2 summarizes the differences between the *Gemeinschaft* and the *Gesellschaft.* Sociologists have used these terms to compare social

summing UP

Table 3–2 Comparison of the *Gemeinschaft* and *Gesellschaft*

Gemeinschaft	Gesellschaft
Rural life typifies this form	Urban life typifies this form
People share a feeling of community that results from their similar backgrounds and life experiences	People have little sense of commonality; their differences appear more striking than their similarities
Social interactions are intimate and familiar	Social interactions are likely to be impersonal and task-specific
People maintain a spirit of cooperation and unity of will	Self-interest dominates
Tasks and personal relationships cannot be separated	The task being performed is paramount; relationships are subordinate
People place little emphasis on individual privacy	Privacy is valued
Informal social control predominates	Formal social control is evident
People are not very tolerant of deviance	People are more tolerant of deviance
Emphasis is on ascribed statuses	Emphasis is on achieved statuses
Social change is relatively limited	Social change is very evident, even within a generation

Think About It
How would you classify the communities with which you are familiar? Are they more *Gemeinschaft* or *Gesellschaft?*

structures that stress close relationships with those that emphasize less personal ties. It is easy to view the *Gemeinschaft* with nostalgia, as a far better way of life than the rat race of contemporary existence. However, the more intimate relationships of the *Gemeinschaft* come at a price. The prejudice and discrimination found there can be quite confining; ascribed statuses such as family background often outweigh a person's unique talents and achievements. In addition, the *Gemeinschaft* tends to distrust individuals who seek to be creative or just to be different.

LENSKI'S SOCIOCULTURAL EVOLUTION

Sociologist Gerhard Lenski takes a very different view of society and social structure. Rather than distinguishing between two opposite types of society, as Tönnies did, Lenski sees human societies as undergoing a process of change characterized by a dominant pattern known as *sociocultural evolution.* This term refers to long-term social trends resulting from the interplay of continuity, innovation, and selection (Nolan and Lenski 2015:415).

In Lenski's view, a society's level of technology is critical to the way it is organized. Lenski defines *technology* as "cultural information about the ways in which the material resources of the environment may be used to satisfy human needs and desires" (Nolan and Lenski 2015). The available technology does not completely define the form that a particular society and its social structure take. Nevertheless, a low level of technology may limit the degree to which a society can depend on such things as irrigation or complex machinery. As technology advances, society evolves from a preindustrial to an industrial and then a post-industrial stage.

Preindustrial Societies   How does a preindustrial society organize its economy? If we know that, it is possible to categorize the society. The first type of preindustrial society to emerge in human history was the *hunting-and-gathering society,* in which people simply rely on whatever foods and fibers are readily available. Technology in such societies is minimal. Organized in groups, people move constantly in search of food. There is little division of labor into specialized tasks.

Hunting-and-gathering societies are composed of small, widely dispersed groups. Each group consists almost entirely of people related to one another. As a result, kinship ties are the source of authority and influence, and the social institution of the family takes on a particularly important role. Tönnies would certainly view such societies as examples of *Gemeinschaft.*

Since resources are scarce in hunting-and-gathering societies, there is relatively little inequality in terms of material goods. Social differentiation is based on ascribed statuses such as gender, age, and family background. By the close of the 20th century, the last hunting-and-gathering societies had virtually disappeared (Nolan and Lenski 2009).

Horticultural societies, in which people plant seeds and crops rather than merely subsist on available foods, emerged about 12,000 years ago. Members of horticultural societies are much less nomadic than hunters and gatherers. They place greater emphasis on the production of tools and household objects. Yet their technology remains rather limited: They cultivate crops with the aid of digging sticks or hoes (Wilford 1997).

The last stage of preindustrial development is the *agrarian society,* which emerged about 5,000 years ago. As in horticultural societies, members of agrarian societies are engaged primarily in the production of food. However, the introduction of technological innovations such as the plow allows farmers to dramatically increase their crop yields. Farmers can cultivate the same fields over generations, allowing the emergence of still larger settlements.

Industrial Societies   Although the Industrial Revolution did not topple monarchs, it produced changes every bit as significant as those resulting from political revolutions. The Industrial Revolution, which took place largely in England during the period 1760 to 1830, was a scientific revolution focused on the application of nonanimal (mechanical) sources of power to labor tasks. An *industrial society* is a society that depends on mechanization to produce its goods and services. Industrial societies rely on inventions that facilitate agricultural and industrial production, and on new sources of energy, such as steam.

As the Industrial Revolution proceeded, a new form of social structure emerged. Many societies underwent an irrevocable shift from an agrarian-oriented economy to an industrial base. No longer did a typical individual or a family make an entire product. Instead, specialization of tasks and manufacturing of goods became increasingly common. Workers, generally men but also women and even children, left their family homesteads to work in central locations such as factories.

The process of industrialization had distinctive social consequences. Families and communities could not continue to function as self-sufficient units. Individuals, villages, and regions began to exchange goods and services and to become interdependent. As people came to rely on the labor of members of other communities, the family lost its unique position as the source of power and authority. The need for specialized knowledge led to more formalized education, and education emerged as a social institution distinct from the family.

Postindustrial and Postmodern Societies   When Lenski first proposed the sociocultural evolutionary approach in the 1960s, he paid relatively little attention to how maturing industrialized societies may change with the emergence of even more advanced forms of technology. More recently, he and other sociologists have studied the significant changes in the occupational structure of industrial societies as they shift from manufacturing to service economies. In the 1970s, sociologist Daniel Bell wrote about the technologically advanced *postindustrial society,* whose economic system is engaged primarily in the processing and control of information. The main output of a postindustrial society is services rather than manufactured goods. Large numbers of people become involved in occupations devoted to the teaching, generation, or dissemination of ideas. Jobs in fields such as advertising, public relations, human resources, and computer information systems would be typical of a postindustrial society (D. Bell [1973] 1999).

Bell views this transition from industrial to postindustrial society as a positive development. He sees a general decline in organized working-class groups and a rise in interest groups concerned with such national issues as health, education, and the environment. Bell's outlook is functionalist because he portrays postindustrial society as basically consensual. As organizations and interest groups engage in an open and competitive process of decision making, Bell believes, the level of conflict between diverse groups will diminish, strengthening social stability.

More recently, sociologists have gone beyond discussion of postindustrial societies to the postmodern society. A *postmodern society* is a technologically sophisticated society that is preoccupied with consumer goods and media images (Brannigan 1992). Such societies consume goods and information on a mass scale. Postmodern theorists take a global perspective, noting the ways that aspects of culture cross national boundaries. For example, residents of the United States may listen to reggae music from Jamaica, eat sushi and other types of Japanese food, and wear clogs from Sweden. Table 3–3 summarizes the six stages of sociocultural evolution.

Table 3–3 Stages of Sociocultural Evolution

Societal Type	First Appearance	Characteristics
Hunting-and-gathering	Beginning of human life	Nomadic; reliance on readily available food and fibers
Horticultural	About 12,000 years ago	More settled; development of agriculture and limited technology
Agrarian	About 5,000 years ago	Larger, more stable settlements; improved technology and increased crop yields
Industrial	1760–1850	Reliance on mechanical power and new sources of energy; centralized workplaces; economic interdependence; formal education
Postindustrial	1960s	Reliance on services, especially the processing and control of information; expanded middle class
Postmodern	Latter 1970s	High technology; mass consumption of consumer goods and media images; cross-cultural integration

Durkheim, Tönnies, and Lenski present three visions of society's social structure. While they differ, each is useful, and this textbook will draw on all three. The sociocultural evolutionary approach emphasizes a historical perspective. It does not picture different types of social structure coexisting within the same society. Consequently, one would not expect a single society to include hunters and gatherers along with a postmodern culture. In contrast, Durkheim's and Tönnies's theories allow for the existence of different types of community—such as a *Gemeinschaft* and a *Gesellschaft*—in the same society. Thus, a rural New Hampshire community located 100 miles from Boston can be linked to the city by modern information technology. The main difference between these two theories is a matter of emphasis. While Tönnies emphasized the overriding concern in each type of community—one's own self-interest or the well-being of the larger society—Durkheim emphasized the division (or lack of division) of labor.

The work of these three thinkers reminds us that a major focus of sociology has been to identify changes in social structure and the consequences for human behavior. At the macro level, we see society shifting to more advanced forms of technology. The social structure becomes increasingly complex, and new social institutions emerge to assume some functions that once were performed by the family. On the micro level, these changes affect the nature of social interactions. Each individual takes on multiple social roles, and people come to rely more on social networks and less on kinship ties. As the social structure becomes more complex, people's relationships become more impersonal, transient, and fragmented. The development of formal organizations and bureaucracies, the subject of the next section, is another outcome of this process.

Use Your Sociological Imagination

Describe any personal experiences you have had with a nonindustrial, or developing, society. If you have not had that kind of experience, how do you think you would prepare for it?

Understanding Organizations

FORMAL ORGANIZATIONS AND BUREAUCRACIES

As industrial and postmodern societies have shifted to more advanced forms of technology and their social structures have become more complex, our lives have become increasingly dominated by large secondary groups referred to as *formal organizations*. A ***formal organization*** is a group designed for a special purpose and structured for maximum efficiency. The United States Postal Service, the McDonald's fast-food chain, the Boston Pops orchestra, and the college you attend are all examples of formal organizations. Organizations vary in their size, specificity of goals, and degree of efficiency, but all are structured to facilitate the management of large-scale operations. All have a bureaucratic form of organization.

In our society, formal organizations fulfill an enormous variety of personal and societal needs, shaping the lives of every one of us. In fact, formal organizations have become such a dominant force that we must create organizations to supervise other organizations, such as the Securities and Exchange Commission (SEC), which regulates the stock market. Though it sounds much more exciting to say that we live in a "computer age" than in an "age of formal organizations," the latter is probably a more accurate description of our times (Azumi and Hage 1972; Etzioni 1964).

Ascribed statuses such as gender, race, and ethnicity can influence how we see ourselves within formal organizations. For example, a study followed the careers of nearly 4,000 women and men who entered the bar in 2000 and found that among full-time lawyers, women earned an average of $6,000 less per year than men who were at the same stage of the profession. The discrepancy held even after considering type of firm, specialization within law, and work history (whether the lawyer had taken family leave, for example).

This consistent gender wage inequality appeared to stem from a devaluation of women and their work within legal organizations. Regrettably, women lawyers operating in this work culture may come to perceive themselves as worth less and entitled to less, which in turn creates further gendered compensatory practices. For example, over time, women and men record billable hours differently: men bill for every snippet of conversation, while women bill more selectively. This pattern of organizational culture, which perpetuates salary differences and ultimately discourages women from being as tough as men at salary negotiation, has been documented in a variety of occupations (Dinovitzer et al. 2009; Sandberg 2015).

CHARACTERISTICS OF A BUREAUCRACY

A *bureaucracy* is a component of formal organization in which rules and hierarchical ranking are used to achieve efficiency. Rows of desks staffed by seemingly faceless people, endless lines and forms, impossibly complex language, and frustrating encounters with red tape—all these unpleasant images have combined to make *bureaucracy* a dirty word and an easy target in political campaigns. As a result, few people want to identify their occupation as "bureaucrat," despite the fact that all of us perform various bureaucratic tasks. Elements of bureaucracy enter into almost every occupation in an industrial society.

Max Weber ([1913–1922] 1947) first directed researchers to the significance of bureaucratic structure. In an important sociological advance, Weber emphasized the basic similarity of structure and process found in the otherwise dissimilar enterprises of religion, government, education, and business. Weber saw bureaucracy as a form of organization quite different from the family-run business. For analytical purposes, he developed an ideal type of bureaucracy that would reflect the most characteristic aspects of all human organizations. By *ideal type* Weber meant a construct or model that serves as a measuring rod against which actual cases can be evaluated. In actuality, perfect bureaucracies do not exist; no real-world organization corresponds exactly to Weber's ideal type.

Weber proposed that whether the purpose is to run a church, a corporation, or an army, the ideal bureaucracy displays five basic characteristics. A discussion of those characteristics, as well as the dysfunctions (or potential negative consequences) of a bureaucracy, follows.

1. *Division of Labor.*   Specialized experts perform specific tasks. In your college bureaucracy, the admissions officer does not do the job of registrar; the dean doesn't see to the maintenance of buildings. By working at a specific task, people are more likely to become highly skilled and carry out a job with maximum efficiency. This emphasis on specialization is so basic a part of our lives that we may not realize it is a fairly recent development in Western culture.

    Although the division of labor has certainly enhanced the performance of many complex bureaucracies, in some cases it can lead to ***trained incapacity.*** That is, workers become so specialized that they develop blind spots and fail to notice obvious problems. Even worse, they may not care about what is happening in the next department. Some observers believe that such developments have caused workers in the United States to become less productive on the job.

    In some cases, the bureaucratic division of labor can have tragic results. In the wake of the coordinated attacks on the World Trade Center and the Pentagon on September 11, 2001, Americans wondered aloud how the FBI and CIA could have failed to detect the terrorists' elaborately planned operation. The problem, in part, turned out to be the division of labor between the FBI, which focuses on domestic matters, and the CIA, which operates overseas. Officials at these intelligence-gathering organizations, both of which are huge bureaucracies, are well known for jealously guarding information from one another. Subsequent investigations revealed that they knew about Osama bin Laden and his al-Qaeda terrorist network in the early 1990s. Unfortunately, five federal agencies—the CIA, FBI, National Security Agency, Defense Intelligence Agency, and National Reconnaissance Office—failed to share their leads on the network. Although the hijacking of the four commercial airliners used in the massive attacks may not have been preventable, the bureaucratic division of labor definitely hindered efforts to defend against terrorism and actually undermined U.S. national security.

2. *Hierarchy of Authority.*   Bureaucracies follow the principle of hierarchy; that is, each position is under the supervision of a higher authority. A president heads a college bureaucracy; he or she selects members of the administration, who in turn hire their own staff. In the Roman Catholic Church, the pope is the supreme authority; under him sit cardinals, bishops, and so forth.

3. *Written Rules and Regulations.*   What if your sociology professor gave your classmate an A for having such a friendly smile? You might think that wasn't fair—that it was "against the rules." Through written rules and regulations, bureaucracies generally offer employees clear

"Frankly, at this point in the flow chart,
we don't know what happens to these people..."

standards for an adequate (or exceptional) performance. In addition, procedures provide a valuable sense of continuity in a bureaucracy. Individual workers will come and go, but the organization's structure and past records give it a life of its own that outlives the services of any one bureaucrat.

Of course, rules and regulations can overshadow the larger goals of an organization to the point that they become dysfunctional. What if a hospital emergency room physician failed to treat a seriously injured person because he or she had no valid proof of U.S. citizenship? If blindly applied, rules no longer serve as a means to achieving an objective but instead become important (and perhaps too important) in their own right. Robert Merton (1968) has used the term *goal displacement* to refer to overzealous conformity to official regulations.

4. *Impersonality.*   Max Weber wrote that in a bureaucracy, work is carried out *sine ira et studio,* "without hatred or passion." Bureaucratic norms dictate that officials perform their duties without the personal consideration of people as individuals. Although this approach is intended to guarantee equal treatment for each person, it also contributes to the often cold and uncaring feeling associated with modern organizations. We typically think of big government and big business when we think of impersonal bureaucracies. But today even small firms use electronically automated menus to screen callers.

5. *Employment Based on Technical Qualifications.*   Within the ideal bureaucracy, hiring is based on technical qualifications rather than on favoritism, and performance is measured against specific standards. Written personnel policies dictate who gets promoted; people often have a right to appeal if they believe that particular rules have been violated.

Your school or workplace suddenly ceases to exhibit one of the five characteristics of bureaucracy. Which characteristic is it, and what are the consequences?

Such procedures protect bureaucrats against arbitrary dismissal, provide a measure of security, and encourage loyalty to the organization.

Although ideally any bureaucracy will value technical and professional competence, personnel decisions do not always follow this ideal pattern. Bureaucratic dysfunctions have become well publicized, particularly because of the work of Laurence J. Peter. According to the *Peter Principle,* every employee within a hierarchy tends to rise to his or her level of incompetence (Peter and Hull 1969).

These five characteristics of bureaucracy, developed by Max Weber more than 90 years ago, describe an ideal type rather than offering a precise definition of an actual bureaucracy. Not every formal organization will possess all five of Weber's characteristics. In fact, actual bureaucratic organizations can vary widely. (Table 3–4 summarizes the characteristics of a bureaucracy.)

BUREAUCRACY AND ORGANIZATIONAL CULTURE

How does bureaucratization affect the average individual who works in an organization? Early theorists of formal organizations tended to neglect this question. Max Weber, for example, focused on managerial personnel within bureaucracies but had little to say about workers in industry or clerks in government agencies.

According to the *classical theory* of formal organizations, also known as the *scientific management approach,* workers are motivated almost entirely by economic rewards. This theory stresses that only the physical constraints on workers limit their productivity. Therefore, workers are treated as a resource, much like the machines that began to replace them

summing UP

Table 3–4 Characteristics of a Bureaucracy

Characteristic	Positive Consequence	Negative Consequence	
		For the Individual	For the Organization
Division of labor	Produces efficiency in large-scale organizations	Produces trained incapacity	Produces a narrow perspective
Hierarchy of authority	Clarifies who is in command	Deprives employees of a voice in decision making	Permits concealment of mistakes
Written rules and regulations	Let workers know what is expected of them	Stifle initiative and imagination	Lead to goal displacement
Impersonality	Reduces bias	Contributes to cold and uncaring atmosphere	Discourages loyalty to company
Employment based on technical qualifications	Discourages favoritism and reduces petty rivalries	Discourages ambition to improve oneself elsewhere	Fosters Peter Principle

in the 20th century. Management attempts to achieve maximum work efficiency through scientific planning, established performance standards, and careful supervision of workers and production. Under the scientific management approach, planning includes efficiency studies but not studies of workers' attitudes or job satisfaction.

Not until workers organized unions—and forced management to recognize that they were not objects—did theorists of formal organizations begin to revise the classical approach. Along with management and administrators, social scientists became aware that informal groups of workers have an important impact on organizations. An alternative way of considering bureaucratic dynamics, the *human relations approach,* emphasizes the roles of people, communication, and participation within a bureaucracy. This type of analysis reflects the interest of interactionist theorists in small-group behavior. Unlike planning under the scientific management approach, planning based on the human relations perspective focuses on workers' feelings, frustrations, and emotional need for job satisfaction.

Today, research on formal organizations is following new avenues. Among them are:

- The recent arrival of a small number of women and minority group members in high-level management

- In large corporations, the decision-making role of groups that lie outside the top ranks of leadership

- The loss of fixed boundaries in organizations that have outsourced key functions

- The role of the Internet in influencing business and consumer preferences

Though research on organizations still embraces Max Weber's insights, it has gone well beyond them (Hamm 2007; Kleiner 2003; W. Scott and Davis 2007).

Sociology Matters

Sociology matters because it defines your social status in terms of a variety of social characteristics and groups.

- What is your ascribed status? What do you hope your achieved status will be someday? Do you have a master status, and if so, how might it impact your achievements?

- What primary and secondary groups do you belong to, and why? How do those groups affect your behavior?

- What social networks and institutions are you involved in? Do you belong to any virtual networks? What are the functions of those networks, and how can they help you?

CHAPTER RESOURCES

Summary

Through **social structure,** society is organized into predictable relationships that facilitate **social interaction.** The transmission of culture and even the survival of society depend on social interaction. This chapter has presented the six basic elements of social structure, from individual **statuses** and the **social roles** that go with them to **groups, social networks,** virtual worlds, and **social institutions.** It has examined several theories of social structure and **formal organizations,** including **bureaucracies.**

1. An **ascribed status** is generally assigned to a person at birth, whereas an **achieved status** is attained largely through one's own effort. In the United States, ascribed statuses such as race and gender can function as **master statuses** that affect one's potential for achievement.

2. The statuses people carry determine the **social roles** they play. People who play more than one social role often suffer from **role conflict,** but even a single role can create **role strain. Role exit** is the process of disengagement from a role that is central to one's self-identity in order to establish a new role and identity.

3. Much of our social behavior takes place within **groups.** When we find ourselves identifying closely with a group, it is probably a **primary group.** A **secondary group** is more formal and impersonal.

4. People tend to see the world in terms of **in-groups** (groups to which they belong) and **out-groups** (groups they do not belong to or identify with). **Reference groups** set and enforce standards of social conduct, allowing members to compare themselves to others.

5. Groups serve as links to **social networks** and their vast resources. Today, more and more networking is being done online.

6. **Social institutions,** such as government and the family, fulfill essential social functions that other groups cannot, such as preserving order and perpetuating society.

7. Émile Durkheim thought that social structure depends on the division of labor in a society. According to Durkheim, societies with minimal division of labor have a collective consciousness called **mechanical solidarity;** those with greater division of labor show an interdependence called **organic solidarity.**

8. The sociologist Ferdinand Tönnies contrasted the close-knit type of community that characterizes rural life, which he called *Gemeinschaft,* with the impersonal type of mass society that characterizes urban life, which he called *Gesellschaft.*

9. In his theory of **sociocultural evolution,** Gerhard Lenski linked the historical development of societies to the technological advances they achieved. Lenski traced their evolution from primitive **hunting-and-gathering societies** to modern-day **postindustrial** and **postmodern societies.**

10. As societies have become more complex, large **formal organizations** and **bureaucracies** have become more powerful and pervasive. Max Weber theorized that in its **ideal type,** every bureaucracy has five basic characteristics: division of labor, hierarchical authority, written rules and regulations, impersonality, and employment based on technical qualifications.

Key Terms

achieved status, 76

agrarian society, 86

ascribed status, 75

bureaucracy, 89

classical theory, 92

formal
  organization, 88

Gemeinschaft, 83

Gesellschaft, 84

goal
  displacement, 91

group, 79

horticultural
  society, 86

human relations
  approach, 93

hunting-and-gathering
  society, 85

ideal type, 89

industrial society, 86

in-group, 80

master status, 76

mechanical
  solidarity, 83

organic solidarity, 83

out-group, 80

Peter Principle, 92

postindustrial
  society, 87

postmodern society, 87

primary group, 79

reference group, 80

role conflict, 77

role exit, 78

role strain, 78

scientific management
  approach, 92

secondary group, 79

social institution, 82

social interaction, 73

social network, 81

social role, 77

social structure, 73

sociocultural
  evolution, 85

status, 75

technology, 85

trained incapacity, 90

Deviance and Social Control

©druvo/Getty Images

Social Control

What Is Deviance?

Sociological Perspectives on Deviance

Crime: A Sociological Approach

Crime Statistics

Rachel came from a happy family. She began wounding herself with a coat hanger when her friends turned against her. She stayed home from school for a week, couldn't stop crying, after they began spreading malicious rumors about her. Natalie, a college student, started injuring herself in eighth grade. She was hanging around the bridge with a group of stoners and punks, smoking and taking drugs, when she began imitating the ones who cut themselves.

These descriptions of the covert practice of self-injury are taken from Patricia A. Adler and Peter Adler's extensive research on the little-known behavior and its social underpinnings. Over a six-year period, the Adlers conducted lengthy, emotionally intense interviews with self-injurers, becoming friends with many. They met others in virtual space, through Internet-based support groups and Web postings. "Rather than remaining strictly detached from our subjects, we became involved in their lives, helping them and giving voice to their experiences and beliefs," the Adlers admit (2007:542).

The Adlers' work on self-injury reflects all three major sociological approaches. For self-injurers, who rarely come into contact with others like themselves, the Internet functions as a meeting place, a refuge from their self-imposed social isolation. As conflict theorists would point out, their unconventional behavior marginalizes them, preventing them from receiving assistance even when they would welcome it. Interactionists would recognize the critical nature of self-injurers' interpersonal contacts, in person and often online.

Though many people would like to ignore the phenomenon of self-injury, believing that those who practice it will eventually "grow out of it," the Adlers' research allows us to consider it intelligently and scientifically, within the social context. Self-injurers, the Adlers found, are a diverse group, most of whom have never been treated for psychological problems. They include older adults, who communicate with one another online, as well as teens and young adults. Far from being impulsive or pathological, self-injury is a carefully planned and considered behavior. Surprisingly, members often begin to injure themselves in the company of others rather than in secret. They have recently begun to coalesce as a subculture.

Who decides what is and is not normal behavior, and how does society attempt to control what people say and do? In this chapter we will study various mechanisms of *social control,* both formal and informal. We will examine several theoretical explanations for *deviance* from social norms. And we will discuss one form of deviance that is subject to strict formal controls: *crime.*

Social Control

As we saw in Chapter 2, each culture, subculture, and group has distinctive norms governing what is deemed appropriate behavior. Laws, dress codes, organizational bylaws, course requirements, and the rules of sports and games all express social norms.

How does a society bring about acceptance of basic norms? The term *social control* refers to the techniques and strategies for preventing deviant behavior in any society. Social control occurs on all levels of society. In the family, we are socialized to obey our parents simply because they are our parents. Peer groups introduce us to informal norms, such as dress codes, that govern the behavior of members. Colleges establish standards they expect their students to meet. In bureaucratic organizations, workers encounter a formal system of rules and regulations. Finally, the government of every society legislates and enforces social norms.

Most of us respect and accept basic social norms and assume that others will do the same. Even without thinking, we obey the instructions of police officers, follow the day-to-day rules at our jobs, and move to the rear of elevators when people enter. Such behavior reflects an effective process of socialization to the dominant standards of a culture. At the same time, we are well aware that individuals, groups, and institutions

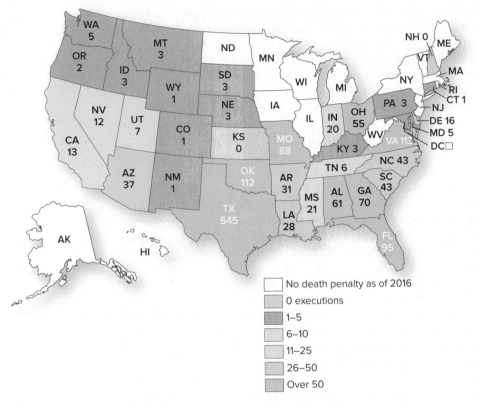

No death penalty as of 2016
0 executions
1–5
6–10
11–25
26–50
Over 50

Figure 4–1

Executions by State Since 1976

NOTES: *Number of executions carried out from January 17, 1977, to November 9, 2017, not including three federal executions. Illinois carried out 12 executions before abolishing the death penalty. Nebraska, which abolished the death penalty in 2015, had executed 3 people. The U.S. government has 62 people on death row; the military has 5.*

SOURCE: Death Penalty Information Center, 2017.

Think About It

Why is there so much variation in the number of executions from one state to the next? What might cause that variation?

expect us to act "properly." This expectation carries with it *sanctions,* penalties and rewards for conduct concerning a social norm. If we fail to live up to the norm, we may face punishment through informal sanctions such as fear and ridicule or formal sanctions such as jail sentences or fines.

The ultimate formal sanction is the death penalty, which has been the subject of much controversy recently. Figure 4–1 shows the number of executions carried out in the United States from 1976 through February 2017. Is this sanction an effective form of social control? Other than eliminating the person who is executed, what does the death penalty accomplish? Does it actually control others' behavior by deterring them from committing a capital offense? To answer these questions, researchers must consider the motivation behind capital crimes as well as the criminal's understanding of the resulting penalties. Taking these factors into consideration, researchers have found little evidence that execution is any more a deterrent to capital crimes than an extended prison term (Nagen and Pepper 2012).

The challenge to effective social control is that people often receive competing messages about how to behave. While the state or government may clearly define acceptable behavior, friends or fellow employees may encourage quite different behavior patterns. Historically, legal measures aimed at blocking discrimination based on race, religion, gender, age, and sexual orientation have been difficult to implement because many people tacitly encourage the violation of such measures.

As with other topics, sociologists who study social control tend to speak from one of the major theoretical perspectives. Functionalists contend that people must respect social norms if a group or society is to survive. In their view, societies literally could not function if massive numbers of people defied standards of appropriate conduct. By contrast, conflict theorists maintain that "successful functioning" of a society will consistently benefit the powerful and work to the disadvantage of other groups. They point out, for example, that in the United States, widespread resistance to social norms was necessary to overturn the institution of slavery, to win independence from England, to secure civil rights, to allow women to vote, and to force an end to the war in Vietnam.

CONFORMITY AND OBEDIENCE

Techniques for social control operate on both the group level and the societal level. People we think of as peers or equals influence us to act in particular ways; the same is true of people who hold authority over us or occupy awe-inspiring positions. Stanley Milgram (1975) made a useful distinction between these two important levels of social control.

Milgram defined *conformity* as going along with peers—individuals of our own status, who have no special right to direct our behavior. By contrast, *obedience* is defined as compliance with higher authorities in a hierarchical structure. Thus, a recruit entering military service will typically *conform* to the habits and language of other recruits and will *obey* the orders of superior officers. Students will *conform* to the behavior of their peers and will *obey* the requests of campus security officers.

If ordered to do so, would you comply with an experimenter's instruction to give people increasingly painful electric shocks? Most people would say no, yet the research of social psychologist Stanley Milgram (1963, 1975) suggests that most of us *will* obey such orders. In Milgram's words (1975:xi), "Behavior that is unthinkable in an individual . . . acting on his own may be executed without hesitation when carried out under orders."

Milgram placed advertisements in New Haven, Connecticut, newspapers to recruit subjects for what was described as a learning experiment at Yale University. Participants included postal clerks, engineers, high school teachers, and laborers. They were told that the purpose of the research was to investigate the effects of punishment on learning. The experimenter, dressed in a gray technician's coat, explained that in each testing, one subject would be randomly selected as the "learner" and another would function as the "teacher." However, the experiment was rigged so that the "real" subject would always be the teacher, while an associate of Milgram's served as the learner.

At this point, the learner's hand was strapped to an electric apparatus. The teacher was taken to an electronic "shock generator" with 30 graduated lever switches labeled from 15 to 450 volts. Before beginning the experiment, all subjects were given sample shocks of 45 volts, to convince them of the authenticity of the experiment. The experimenter then instructed the teacher to apply shocks of increasing voltage each time the learner gave an incorrect answer on a memory test. Teachers were told that "although the shocks can be extremely painful, they cause no permanent tissue damage." In reality, the learner did not receive any shocks.

The learner acted out a prearranged script, deliberately giving incorrect answers and pretending to be in pain. For example, at 150 volts, the learner would cry out, "Get me out of here!" At 270 volts, the learner would scream in agony. When the shock reached 350 volts, the learner would fall silent. If the teacher wanted to stop the experiment, the experimenter would insist that the teacher continue, using such statements as "The experiment requires that you continue" and "You have no other choice; you *must* go on" (Milgram 1975:19–23).

The results of this unusual experiment stunned and dismayed Milgram and other social scientists. Almost *two-thirds* of participants fell into the category of "obedient subjects." Why did these subjects obey? Why were they willing to inflict seemingly painful shocks on innocent victims who had never done them any harm? There is no evidence that these subjects were unusually sadistic; few seemed to enjoy administering the shocks. Instead, in Milgram's view, the key to obedience was the experimenter's social role as a "scientist" and "seeker of knowledge."

Milgram pointed out that in the modern industrial world, we are accustomed to submitting to impersonal authority figures whose status is indicated by a title (professor, lieutenant, doctor) or a uniform (the technician's coat). Because we view the authority as larger and more important than the individual, we shift responsibility for our behavior to the authority figure. Milgram's subjects frequently stated, "If it were up to me, I would not have administered shocks." They saw themselves as merely doing their duty (Milgram 1975).

From a conflict perspective, our obedience may be affected by the value we place on those whom our behavior affects. While Milgram's experiment shows that in general, people are willing to obey authority figures, other studies show that they are even more willing to obey if they feel the "victim" is deserving of punishment. Sociologist Gary Schulman (1974) re-created Milgram's experiment and found that White students were significantly more likely to shock Black "learners" than White "learners." By a margin of 70 percent to 48 percent, they imposed more shocks on the Black learners than on the White learners.

Use Your Sociological Imagination

If you were a participant in Milgram's research on obedience, how far do you think you would go in carrying out "orders"? Do you see any ethical problem with the experimenter's manipulation of the subjects? Explain your answers.

From an interactionist perspective, one important aspect of Milgram's findings is the fact that in follow-up studies, subjects were less likely to inflict the supposed shocks as they were moved physically closer to their victims. Moreover, interactionists emphasize the effect of *incrementally* administering additional dosages of 15 volts. In effect, the experimenter gradually persuaded the teacher to continue inflicting higher levels of punishment. It is doubtful that anywhere near the two-thirds rate of obedience would have been reached had the experimenter told the teachers to immediately administer 450 volts to the learners (B. Allen 1978; Katovich 1987).

How willing would participants in this experiment be to shock learners today? Although many people may be skeptical of the high levels of conformity Milgram found, recent replications of his experiment confirm his findings. In 2006, using additional safeguards to protect participants' welfare, psychologist Jerry Burger (2009) repeated part of Milgram's experiment with college undergraduates. To avoid biasing the participants, Burger was careful to screen out students who had heard of Milgram's study. The results of the replication were startlingly similar to Milgram's: participants showed a high level of willingness to shock the learner, just as the participants in Milgram's experiment had almost half a century earlier. At the most comparable point in the two studies, Burger measured a rate of 70 percent full obedience—lower, but not significantly so, than the rate of 82.5 percent measured two generations earlier.

INFORMAL AND FORMAL SOCIAL CONTROL

The sanctions used to encourage conformity and obedience—and to discourage violation of social norms—are carried out through both informal and formal social control. As the term implies, people use ***informal social control*** casually to enforce norms. Examples include smiles, laughter, a raised eyebrow, and ridicule.

In the United States and many other cultures, adults often view spanking, slapping, or kicking children as a proper and necessary means of informal social control. Child development specialists counter that such corporal punishment is inappropriate because it teaches children to solve problems through violence. They warn that slapping and spanking can escalate into more serious forms of abuse. Yet, despite a 1998 policy statement by the American Academy of Pediatrics that corporal punishment is not effective and can indeed be harmful, 59 percent of pediatricians support the use of corporal punishment, at least in certain situations. Our culture widely accepts this form of informal social control (Chung et al. 2009).

Formal social control is carried out by authorized agents, such as police officers, physicians, school administrators, employers, military officers, and managers of movie theaters. It can serve as a last resort when socialization and informal sanctions do not bring about desired behavior. An increasingly significant means of formal social control in the United States is to imprison people. During the course of a year, over 7 million adults undergo some form of correctional supervision—jail, prison, probation, or parole. Put another way, almost 1 out of every 30 adult Americans is subject to this very formal type of social control every year (Sabol et al. 2009).

LAW AND SOCIETY

Some norms are so important to a society that they are formalized into laws controlling people's behavior. *Law* may be defined as governmental social control (Black 1995). Some laws, such as the prohibition against murder, are directed at all members of society. Others, such as fishing and hunting regulations, affect particular categories of people. Still others govern the behavior of social institutions (corporate law and laws regarding the taxation of nonprofit enterprises).

Sociologists see the creation of laws as a social process. Laws are created in response to a perceived need for formal social control. Sociologists have sought to explain how and why such perceptions arise. In their view, law is not merely a static body of rules handed down from generation to generation. Rather, it reflects continually changing standards of what is right and wrong, how violations are to be determined, and what sanctions are to be applied (Schur 1968).

Sociologists representing varying theoretical perspectives agree that the legal order reflects the values of those in a position to exercise authority. Therefore, the creation of criminal law can be a most controversial matter. Should it be against the law to employ illegal immigrants in a factory or to have an abortion? Such issues have been bitterly debated because they require a choice among competing values. Not surprisingly, laws that are unpopular—such as the prohibition of alcohol under the 18th Amendment in 1919 and the widespread establishment of a 55-mile-per-hour speed limit on the highway—become difficult to enforce when there is no consensus supporting the underlying norms.

Socialization is actually the primary source of conforming and obedient behavior, including obedience to law. Generally, it is not external pressure from a peer group or authority figure that makes us go along with social norms. Rather, we have internalized such norms as valid and desirable and are committed to observing them. In a profound sense, we want to see ourselves (and to be seen) as loyal, cooperative, responsible, and respectful of others. In the United States and other societies around the world, people are socialized both to want to belong and to fear being viewed as different or deviant.

What Is Deviance?

For sociologists, the term *deviance* does not mean perversion or depravity. Rather, *deviance* is behavior that violates the standards of conduct or expectations of a group or society. In the United States, persons who abuse alcohol or who are compulsive gamblers, and those with mental illness would all be classified as deviant. Being late for class is a deviant act; the same is true of wearing jeans to a formal wedding. On the basis of the sociological definition, we are all deviant from time to time. Each of us violates common social norms in certain situations (Best 2004).

Is being overweight an example of deviance? In the United States and many other cultures, unrealistic standards of appearance and body image place a huge strain on people, especially women and girls. Journalist Naomi Wolf (1992) has used the term *beauty myth* to refer to an exaggerated ideal of beauty, beyond the reach of all but a few females. The beauty myth can have unfortunate consequences. In order to shed their "deviant" image and conform to (unrealistic) societal norms, many women and girls become consumed with adjusting their appearance. Yet what is deviant in one culture may be celebrated in another.

Deviance involves the violation of group norms, which may or may not be formalized into law. It is a comprehensive concept that includes not only criminal behavior but also many actions not subject to prosecution. The public official who takes a bribe has defied social norms, but so has the high school student who refuses to sit in an assigned seat or cuts class. Of course, deviation from norms is not always negative, let alone criminal. A member of an exclusive social club who speaks out against a traditional policy of excluding women, Blacks, and Jews from admittance is deviating from the club's norms. So is a police officer who blows the whistle on police corruption or brutality.

A person can acquire a deviant identity in many ways. Because of physical or behavioral characteristics, some people are unwillingly cast in negative social roles. Once they have been assigned a deviant role, they have trouble presenting a positive image to others and may even experience lowered self-esteem. Whole groups of people—for instance, "short people" or "redheads"—may be labeled in this way. The interactionist Erving Goffman coined the term *stigma* to describe the labels society uses to devalue members of certain social groups (Goffman 1963; Heckert and Best 1997).

Prevailing expectations about beauty and body shape may prevent people who are regarded as ugly or obese from advancing as rapidly as their abilities permit. Both overweight and anorexic people are assumed to be weak in character, slaves to their appetites or to media images. Because they do not conform to the beauty myth, these people may be viewed as "disfigured" or "strange" in appearance, bearers of what Goffman calls a "spoiled identity." However, what constitutes disfigurement is a matter of interpretation. Of the millions of cosmetic procedures done every year in the United States alone, many are performed on women who would be objectively defined as having a normal appearance. And while feminist sociologists have accurately noted that the beauty myth makes many

You are a reporter who is investigating gambling activities in your community. How do people react to those who engage in highly stigmatized forms of gambling? How do they encourage other forms of gambling?

women feel uncomfortable with themselves, men too lack confidence in their appearance. The number of males who choose to undergo cosmetic procedures has risen sharply in recent years.

Often people are stigmatized for deviant behaviors they may no longer engage in. The labels "compulsive gambler," "ex-convict," "recovering alcoholic," and "ex-mental patient" can stick to a person for life. Goffman draws a useful distinction between a prestige symbol that calls attention to a positive aspect of one's identity, such as a wedding band or a badge, and a stigma symbol that discredits or debases one's identity, such as a conviction for child molestation. While stigma symbols may not always be obvious, they can become a matter of public knowledge. Since 1994, many states have required convicted sex offenders to register with local police departments. Some communities publish the names and addresses, and in some instances even the pictures, of convicted sex offenders on the Web.

From a sociological perspective, deviance is hardly objective or set in stone. Rather, it is subject to social definition within a particular society and at a particular time. For that reason, what is considered deviant can shift from one social era to another. In most instances, those individuals and groups with the greatest status and power define what is acceptable and what is deviant.

Sociological Perspectives on Deviance

Why do people violate social norms? We have seen that deviant acts are subject to both informal and formal sanctions. The nonconforming or disobedient person may face disapproval, loss of friends, fines, or even imprisonment. Why, then, does deviance occur?

Early explanations for deviance blamed supernatural causes or genetic factors (such as "bad blood" or evolutionary throwbacks to primitive ancestors). In the 1800s, substantial efforts were made to identify biological factors that lead to deviance and especially to criminal activity. Although such research was discredited in the 20th century, contemporary researchers, primarily biochemists, have sought to isolate genetic factors connected to certain personality traits. Although criminality (much less deviance) is hardly a personality characteristic, researchers have focused on traits that might lead to crime, such as aggression. Of course, aggression can also lead to success in the corporate world, professional sports, and other pursuits.

The contemporary search for biological roots of criminality is but one aspect of the larger sociobiology debate. In general, sociologists reject any emphasis on genetic roots of crime and deviance. The limitations of current knowledge, the possibility of reinforcing racist and sexist assumptions, and the disturbing implications for the rehabilitation of criminals have led sociologists to draw largely on other approaches to explain deviance (Walsh 2000).

FUNCTIONALIST PERSPECTIVE

According to functionalists, deviance is a common part of human existence, with positive (as well as negative) consequences for social stability. Deviance helps to define the limits of proper behavior. Children who see one parent scold the other for belching at the dinner table learn about approved conduct. The same is true of the driver who receives a speeding ticket, the department store cashier who is fired for yelling at a customer, and the college student who is penalized for handing in papers weeks overdue.

Durkheim's Legacy Émile Durkheim ([1895] 1964) focused his sociological investigations mainly on criminal acts, yet his conclusions have implications for all types of deviant behavior. In Durkheim's view, the punishments established within a culture (including both formal and informal mechanisms of social control) help to define acceptable behavior and thus contribute to social stability. If improper acts were not sanctioned, people might stretch their standards of what constitutes appropriate conduct.

Durkheim ([1897] 1951) introduced the term *anomie* into sociological literature to describe the loss of direction felt in a society when social control of individual behavior has become ineffective. Anomie is a state of normlessness that typically occurs during a period of profound social change and disorder, such as a time of economic collapse. People become more aggressive or depressed, which results in higher rates of violent crime and suicide. Since there is much less agreement on what constitutes proper behavior during times of revolution, sudden prosperity, or economic depression, conformity and obedience become less significant as social forces. Stating exactly what constitutes deviance also becomes much more difficult.

Merton's Theory of Deviance What do a mugger and a teacher have in common? Each is "working" to obtain money that can be exchanged for desired goods. As this example illustrates, behavior that violates accepted norms (such as mugging) may be based on the same objectives as the behavior of people who pursue conventional lifestyles.

Using this kind of analysis, sociologist Robert Merton (1968) adapted Durkheim's concept of anomie to explain why people accept or reject the goals of a society, the socially approved means of meeting those goals, or both. Merton maintained that one important cultural goal in the United States is success, measured largely in terms of money. In addition to setting this goal for people, our society offers specific instructions on how to reach it—go to school, work hard, do not quit, take advantage of opportunities, and so forth.

What happens in a society with a heavy emphasis on wealth as a basic symbol of success? Merton reasoned that people adapt in certain ways, by conforming to or deviating from such cultural expectations. In his *anomie theory of deviance,* he posited five basic forms of adaptation (see Table 4–1).

Conformity to social norms, the most common adaptation in Merton's typology, is the opposite of deviance. It involves acceptance of both the overall societal goal ("become affluent") and the approved means ("work hard"). In Merton's view, there must be some consensus regarding accepted cultural goals and legitimate means for attaining them. Without such consensus, societies could exist only as collectives of people rather than as unified cultures, and might experience continual chaos.

summing UP

Table 4–1   Merton's Deviance Theory

	Type of Behavior				
	Nondeviant	*Deviant*			
Does the individual accept:	*Conformity*	*Retreatism*	*Innovation*	*Ritualism*	*Rebellion*
the goals of society, such as acquisition of wealth?	👍	👎	👍	👎	👎 👍
the use of acceptable means, such as hard work?	👍	👎	👎	👍	👎 👍

Source: Adapted from Merton, Robert K., "Social Structure and Anomie," *American Sociological Review,* 1938.
Photos: (Moneybag): ©Shutterstock/Billion Photos; (Timeclock): ©Alamy Images.

Of course, in a varied society such as the United States, conformity is not universal. For example, the means for realizing objectives are not equally distributed. People in the lower social classes often identify with the same goals as those of more powerful and affluent citizens, yet they lack equal access to high-quality education and training for skilled work. Moreover, even within a society, institutionalized means for realizing objectives vary. For instance, it is legal to win money by playing roulette or poker in Nevada, but not in neighboring Utah.

The other four types of behavior represented in Table 4–1 all involve some departure from conformity. The "innovator" accepts society's goals but pursues them with means regarded as improper. For example, a professional thief who specializes in safecracking may steal money to buy consumer goods and expensive vacations.

In Merton's typology, the "ritualist" has abandoned the goal of material success and become compulsively committed to the institutional means. Work becomes simply a way of life rather than a means to achieving success. An example is the bureaucratic official who blindly applies rules and regulations without remembering the larger goals of an organization. Such would be true of a welfare caseworker who refuses to assist a homeless family because their last apartment was in another district.

The "retreatist," as described by Merton, has basically withdrawn (or "retreated") from both the goals *and* the means of society. In the United States, drug addicts and vagrants are typically portrayed as retreatists. Some social workers worry that adolescents who are addicted to alcohol will become retreatists at an early age.

The final adaptation identified by Merton reflects people's attempts to create a new social structure. The "rebel" who feels alienated from dominant means and goals may seek a dramatically different social order. Members of a revolutionary political organization, such as a militia group, can be categorized as rebels according to Merton's model.

Although Merton's theory of deviance is popular, it has not been applied systematically to real-world crime. Nevertheless, Merton made a key contribution to the sociological understanding of deviance by pointing out that deviants (such as innovators and ritualists) share a great deal with conforming people. The convicted felon may hold many of the same aspirations as people with no criminal background. Thus, the theory helps us to understand deviance as socially created behavior, rather than as the result of momentary pathological impulses.

You are a young person growing up in a poor neighborhood. You yearn for the flashy, expensive lifestyle you see portrayed in the media. How will you get it?

INTERACTIONIST PERSPECTIVE

The functionalist approach to deviance explains why rule violation continues to exist in societies, despite pressure to conform and obey. However, functionalists do not indicate how a given person comes to commit a deviant act, or why on some occasions crimes do or do not occur. The emphasis on everyday behavior that is the focus of the interactionist perspective provides two such explanations of crime: cultural transmission and social disorganization theory.

Cultural Transmission   In the course of studying graffiti writing by gangs in Los Angeles, sociologist Susan A. Phillips (1999) discovered that the writers learned from one another. In fact, Phillips was surprised by how stable their focus was over time. She also noted how other ethnic groups built on the models of the African American and Chicano gangs, superimposing Cambodian, Chinese, or Vietnamese symbols.

These teenagers demonstrate that humans *learn* how to behave in social situations, whether properly or improperly. There is no natural, innate manner in which people interact with one another. Though these simple ideas are not disputed today, such was not the case when sociologist Edwin Sutherland (1883–1950) first advanced the argument that an individual undergoes the same basic socialization process whether learning conforming or deviant acts.

Sutherland, whose ideas have been the dominating force in criminology, drew on the *cultural transmission* school, which emphasizes that people learn criminal behavior through their social interactions. Such learning includes not only the techniques of lawbreaking (for example, how to break into a car quickly and quietly) but also the motives, drives, and rationalizations of criminals. The cultural transmission approach can also be used to explain the behavior of those who habitually abuse alcohol or drugs.

Sutherland maintained that people acquire their definitions of proper and improper behavior through interactions with a primary group and significant others. He used the term *differential association* to describe the process through which exposure to attitudes *favorable* to criminal acts leads to rule violations. Research suggests that this process also applies to such noncriminal deviant acts as smoking, truancy, and early sexual behavior.

Sutherland offers the example of a boy who is sociable, outgoing, and athletic and who lives in an area with a high delinquency rate. The youth is very likely to come into contact with peers who commit acts of vandalism, fail to attend school, and so forth and may come to adopt such behavior. However, an introverted boy living in the same neighborhood may stay away from his peers and avoid delinquency. In another community, an outgoing and athletic boy may join a Little League baseball team or a scout troop because of his interactions with peers. Thus, Sutherland views deviant behavior as the result of the types of groups to which one belongs and the kinds of friendships one has.

According to critics, though the cultural transmission approach may explain the deviant behavior of juvenile delinquents or graffiti artists, it fails to explain the conduct of the first-time impulsive shoplifter or the impoverished person who steals out of necessity. While the theory is not a precise statement of the process through which one becomes a criminal, it does stress the paramount role of social interaction in increasing a person's motivation to engage in deviant behavior (Loughran et al. 2013; Sutherland et al. 1992).

Social Disorganization Theory   The social relationships that exist in a community or neighborhood affect people's behavior. Philip Zimbardo (2007:24–25), author of the mock prison experiment described in Chapter 3, once did an experiment that demonstrated the power of communal relationships. He abandoned a car in each of two different neighborhoods, leaving its hood up and removing its hubcaps. In one neighborhood, people started to strip the car for parts before Zimbardo had finished setting up a remote video camera to record their behavior. In the other neighborhood, weeks passed without the car being touched, except for a pedestrian who stopped to close the hood during a rainstorm.

What accounts for the strikingly different outcomes of Zimbardo's experiment in the two communities? According to *social disorganization theory,* increases in crime and deviance can be attributed to the absence or breakdown of communal relationships and social institutions, such as the family, school, church, and local government. This theory was developed at the University of Chicago in the early 1900s to describe the apparent disorganization that occurred as cities expanded with rapid immigration and migration from rural areas. Using the latest survey techniques, Clifford Shaw and Henry McKay literally mapped the distribution of social problems in Chicago. They found high rates of social problems in neighborhoods where buildings had deteriorated and the population had declined. Interestingly, the patterns persisted over time, despite changes in the neighborhoods' ethnic and racial composition.

This theory is not without its critics. To some, social disorganization theory seems to "blame the victim," leaving larger societal forces, such as the lack of jobs or high-quality schools, unaccountable. Critics also argue that even troubled neighborhoods have viable, healthy organizations, which persist despite the problems that surround them.

More recently, social disorganization theorists have taken to emphasizing the effect of social networks on communal bonds. These researchers acknowledge that communities are not isolated islands. Residents' bonds may be enhanced or weakened by their ties to groups outside the immediate community (Jensen 2003; Sampson and Groves 1989; Shaw and McKay 1942).

LABELING PERSPECTIVE

The Saints and Roughnecks were two groups of high school males continually engaged in excessive drinking, reckless driving, truancy, petty theft, and vandalism. There the similarity ended. None of the Saints was ever arrested, but every Roughneck was frequently in trouble with police and townspeople. Why the disparity in their treatment? On the basis of his observation research in their high school, sociologist William Chambliss (1973) concluded that social class played an important role in the varying fortunes of the two groups.

The Saints hid behind a facade of respectability. They came from "good families," were active in school organizations, planned on attending college, and received good grades. People generally viewed their delinquent acts as isolated cases of "sowing wild oats." By contrast, the Roughnecks had no such aura of respectability. They drove around town in beat-up cars, were generally unsuccessful in school, and aroused suspicion no matter what they did.

We can understand such discrepancies by using an approach to deviance known as **labeling theory.** Unlike Sutherland's work, labeling theory does not focus on why some individuals come to commit deviant acts. Instead, it attempts to explain why certain people (such as the Roughnecks) are *viewed* as deviants, delinquents, "bad kids," "losers," and criminals, while others whose behavior is similar (such as the Saints) are not seen in such harsh terms. Reflecting the contribution of interactionist theorists, labeling theory emphasizes how a person comes to be labeled as deviant or to accept that label. Sociologist Howard Becker ([1953] 2015; 1963:9; 1964), who popularized this approach, summed it up with this statement: "Deviant behavior is behavior that people so label."

Labeling theory is also called the *societal-reaction approach,* reminding us that it is the *response* to an act, not the behavior itself, that determines deviance. For example, studies have shown that some school personnel and therapists expand educational programs designed for students with learning disabilities to include students with behavioral problems. Consequently, a "troublemaker" can be improperly labeled as learning disabled, and vice versa (Grattet 2011).

Traditionally, research on deviance has focused on people who violate social norms. In contrast, labeling theory focuses on police, probation officers, psychiatrists, judges, teachers, employers, school officials, and other regulators of social control. These agents, it is argued, play a significant role in creating the deviant identity by designating certain people (and not others) as "deviant." An important aspect of labeling theory is the recognition that some individuals or groups have the power to *define* labels and apply them to others. This view ties into the conflict perspective's emphasis on the social significance of power.

In recent years, the practice of *racial profiling,* in which people are identified as criminal suspects purely on the basis of their race, has come under public scrutiny. Studies confirm the public's suspicions that in some jurisdictions, police officers are much more likely to stop African American males than White males for routine traffic violations, in the expectation of finding drugs or guns in their cars. Civil rights activists refer to these cases sarcastically as DWB ("Driving While Black") violations. After the September 11, 2001, attacks on the World Trade Center and the Pentagon, profiling took a new turn as people who appeared to be Arab or Muslim came under special scrutiny.

Use Your Sociological Imagination

You are a teacher. What kinds of labels, freely used in education, might be attached to your students?

CONFLICT PERSPECTIVE

Conflict theorists point out that people with power protect their own interests and define deviance to suit their own needs. Sociologist Richard Quinney (1974, 1979, 1980) is a leading proponent of the view that the criminal justice system serves the interests of the powerful. Crime, according to Quinney (1970), is a definition of conduct created by authorized agents of social control—such as legislators and law enforcement officers—in a politically organized society. Quinney and other conflict theorists argue that lawmaking is often an attempt by the powerful to coerce others into their own morality (see also Spitzer 1975).

Conflict theory helps to explain why our society has laws against gambling, drug usage, and prostitution, many of which are violated on a massive scale. (We will examine these "victimless crimes" later in the chapter.) According to the conflict school, criminal law does not represent a consistent application of societal values but instead reflects competing values and interests. Thus, marijuana is outlawed by the federal government because it is alleged to be harmful to users, yet cigarettes and alcohol are sold legally almost everywhere.

In fact, conflict theorists contend that the entire criminal justice system in the United States treats suspects differently based on their racial, ethnic, or social-class background. In many cases, officials in the system use their own discretion to make biased decisions about whether to press charges or drop them, whether to set bail and how much, whether to offer parole or deny it. Researchers have found that this kind of *differential justice*—differences in the way social control is exercised over different groups—puts African Americans and Latinos at a disadvantage in the justice system, both as juveniles and as adults. On average, White offenders receive shorter sentences than comparable Latino and African American offenders, even when prior arrest records and the relative severity of the crime are taken into consideration (Brewer and Heitzeg 2008; Sandefur 2008; Schlesinger 2011).

The perspective advanced by labeling and conflict theorists forms quite a contrast to the functionalist approach to deviance. Functionalists view standards of deviant behavior as merely reflecting cultural norms, whereas conflict and labeling theorists point out that the most powerful groups in a society can shape laws and standards and determine who is (or is not) prosecuted as a criminal. Those groups would be unlikely to apply the label "deviant" to the corporate executive whose decisions lead to large-scale environmental pollution. In the opinion of conflict theorists, agents of social control and powerful groups can generally impose their own self-serving definitions of deviance on the general public.

FEMINIST PERSPECTIVE

Feminist criminologists such as Freda Adler and Meda Chesney-Lind have suggested that many of the existing approaches to deviance and crime were developed with only men in mind. For example, in the United States, for many years any husband who forced his wife to have sexual intercourse–without her consent and against her will–was not legally considered to have committed rape. The law defined rape as pertaining only to sexual relations between people who were not married to each other, reflecting the overwhelmingly male composition of state legislatures at the time.

It took repeated protests by feminist organizations to change the criminal law defining rape. Beginning in 1993, husbands in all 50 states could be prosecuted under most circumstances for the rape of their wives. There remain alarming exceptions in no fewer than eight states, however. For example, the husband is exempt when he does not need to use force because his wife is asleep, unconscious, or mentally or physically impaired. These interpretations rest on the notion that the marriage contract entitles a husband to sex (Allen 2015).

In the future, feminist scholarship can be expected to grow dramatically. Particularly on topics such as white-collar crime, drinking behavior, drug abuse, and differential sentencing rates between the genders, as well as on the fundamental question of how to define deviance, feminist scholars will have much to say.

Table 4-2 summarizes the various approaches sociologists have used in studying deviance.

Tracking Perspectives

Table 4-2 Approaches to Deviance

Approach	Perspective	Proponent	Emphasis
Anomie	Functionalist	Émile Durkheim Robert Merton	Adaptation to societal norms
Cultural transmission/ differential association	Interactionist	Edwin Sutherland	Patterns learned through others
Social disorganization	Interactionist	Clifford Shaw Henry McKay	Communal relationships
Labeling/societal reaction	Interactionist	Howard Becker William Chambliss	Societal response to acts
Conflict	Conflict	Richard Quinney	Dominance by authorized agents Discretionary justice
Feminist	Conflict/ feminist	Freda Adler Meda Chesney-Lind	Role of gender Women as victims and perpetrators

Think About It
Which sociological perspective is most useful in analyzing white collar crime? Vandalism? Cocaine use?

Crime: A Sociological Approach

Crime is a violation of criminal law for which some governmental authority applies formal penalties. It represents a deviation from formal social norms administered by the state. Laws divide crimes into various categories, depending on the severity of the offense, the age of the offender, the potential punishment that can be levied, and the court that holds jurisdiction over the case.

Rather than relying solely on legal categories, sociologists classify crimes in terms of how they are committed and how society views the offenses. In this section we will examine six types of crime differentiated by sociologists: victimless crimes, professional crime, organized crime, white-collar and technology-based crime, hate crime, and transnational crime.

VICTIMLESS CRIMES

When we think of crime, we tend to think of acts that endanger people's economic or personal well-being against their will (or without their direct knowledge). By contrast, sociologists use the term *victimless crime* to describe the willing exchange among adults of widely desired but illegal goods and services. For example, prostitution is widely regarded as a victimless crime (Schur 1965, 1985).

Some activists are working to decriminalize many of these illegal practices. Supporters of decriminalization are troubled by the attempt to legislate a moral code of behavior for adults. In their view, it is impossible to prevent prostitution, drug abuse, gambling, and other victimless crimes. The already overburdened criminal justice system should instead devote its resources to "street crimes" and other offenses with obvious victims.

Despite the wide use of the term *victimless crime,* many people object to the notion that there is no victim other than the offender in such crimes. Excessive drinking, compulsive gambling, and illegal drug use contribute to an enormous amount of personal and property damage. A person with a drinking problem can become abusive to a spouse or children; an individual with a compulsive gambling or drug abuse problem may steal to pursue his obsession. And feminist sociologists contend that prostitution, as well as the more disturbing aspects of pornography, reinforce the misconception that women are "toys" who can be treated as objects rather than people. According to critics of decriminalization, society must not give tacit approval to conduct that has such harmful consequences (Farley and Malarek 2008).

The controversy over decriminalization reminds us of the important insights of labeling and conflict theorists presented earlier. Underlying this debate are two interesting questions: Who has the power to define gambling, prostitution, and public drunkenness as "crimes"? And who has the power to label such behaviors as "victimless"? The answer, in both cases, is generally the state legislatures and sometimes the police and the courts.

PROFESSIONAL CRIME

Although the adage "crime doesn't pay" is familiar, many people do make a career of illegal activities. A *professional criminal* (or career criminal) is a person who pursues crime as a day-to-day occupation, developing skilled techniques and enjoying a certain degree of status among other criminals. Some professional criminals specialize in burglary, safecracking, hijacking of cargo, pickpocketing, and shoplifting. Such people have acquired skills that reduce the likelihood of arrest, conviction, and imprisonment. As a result, they may have long careers in their chosen "professions."

Edwin Sutherland (1937) offered pioneering insights into the behavior of professional criminals by publishing an annotated account written by a professional thief. Unlike the person who engages in crime only once or twice, professional thieves make a business of stealing. They devote their entire working time to planning and executing crimes, and sometimes travel across the nation to pursue their "professional duties." Like people in regular occupations, professional thieves consult with their colleagues concerning their work, becoming part of a subculture of similarly occupied individuals. They exchange information on good places to burglarize, outlets for stolen goods, and ways of securing bail bonds.

ORGANIZED CRIME

A 1976 government report takes three pages to define the term *organized crime.* For our purposes, we will consider *organized crime* to be the work of a group that regulates relations between various criminal enterprises involved in various illegal activities, including the smuggling and sale of drugs, prostitution, and gambling. Organized crime dominates the world of illegal business just as large corporations dominate the conventional business world. It allocates territory, sets prices for goods and services, and arbitrates internal disputes. A secret, conspiratorial activity that generally evades law enforcement, it takes over legitimate businesses, gains influence over labor unions, corrupts public officials, intimidates witnesses in criminal trials, and even "taxes" merchants in exchange for "protection" (National Advisory Commission on Criminal Justice 1976).

Organized crime serves as a means of upward mobility for groups of people struggling to escape poverty. Sociologist Daniel Bell (1953) used the term *ethnic succession* to describe the sequential passage of leadership from Irish Americans in the early part of the 20th century to Jewish Americans in the 1920s and then to Italian Americans in the early 1930s. Since then ethnic succession has become more complex, reflecting the diversity of the nation's latest immigrants. Colombian, Mexican, Russian, Chinese, Pakistani, and Nigerian immigrants are among those who have begun to play a significant role in organized crime activities (Chin 1996; Kleinknecht 1996).

WHITE-COLLAR AND TECHNOLOGY-BASED CRIME

Income tax evasion, stock manipulation, consumer fraud, bribery and extraction of "kickbacks," embezzlement, and misrepresentation in advertising—these are all examples of *white-collar crime,* illegal acts committed in the course of business activities, often by affluent, "respectable" people. Edwin Sutherland (1949, 1983) likened these crimes to organized crime because they are often perpetrated through people's occupational roles.

A new type of white-collar crime has emerged in recent decades: cybercrime. *Cybercrime* is illegal activity primarily conducted through the use of computer hardware or software. Encompassed within cybercrime is cyberespionage and cyberterrorism. Cybercrime is a global problem, but the United States is victim to 80 percent of the data breaches. Because of the high value of U.S. targets, it is estimated that this country accounts for over 90 percent of the global cost of these breaches. By 2019 the annual cost of criminal data breaches in the United States is estimated to reach 2 trillion dollars (Juniper Research 2015).

When Charles Horton Cooley spoke of the self and Erving Goffman of impression management, surely neither scholar could have envisioned the insidious crime of identity theft. Each year about 7 percent of all adults find that their personal information has been misused for criminal purposes. Unfortunately, with our society's growing reliance on electronic financial transactions, assuming someone else's identity has become increasingly easy (Harrel 2015).

Identity theft does not necessarily require technology. A criminal can obtain someone's personal information by pickpocketing or by intercepting mail. However, the widespread exchange of information online has allowed criminals to access large amounts of personal information. Public awareness of the potential harm from identity theft took a giant leap in the aftermath of September 11, 2001, when investigations revealed that several hijackers had used fraudulent IDs to open bank accounts, rent apartments, and board planes. A law enacted in 2004 makes identity theft punishable by a mandatory prison sentence if it is linked to other crimes. Still, unauthorized disclosures of information, even if accidental, persist.

Sutherland (1940) coined the term *white-collar crime* in 1939 to refer to acts by individuals, but the term has been broadened recently to include offenses by businesses and corporations. *Corporate crime,* or any act by a corporation that is punishable by the government, takes many forms and includes individuals, organizations, and institutions among its victims. Corporations may engage in anticompetitive behavior, environmental pollution, tax fraud, accounting fraud, stock fraud and manipulation, the production of unsafe goods, bribery and corruption, and worker health and safety violations (J. Coleman 2006).

As the editor of an online news service, how might you treat stories about corporate or white-collar crime differently from those about violent crime?

"BUT IF WE GO BACK TO SCHOOL AND GET A GOOD EDUCATION, THINK OF ALL THE DOORS IT'LL OPEN TO WHITE-COLLAR CRIME."

©ScienceCartoonsPlus.com

For many years, corporate wrongdoers got off lightly in court by documenting their long history of charitable contributions and agreeing to help law enforcement officials find other white-collar criminals. Unfortunately, that is still the case. The highly visible jailing of multimedia personality Martha Stewart in 2004, as well as recent disclosures of "Wall Street greed," may lead the casual observer to think that government is cracking down on white-collar crime. However, an independent analysis found that from 2000 through 2014, the number of white-collar crimes that were prosecuted fell by 29 percent (Transactional Records Access Clearinghouse 2015).

Even when a person is convicted of corporate crime, the verdict generally does not harm his or her reputation and career aspirations nearly so much as conviction for street crime would. Apparently, the label "white-collar criminal" does not carry the stigma of the label "felon convicted of a violent crime." Conflict theorists don't find such differential labeling and treatment surprising. They argue that the criminal justice system largely disregards the white-collar crimes of the affluent, while focusing instead on crimes committed by the poor. If an offender holds a position of status and influence, his or her crime is treated as less serious, and the sanction is much more lenient.

HATE CRIME

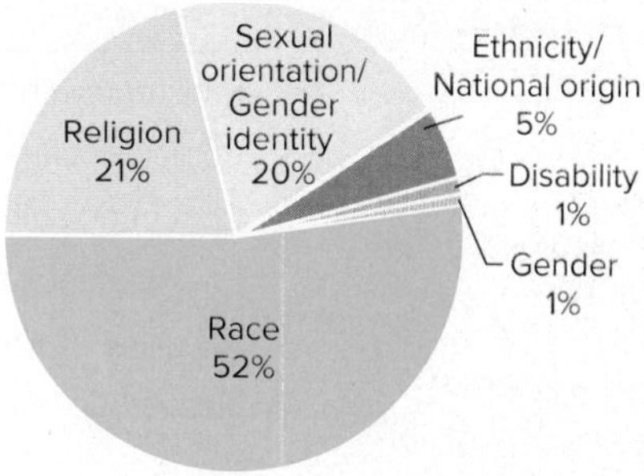

In contrast to other crimes, hate crimes are defined not only by the perpetrators' actions, but also by their purpose. The government considers an ordinary crime to be a *hate crime* when the offender is motivated to choose a victim based on race, religion, ethnic group, national origin, or sexual orientation, and when evidence shows that hatred prompted the offender to commit the crime. Hate crimes are sometimes referred to as *bias crimes* (Department of Justice 2008).

In 1990, Congress passed the Hate Crimes Statistics Act, which created a national mandate to identify crimes based on race, religion, ethnic group, and national origin. (Before that time, only 12 states had monitored such crimes.) Since then the act has been broadened to include disabilities, both physical and mental, and sexual orientation. In addition, some jurisdictions impose harsher sanctions (jail time or fines) for hate crimes than for other crimes. For example, if the penalty for assault is a year in jail, the penalty for an assault identified as a hate crime might be two years.

In 2016, law enforcement agencies submitted data on hate crimes to the federal government. The statistics included official reports of 5,850 hate crimes and bias-motivated offenses. As Figure 4–2 shows, race was the apparent motivation in approximately 57 percent of the reports. Although vandalism and intimidation were the most common crimes, 37 percent of the incidents involved assault, rape, or murder.

The vast majority of hate crimes, although not all of them, are committed by members of the dominant group against those who are relatively powerless. One in every five racially based hate crimes is an anti-White incident. Except for the most horrific hate crimes, these offenses receive little media attention. Clearly, hostility based on race knows no boundaries.

Figure 4–2
Reported Hate Crimes, by Category
SOURCE: Incidents reported for 2013 in 2014. Federal Bureau of Investigation 2016.

TRANSNATIONAL CRIME

More and more, scholars and police officials are turning their attention to *transnational crime,* or crime that occurs across multiple national borders. In the past, international crime was often limited to the clandestine shipment of goods across the border between two countries. But increasingly, crime is no more restricted by such borders than is legal commerce. Rather than concentrating on specific countries, international crime now spans the globe.

Historically, probably the most dreaded example of transnational crime has been slavery. At first, governments did not regard slavery as a crime but merely regulated it as they would the trade in goods. In the 20th century, transnational crime grew to embrace trafficking in endangered species, drugs, and stolen art and antiquities.

Table 4–3 Types of Transnational Crime

Bankruptcy and insurance fraud

Computer crime (treating computers as both a tool and a target of crime)

Corruption and bribery of public officials

Environmental crime

Hijacking of airplanes ("skyjacking")

Illegal drug trade

Illegal money transfers ("money laundering")

Illegal sales of firearms and ammunition

Infiltration of legal businesses

Intellectual property crime

Migrant smuggling

Networking of criminal organizations

Sea piracy

Terrorism

Theft of art and cultural objects

Trafficking in body parts (includes illegal organ transplants)

Trafficking in human beings (includes sex trade)

SOURCE: Adapted from Mueller 2001 and United Nations Office on Drugs and Crime 2012.

Transnational crime is not exclusive of some of the other types of crime we have discussed. For example, organized criminal networks are increasingly global. Technology definitely facilitates their illegal activities, such as trafficking in child pornography. In the 1990s, the United Nations began to categorize transnational crimes; Table 4–3 lists some of the more common types.

Crime Statistics

Crime statistics are not as accurate as social scientists would like. Unfortunately, they are frequently cited as if they were completely reliable. Such data do serve as an indicator of police activity, as well as of the approximate level of certain crimes. Yet it would be a mistake to interpret these data as an exact representation of the incidence of crime.

INDEX CRIMES AND VICTIMIZATION SURVEYS

Typically, the crime data reported in the United States are based on *index crimes,* or the eight types of crime tabulated each year by the Federal Bureau of Investigation (FBI). This category of criminal behavior generally consists of those serious offenses that people think of when they express concern about the nation's crime problem. Index crimes include

Table 4–4 National Crime Rates and Percentage Change

Crime Index Offenses in 2014	Number Reported	Rate per 100,000 Inhabitants	Percentage Change in Rate Since 2005
Violent crime			
Murder	14,249	5	−15
Forcible rape	116,645	37	−11
Robbery	325,802	103	−27
Aggravated assault	741,291	233	−14
Total	1,165,383	366	−22
Property crime			
Burglary	1,729,806	543	−25
Larceny-theft	5,858,496	1,839	−20
Motor vehicle theft	689,527	216	−48
Total	8,299,829	2,590	−24

NOTE: Arson was designated an index offense beginning in 1979; data on arson were still incomplete as of 2014. Because of rounding, the offenses may not add to totals. Beginning in 2011, the FBI broadened the definition of rape, and use of the term is being phased out. The 2014 data use the new definition; the "Change since 2005" column uses the legacy definition.

SOURCE: Department of Justice 2014.

murder, rape, robbery, and assault—all of which are violent crimes committed against people—as well as the property crimes of burglary, larceny-theft, motor vehicle theft, and arson (see Table 4-4). The crime index is published annually by the FBI as part of the *Uniform Crime Reports.*

Obviously, many serious offenses, such as white-collar crimes, are not included in this index (although they are recorded elsewhere). In addition, the crime index is disproportionately devoted to property crimes, whereas most citizens are more worried about violent crimes. Thus, a significant decrease in the number of rapes and robberies could be overshadowed by a slightly larger increase in the number of automobiles stolen, leading to the mistaken impression that *personal* safety is more at risk than before.

The most serious limitation of official crime statistics is that they include only those crimes actually *reported* to law enforcement agencies. Because members of racial and ethnic minority groups often distrust law enforcement agencies, they may not contact the police. Feminist sociologists and others have noted that many women do not report rape or spousal abuse out of fear they will be blamed for the crime.

Partly because of these deficiencies in official statistics, the National Crime Victimization Survey was initiated in 1972. The Bureau of Justice Statistics, in compiling this annual report, seeks information from law enforcement agencies, but also interviews households across the nation and asks if they were victims of a specific set of crimes during the preceding year. In general, those who administer *victimization surveys* question ordinary people, not police officers, to determine whether they have been victims of crime.

Unfortunately, like other crime data, victimization surveys have particular limitations. They require that victims understand what has happened to them and are willing to disclose such information to interviewers. Fraud, income tax evasion, and blackmail are examples of crimes that are unlikely to be reported in victimization studies.

CRIME TRENDS

Crime fills the news reports on television, over the Internet, and in the newspaper. As a result, the public regards crime as a major social problem. Yet there has been a significant decline in violent crime in the United States in recent years, after many years of increases.

How much has crime declined? Consider this: the rate of crime being reported in 2014 was comparable to what it was back when gasoline cost 29 cents a gallon and the average person earned less than $6,000 a year. That was 1963.

Dramatic declines have occurred within the last decade. As Table 4–4 shows, both violent crime and property crime dropped over 20 percent in the last 10 years. Although a tragic 14,249 people were murdered in 2014, in 1991 that number was a staggering 24,700. Declines have also been registered in victimization surveys (see Figure 4–3).

Figure 4–3

Victimization Rates, 1993–2014

Source: Truman and Langton 2015.

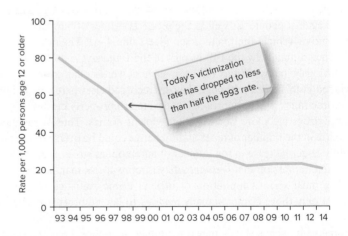

Think About It

What might have caused the victimization rate to drop so dramatically beginning in the mid-1990s?

What explains these declines in both index crimes and victimization rates? Possible explanations include the following:

- Community-oriented policing and crime prevention programs
- New gun control laws
- A massive increase in the prison population, which at least prevents inmates from committing crimes outside prison
- New surveillance technologies
- Better residential and business security
- The decline of the crack cocaine epidemic, which soared in the late 1980s
- The aging of the population, as the number of people in their 50s increased and the number in their 20s decreased

No single explanation could account for such a marked change in crime rates. Taken together, however, these changes in public policy, public health, technology, and demographics may well explain it (Tonry 2014).

Feminist scholars draw our attention to one significant countertrend: the proportion of major crimes committed by women has increased. However, violent crimes committed by women, which have never been common, have declined. Despite the "mean girls" headlines in the tabloid magazines, every reliable measure shows that among women, fights, weapons possession, assaults, and violent injuries have plunged over the last decade (Males and Chesney-Lind 2010).

INTERNATIONAL CRIME RATES

If developing reliable crime data in the United States is difficult, making useful cross-national comparisons is even more difficult. Nevertheless, with some care, we can offer preliminary conclusions about how crime rates differ around the world.

During the 1980s and 1990s, violent crimes were much more common in the United States than in Western Europe. Murders, rapes, and robberies were reported to the police at much higher rates in the United States. Yet the incidence of certain other types of crime appears to be higher elsewhere. For example, England, Ireland, Denmark, and New Zealand all have higher rates of car theft than the United States (United Nations Office on Drugs and Crime 2015b).

Why are violent crime rates so much higher in the United States than in Western Europe? Sociologist Elliot Currie (1985, 1998) has suggested that our society places greater emphasis on individual economic achievement than other societies. At the same time, many observers have noted that the culture of the United States has long tolerated, if not condoned, many forms of violence. Coupled with sharp disparities between poor and affluent citizens, significant unemployment, and substantial alcohol and drug abuse, all these factors combine to produce a climate conducive to crime.

Finally, a particularly worrisome development has been the rapid escalation in homicide rates in developing countries that supply drugs to industrialized countries, especially the United States. The huge profits generated by cocaine exports to North America and Europe have allowed drug gangs to arm themselves to the point of becoming illegal armies. Homicide rates in Mexico are now about twice as high as those in the United States. Honduras, Guatemala, Venezuela, and El Salvador's homicide rates are three to five times those of Mexico (Luhnow 2014).

Sociology Matters

Sociology matters because it explains why you accept certain social norms almost without thinking—and why you pay a price if you break those norms.

- What social norms were you expected to conform to when you became a student at your college or university? Are they similar to or different from the norms you grew up with?
- What happens to students who do not conform to accepted social norms? Is social control on your campus stricter or more lenient than social control in other parts of society?
- Is crime a problem on your campus? If so, what social forces might underlie it?

CHAPTER RESOURCES

Summary

Conformity and **deviance** are two ways in which people respond to real or imagined pressure from others. This chapter examined the mechanisms of **social control** that society uses to encourage conformity to social norms. We defined deviance and offered several theories to explain its existence. The chapter closed with a discussion of **crime** and statistics on criminal activity in the United States and other nations.

1. Stanley Milgram defined **conformity** as going along with one's peers. **Obedience,** on the other hand, means compliance with higher authorities in a hierarchical structure.
2. Some norms are so important to a society that they are formalized in **law.** Socialization is the primary source of both conformity and obedience to law.

3. **Deviance** is behavior that violates any social norm, whether it concerns conduct or personal appearance. Some forms of deviance carry a negative social **stigma,** while others are more or less accepted.

4. The sociologist Robert Merton noted that people who engage in deviant behavior share many of the same goals and values as people who conform to social norms, though they may differ in the means by which they pursue their goals. Merton's theory is called the **anomie theory of deviance.**

5. The interactionist theorist Edwin Sutherland believed that people learn criminal behavior by associating with others, an approach called **cultural transmission.** In his theory of **differential association,** Sutherland proposed that deviance results from a person's exposure to individuals who approve of criminal acts.

6. Other interactionists attribute increases in crime and deviance to the absence or breakdown of communal relationships and social institutions, such as the family, school, church, and local government. This approach is called **social disorganization theory.**

7. **Labeling theory** emphasizes that society brands some people who engage in a behavior as deviant, but not others, based largely on a person's social class, race, or ethnicity. This theory of deviance is also called the **societal-reaction approach.**

8. Conflict theorists stress that laws and the **sanctions** imposed on criminals for breaking them reflect the interests of the powerful. For example, feminists note that the lenient treatment of some crimes against women, such as marital rape, reflects the relative powerlessness of women.

9. **Crime** is a violation of criminal law for which some governmental authority applies formal penalties. Sociologists differentiate among **victimless crimes,** such as drug use and prostitution, **professional crime, organized crime, white-collar crime, hate crime,** and **transnational crime.**

10. Crime statistics are among the least reliable social data, partly because many crimes are not reported to law enforcement agencies. Rates of violent crime are higher in the United States than in most other Western societies.

Key Terms

Stratification in the United States and Global Inequality

©Lissa Harrison

Sani Abdu, age 11, travels for two hours on donkey before the school day begins. Carrying large plastic cans, he rides to a muddy well to fetch water for his family. While watching his footing—children have fallen into the well—he carefully lowers the bucket down to the bottom by rope. By the time Sani returns home with the water, he is late for school.

Sani is not the only child who makes this daily water run. One of his classmates rises at 4 A.M. to walk to the well, then repeats the trek after school. By evening, he is worn out. These two 11-year-olds are typical of schoolchildren in Niger, where 90 percent of the population lacks easy access to drinkable water. Unfortunately, they are typical of children in many parts of the world, where the time-consuming mission to secure freshwater is a daily struggle (Nossiter 2012; UN Office for the Coordination of Humanitarian Affairs 2006; UNICEF 2011).

The per capita income in Niger is now $295 a year—28 percent lower than it was in 1975. In the same period, per capita income in the United States rose 550 percent, to almost $56,000. These data and the daily struggle for water in Niger highlight the global divide between the haves and the have-nots. In the United States, people think of plastic water bottles more as an environmental concern than a vital survival tool.

The global divide separates individuals as well as nations. On one side are the world's wealthy, including Microsoft cofounder Bill Gates, in 2016 the world's richest person with a net worth of $86 billion. Today, the world has at least 1,844 billionaires (a billion equals *one thousand million*) in 67 countries. Gates's fortune alone is 11 times the gross national income of Niger, home to 19 million people (*Forbes* 2017; World Bank 2017).

The condition in which members of a society enjoy different amounts of wealth, prestige, or power is termed **social inequality.** Every society manifests some degree of social inequality. Sociologists refer to the structured ranking of entire groups of people that perpetuates unequal economic rewards and power as **stratification.** In industrial societies, these unequal rewards are evident both in people's **income**—in their salaries and wages—and in their **wealth**—in material assets such as land, stocks, and other property.

In this chapter we will examine several stratification systems, paying particular attention to the theories of Karl Marx and Max Weber. We will see how a person's social class affects his or her opportunities, including the chance to move up the social ladder. And we will look at stratification in developing countries, where multinational corporations based in developed nations have been charged with exploiting those who work in their factories.

Systems of Stratification

Not all societies are stratified in the same way. Sociologists have studied stratification in ancient as well as modern times, in Western and non-Western societies. In the following section we will compare four different general systems of stratification. Then we will discuss several theoretical approaches to stratification, its purpose and desirability.

Look at the four general systems of stratification examined here—slavery, castes, estates, and social classes—as ideal types useful for purposes of analysis. In reality, any stratification system may include elements of more than one type. For example, prior to the Civil War, you could find in the southern states of the United States social classes dividing Whites as well as the institutionalized enslavement of Blacks.

To understand these systems better, it may be helpful to review the distinction between *achieved status* and *ascribed status,* discussed in Chapter 3. *Ascribed status* is a social position "assigned" to a person by society without regard for that person's unique talents or characteristics. By contrast, *achieved status* is a social position attained by a person largely through his or her own efforts. The two are closely linked.

The nation's most affluent families generally inherit wealth and status, while many members of racial and ethnic minorities inherit disadvantaged status. Age and gender, as well, are ascribed statuses that influence a person's wealth and social position.

The most extreme form of legalized social inequality for individuals or groups is *slavery*. What distinguishes this oppressive system of stratification is that enslaved individuals are *owned* by other people, who treat these human beings as property, just as if they were household pets or appliances.

Slavery has varied in the way it has been practiced. In ancient Greece, the main source of slaves was captives of war and piracy. Although succeeding generations could inherit slave status, it was not necessarily permanent. A person's status might change depending on which city-state happened to triumph in a military conflict. In effect, all citizens had the potential of becoming slaves or of being granted freedom, depending on the circumstances of history. By contrast, in the United States and Latin America, where slavery was an ascribed status, racial and legal barriers prevented the freeing of slaves.

Today, the Universal Declaration of Human Rights, which is binding on all members of the United Nations, prohibits slavery in all its forms. Yet more people are enslaved today than at any point in world history. In many developing countries, bonded laborers are imprisoned in virtual lifetime employment; in some countries, human beings are owned outright. But a form of slavery also exists in Europe and the United States, where guest workers and illegal immigrants have been forced to labor for years under terrible conditions, either to pay off debts or to avoid being turned over to immigration authorities.

Both these situations are likely to involve the transnational crime of trafficking in humans. Data on human trafficking and slavery are difficult to assess since no government is voluntarily and publicly going to disclose such numbers. According to the Walk Free Foundation, 29.8 people are enslaved worldwide at any given time. The International Labour Organization places the number forced to work at any given time in the private economy at 4.5 million for sexual exploitation and 14.2 million for other forms of labor (agriculture, construction, domestic work, or manufacturing), for a total of 18.7 million people exploited globally. Whatever the estimate, clearly slavery as a form of stratification has not vanished. Indeed, for several years faith-based groups have organized under the banner of "Abolition Now" to fight trafficking (Abolition Now 2016; McCarthy 2014).

In 2000, the U.S. Congress passed the Trafficking Victims Protection Act, which established minimum standards for the elimination of human trafficking. The act requires the State Department to monitor other

Table 5–1 Human Trafficking Report

Tier 1 Full Compliance	Tier 2 Significant Effort	Tier 2 Watch List, Some Effort, But Trafficking Remains a Concern	Tier 3 Noncompliant, No Effort
Australia	Bolivia	Afghanistan	Algeria
Canada	Brazil	Burma	Congo (Dem. Rep.)
Colombia	Chile	China	Libya
France	Greece	Costa Rica	Cuba
Germany	India	Haiti	Iran
Great Britain	Japan	Iraq	Kuwait
Norway	Mexico	Lebanon	North Korea
Poland	Philippines	Malaysia	Russia
South Korea	South Africa	Panama	Saudi Arabia
Spain	Turkey	Thailand	Sudan
Zimbabwe	Vietnam	Ukraine	Syria

NOTE: Each tier lists only a sample of all nations classified. The *Human Trafficking Report* is created by the State Department. In the report the level of compliance by the United States is considered to be "full compliance."

SOURCE: Department of State 2015:54.

countries' efforts to vigorously investigate, prosecute, and convict individuals who participate in trafficking—including government officials. Each year, the department reports its findings, some of which are shown in Table 5-1. Tier 1 and Tier 2 countries are thought to be largely in compliance with the act. Tier 2 Watch countries are making efforts to comply, though trafficking remains a significant concern. Tier 3 countries are not compliant and are not making significant efforts to comply.

CASTES

Castes are hereditary systems of rank, usually religiously dictated, that tend to be fixed and immobile. The caste system is generally associated with Hinduism in India and other countries. In India there are four major castes, called *varnas*. A fifth category of outcastes, referred to as *untouchables,* is considered to be so lowly and unclean as to have no place within this system of stratification. There are also many minor castes. Caste membership is an ascribed status (at birth, children automatically assume the same position as their parents). Each caste is quite sharply defined, and members are expected to marry within that caste.

In recent decades, industrialization and urbanization have taken their toll on India's rigid caste system. Many villagers have moved to urban areas, where their low-caste status is unknown. The anonymity of city life allows these families to take advantage of opportunities they would not otherwise have had, and eventually to move up the social ladder.

The term *caste* can also be applied in recent historical contexts outside India. For example, the system of stratification that characterized the southern United States from the end of the Civil War through the 1960s resembled a caste system. So did the rigid system of segregation that prevailed in the Republic of South Africa under apartheid, from 1948 through the 1990s. In both cases, race was the defining factor that placed a person in the social hierarchy.

ESTATES

A third type of stratification system, called *estates,* was associated with feudal societies during the Middle Ages. The **estate system,** or *feudalism,* required peasants to work land leased to them by nobles in exchange for military protection and other services. The basis for the system was the nobles' ownership of land, which was critical to their superior and privileged status. As in systems based on slavery and caste, inheritance of one's position largely defined the estate system. The nobles inherited their titles and property; the peasants were born to a subservient position in an agrarian society.

SOCIAL CLASSES

A **class system** is a social ranking based primarily on economic position in which achieved characteristics can influence social mobility. In contrast to slavery and the caste and estate systems, the boundaries between classes are imprecisely defined; one can move from one stratum, or level, of society to another. Yet class systems maintain stable stratification hierarchies and patterns of class divisions, and they, too, are marked by unequal distribution of wealth and power.

Sociologist Daniel Rossides (1997) uses a five-class model to describe the class system of the United States: the upper class, the upper-middle class, the lower-middle class, the working class, and the lower class. Although the lines separating social classes in his model are not so sharp as the divisions between castes, he shows that members of the five classes differ significantly in ways other than just income level.

Rossides categorizes about 1 to 2 percent of the people of the United States as *upper class,* a group limited to the very wealthy. These people associate in exclusive clubs and social circles. By contrast, the *lower class,* consisting of approximately 20 to 25 percent of the population, disproportionately consists of Blacks, Hispanics, single mothers with dependent children, and people who cannot find regular work or must make do with low-paying work. This class lacks both wealth and income and is too politically weak to exercise significant power.

Today, the once broadly based middle class is on the defensive and is slowly being squeezed by two growing groups, the rich and the poor.

©Cagle Cartoons, Inc.

Both these classes, at opposite ends of the nation's social hierarchy, reflect the importance of ascribed status and achieved status. Ascribed statuses such as race and disability clearly influence a person's wealth and social position. Sociologist Richard Jenkins (1991) has researched how being disabled marginalizes a person in the labor market of the United States. People with disabilities are particularly vulnerable to unemployment, are often poorly paid, and in many cases occupy the lower rungs of the occupational ladder. Regardless of their actual performance on the job, people with disabilities are stigmatized as not "earning their keep." Such are the effects of ascribed status.

Sandwiched between the upper and lower classes in Rossides's model are the upper-middle class, the lower-middle class, and the working class. The *upper-middle class,* numbering about 10 to 15 percent of the population, is composed of professionals such as doctors, lawyers, and architects. They participate extensively in politics and take leadership roles in voluntary associations. The *lower-middle class,* which accounts for approximately 30 to 35 percent of the population, includes less affluent professionals (such as elementary school teachers and nurses), owners of small businesses, and a sizable number of clerical workers. While not all members of this varied class hold degrees from a college, they share the goal of sending their children there.

The middle class is currently under a great deal of economic pressure. Close analysis indicates that of those who lost their middle-class standing during the latter 20th century, about half rose to a higher ranking in the social class system, while half dropped to a lower position. These data mean that the United States is moving toward a "bipolar income distribution." That is, a broadly based middle class is slowly being replaced by two growing groups of rich and poor.

Rossides describes the *working class*—about 40 to 45 percent of the population—as people holding regular manual or blue-collar jobs. Certain members of this class, such as electricians, may have higher incomes than people in the lower-middle class. Yet even if they have achieved some degree of economic security, they tend to identify with manual workers and their long history of involvement in the labor movement of the United States. Of Rossides's five classes, the working class is declining most noticeably in size. In the economy of the United States, service and technical jobs are replacing positions involved in the actual manufacturing or transportation of goods.

How can you tell someone's social class? What indicators can be misleading?

Sociological Perspectives on Stratification

Sociologists have hotly debated stratification and social inequality and have reached varying conclusions. No theorist stressed the significance of class for society—and for social change—more strongly than Karl Marx. Marx viewed class differentiation as the crucial determinant of social, economic, and political inequality. By contrast, Max Weber questioned Marx's emphasis on the overriding importance of the economic sector and argued that stratification should be viewed as having many dimensions.

KARL MARX'S VIEW OF CLASS DIFFERENTIATION

Karl Marx was concerned with stratification in all types of human societies, beginning with primitive agricultural tribes and continuing into feudalism. But his main focus was on the effects of economic inequality on all aspects of 19th-century Europe. The plight of the working class made him feel that it was imperative to strive for changes in the social class structure.

In Marx's view, social relations during any period of history depend on who controls the primary mode of economic production, such as land or factories. Differential access to scarce resources shapes the relationship between groups. Thus, under the estate system, most production was agricultural, and the land was owned by the nobility. Peasants had little choice but to work according to terms dictated by those who owned the land.

Using this type of analysis, Marx examined social relations within *capitalism*—an economic system in which the means of production are held largely in private hands, and the main incentive for economic activity is the accumulation of profits (Rosenberg 1991). Marx focused on the two classes that began to emerge as the estate system declined—the bourgeoisie and the proletariat. The *bourgeoisie,* or capitalist class, owns the means of production, such as factories and machinery; the *proletariat* is the working class. In capitalist societies, the members of the bourgeoisie maximize profit in competition with other firms. In the process, they exploit workers, who must exchange their labor for subsistence wages. In Marx's view, members of each class share a distinctive culture. He was most interested in the culture of the proletariat, but he also examined the ideology of the bourgeoisie, through which it justifies its dominance over workers.

According to Marx, exploitation of the proletariat will inevitably lead to the destruction of the capitalist system, because the workers will revolt. But first, the working class must develop *class consciousness*—a subjective awareness of common vested interests and the need for collective political action to bring about social change. Workers must often overcome what Marx termed *false consciousness,* or an attitude held by members of a class that does not accurately reflect its objective position. A worker with false consciousness may adopt an individualistic viewpoint toward capitalist exploitation ("*I* am being exploited by *my* boss"). By contrast, the class-conscious worker realizes that *all* workers are being exploited by the bourgeoisie and have a common stake in revolution.

For Karl Marx, class consciousness is part of a collective process in which the proletariat comes to identify the bourgeoisie as the source of its oppression. Revolutionary leaders will guide the proletariat in its class struggle. Ultimately, the proletariat will overthrow the rule of the bourgeoisie and the government (which Marx saw as representing the interests of capitalists) and eliminate private ownership of the means of production. In Marx's rather utopian view, classes and oppression will cease to exist in the postrevolutionary workers' state.

How accurate were Marx's predictions? He failed to anticipate the emergence of labor unions, whose power in collective bargaining weakens the stranglehold that capitalists maintain over workers. Moreover, as contemporary conflict theorists note, he did not foresee the extent to which political liberties and relative prosperity could contribute to "false consciousness." Many people have come to view themselves as individuals striving for improvement within "free" societies that offer substantial mobility rather than as downtrodden members of a working class facing a collective fate. Finally, Marx did not predict that Communist Party rule would be established and later overthrown in the former Soviet Union and Eastern Europe. Still, the Marxist approach to the study of class is useful in stressing the importance of stratification as a determinant of social behavior, and of the fundamental separation in many societies between two distinct groups, the rich and the poor.

Have you ever been unaware of your true position in society— that is, have you experienced false consciousness? Explain.

MAX WEBER'S VIEW OF STRATIFICATION

Unlike Karl Marx, Max Weber insisted that no single characteristic (such as class) totally defines a person's position within the stratification system. Instead, writing in 1916, Weber identified three analytically distinct components of stratification: class, status, and power.

Weber used the term *class* to refer to a group of people who have a similar level of wealth and income. For example, certain workers in the United States try to support their families through minimum-wage jobs. According to Weber's definition, these wage earners constitute a class because they share the same economic position and fate. Although Weber agreed with Marx on the importance of this economic dimension of stratification, he argued that the actions of individuals and groups could not be understood *solely* in economic terms.

Weber used the term *status group* to refer to people who have the same prestige or lifestyle. An individual gains status through membership in a desirable group, such as the medical profession. But status is not the same as economic class standing. In our culture, a successful pickpocket may earn the same income as a college professor. Yet the thief is widely regarded as a member of a low-status group, whereas the professor holds high status.

For Weber, the third major component of stratification reflects a political dimension. *Power* is the ability to exercise one's will over others. In the United States, power stems from membership in particularly influential groups, such as corporate boards of directors, government bodies, and interest groups. Conflict theorists generally agree that two major sources of power—big business and government—are closely interrelated.

In Weber's view, then, each of us has not one rank in society but three. Our position in a stratification system reflects some combination of class, status, and power. Each factor influences the other two, and in fact the rankings on these three dimensions often tend to coincide. John F. Kennedy came from an extremely wealthy family, attended exclusive preparatory schools, graduated from Harvard University, and went on to become president of the United States. Like Kennedy, many people from affluent backgrounds achieve impressive status and power.

INTERACTIONIST PERSPECTIVE ON STRATIFICATION

Both Karl Marx and Max Weber looked at inequality primarily from a macrosociological perspective, considering the entire society or even the global economy. Marx did suggest the importance of a more microsociological analysis, however, when he stressed the ways in which individuals develop a true class consciousness.

Interactionists, as well as economists, have long been interested in the importance of social class in shaping a person's lifestyle. The theorist Thorstein Veblen (1857–1929) noted that those at the top of the social hierarchy typically convert part of their wealth into *conspicuous consumption,* purchasing more automobiles than they can reasonably use and building houses with more rooms than they can possibly occupy. Or they may engage in *conspicuous leisure,* jetting to remote destinations and staying just long enough to have dinner or view a sunset over some historic locale (Veblen [1899] 1964).

Give some examples of conspicuous consumption among your fellow college students. Which are obvious and which more subtle?

Today, conspicuous consumption has found a new outlet in the cyberworld. Users of social media can now see their friends' vacations and snazzy new cars online—an experience that can provoke what researchers call *Facebook envy*. Studies done in the United States and Germany show that even otherwise happy people can suffer envy and distress over this kind of digitally shared conspicuous consumption (Shea 2013).

At the other end of the spectrum, behavior that is judged to be typical of the lower class is subject not only to ridicule but even to legal action. Communities have, from time to time, banned trailers from people's front yards and sofas from their front porches. In some communities, it is illegal to leave a pickup truck in front of the house overnight.

Is Stratification Universal?

Must some members of society receive greater rewards than others? Do people need to feel socially and economically superior to others? Can social life be organized without structured inequality? These questions have been debated for centuries, especially among political activists. Utopian socialists, religious minorities, and members of recent countercultures have all attempted to establish communities that to some extent or other would abolish inequality in social relationships.

Social science researchers have found that inequality exists in all societies—even the simplest. For example, when anthropologist Gunnar Landtman ([1938] 1968) studied the Kiwai Papuans of New Guinea, he initially noticed little differentiation among them. Every man in the village did the same work and lived in similar housing. However, on closer inspection, Landtman observed that certain Papuans—the men who were warriors, harpooners, and sorcerers—were described as "a little more high" than others. By contrast, villagers who were female, unemployed, or unmarried were considered "down a little bit" and were barred from owning land.

Stratification is universal, then, in that all societies maintain some form of social inequality among members. Depending on its values, a society may assign people to distinctive ranks based on their religious knowledge, skill in hunting, beauty, trading expertise, or ability to provide health care. But *why* has such inequality developed in human societies? And how much differentiation among people, if any, is actually essential?

Functionalist and conflict theorists offer contrasting explanations for the existence and necessity of social stratification. Functionalists maintain that a differential system of rewards and punishments is necessary for the efficient operation of society. Conflict theorists argue that competition for scarce resources results in significant political, economic, and social inequality.

FUNCTIONALIST PERSPECTIVE

Would people go to school for many years to become physicians if they could make as much money and gain as much respect working as street cleaners? Functionalists say no, which is partly why they believe that a stratified society is universal.

In the view of Kingsley Davis and Wilbert Moore (1945), society must distribute its members among a variety of social positions. It must not only make sure that these positions are filled but also see that they are staffed by people with the appropriate talents and abilities. Rewards, including money and prestige, are based on the importance of a position and the relative scarcity of qualified personnel. Yet this assessment often devalues work performed by certain segments of society, such as women's work as homemakers or in occupations traditionally filled by women, as well as low-status work such as fast-food jobs.

Davis and Moore argue that stratification is universal and that social inequality is necessary so that people will be motivated to fill function-ally important positions. But unequal rewards are not the only means of encouraging people to fill critical positions and occupations. Personal pleasure, intrinsic satisfaction, and value orientations also motivate peo-ple to enter particular careers. Functionalists agree but note that society must use some type of reward to motivate people to enter unpleasant or dangerous jobs and jobs that require a long training period. This response does not address stratification systems in which status is largely inher-ited, such as slave, caste, or estate systems. Moreover, even if stratifica-tion is inevitable, the functionalist explanation for differential rewards does not explain the wide disparity between the rich and the poor (R. Collins 1975; Kerbo 2012).

In your view, is the extent of social inequality in the United States helpful or harmful to society as a whole? Explain.

CONFLICT PERSPECTIVE

The writings of Karl Marx lie at the heart of conflict theory. Marx viewed history as a continuous struggle between the oppressors and the oppressed—one that would ultimately culminate in an egalitarian, classless society. In terms of stratification, he argued that the dominant class under capitalism—the bourgeoisie—manipulated the economic and political systems in order to maintain control over the exploited proletariat. Marx did not believe that stratification was inevitable, but he did see inequality and oppression as inherent in capitalism (E. O. Wright et al. 1982; E. O. Wright 2011).

Like Marx, contemporary conflict theorists believe that human beings are prone to conflict over such scarce resources as wealth, status, and power. However, while Marx focused primarily on class conflict, more recent theorists have extended the analysis to include conflicts based on gender, race, age, and other dimensions. The British sociologist Ralf Dahrendorf has been one of the most influential contributors to the con-flict approach.

Dahrendorf (1959) modified Marx's analysis of capitalist society to apply to *modern* capitalist societies. For Dahrendorf, social classes are groups of people who share common interests resulting from their authority relationships. In identifying the most powerful groups in society, he includes not only the bourgeoisie—the owners of the means of production—but also industrial managers, legislators, the judiciary, heads of the government bureaucracy, and others. In that respect, Dahrendorf has merged Marx's emphasis on class conflict with Weber's recognition that power is an important element of stratification (Cuff et al. 1990).

Conflict theorists, including Dahrendorf, contend that the powerful of today, like the bourgeoisie of Marx's time, want society to run smoothly so that they can enjoy their privileged positions. Because the status quo suits those with wealth, status, and power, they have a clear interest in preventing, minimizing, or controlling societal conflict. One way for the powerful to maintain the status quo is to define society's ***dominant ideology***—the set of cultural beliefs and practices that supports powerful social, economic, and political interests. From a conflict perspective, society's most powerful groups and institutions control not only wealth and property but the means of influencing people's cultural beliefs through religion, education, and the media (Abercrombie et al. 1980, 1990; Robertson 1988).

The powerful, such as leaders of government, also use limited social reforms to buy off the oppressed and reduce the danger of challenges to their dominance. For example, minimum wage laws and unemployment compensation unquestionably give some valuable assistance to needy men and women. Yet these reforms also serve to pacify those who might otherwise rebel. Of course, in the view of conflict theorists, such maneuvers can never entirely eliminate conflict, since workers will continue to demand equality, and the powerful will not give up their control of society.

Conflict theorists see stratification as a major source of societal tension and conflict. They do not agree with Davis and Moore that stratification is functional for a society or that it serves as a source of stability. Rather, conflict sociologists argue that stratification will inevitably lead to instability and social change. Table 5-2 summarizes the three major sociological perspectives on social stratification (R. Collins 1975; Coser 1977).

LENSKI'S VIEWPOINT

Let's return to the question posed earlier—Is stratification universal?—and consider the sociological response. Some form of differentiation is found in every culture, from the most primitive to the most advanced industrial societies of our time. Sociologist Gerhard Lenski, in his sociocultural evolution approach, described how economic systems change as their level of technology becomes more complex, beginning with hunting and gathering and culminating eventually with industrial society.

Table 5–2 Three Major Perspectives on Social Stratification

	Functionalist	Conflict	Interactionist
Purpose of Social Stratification	Facilitates filling of social positions	Facilitates exploitation	Influences people's lifestyles
Attitude toward Social Inequality	Necessary to some extent	Excessive and growing	Influences intergroup relations
Analysis of the Wealthy	Talented and skilled, creating opportunities for others	Use the dominant ideology to further their own interests	Exhibit conspicuous consumption and conspicuous leisure

Tracking Perspectives

Think About It
Which perspective seems to best account for the stratification you see in society? Explain your choice.

In subsistence-based hunting-and-gathering societies, people focus on survival. While some inequality and differentiation is evident, a stratification system based on social class does not emerge because there is no real wealth to be claimed. As a society advances in technology, it becomes capable of producing a considerable surplus of goods. The emergence of surplus resources greatly expands the possibilities for inequality in status, influence, and power and allows a well-defined, rigid social class system to develop. In order to minimize strikes, slowdowns, and industrial sabotage, the elites may share a portion of the economic surplus with the lower classes, but not enough to reduce their own power and privilege.

As Lenski argued, the allocation of surplus goods and services controlled by those with wealth, status, and power reinforces the social inequality that accompanies stratification systems. While this reward system may once have served the overall purposes of society, as functionalists contend, the same cannot be said for the large disparities separating the haves from the have-nots in current societies. In contemporary industrial society, the degree of social and economic inequality far exceeds the need to provide for goods and services (Lenski 1966; Nolan and Lenski 2015).

Stratification by Social Class

MEASURING SOCIAL CLASS

We assess how wealthy people are by looking at the cars they drive, the houses they live in, the clothes they wear, and so on. Yet it is not so easy to locate an individual within our social hierarchies as it would be in slavery, caste, or estate systems of stratification. To determine someone's class position, sociologists generally rely on the objective method.

Objective Method   The *objective method* of measuring social class views class largely as a statistical category. Researchers assign individuals to social classes on the basis of criteria such as occupation, education, income, and place of residence. The key to the objective method is that the *researcher,* rather than the person being classified, identifies an individual's class position.

The first step in using this method is to decide what indicators or causal factors will be measured objectively, whether wealth, income, education, or occupation. The prestige ranking of occupations has proved to be a useful indicator of a person's class position. For one thing, it is much easier to determine accurately than income or wealth. The term *prestige* refers to the respect and admiration that an occupation holds in a society. "My daughter, the physicist" connotes something very different from "my daughter, the bus driver." Prestige is independent of the particular individual who occupies a job, a characteristic that distinguishes it from esteem. *Esteem* refers to the reputation that a specific person has earned within an occupation. Therefore, one can say that the position of president of the United States has high prestige, even though it has been occupied by people with varying degrees of esteem. A hairdresser may have the esteem of his clients, but he lacks the prestige of a corporate executive.

Table 5–3 shows the prestige rankings of a number of occupations. In a series of national surveys, sociologists assigned prestige rankings to about 500 occupations, ranging from physician to newspaper vendor. The highest possible prestige score was 100; the lowest was 0. Physician, lawyer, dentist, and college professor were the most highly regarded occupations. Sociologists have used such data to assign prestige rankings to virtually all jobs and have found stability in rankings from 1925 to 1991. Similar studies in other countries have also developed useful prestige rankings for occupations (Nakao and Treas 1994).

For many years, sociologists tended to neglect the occupations and incomes of *women* as determinants of social rank. With more than half of all married women now working outside the home (see Chapter 7), this approach seems outmoded. How should we judge class or status in dual-career families? One approach is to focus on the individual (rather than the family or household). Thus, a woman would be classified according to her own occupational status rather than that of her spouse. Another approach would place a monetary value on women's unpaid work at home (Mandel 2016; McCall 2008).

Multiple Measures   One complication in measuring social class is that advances in statistical methods and computer technology have multiplied the factors used to define class under the objective method. No longer

Table 5–3 Prestige Rankings of Occupations

Occupation	Score	Occupation	Score
Physician	86	Bank teller	50
College professor	78	Electrician	49
Lawyer	76	Farm manager	48
Dentist	74	Insurance agent	47
Banker	72	Secretary	46
Architect	71	Mail carrier	42
Airline pilot	70	Farmer	41
Clergy	69	Correctional officer	40
Registered nurse	66	Carpenter	40
High school teacher	63	Receptionist	39
Dental hygienist	61	Barber	38
Legislator	61	Child care worker	36
Pharmacist	61	Hotel clerk	32
Elementary school teacher	60	Bus driver	32
Veterinarian	60	Auto body repairer	31
Police officer or detective	60	Truck driver	30
Prekindergarten teacher	60	Salesworker (shoes)	28
Accountant	57	Waiter and waitress	28
Librarian	55	Cook (short-order)	28
Firefighter	53	Bartender	25
Funeral director	52	Garbage collector	17
Social worker	52	Janitor	16
Optician	51	Newspaper vendor	15

NOTE: 100 is the highest and 0 the lowest possible prestige score.

SOURCE: General Social Survey 2015 in T. Smith et al. 2015: Appendix F.

> Think About It
> Can you name what you think are two more high-prestige occupations? Two more low-prestige occupations?

are sociologists limited to annual income and education in evaluating a person's class position. Today, studies use as criteria the value of homes, sources of income, assets, years in present occupation, neighborhoods, and considerations regarding dual careers. Adding these variables will not necessarily paint a different picture of class differentiation in the United States, but it does allow sociologists to measure class in a more complex and multidimensional way. When researchers use multiple measures, they typically speak of *socioeconomic status (SES),* a measure of social class that is based on income, education, and occupation. To determine the socioeconomic status of a young person, such as a college student under the age of 25, they use *parental* income, education, and occupation.

Whatever the technique used to measure class, the sociologist is interested in real and often dramatic differences in power, privilege, and opportunity in a society. The study of stratification is a study of inequality. Nowhere is this more evident than in the distribution of wealth and income.

INCOME AND WEALTH

By all measures, income in the United States is distributed unevenly. Nobel Prize–winning economist Paul Samuelson has described the situation in the following words: "If we made an income pyramid out of building blocks, with each layer portraying $500 of income, the peak would be far higher than Mount Everest, but most people would be within a few feet of the ground" (Samuelson and Nordhaus 2010:324).

Recent data support Samuelson's analogy. In 2014, the median household income in the United States was $53,657. In other words, half of all households had higher incomes that year and half had lower incomes. However, this fact does not fully convey the income disparities in our society.

We can gain some insight into income inequality in the United States by looking at the relative placement of households within the income distribution. One of the most common ways of doing so is to line up all income-earning households from low to high and then break them into quintiles, or fifths. Because there are approximately 125 million households in the United States, each quintile includes an equal number of about 25 million households. This method gives us a sense of the average income within each quintile, along with the percentage of the nation's total income earned in each quintile.

As Figure 5-1 shows, looking at the population in this way reveals a significant degree of income inequality. The mean income for households in the lowest quintile is $12,457; in the top quintile, it is $202,366. If we were to move up to the highest end of the income distribution, we would find that the top 0.01 percent of taxpayers—about 15,000 households— make incomes of at least $11.5 million a year. Collectively, they control 6 percent of the nation's total income (DeNavas-Walt and Proctor 2015:40; Sloan 2009:27).

There has been a modest redistribution of income in the United States over the past 80 years, but not always to the benefit of the poor or even the middle class. From 1929 through 1970, the government's economic and tax policies shifted some income to the poor. However, in

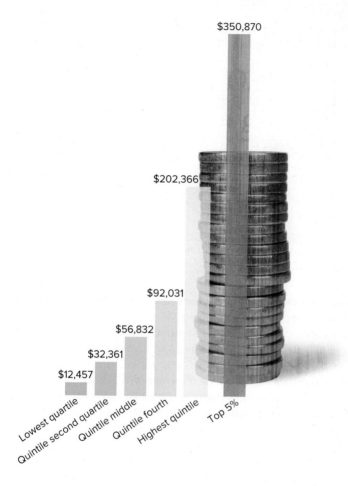

$350,870

$202,366

$92,031

$56,832

$32,361

$12,457

Lowest quartile

Quintile second quartile

Quintile middle

Quintile fourth

Highest quintile

Top 5%

Figure 5–1

Household Income
by Quintile

SOURCE OF DATA: 2015 in
Proctor et al. 2016:31.

(Coins): ©amphotora/
Getty Images

the past four decades—especially in the 1980s and in the decade from 2001 through 2012—federal tax policies have favored the affluent. Moreover, while the salaries of highly skilled workers and professionals have continued to rise, the wages of less skilled workers have *decreased* when controlled for inflation.

Just how dramatic has this growth in inequality been? Consider the pre-recession period between 1984 and 2008. In just 25 years, the following changes occurred in real household income (adjusted for inflation):

- For the lowest 20 percent of the population, income rose 9 percent.
- For the next lowest 20 percent of the population, income rose 10 percent.
- For the middle 20 percent of the population, income rose 13 percent.
- For the next highest 20 percent of the population, income rose 20 percent.
- For the top 20 percent of the population, income rose a whopping 40 percent.

142

CHAPTER 5: STRATIFICATION IN THE UNITED STATES AND GLOBAL INEQUALITY

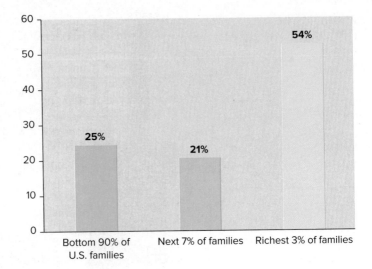

Figure 5–2
Distribution of Wealth in the United States
SOURCE OF DATA: 2013 from Institute for Policy Studies 2015.

The pattern is clear. Though everyone has done better, by far the biggest winners have been the affluent.

Careful economic analysis has shown that over the past 30 years, federal and state tax policies have tended to accentuate this trend toward income inequality. During one 25-year period, the top 1 percent of income earners *after taxes* saw their incomes rise 228 percent, compared to only 21 percent for households in the middle quintile. Little wonder that the middle class is shrinking (Billitteri 2009; Sherman 2007).

Indeed, wealth is distributed much more unevenly than income in the United States. A 2013 Federal Reserve Bank study showed that 3 percent of the nation's families control 54 percent of the nation's wealth (see Figure 5–2). Put another way, the wealth of the top 3 percent exceeds the collective wealth of the bottom 97 percent.

POVERTY

About 11 percent of the people in the United States live below the poverty line established by the federal government. In 2015, no fewer than 43.1 million people were living in poverty. The economic correction that followed the Great Recession passed these people by. A Bureau of the Census report shows that one in five households has trouble meeting basic needs, from paying the utility bills to buying dinner (Proctor et al. 2016:31).

One contributor to the United States' high poverty rate has been the large number of workers employed at minimum wage. The federal government raised the minimum wage over the last 60 years from 75 cents in 1950 to $7.25 in 2009. But in terms of its real value, adjusted for inflation, the minimum wage has failed to keep pace with the cost of living. In fact, its real value today is *lower* than it was at any time from 1956 to 1984.

Little wonder, then, that low-income workers can barely scrape by. In this section, we'll consider just how social scientists define *poverty*. We'll also take a closer look at the people who fall into that category, including the working poor.

Studying Poverty   Sociologists' efforts to better understand poverty are complicated by the difficulty of defining it. This problem is evident even in government programs that conceive of poverty in either absolute or relative terms. ***Absolute poverty*** refers to a minimum level of subsistence that no family should be expected to live below.

One commonly used measure of absolute poverty is the federal government's *poverty line,* a money income figure that is adjusted annually to reflect the consumption requirements of families based on their size and composition. The poverty line serves as an official definition of which people are poor. In 2015, for example, any family of four (two adults and two children) with a combined income of $24,036 or less fell below the poverty line. This definition determines which individuals and families will be eligible for certain government benefits (Proctor et al. 2016:43).

By contrast, ***relative poverty*** is a floating standard of deprivation by which people at the bottom of a society, whatever their lifestyles, are judged to be disadvantaged *in comparison with the nation as a whole.* Therefore, even if the poor of 2018 are better off in absolute terms than the poor of the 1930s or 1980s, they are still seen as deserving special assistance.

Debate has been growing over the accuracy of the federal government's measure of poverty, which has remained largely unchanged since 1963. If noncash benefits such as Medicare, Medicaid, tax credits, food stamps (Supplemental Nutritional Assistance Program, or SNAP), public housing, and health care and other employer-provided fringe benefits were included, the reported poverty rate would be lower. On the other hand, if out-of-pocket medical expenses and mandatory work expenses for transportation and child care were included, the poverty rate would be higher. Although the current poverty measure does consider family size, it does not consider a household's location, whether in a relatively expensive city like New York or in a less expensive rural area. Nor does it consider whether a householder pays rent or a mortgage installment, lives at home or with someone else.

To address some of these shortcomings, in 2010 the federal government launched a second statistic called the Supplemental Poverty Measure (SPM), which will be used to estimate economic hardship. The SPM is a relative poverty measure that is based on a broad range of changing household resources and expenses. This calculation shows a larger number of people in poverty than the government's official measure. However, it does not change the poverty line, which determines a household's eligibility for benefits (Blank 2011; Short 2015).

Who Are the Poor?   Not only does the category of the poor defy any simple definition, but it counters common stereotypes about poor people. For example, many people in the United States believe that the vast majority of the poor are able to work but will not. Yet many poor adults do work outside the home, although only a small proportion work full-time throughout the year. In 2015, about 39 percent of all poor working adults worked full-time, compared to 53 percent of all adults. Of those poor adults who do not work, most are ill or disabled, or are occupied in maintaining a home (Proctor et al. 2016:13).

Though many of the poor live in urban slums, a majority live outside those areas. Poverty is no stranger to rural areas, from Appalachia to hard-hit farming regions and Native American reservations. Table 5–4 provides additional statistical information regarding these low-income people.

Table 5–4 Who Are the Poor in the United States?

Group	Percentage of the Population of the United States	Percentage of the Poor of the United States
Age		
Under 18 years old	24%	34%
18 to 64 years old	63	56
65 years and older	13	10
Race-Ethnicity		
Whites (non-Hispanic)	63	41
Blacks	13	23
Hispanics	17	28
Asians and Pacific Islanders	5	5
Family Composition		
Married couples with both members present	72	35
Female householders	20	54
Nativity		
Native born	87	83
Foreign born (naturalized citizen)	6	5
Foreign born (not citizens)	6	12
People with Disabilities	8	10

NOTE: People with disabilities refers to ages 18 to 64.

SOURCE: Data for 2011 in DeNavas-Walt et al. 2012:14, 17.

Since World War II, women have constituted an increasing propor-tion of the poor people of the United States. Many of them are divorced or never-married mothers. In 1959 female householders accounted for 26 percent of the nation's poor; by 2011 that figure had risen to 51 percent (see Table 5-4). This alarming trend, known as the *feminization of poverty,* is evident not just in the United States but around the world.

About half of all women in the United States who are living in poverty are "in transition," coping with an economic crisis caused by the depar-ture, disability, or death of a husband. The other half tend to be economi-cally dependent either on the welfare system or on friends and relatives living nearby. A major factor in the feminization of poverty has been the increase in families with women as single heads of the household (see Chapter 7). Conflict theorists and other observers trace the higher rates of poverty among women to three distinct factors: the difficulty in find-ing affordable child care, sexual harassment, and sex discrimination in the labor market (Burns 2010; Porter 2013).

Analyses of the poor in general reveal that they are not a static social class. The overall composition of the poor changes continually, because some individuals and families near the top edge of poverty move above the poverty level after a year or two, while others slip below it. Still, hun-dreds of thousands of people remain in poverty for many years at a time. Blacks and Latinos are more likely than Whites to be persistently poor. Both Latinos and Blacks are less likely than Whites to leave the welfare rolls as a result of welfare reform (Jäntti 2009).

Explaining Poverty   Why does poverty pervade a nation of such vast wealth? Sociologist Herbert Gans (1995) has applied functionalist analysis to this question; he argues that various segments of society actually *benefit* from the existence of the poor. Gans has identified a number of social, economic, and political functions that the poor perform for society:

- The presence of poor people means that society's dirty work—physically dirty or dangerous, underpaid and undignified, dead-end and menial jobs—will be performed at low cost.

- Poverty creates jobs for occupations and professions that "service" the poor. It creates both legal employment (public health experts, welfare caseworkers) and illegal jobs (drug dealers, numbers runners).

- The identification and punishment of the poor as deviants upholds the legitimacy of conventional social norms and mainstream values regarding hard work, thrift, and honesty.

- Within a relatively hierarchical society, the existence of poor people guarantees the higher status of the affluent. As psychologist William Ryan (1976) has noted, affluent people may justify inequality (and gain a measure of satisfaction) by "blaming the victims" of poverty for their disadvantaged condition.

- Because of their lack of political power, the poor often absorb the costs of social change. Under the policy of deinstitutionalization, mental patients released from long-term hospitals have been "dumped" primarily into low-income communities and neighborhoods. Similarly, halfway houses for rehabilitated drug abusers, often rejected by more affluent communities, tend to end up in poorer neighborhoods.

In Gans's view, then, poverty and the poor actually perform positive functions for many nonpoor groups in the United States.

LIFE CHANCES

Max Weber thought that class was closely related to one's *life chances*—that is, the opportunities people have to provide themselves with material goods, positive living conditions, and favorable life experiences (Gerth and Mills 1958). Life chances are reflected in such measures as housing, education, and health. Occupying a higher position in society improves a person's life chances and brings greater access to social rewards. Occupying a lower position forces a person to devote more energy and resources to the necessities of life. In some cases, life chances are a matter of life and death. According to a medical study published in 2011, in the United States, approximately 133,000 deaths a year can be attributed to individual poverty, and another 119,000 to income inequality. That is over a quarter million deaths per year caused by severely limited resources (Galea et al. 2011).

In times of danger, the affluent and powerful have a better chance of surviving than people of ordinary means. When the supposedly unsinkable British ocean liner *Titanic* hit an iceberg in 1912, it was not carrying enough lifeboats to accommodate all passengers. Plans had been made to evacuate only first- and second-class passengers. About 62 percent of the first-class passengers survived the disaster. Despite a rule that women and children would go first, about a third of those passengers were male. In contrast, only 25 percent of the third-class passengers survived. The first attempt to alert them to the need to abandon ship came well after other passengers had been notified. In an ironic demonstration of continuing social inequality, a luxury travel organization called Bluefish recently charged passengers $60,000 each to view the underwater remains of the *Titanic* from a deep-sea submersible (Butler 1998; Crouse 1999; Dickler 2011; Riding 1998).

Wealth, status, and power may not ensure happiness, but they certainly provide additional ways of coping with problems and disappointments. For this reason, the opportunity for advancement—for social mobility—is of special significance to those on the bottom of society. These people want the rewards and privileges that are granted to high-ranking members of a culture. What can society do to increase their social mobility? One strategy is to offer financial aid to college students from low-income families, on the theory that education lifts people out of poverty. Yet such programs are not having as great an effect as their authors once hoped, because many of today's graduates will be paying off their college loans for years to come.

Imagine a society in which there are no social classes—no differences in people's wealth, income, and life chances. What would such a society be like? Would it be stable, or would its social structure change over time?

Social Mobility

In the movie *Maid in Manhattan,* Jennifer Lopez plays the lead in a modern-day Cinderella story, rising from the lowly status of chambermaid in a big-city hotel to become a company supervisor and the girlfriend of a well-to-do politician. The ascent of a person from a poor background to a position of prestige, power, or financial reward is an example of social mobility. Formally defined, the term ***social mobility*** refers to the movement of individuals or groups from one position in a society's stratification system to another. But how significant—how frequent, how dramatic—is mobility in a class society such as the United States?

OPEN VERSUS CLOSED STRATIFICATION SYSTEMS

Sociologists use the terms *open stratification system* and *closed stratification system* to indicate the degree of social mobility in a society. An ***open system*** implies that the position of each individual is influenced by his or her *achieved* status. Such a system encourages competition among members of society. The United States is moving toward this ideal type as the nation attempts to reduce the barriers facing women, racial and ethnic minorities, and people born in the lower social classes. Even in the midst of the economic downturn of 2008–2009, nearly 80 percent of people in the United States felt they could get ahead (Economic Mobility Project 2009).

At the other extreme of social mobility is the ***closed system,*** which allows little or no possibility of moving up. The slavery, caste, and estate systems of stratification are examples of closed systems. In such societies, social placement is based on *ascribed* statuses that cannot be changed, such as race or family background.

TYPES OF SOCIAL MOBILITY

An elementary school teacher who becomes a police officer moves from one social position to another of the same rank. Each occupation has the same prestige ranking: 60 on a scale ranging from a low of 0 to a high of 100 (see Table 5-3). Sociologists call this kind of movement ***horizontal mobility.*** However, if the teacher were to become a lawyer (prestige ranking of 76), he or she would experience ***vertical mobility,*** the movement of a person from one social position to another of a different rank. Vertical mobility can also involve moving *downward* in a society's stratification system, as would be the case if the teacher became a bank teller (prestige ranking of 50). Pitirim Sorokin ([1927] 1959) was the first sociologist to distinguish between horizontal and vertical mobility.

Most sociological analysis focuses on vertical social mobility. One way of examining vertical mobility is to contrast intergenerational and intragenerational mobility. ***Intergenerational mobility*** involves changes in the social position of children relative to their parents. Thus, a plumber whose father was a physician provides an example of downward intergenerational mobility. A film star whose parents were both factory workers illustrates upward intergenerational mobility. Because education contributes significantly to upward mobility, any barrier to the pursuit of advanced degrees can definitely limit intergenerational mobility.

In the United States, men born in the 1960s experienced considerable intergenerational mobility as a result of economic growth. On average, they earned more than their fathers did at the same age; their family incomes improved as well. However, the trend did not continue into the next generation. Currently, young men are earning less than their fathers did at the same age—about 12 percent less. Family incomes are slightly higher than in the last generation, but only because women have moved into the paid labor force to supplement their husbands' earnings (Sawhill and Haskins 2009).

Intragenerational mobility involves changes in a person's social position within his or her adult life. A woman who enters the paid labor force as a teacher's aide and eventually becomes superintendent of the school district experiences upward intragenerational mobility. A man who becomes a taxicab driver after his accounting firm goes bankrupt undergoes downward intragenerational mobility.

SOCIAL MOBILITY IN THE UNITED STATES

The belief in upward mobility is an important value in our society. Does that mean the United States is indeed the land of opportunity? Not unless such ascriptive characteristics as race, gender, and family background have ceased to be significant in determining one's future prospects. We can see the impact of these factors in the occupational structure.

Occupational Mobility   Two sociological studies conducted a decade apart offer insight into the degree of social mobility in the nation's occupational structure (Blau and Duncan 1967; Featherman and Hauser 1978). Taken together, these investigations lead to several noteworthy conclusions. First, occupational mobility (both intergenerational and intragenerational) has been common among males. Approximately 60 to 70 percent of sons are employed in higher-ranked occupations than their fathers.

Second, although there is a great deal of social mobility in the United States, much of it covers a very short distance. That is, people who reach an occupational level different from that of their parents usually advance or fall back only one or two out of a possible eight occupational levels. Thus, the child of a laborer may become an artisan or a technician, but he or she is less likely to become a manager or professional. The odds against reaching the top are extremely high unless one begins from a relatively privileged position.

The Impact of Education   Another conclusion of both studies is that education plays a critical role in social mobility. The impact of formal schooling on adult status is even greater than that of family background (although as we have seen, family background influences the likelihood that one will receive higher education). Furthermore, education represents an important means of intergenerational mobility. A person who was born into a poor family but who graduates from college has a 1 in 5 chance of entering the top fifth of all income earners as an adult (Isaacs et al. 2008).

Education's impact on social mobility has diminished somewhat in the last decade, however. An undergraduate degree—a B.A. or a B.S.— serves less as a guarantee of upward mobility today than it did in the past simply because more and more entrants into the job market now hold such a degree. Moreover, intergenerational mobility is declining, since there is no longer such a stark difference between generations. In earlier decades many high school–educated parents successfully sent their children to college, but today's college students are increasingly likely to have college-educated parents (Greenstone et al. 2013; Sawhill and Morton 2007).

The Impact of Race and Ethnicity   Sociologists have long documented the fact that the class system is more rigid for African Americans than it is for members of other racial groups. Black men who have good jobs, for example, are less likely than White men to see their adult children attain the same status. The cumulative disadvantage of discrimination plays a significant role in the disparity between the two groups' experience.

Which factor—occupation, education, race and ethnicity, or gender—do you expect will have the greatest impact on your own social mobility? Explain.

Compared to White households, the relatively modest wealth of African American households means that adult Black children are less likely than adult White children to receive financial support from their parents. Indeed, young Black couples are much more likely than young White couples to be assisting their parents—a sacrifice that hampers their social mobility.

African American rates of upward intergenerational social mobility are lower. Based on national income data beginning in 1968 and following three generations, Black children are more likely to be born into poverty than White children, and they are less likely to escape their dire circumstance. In fact, the majority of Black children raised at the bottom of the stratification system remain stuck there as adults, compared to only a third of Whites. In summary, Black Americans are more likely to stay in the bottom and fall from the middle (Pew Charitable Trust 2012; Reeves and Venator 2014).

Latino social mobility shows a more mixed picture. Hispanics whose parents were both born outside the United States are substantially better off than their immigrant parents. They have higher incomes, more are college graduates and homeowners, and fewer live in poverty. The immigrants themselves often face work situations that have significantly lower prestige than what they left behind, even if their absolute incomes are higher (Nicklett and Burgard 2009; Pew Research Center 2013).

The Latino wealth and asset picture is bleaker and more resembles that of African Americans. According to one analysis, the median wealth of White non-Hispanic households is 18 times that of Hispanic households. This lopsided wealth ratio is the largest since the government first published these data in the 1980s. Continuing immigration accounts for part of the disparity: most of the new arrivals are destitute. But even the wealthiest 10 percent of Latino households have only a third as much net worth as the top 5 percent of White households (Kochhar et al. 2011).

The Impact of Gender   Studies of mobility, even more than those of class, have traditionally ignored the significance of gender, but some research findings are now available that explore the relationship between gender and mobility.

Women's employment opportunities are much more limited than men's (as Chapter 7 will show). Moreover, according to recent research, women whose skills far exceed the jobs offered them are more likely than men to withdraw entirely from the paid labor force. Their withdrawal violates an assumption common to traditional mobility studies: that most people will aspire to upward mobility and seek to make the most of their opportunities.

In contrast to men, women have a rather large range of clerical occupations open to them. But modest salary ranges and small prospects for advancement limit their chance of upward mobility. Moreover, self-employment as shopkeepers, entrepreneurs, independent professionals, and the like—an important road to upward mobility for men—is more difficult for women, who find it harder to secure the necessary financing. Although sons commonly follow in the footsteps of their fathers, women are unlikely to move into their fathers' positions. Consequently, gender remains an important factor in shaping social mobility within the United States. Women in the United States (and in other parts of the world) are especially likely to be trapped in poverty, unable to rise out of their low-income status (Beller 2009; Heilman 2001).

On the positive side, though today's women lag behind men in employment, their earnings have increased faster than their mothers' did at a comparable age, so that their incomes are substantially higher. The one glaring exception to this trend is the daughters of low-income parents. Because these women typically care for children—many as single parents—and sometimes for other relatives as well, their mobility is severely restricted (Isaacs 2007b).

The Global Divide

In some parts of the world, the people who have dedicated their lives to fighting starvation refer to what they call "coping mechanisms"—ways in which the desperately poor attempt to control their hunger. Eritrean women will strap flat stones to their stomachs to lessen their hunger pangs. In Mozambique, people eat the grasshoppers that have destroyed their crops, calling them "flying shrimp." Though dirt eating is considered a pathological condition (called *pica*) among the well fed, the world's poor eat dirt to add minerals to their diet. And in many countries, mothers have been known to boil stones in water, to convince their hungry children that supper is almost ready. As they hover over the pot, these women hope that their malnourished children will fall asleep (McNeil 2004).

Imagine that the United States borders a country with a much higher standard of living. In this neighboring country, the salaries of workers with a college degree start at $120,000 a year. What is life in the United States like?

Around the world, inequality is a significant determinant of human behavior, opening doors of opportunity to some and closing them to others. Indeed, disparities in life chances are so extreme that in some places, the poorest of the poor may not be aware of them. Western media images may have circled the globe, but in extremely depressed rural areas, those at the bottom of society are not likely to see them.

A few centuries ago, such vast divides in global wealth did not exist. Except for a very few rulers and landowners, everyone in the world was poor. In much of Europe, life was as difficult as it was in Asia or South America. This was true until the Industrial Revolution and rising agricultural productivity produced explosive economic growth. The resulting rise in living standards was not evenly distributed across the world.

Although the divide between industrialized and developing nations is sharp, sociologists recognize a continuum of nations, from the richest of the rich to the poorest of the poor. For example, in 2015 the average value of goods and services produced per citizen (or per capita gross national income) in the industrialized countries of the United States, the Netherlands, Switzerland, France, and Norway was more than $47,000. In at least 18 poorer countries, the value was just $2,000 or less. However, most countries fell somewhere between those extremes (Kaneda and Bietsch 2015).

Still, the contrasts are stark. Three forces discussed here are particularly responsible for the domination of the world marketplace by a few nations: the legacy of colonialism, the advent of multinational corporations, and modernization.

LEGACY OF COLONIALISM

Colonialism occurs when a foreign power maintains political, social, economic, and cultural domination over a people for an extended period. In simple terms, it is rule by outsiders. The long reign of the British Empire over much of North America, parts of Africa, and India is an example of colonial domination. The same can be said of French rule over Algeria, Tunisia, and other parts of North Africa. Relations between the colonial nation and colonized people are similar to those between the dominant capitalist class and the proletariat, as described by Karl Marx.

You are traveling through a developing country. What evidence do you see of neocolonialism?

By the 1980s, colonialism had largely disappeared. Most of the nations that were colonies before World War I had achieved political independence and established their own governments. However, for many of these countries, the transition to genuine self-rule was not yet complete. Colonial domination had established patterns of economic exploitation that continued even after the colonies achieved their nationhood—in part because they were unable to develop their own industry and technology. Their dependence on more industrialized nations, including their former colonial masters, for managerial and technical expertise, investment capital, and manufactured goods kept former colonies in a subservient position. Such continuing dependence and foreign domination constitute *neocolonialism.*

The economic and political consequences of colonialism and neocolonialism are readily apparent. Drawing on the conflict perspective, sociologist Immanuel Wallerstein (1974, 1979a, 2000, 2012) views the global economic system as one divided between nations that control wealth and nations from which resources are taken. Through his *world systems analysis,* Wallerstein has described an interdependent global economy resting on unequal economic and political relationships. Critical to his analysis is the understanding that by themselves, nations do not, nor have they ever constituted whole systems. Instead, they exist within a larger, global social context.

In Wallerstein's view, certain industrialized nations (among them the United States, Japan, and Germany) and their global corporations

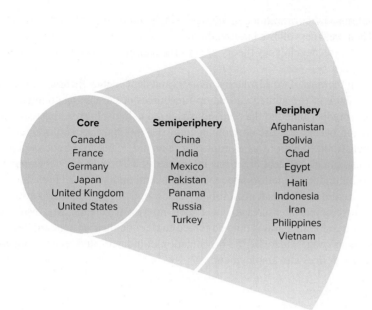

Figure 5–3
World Systems Analysis
NOTE: *Figure shows only a partial listing of countries, selected by the author.*

Core
Canada
France
Germany
Japan
United Kingdom
United States

Semiperiphery
China
India
Mexico
Pakistan
Panama
Russia
Turkey

Periphery
Afghanistan
Bolivia
Chad
Egypt
Haiti
Indonesia
Iran
Philippines
Vietnam

dominate the *core* of the world's economic system (see Figure 5-3). At the *semiperiphery* of the system are countries with marginal economic status, such as Israel, Ireland, and South Korea. Wallerstein suggests that the poor developing countries of Asia, Africa, and Latin America are on the *periphery* of the world's economic system. The key to Wallerstein's macro-level analysis is the exploitative relationship of *core* nations toward *noncore* nations. Core nations and their corporations control and exploit noncore nations' economies. Unlike other nations, they are relatively independent of outside control (Chase-Dunn and Grimes 1995; G. Williams 2013).

The division between core and periphery nations is significant and remarkably stable. A study by the International Monetary Fund (2000; Alvaredo 2011) found little change over the course of the *past 115 years* for the more than 24 economies that were studied. The only changes were Japan's movement up into the group of core nations and China's movement down toward the margins of the semiperiphery nations. Yet Immanuel Wallerstein (2012:9) speculates that the world system as we currently understand it may soon undergo unpredictable changes. The world is becoming increasingly urbanized, a trend that is gradually eliminating the large pools of low-cost workers in rural areas. In the future, core nations will have to find other ways to reduce their labor costs. Exhaustion of land and water resources through clear-cutting and pollution is also driving up the costs of production.

Wallerstein's world systems analysis is the most widely used version of ***dependency theory.*** According to this theory, even as developing countries make economic advances, they remain weak and subservient to core

When you see a developing country on television or in the movies, does the film or program emphasize the country's progress or its problems?

nations and corporations in an increasingly intertwined global economy. Their weakness allows industrialized nations to continue to exploit them. In a sense, dependency theory applies the conflict perspective on a global scale.

In the view of world systems analysts and dependency theorists, a growing share of the human and natural resources of developing countries is being redistributed to the core industrialized nations. In part, this redistribution occurs because developing countries owe huge sums of money to industrialized nations as a result of foreign aid, loans, and trade deficits. Thus, the global debt crisis has intensified the Third World dependency begun under colonialism, neocolonialism, and multi-national investment. International financial institutions are now pressuring indebted countries to take severe measures to meet their interest payments. The result is that developing nations may be forced to devalue their currencies, freeze workers' wages, increase the privatization of industry, and reduce government services and employment.

GLOBALIZATION

Closely related to these problems is *globalization,* or the worldwide integration of government policies, cultures, social movements, and financial markets through trade and the exchange of ideas.

Because world financial markets transcend governance by conventional nation-states, international organizations such as the World Bank and the International Monetary Fund have emerged as major players in the global economy. The function of these institutions, which are heavily funded and influenced by core nations, is to encourage economic trade and development and to ensure the smooth operation of international financial markets. As such, they are seen as promoters of globalization and defenders primarily of the interests of core nations.

Critics call attention to a variety of issues, including violations of workers' rights, the destruction of the environment, the loss of cultural identity, and discrimination against minority groups in periphery nations. The impact of globalization appears to be most problematic for developing countries in Latin America and Africa. In Asia, foreign investment involves the high-tech sector, which produces more sustainable economic growth (Kerbo 2006). Even there, however, globalization definitely has not reduced income disparities, either between nations or within countries.

Some observers see globalization and its effects as the natural result of advances in communications technology, particularly the Internet and satellite transmission of the mass media. Others view it more critically, as a process that allows multinational corporations to expand unchecked. We will examine this issue more fully in the next section (Chase-Dunn et al. 2000; Guenther and Kasi 2015).

MULTINATIONAL CORPORATIONS

We have seen that globalization has not necessarily improved the lives of the poor in the developing world. Another development that does not always serve developing countries well has been the rise of multinational corporations. The term *multinational corporations* refers to commercial organizations that are headquartered in one country but do business throughout the world. Such private trade and lending relationships are not new; merchants have conducted business abroad for hundreds of years, trading gems, spices, garments, and other goods. However, today's multinational giants are not merely buying and selling overseas; they are also *producing* goods all over the world, from sneakers to sewing machines (Wallerstein 1974).

Moreover, today's "global factories" (factories throughout the developing world that are run by multinational corporations) now sit alongside the "global office." Multinationals based in core countries are beginning to establish reservations services, claims adjustment offices, and data processing centers in periphery nations. As service industries become more important in the international marketplace, many companies are concluding that the low costs of overseas operations more than offset the expense of transmitting information around the world.

Do not underestimate the size of these global corporations. As Figure 5–4 shows, the total revenues of many multinational businesses are equivalent to the total value of goods and services exchanged in *entire nations*. Foreign sales represent an important source of profit for multinational corporations, a fact that encourages them to expand into other countries (in many cases, the developing nations). The economy of the United States is heavily dependent on foreign commerce, much of which is conducted by multinationals. Over 12 percent of all goods and services produced in the United States relates to the export of goods to foreign countries, which supports an estimated 11 million jobs (U.S. Office of Trade Representative 2016).

Sociologists differ in their appraisal of the economic and social effects of these behemoth organizations. We'll examine two perspectives on multinational corporations, the functionalist view and the conflict view.

Functionalist Perspective   Functionalists believe that multinational corporations can actually help the developing nations of the world. They bring jobs and industry to areas where subsistence agriculture previously served as the only means of survival. Multinationals promote rapid development through the diffusion of inventions and innovations from industrial nations. Viewed from a functionalist perspective, the combination of skilled technology and management provided by multinationals and the relatively cheap labor available in developing nations is ideal for a global enterprise. Multinationals can take maximum advantage of technology while reducing costs and boosting profits.

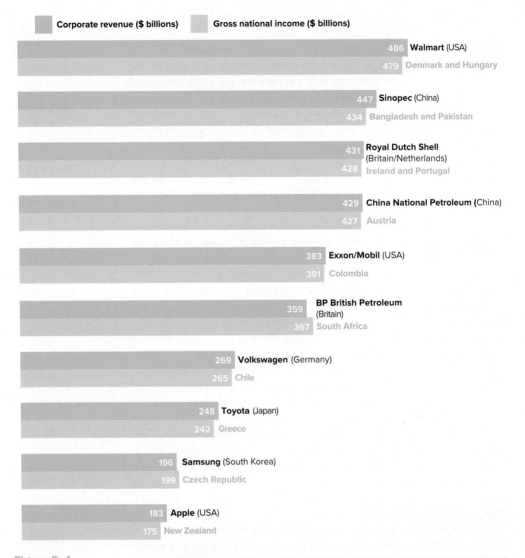

Figure 5–4
Multinational Corporations Compared to Nations

Source of data: Adapted from corporate quarterly report statements for 2014 (World Bank 2015c).

Think About It
What happens to society when corporations grow richer than countries and spill across international borders?

  Through their international ties, multinational corporations also facilitate the global exchange of ideas and technology, making the nations of the world more interdependent. These ties may prevent certain disputes from reaching the point of serious conflict. A country cannot afford to sever diplomatic relations, or engage in warfare, with a nation that is the headquarters for its main business suppliers or a key outlet for its exports.

Conflict Perspective Conflict theorists challenge this favorable evaluation of the impact of multinational corporations. They emphasize that multinationals exploit local workers to maximize profits.

The pool of cheap labor in the developing world prompts multinationals to move their factories out of core countries. An added bonus for the multinationals is the fact that the developing world discourages strong trade unions. In industrialized countries, organized labor insists on decent wages and humane working conditions, but governments seeking to attract or keep multinationals may develop a "climate for investment" that includes repressive antilabor laws—laws that restrict union activity and collective bargaining. These governments know that if labor's demands become too threatening, the multinational firm will simply move its plant elsewhere.

Several sociologists who have surveyed the effects of foreign investment conclude that although it may initially contribute to a host nation's wealth, it eventually increases economic inequality within developing nations. In both income and ownership of land, the upper and middle classes benefit most from economic expansion; the lower classes are less likely to benefit. Multinationals invest in limited industries and restricted regions. Although certain sectors of the host nation's economy, such as hotels and expensive restaurants, expand, their very expansion appears to retard growth in agriculture and other economic sectors. Moreover, multinational corporations often buy out or force out local entrepreneurs and companies, increasing a nation's economic and cultural dependence (Chase-Dunn and Grimes 1995; Kerbo 2012; Wallerstein 1979b).

Think of something you bought recently that was made by a multinational corporation. How do you know the maker was a multinational?

MODERNIZATION

Globalization and the rise of multinational corporations have affected developing countries not just economically, but culturally. Around the world, millions of people are witnessing a revolutionary transformation of their day-to-day life. Contemporary social scientists use the term *modernization* to describe the far-reaching process through which developing nations move from traditional or less developed institutions to those characteristic of more developed societies.

Sociologist Wendell Bell (1981), whose definition of modernization we are using, notes that modern societies tend to be urban, literate, and industrial. They have sophisticated transportation and media systems. Their families tend to be organized on the nuclear-family rather than the extended-family model. Members of societies that have undergone modernization shift their allegiance from traditional sources of authority, such as parents and priests, to newer authorities, such as government officials.

Many sociologists are quick to note that terms such as *modernization* and even *development* contain an ethnocentric bias. The unstated assumption behind these terms is that "they" (people living in developing countries) are struggling to become more like "us" (in the core industrialized nations). Viewed from a conflict perspective, these terms perpetuate the dominant ideology of capitalist societies.

The term *modernization* also suggests positive change. Yet change, if it comes, often comes slowly, and when it does it tends to serve the affluent segments of industrial nations. This truism seems to apply to the spread of the latest electronic technologies to the developing world.

A similar criticism has been made of **modernization theory,** the functionalist view that modernization and development will gradually improve the lives of people in developing nations. According to this theory, though countries develop at uneven rates, the development of peripheral countries is assisted by innovations transferred from the industrialized world. Critics of modernization theory, including dependency theorists, counter that any such technology transfer only increases the dominance of core nations over developing countries and facilitates further exploitation. Table 5–5 summarizes the sociological perspectives on global inequality.

When we see all the Coca-Cola and Dunkin' Donuts signs going up in developing countries, it is easy to assume that globalization and economic change are effecting cultural change. But that is not always the case, researchers note. Distinctive cultural traditions, such as a particular religious orientation or a nationalistic identity, often persist in developing nations and can soften the impact of modernization. Some contemporary sociologists emphasize that both industrialized and developing countries are "modern." Increasingly, researchers are viewing modernization as movement along a series of social indicators—among them degree of urbanization, energy use, literacy, political democracy, and use of birth control. Clearly, these are subjective indicators; even in industrialized nations, not everyone would agree that wider use of birth control represents "progress" (Armer and Katsillis 1992; Hedley 1992; Inglehart and Baker 2000).

Current modernization studies generally take a convergence perspective. Using the indicators just noted, researchers focus on how societies

Table 5–5 Sociological Perspectives on Global Inequality

Approach	Sociological Perspective	Explanation
World systems analysis	Functionalist and conflict	Unequal economic and political relationships maintain sharp divisions between nations.
Dependency theory	Conflict	Industrial nations exploit developing countries through colonialism and multinational corporations.
Modernization theory	Functionalist	Developing countries are moving away from traditional cultures and toward the cultures of industrialized nations.

Tracking Perspectives

are moving closer together, despite their traditional differences. From a conflict perspective, however, the modernization of developing countries often perpetuates their dependence on—and continued exploitation by—more industrialized nations. Conflict theorists view such continuing dependence on foreign powers as a form of contemporary neocolonialism.

Sociology Matters

Sociology matters because it defines your social class, an important part of your place in the social system.

- Do wide differences in family wealth and income separate students on your campus? What about the people in your hometown? How do sociologists explain these differences?
- What is your family's social class, and what measures of social class do you base your answer on? How does your family's social class affect your life chances?
- Where do you fit in the global stratification system? How many of the products you use were made by workers in developing nations? Would your social standing be different if you couldn't afford to buy those products?

CHAPTER RESOURCES

Summary

Stratification is the structured ranking of entire groups of people in a society, so as to perpetuate **social inequality.** Worldwide, stratification can be seen in the unequal distribution of **income** and **wealth** within countries, as well as in the gap between rich and poor nations. This chapter examined four systems of stratification, including the **class system** that prevails in the United States. It considered two theoretical explanations for the existence of social inequality, as well as the relationship between stratification and **social mobility.** It closed with a discussion of stratification in developing countries.

1. All cultures manifest some degree of **social inequality** through stratification systems such as **slavery, castes, estates,** and **classes.**
2. Karl Marx wrote that **capitalism** created two distinct social classes, the **bourgeoisie** (owners of the means of production) and the **proletariat** (workers).

3. Max Weber identified three analytically distinct components of **stratification: class, status group,** and **power.**

4. Functionalists assert that stratification benefits society by motivating people to fill demanding positions. Conflict theorists, however, see stratification as a major source of societal tension. Interactionists stress the way in which stratification shapes an individual's lifestyle.

5. Sociologists distinguish between **absolute poverty,** which is defined as a minimum level of subsistence, and **relative poverty,** a floating standard of deprivation that is based on comparison with society as a whole.

6. One's **life chances**–opportunities to obtain material goods, positive living conditions, and favorable life experiences–are related to one's social class. The higher a person's social class, the better one's life chances.

7. **Social mobility** is more likely to be found in an **open system** that emphasizes a person's **achieved status** than in a **closed system** that focuses on a person's **ascribed status.**

8. In 2010 the per capita gross national income of several developing countries was $1,000 or less. Many such countries, former colonies of developed nations, are still subject to foreign domination through the process of **neocolonialism.**

9. According to sociologist Immanuel Wallerstein, the global economic system is divided between industrialized nations that control the world's wealth, called *core nations,* and the developing nations they exploit, called *periphery nations.* Wallerstein's teaching, a version of **dependency theory,** is referred to as **world systems analysis.**

10. Critics blame the process of **globalization**–the worldwide integration of government policies, cultures, social movements, and financial markets through trade and the exchange of ideas–for contributing to the cultural domination of periphery nations by core nations. They also charge that **multinational corporations** exploit workers in developing countries in order to maximize their profits.

Key Terms

absolute poverty, 143

achieved status, 126

ascribed status, 126

bourgeoisie, 131

capitalism, 131

caste, 128

class, 133

class consciousness, 132

class system, 129

closed system, 147

colonialism, 152

dependency theory, 153

dominant ideology, 136

estate system, 129

esteem, 138

6

Inequality by Race and Ethnicity

©Ariel Skelley/Getty Images

The Privileges of the Dominant

The Social Construction of Race and Ethnicity

Immigration and New Ethnic Groups

Sociological Perspectives on Race and Ethnicity

Patterns of Prejudice and Discrimination

In 1900, in an address to the Anti-Slavery Union in London, scholar W. E. B. DuBois predicted that "the color line" would become the foremost problem of the 20th century. DuBois, born a free Black man in 1868, had witnessed prejudice and discrimination throughout the United States. His comment was prophetic. Today, over a century later, race and ethnicity still carry enormous weight in the United States (DuBois [1900] 1969).

The color line has blurred significantly since 1900, however. Interracial marriage is no longer forbidden by law and custom. Thus, Geetha Lakshmi-narayanan, a native of Ann Arbor, Michigan, is both White and Asian Indian. Often mistaken for a Filipina or Latina, she has grown accustomed to the blunt question "What are you?" (Navarro 2005). Public figures, rather than hide their mixed ancestry, now flaunt it. Singer Mariah Carey celebrates her Irish American background, and Barack Obama speaks of being born in Hawai'i to a Kenyan father and a White mother from Kansas.

Today, the color line is drawn more clearly between the young and the old. In 2011, for the first time, more non-White and Hispanic babies were born in the United States than White babies. In a nation founded by White Europeans, who struggled for over two centuries to maintain their dominance over tribal peoples, slaves, immigrants, and acquired territories like Hawai'i and Alaska, this was a demographic milestone. Although the U.S. population as a whole remains predominantly White, the trend is clearly toward a "majority minority." That is, as the babies born beginning in 2011 mature, the demographic pattern that we see today in hospital nurseries will gradually move through the nation's schools and into the labor force. At some point in the future, the nation's minority racial and ethnic groups, taken together, will grow to more than 50 percent of the total population.

The composition of the nation's minority population is changing as well. Only among adults over age 50 are African Americans still the largest minority group in the United States. Among younger Americans, including newborns, Latinos are now the largest minority group. This change is visible not just in large cities but in rural areas as well.

These demographic changes have not made the lives of racial and ethnic minorities any easier. Clearly, race and ethnicity still matter in the United States. On a collective level, our racial biases underlie the societal prejudice that members of some ethnic and racial groups encounter every day. In this chapter we will see how the ascribed characteristics of race and ethnicity create social privilege for some and discrimination for others. We will see that race and ethnicity are socially constructed concepts rather than genetically determined traits. Though functionalists, conflict theorists, labeling theorists, and interactionists have offered different explanations for the unequal treatment of Whites and Blacks, all agree that prejudice and discrimination are real, on both an individual and an institutional level.

The Privileges of the Dominant

One aspect of discrimination that is often overlooked is the privileges that dominant groups enjoy at the expense of others. For instance, we tend to focus more on the difficulty women have getting ahead at work and getting a hand at home than on the ease with which men avoid household chores and manage to make their way in the world. Similarly, we concentrate more on discrimination against racial and ethnic minorities than on the advantages members of the White majority enjoy. Indeed, most White people rarely think about their "Whiteness," taking their status for granted.

Sociologists and other social scientists are becoming increasingly interested in what it means to be "White," for White privilege is the other side of the proverbial coin of racial discrimination. In this context, *White privilege* refers to rights or immunities granted to people as a particular benefit or favor simply because they are White (Ferber and Kimmel 2008).

This view of Whiteness as a privilege echoes an observation by W. E. B. DuBois. Rather than wanting fair working conditions for all laborers, DuBois wrote, White workers had accepted the "public and psychological wage" of Whiteness ([1935] 1962:700).

The feminist scholar Peggy McIntosh (1988) became interested in White privilege after noticing that most men would not acknowledge that there were privileges attached to being male—even if they would agree that being female had its disadvantages. Did White people suffer from a similar blind spot regarding their own racial privilege? she wondered. Intrigued, McIntosh began to list all the ways in which she benefited from her Whiteness. She soon realized that the list of unspoken advantages was long and significant.

McIntosh found that as a White person, she rarely needed to step out of her comfort zone, no matter where she went. If she wished to, she could spend most of her time with people of her own race. She could find a good place to live in a pleasant neighborhood and get the foods she liked to eat in almost any grocery store. She could attend a public meeting without feeling that she did not belong, that she was different from everyone else.

How often do you think people are privileged because of their race or ethnicity? How about yourself— how often are you privileged?

McIntosh discovered, too, that her skin color opened doors for her. She could cash checks and use credit cards without suspicion, browse through stores without being shadowed by security guards. She could be seated without difficulty in a restaurant. If she asked to see the manager, she could assume he or she would be of her own race. If she needed help from a doctor or a lawyer, she could get it.

McIntosh also realized that her Whiteness made the job of parenting easier. She did not need to worry about protecting her children from people who did not like them. She could be sure that their textbooks would show pictures of people who looked like them, and that their history texts would describe White people's achievements. She knew that the television programs they watched would include White characters.

Finally, McIntosh had to admit that others did not constantly evaluate her in racial terms. When she appeared in public, she didn't need to worry that her clothing or behavior might reflect poorly on White people. If she was recognized for an achievement, it was seen as her achievement, not that of an entire race. And no one ever assumed that the personal opinions she voiced should be those of all White people. Because McIntosh blended in with the people around her, she wasn't always onstage.

These are only some of the privileges McIntosh found she took for granted as a result of her membership in the dominant racial group in the United States. Whiteness *does* carry privileges—to a much greater extent than most White people realize. In the following section we will examine the social construction of race and ethnicity—abstract concepts that have enormous practical consequences for millions of people throughout the world (Fitzgerald 2008; Picca and Feagin 2007).

The Social Construction of Race and Ethnicity

Racial definitions are crystallized through what Michael Omi and Howard Winant (1994) have called *racial formation,* a sociohistorical process in which racial categories are created, inhibited, transformed, and destroyed. In this process, those who have power define groups of people according to a racist social structure. The creation of a reservation system for Native Americans in the late 1800s is one example of racial formation. Federal officials combined what were distinctive tribes into a single racial group, which we refer to today as Native Americans. The extent and frequency to which peoples are subject to racial formation is such that no one escapes it.

Another example of racial formation from the 1800s was known as the "one-drop rule." If a person had even a single drop of "Black blood," that person was defined and viewed as Black, even if he or she appeared to be White. Clearly, race had social significance, enough so that White legislators established official standards about who was "Black" and who was "White."

The one-drop rule was a vivid example of the *social construction of race*—the process by which people come to define a group as a race based in part on physical characteristics, but also on historical, cultural, and economic factors. For example, in the 1800s, immigrant groups such as Italian and Irish Americans were not at first seen as being "White," but as foreigners who were not necessarily trustworthy. The social construction of race is an ongoing process that is subject to debate, especially in a diverse society such as the United States, where each year increasing numbers of children are born to parents of different racial backgrounds.

In the late 20th century, with immigration from Latin America rising, the fluid nature of racial formation became evident. Suddenly, people were speaking about the "Latin Americanization" of the United States, or about a biracial, Black–White society being replaced by a triracial one. In the 2010 census, over 9 million people in the United States (or about 2.9 percent of the population) reported that they were of two or more races. Half the people classified as multiracial were under age 18, suggesting that this segment of the population will grow in the years to come. People who claimed both White and American Indian ancestry were the largest group of multiracial residents (Bonilla-Silva 2004; Humes et al. 2011).

This statistical finding of millions of multiracial people obscures how individuals handle their identity. The prevailing social construction of race pushes people to choose just one race, even if they acknowledge a broader cultural background. Still, many individuals, especially young adults, struggle against social pressure to choose a single identity and instead openly embrace multiple heritages.

Ethnicity, too, is subject to social construction. Which ethnic groups are White, for instance? Do we consider Turkish and Arab Americans to be White? We have seen that in the 1800s, Irish and Italian Americans were viewed as non-White and treated as such. But gradually, as other ethnic groups came to see them as White, Irish and Italian Americans became accepted members of mainstream society.

Social construction of race and ethnicity occurs throughout the world, as people in virtually all societies define their positions in the social hierarchy in terms of race, ethnicity, and nationality. Thus, a dominant or majority group has the power not only to define itself legally but to define a society's values. Sociologist William I. Thomas (1923), an early critic of theories of racial and gender differences, wrote that the "definition of the situation" could even mold the individual personality. To put it another way, people respond not only to the objective features of a situation or person but also to the *meaning* that situation or person has for them. In this way, we can create false images or stereotypes that become real in their consequences. *Stereotypes* are unreliable generalizations about all members of a group that do not recognize individual differences within the group.

How do sociologists today conceive of race and ethnicity? Sociologists frequently distinguish between racial and ethnic groups. The term *racial group* is used to describe a group that is set apart from others because of obvious physical differences. Whites, African Americans, and Asian Americans are all considered racial groups in the United States. While race does turn on physical differences, it is the culture of a particular society that constructs and attaches social significance to those differences, as we will see later. Unlike racial groups, an *ethnic group* is set apart from others primarily because of its national origin or distinctive cultural patterns. In the United States, Puerto Ricans, Jews, and Polish Americans are all categorized as ethnic groups (see Table 6-1).

Use Your Sociological Imagination

Using a TV remote control, how quickly do you think you could find a television show in which all the characters share your own racial or ethnic background? What about a show in which all the characters share a different racial or ethnic background from your own—how quickly could you find one?

RACE

The term *racial group* refers to those minorities (and the corresponding dominant groups) set apart from others by obvious physical differences. But what is an "obvious" physical difference? Each society determines which differences are important, while ignoring other characteristics that could serve as a basis for social differentiation. In the United States, we see differences in both skin color and hair color. Yet people learn informally that differences in skin color have a dramatic social and political meaning, while differences in hair color do not.

When observing skin color, people in the United States tend to lump others rather casually into such categories as "Black," "White," and "Asian." More subtle differences in skin color often go unnoticed. However, such is not the case in other societies. In many nations of Central America and South America, people distinguish among color gradients on a continuum from light to dark skin. Brazil has approximately 40 color groupings, while in other countries people may be described as "Mestizo Hondurans," "Mulatto Colombians," or "African Panamanians." What we see as "obvious" differences, then, is subject to each society's social definitions.

Table 6-1 Racial and Ethnic Groups in the United States, 2015

Classification	Number in Thousands	Percentage of Total Population
Racial groups		
Whites (non-Hispanic)	188,568	58.7
Blacks/African Americans	40,695	12.7
Native Americans, Alaskan Natives	2,597	0.8
Asian Americans and Pacific Islanders	21,118	7.0
Chinese	4,761	1.5
Asian Indians	3,982	1.2
Filipinos	3,899	1.2
Vietnamese	1,980	0.6
Koreans	1,822	0.6
Japanese	1,411	0.2
Pacific Islanders, Native Hawaiians	555	0.1
Other Asian Americans	2,708	0.5
Arab Americans	1,963	0.6
Two or more races	9,982	3.1
Ethnic groups		
White ancestry		
Germans	45,526	14.2
Irish	32,713	10.2
English	23,959	7.5
Italians	17,070	5.3
Poles	9,231	2.9
Scottish and Scots-Irish	8,492	2.6
French	7,969	2.5
Jews	7,200	1.8
Hispanics (or Latinos)	56,496	17.6
Mexican Americans	35,797	11.1
Puerto Ricans	5,373	1.7
Salvadorans	2,172	0.7
Cubans	2,107	0.7
Dominicans	1,873	0.6
Guatemalans	1,378	0.4
Colombians	1,082	0.3
Other Hispanics	6,764	2.1
Total (All groups)	**321,419**	

NOTE: Arab American population excluded from White total. All data are for 2015. Percentages do not total 100 percent, and when subcategories are added, they do not match totals in major categories because of overlap between groups (e.g., Polish American Jews or people of mixed ancestry such as Irish and Italian).

SOURCES: American Community Survey 2016a: Tables B02001, B02018, B03001, B03001, B04006; Steinhardt Social Research Institute 2016.

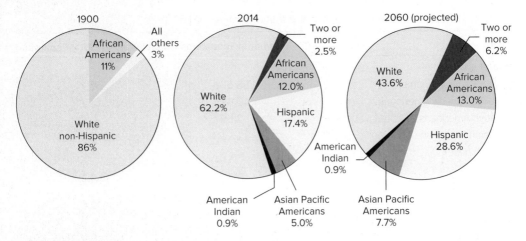

Figure 6–1

U.S. Population by Race and Ethnicity, 1900–2060 (Projected)

According to projections by the Census Bureau, the proportion of U.S. residents who are White and non-Hispanic will decrease significantly by the year 2060. By contrast, the proportion of both Hispanic Americans and Asian Americans will rise significantly.

SOURCES OF DATA: Bureau of the Census 2004a; Colby and Ortman 2015:9.

The largest racial minorities in the United States are African Americans (or Blacks), Native Americans (or American Indians), and Asian Americans (Japanese Americans, Chinese Americans, and other Asian peoples). Figure 6-1 provides information about the changing population of racial and ethnic groups in the United States over the past century. It suggests that the racial and ethnic composition of the U.S. population will change as much in the next 40 years as it has in the last 100.

ETHNICITY

An ethnic group, unlike a racial group, is set apart from others because of its national origin or distinctive cultural patterns. Among the ethnic groups in the United States are peoples with a Spanish-speaking background, referred to collectively as *Latinos* or *Hispanics,* such as Puerto Ricans, Mexican Americans, Cuban Americans, and other Latin Americans. Other ethnic groups in this country include Jewish, Irish, Italian, and Norwegian Americans. While these groupings are convenient, they serve to obscure differences *within* these ethnic categories (as in the case of Hispanics) as well as to overlook the mixed ancestry of so many ethnic people in the United States.

The distinction between racial and ethnic groups is not always clear-cut. Some members of racial groups, such as Asian Americans, may have significant cultural differences from other groups. At the same time, certain ethnic groups, such as Latinos, may have obvious physical differences that set them apart from other residents of the United States.

Despite categorization problems, sociologists continue to feel that the distinction between racial groups and ethnic groups is socially significant. In most societies, including the United States, socially constructed physical differences tend to be more visible than ethnic differences. Partly as a result of this fact, stratification along racial lines is more resistant to change than stratification along ethnic lines. Over time, members of an ethnic minority can sometimes become indistinguishable from the majority—although the process may take generations and may never include all members of the group. In contrast, members of a racial minority find it much more difficult to blend in with the larger society and gain acceptance from the majority.

Immigration

A significant segment of the population of the United States is made up of White ethnics whose ancestors arrived from Europe within the last 160 years. The nation's White ethnic population includes about 46 million people who claim at least partial German ancestry, 33 million Irish Americans, 17 million Italian Americans, and 9 million Polish Americans, as well as immigrants from other European nations (see Table 6-1). Some of these people continue to live in close-knit ethnic neighborhoods, while others have largely assimilated and left the "old ways" behind.

Many White ethnics today identify only sporadically with their heritage. *Symbolic ethnicity* refers to an emphasis on such concerns as ethnic food or political issues rather than on deeper ties to one's ethnic heritage. This identity is reflected in the occasional family trip to an ethnic bakery, in the celebration of a ceremonial event such as St. Joseph's Day among Italian Americans, or among Irish Americans, concern about the future of Northern Ireland. Except in cases in which new immigration reinforces old traditions, symbolic ethnicity tends to decline with each passing generation (Alba 1990; Winter 2008).

HISTORY OF IMMIGRATION

The contemporary diversity of the United States is not accidental, but reflects centuries of immigration. The United States has long had policies to determine who has preference to enter the country. Often, clear racial and ethnic biases are built into these policies. In the 1920s, U.S. policy gave preference to people from western Europe, while making it difficult for residents of southern and eastern Europe, Asia, and Africa to enter the country. During the late 1930s and early 1940s, the federal government refused to lift or loosen restrictive immigration quotas to allow Jewish refugees to escape the terror of the Nazi regime. In line with this policy, the S.S. *St. Louis,* with more than 900 Jewish refugees on board, was denied permission to land in the United States in 1939. The ship was forced to sail back to Europe, where at least a few hundred of its passengers later died at the hands of the Nazis (Morse 1967; G. Thomas and Witts 1974).

Since the 1960s, policies in the United States have encouraged the immigration of people who have relatives here as well as of those who have needed skills. This change has significantly altered the pattern of sending nations. Previously, Europeans dominated, but for the last 40 years, immigrants have come primarily from Latin America and Asia

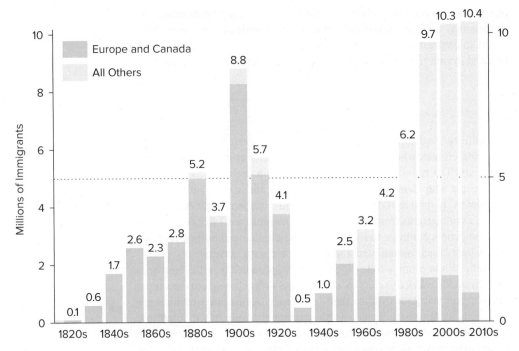

Figure 6–2

Legal Immigration to
the United States,
1820–2020

SOURCE OF DATA: Office of
Immigration Statistics
2016.

(see Figure 6-2). This means that in the future, an ever-growing propor-tion of the United States will be Asian or Hispanic. To a large degree, fear and resentment of this growing racial and ethnic diversity is a key factor in opposition to immigration. Many people are very concerned that the new arrivals do not reflect the nation's cultural and racial heritage.

The source countries of immigrants have changed. First, settlers came from Europe, then Latin America, and now, increasingly, Asia. Europe-ans were the dominant immigrant group through the 1950s. However, the majority of today's 41.7 million foreign-born people are from Latin America. Primarily, they are from Central America and, more specifi-cally, Mexico (although Mexico is sometimes considered a part of North America). By contrast, Europeans, who dominated the early settlement of the United States, now account for fewer than one in seven of the foreign-born. The changing patterns of immigration have continued into the 21st century. Beginning in 2010, the annual immigration from Asia exceeded the level of annual immigration from Latin America for the first time.

The most bitterly debated aspect of U.S. immigration policy has been the control of illegal or undocumented immigrants. These immigrants and their families usually come to the United States in search of higher-paying jobs than their home countries can provide. Because by definition illegal immigrants are in the country illegally, the exact number of these undoc-umented or unauthorized workers is subject to estimates and disputes. Based on the best available information, in late 2016 more than 11.1 million illegal or unauthorized immigrants lived in the United States. This compares with about 3.5 million in 1990 and a peak of 12.2 million in 2007. When employment opportunities dried up during the Great Recession that began in 2008, significantly fewer people tried to enter illegally, and many unauthorized immigrants returned to their countries (Krogstad 2016).

FUNCTIONS OF IMMIGRATION

Despite people's fears about it, immigration performs many valuable functions. For the receiving society, it alleviates labor shortages, such as exist in the fields of health care and technology in the United States. In 1998 Congress debated not whether individuals with technological skills should be allowed into the country, but just how much to increase the annual quota. For the sending nation, migration can relieve economies unable to support large numbers of people.

Remittances, or the monies that immigrants send home to their countries of origin, are significant. They result in the outflow of hundreds of millions of dollars from the United States to other countries, where they provide substantial support for families and even venture capital for new businesses. Immigrants in the United States send about $56 billion to their home countries annually, and worldwide remittances total about $582 billion annually, easily surpassing all other forms of foreign aid. This cash inflow is integral to the economies of many nations, but it can also fluctuate dramatically during times of economic stress. During the Great Recession that began in 2008, low-skilled immigrants (legal or illegal) took the hardest hit, and as a result, remittances immediately declined (Connor 2016; World Bank Group 2016).

Immigration can be dysfunctional as well. Although studies generally show that it has a positive impact on the receiving nation's economy, areas that accept high concentrations of immigrants may have difficulty meeting short-term social service needs. Furthermore, when migrants with skills or educational potential leave developing countries, their absence can be dysfunctional for those nations. No amount of money sent back home can make up for the loss of valuable human resources from poor nations.

THE CONFLICT PERSPECTIVE ON IMMIGRATION

White ethnics and racial minorities have often been antagonistic toward one another because of economic competition—an interpretation rooted in the conflict approach to sociology. As Blacks, Latinos, and Native Americans emerge from the lower class, they compete with working-class Whites for jobs, housing, and educational opportunities. In times of high unemployment or inflation, any such competition can easily generate intense intergroup conflict.

Conflict theorists have noted how much of the debate over immigration is phrased in economic terms. The debate intensifies when the

You have immigrated to another country with a very different culture. What steps might you take to assimilate?

arrivals are of different racial and ethnic backgrounds from the host population. For example, Europeans often refer to "foreigners," but that term does not necessarily mean one of foreign birth. In Germany, "foreigners" refers to people of non-German ancestry, even if they were *born* in Germany; it does not refer to people of German ancestry born in another country, who may choose to immigrate to their "mother country." Fear and dislike of "new" ethnic groups divide countries throughout the world.

REFUGEES

Refugees are people who live outside their country of citizenship for fear of political or religious persecution. Approximately 20 million refugees exist worldwide, enough to populate an entire nation that would be larger than the Netherlands or Guatemala. The United States has seen itself a haven for refugees, but at different times this has been controversial. Examples are the nation's reluctance to accept Jews fleeing Nazi Germany prior to World War II or, more recently, political refugees escaping Vietnam and Cuba.

Public concerns about admitting refugees have come from both ends of the political spectrum—those who lobby vigorously to allow more exiles from a particular country they argue has been especially hard hit, and those who feel we do too much already for noncitizens or feel that our security is threatened by allowing people in from the world's trouble spots.

The U.S. government is officially committed to accepting refugees, although how many and from where is always subject to change. Table 6-2 lists the major sources of refugees in 2005 and 2015. Changing political situations that change policy priorities here and abroad can alter this mix.

Table 6–2 Top Sources of Refugees, 2005 and 2015

2005		2015	
1. Somalia	10,405	Burma (Myanmar)	18,356
2. Laos	8,517	Iraq	12,676
3. Cuba	6,361	Somalia	8,858
4. Russia	5,982	Dem. Rep. of Congo	7,876
5. Liberia	4,289	Bhutan	5,775
Total of All Countries:	53,813		69,920

SOURCES: Jefferys 2006:2; Mossaad 2016:3.

Because of unrest in the Middle East and North Africa, during a single four-month period from October 2016 to January 2017, the United States accepted over 4,000 refugees each from Iraq, Syria, and Somalia (Department of State 2017).

These seem like large numbers. But to place them in perspective, the United States ranks 47th among 170 countries in terms of wealth and 75th in terms of population in the number of refugees admitted. Many smaller and poorer nations have received much larger numbers of refugees, with Lebanon, Pakistan, and Turkey hosting more than 1 million refugees each (Martin and Yankay 2013; United Nations High Commission on Refugees 2015).

In 2017, following through on campaign promises, President Donald Trump cited national security concerns when he issued an executive order instituting an indefinite ban on Syrian refugees and a 120-day ban on refugees from the rest of the world. The administration also indicated that once immigration resumed, the number of refugees allowed into the country would be half those shown in Table 6–2. At the time, national surveys indicated that most people opposed these steps, but a significant minority, about one-third, approved of them. In a matter of days, courts overruled the bans, but the expectation of a significant reduction in the approval process for new refugees looms (Newport 2017).

Sociological Perspectives on Race and Ethnicity

To understand how and why people make social distinctions based on race and ethnicity, we must turn to theory. All the major theoretical perspectives presume that culture, rather than biology, is the major determinant of racial-ethnic distinctions, yet they offer quite different explanations for discrimination. Viewing race from the macro level, functionalists observe that prejudice and discrimination based on race and ethnicity serve positive functions for dominant groups. In contrast, conflict theorists see the economic structure as a central factor in the exploitation of minorities. Interactionists stress the myriad ways in which everyday contact between people of different racial and ethnic backgrounds contributes to tolerance or hostility.

THE FUNCTIONALIST PERSPECTIVE

What possible use could racial bigotry have for society? Functionalist theorists, while agreeing that racial hostility is hardly to be admired, point out that it indeed serves positive functions for those practicing discrimination.

Anthropologist Manning Nash (1962) has identified three functions that racially prejudiced beliefs have for the dominant group:

1. Racist views provide a moral justification for maintaining an unequal society that routinely deprives a subordinate group of its rights and privileges. For example, southern Whites justified slavery by believing that Africans were physically and spiritually subhuman and devoid of souls.

2. Racist beliefs discourage members of the subordinate group from attempting to question their lowly status, which would be to question the very foundations of society.

3. Racial myths encourage support for the existing order by introducing the argument that any major societal change (such as an end to discrimination) would only bring greater poverty to the subordinate group and lower the dominant group's standard of living. As a result, Nash suggests, racial prejudice grows when a society's value system (for example, one underlying a colonial empire or a regime that perpetuates slavery) is being threatened.

Although racial prejudice and discrimination may serve the interests of the powerful, such unequal treatment can also be dysfunctional for a society, and even for the dominant group. Sociologist Arnold Rose (1951) outlined four dysfunctions associated with racism:

1. A society that practices discrimination fails to use the resources of all individuals. Discrimination limits the search for talent and leadership to the dominant group.

2. Discrimination aggravates social problems such as poverty, delinquency, and crime and places the financial burden to alleviate those problems on the dominant group.

3. Society must invest a good deal of time and money to defend the barriers to full participation of all members.

4. Racial prejudice and discrimination often undercut goodwill and friendly diplomatic relations between nations.

THE CONFLICT PERSPECTIVE

Conflict theorists would certainly agree with Arnold Rose that racial prejudice and discrimination have many harmful consequences for society. Sociologists such as Oliver Cox (1948), Robert Blauner (1972), and Herbert M. Hunter (2000) have used *exploitation theory* (also called *Marxist class theory*) to explain the basis of racial subordination in the United States. As we saw in Chapter 5, Karl Marx viewed the exploitation of the lower class as a basic part of the capitalist economic system. From a Marxist point of view, racism keeps members of subordinate groups in low-paying jobs, thereby supplying the capitalist ruling class with a pool of cheap labor. Moreover, by forcing these workers to accept low wages, capitalists can restrict the wages of *all* members of the proletariat. Workers from the dominant group who demand higher wages can always be replaced by those from the subordinate group, who have no choice but to accept low-paying jobs.

The conflict view of race relations seems persuasive in a number of instances. Japanese Americans were the object of little prejudice until they began to enter jobs that brought them into competition with Whites. The movement to keep Chinese immigrants out of the United States became most fervent during the latter half of the 19th century, when Chinese and Whites fought over dwindling work opportunities. Both the enslavement of Blacks and the extermination and removal westward of Native Americans were, to a significant extent, economically motivated.

THE LABELING PERSPECTIVE

The practice of racial profiling fits both the conflict perspective and labeling theory. *Racial profiling* may be defined as any arbitrary action initiated by an authority based on race, ethnicity, or national origin rather than on a person's behavior. Generally, racial profiling occurs when law enforcement officers—customs officials, airport security personnel, and police— assume that people who fit certain descriptions are likely to be engaged in illegal activities. Skin color became a key characteristic of criminal profiles beginning in the 1980s, with the emergence of the crack cocaine market. But profiling can also involve a much more explicit use of stereotypes.

Today, authorities continue to rely on racial profiling, despite overwhelming evidence that it is misleading. A study of New York City's controversial stop-and-frisk procedure, in which police officers temporarily detain, question, and sometimes search citizens on the street for suspected gun and drug violations, showed that in 4.43 million stops between 2004 and mid-2012, Blacks and Latinos accounted for 83 percent of people who were stopped and frisked. In contrast, a related study found that Whites were 50 percent more likely to be carrying weapons. In addition, a 2015 study of the states with the most accurate data tracking stop-and-frisk encounters found that African American drivers were much more likely to be stopped, but except in

Describe an example of labeling that you are personally familiar with.

Rhode Island, they were less likely than Whites to have contraband such as drugs or firearms (Apuzzo and Goldstein 2013; LaFraniere and Lehren 2015).

THE INTERACTIONIST PERSPECTIVE

A Hispanic woman is transferred from a job on an assembly line to a similar position working next to a White man. At first, the White man is patronizing, assuming that she must be incompetent. She is cold and resentful; even when she needs assistance, she refuses to admit it. After a week, the growing tension between the two leads to a bitter quarrel. Yet over time, each slowly comes to appreciate the other's strengths and talents. A year after they begin working together, these two workers become respectful friends. This story is an example of what interactionists call the *contact hypothesis* in action.

The **contact hypothesis** states that interracial contact between people of equal status who are engaged in a cooperative task will cause them to become less prejudiced and to abandon previous stereotypes. People will begin to see one another as individuals and discard the broad generalizations characteristic of stereotyping. Note the phrases *equal status* and *cooperative task*. In the example just given, if the two workers had been competing for one vacancy as a supervisor, the racial hostility between them might have worsened (Allport 1979; Fine 2008).

As Latinos and other subordinate groups slowly gain access to better-paying, more responsible jobs, the contact hypothesis may take on even greater significance. The trend in our society is toward increasing contact between individuals from dominant and subordinate groups. This may be one way of eliminating—or at least reducing—racial and ethnic stereotyping and prejudice. Another may be the establishment of interracial coalitions, an idea suggested by sociologist William Julius Wilson (1999). To work, such coalitions would obviously need to be built on an equal role for all members.

Table 6-3 summarizes the four major sociological perspectives on race. No matter what the explanation for racial and ethnic distinctions—functionalist, conflict, labeling, or interactionist—these socially constructed inequalities can have powerful consequences in the form of prejudice and discrimination. In the next section we will see how inequality based on the ascribed characteristics of race and ethnicity can poison people's interpersonal relations, depriving whole groups of opportunities others take for granted.

Patterns of Prejudice and Discrimination

In recent years, college campuses across the United States have been the scene of bias-related incidents. Student-run newspapers and radio stations have ridiculed subordinate racial and ethnic groups; threatening

Tracking Perspectives

Table 6–3 Sociological Perspectives on Race

Perspective	Emphasis
Functionalist	The dominant majority benefits from the subordination of racial minorities.
Conflict	Vested interests perpetuate racial inequality through economic exploitation.
Labeling	People are profiled and stereotyped based on their racial and ethnic identities.
Interactionist	Cooperative interracial contacts can reduce hostility.

Think About It

Consider an example of discrimination that you are familiar with. Which theoretical view best explains it?

literature has been stuffed under students' doors; graffiti endorsing the views of White supremacist organizations such as the Ku Klux Klan have been scrawled on university walls. In some cases, violent clashes have occurred between groups of White and Black students (Southern Poverty Law Center 2010). What causes such ugly incidents?

PREJUDICE

Prejudice is a negative attitude toward an entire category of people, often an ethnic or racial group. If you resent your roommate because he or she is sloppy, you are not necessarily guilty of prejudice. However, if you immediately stereotype your roommate on the basis of such characteristics as race, ethnicity, or religion, that is a form of prejudice. Prejudice tends to perpetuate false definitions of individuals and groups.

Sometimes prejudice results from *ethnocentrism*—the tendency to assume that one's own culture and way of life represent the norm or are superior to all others. Ethnocentric people judge other cultures by the standards of their own group, which leads quite easily to prejudice against cultures they see as inferior.

One important and widespread form of prejudice is *racism,* the belief that one race is supreme and all others are innately inferior. When racism prevails in a society, members of subordinate groups generally experience prejudice, discrimination, and exploitation. Racism can be subtle and deep-seated. Though many Americans both White and Black condemn racism, research results suggest that racist stereotypes—such as that of the violent Black male—may be rooted in our subconscious thought processes.

How might online social networking maintain prejudice and discrimination?

COLOR-BLIND RACISM

Over the last three generations, nationwide surveys have consistently shown growing support among Whites for integration, interracial dating, and the election of minority group members to public office—including even the presidency of the United States. How can this trend be explained, given the existence of racial and ethnic prejudice? The answer, to some extent, is that racial and ethnic prejudice is no longer expressed as freely as it once was. Often, it is couched in terms of equal opportunity.

Color-blind racism is the use of the principle of race neutrality to defend a racially unequal status quo. Proponents of race neutrality claim they believe that everyone should be treated equally. However, the way in which they apply the principle to government policy is anything but neutral. Proponents of this approach oppose affirmative action, public welfare assistance, and to a large extent, government-funded health insurance, all of which they see largely as favors to minority groups. Yet they do not object to practices that privilege Whites, such as college admissions criteria that give preference to the relatives of alumni. Nor do they oppose tax breaks for homeowners, most of whom are White, or government financial aid to college students, who are also disproportionately White. Though race neutrality is not based on theories of racial superiority or inferiority, then, the idea that society should be color-blind only perpetuates racial inequality.

Color-blind racism has also been referred to as "covert racism." Although its proponents rarely speak of racism, other indicators of social status, such as social class or citizenship, tend to become proxies for race. Thus, many White people can convince themselves that they are not racist—nor do they know anyone who is—and yet remain prejudiced against "welfare mothers" and "immigrants." They can conclude, mistakenly, that racial tolerance, or even racial and ethnic equality, has been achieved.

Researchers who have surveyed White attitudes toward African Americans over the past several decades have come to two inescapable conclusions. First, people's attitudes do change. In periods of social upheaval, dramatic attitudinal shifts can occur within a single generation. Second, less racial progress was made in the late 20th and early 21st centuries than in the relatively brief period of the 1950s and 1960s. Today, economically disadvantaged groups such as African Americans and Latinos have become so closely associated with urban decay, homelessness, welfare, and crime that those problems are now viewed as racial issues, even if they are not labeled as such. The tendency to *blame the victims* of these social ills complicates their resolution, especially at a time when government's ability to address social problems is limited by anti-tax initiatives and concern over terrorism. In short, the color line is still in place, even if more and more people refuse to acknowledge its existence (Ansell 2008; Bonilla-Silva 2014).

DISCRIMINATORY BEHAVIOR

Prejudice often leads to *discrimination,* the denial of opportunities and equal rights to individuals and groups based on some type of arbitrary bias. Say that a White corporate president with a prejudice against Asian Americans has to fill an executive position. The most qualified candidate for the job is a Vietnamese American. If the president refuses to hire this candidate and instead selects an inferior White candidate, he or she is engaging in an act of racial discrimination.

Which would be more socially significant, the elimination of prejudice or the elimination of discrimination?

Prejudiced *attitudes* should not be equated with discriminatory *behavior.* Although the two are generally related, they are not identical; either condition can be present without the other. A prejudiced person does not always act on his or her biases. The White president, for example, might choose to hire the Vietnamese American, despite his or her stereotypes. That would be prejudice without discrimination. On the other hand, a White corporate president with a completely respectful view of Vietnamese Americans might refuse to hire them for executive posts, out of fear that biased clients would take their business elsewhere. In that case, the president's action would constitute discrimination without prejudice.

Discrimination based on racism developed deep roots in the period following the Civil War, as Southern states enacted laws meant to keep former slaves and their descendants in a subordinate status. Through these laws, referred to in slang as *Jim Crow,* segregation became entrenched in the South. The term appears to have originated in a dance tune; by the 1890s it was synonymous with segregation and the statutes that kept African Americans in an inferior position. Jim Crow laws gave White people their ultimate authority over Blacks. In 1896, the U.S. Supreme Court ruled in *Plessy v. Ferguson* that state laws requiring "separate but equal" accommodations for Blacks were a "reasonable" use of state governments' power. Although the statutes were eventually overturned, new laws may have a similar impact in the 21st century, as we will see in the next section on institutional discrimination.

Discrimination persists even for the most educated and qualified people from the best family backgrounds. Despite their talents and experiences, they sometimes encounter attitudinal or organizational bias that prevents them from reaching their full potential. The term *glass ceiling* refers to an invisible barrier that blocks the promotion of a qualified individual in a work environment because of the individual's gender, race, or ethnicity (Schaefer 2012; Yamagata et al. 1997).

INSTITUTIONAL DISCRIMINATION

Discrimination is practiced not only by individuals in one-to-one encounters but also by institutions. Social scientists are particularly concerned with the ways in which structural factors such as employment, housing, health care, and government administration maintain the social significance of race and ethnicity. ***Institutional discrimination*** refers to the denial of opportunities and equal rights to individuals and groups that results from the normal operations of a society. This kind of discrimination consistently affects certain racial and ethnic groups more than others.

The Commission on Civil Rights (1981:9–10) has identified various forms of institutional discrimination, including:

- Rules requiring that only English be spoken at a place of work, even when it is not a business necessity to restrict the use of other languages.
- Preferences shown by law and medical schools in the admission of children of wealthy and influential alumni, nearly all of whom are White.
- Restrictive employment-leave policies, coupled with prohibitions on part-time work, that make it difficult for the heads of single-parent families (most of whom are women) to obtain and keep jobs.

In some cases, even seemingly neutral institutional standards can turn out to have discriminatory effects. For example, significant potential for institutional discrimination exists in local laws that govern voting. Recently, states have begun requiring voters to show a photo ID, presumably to prevent voter fraud. However, there is little evidence that people have been impersonating eligible voters at the polls. Such laws disproportionately disenfranchise members of minority groups, simply because they do not have a driver's license. According to national surveys, 25 percent of African Americans and 16 percent of Latino citizens do not have a valid government-issued photo ID, compared to 8 percent of White citizens (Brennan Center 2006; Dade 2012).

Attempts have been made to eradicate or compensate for discrimination in the United States. The 1960s saw the passage of many pioneering

State laws requiring voters to show a photo ID discriminate against many citizens from racial minority groups. An example of institutional racism, they are reminiscent of Jim Crow practices in the old South, which enforced separate but unequal treatment of African Americans.

©Jim Marguilies 2012

civil rights laws, including the landmark 1964 Civil Rights Act, which prohibits discrimination in public accommodations and publicly owned facilities on the basis of race, color, creed, national origin, and gender. In 1965 the Voting Rights Act outlawed poll taxes and other requirements meant to keep Blacks from voting.

For more than 20 years, affirmative action programs have been instituted to overcome past discrimination. *Affirmative action* refers to positive efforts to recruit members of subordinate groups or women for jobs, promotions, and educational opportunities. Many people resent these programs, arguing that advancing one group's cause merely shifts the discrimination to another group. By giving priority to African Americans in admissions, for example, a school may overlook more qualified White candidates. In many parts of the country and many sectors of the economy, affirmative action is being rolled back, even though it was never fully implemented.

Discriminatory practices continue to pervade nearly all aspects of life in the United States today, in part because various individuals and groups actually *benefit* from them in terms of money, status, and influence. Discrimination permits members of the majority to enhance their wealth, power, and prestige at the expense of others. Less qualified people get jobs and promotions simply because they are members of the dominant group. Such individuals and groups will not surrender these advantages easily. Even ex-convicts who are White are privileged in comparison to non-Whites. A study by sociologist Devah Pager (2003) documents this kind of racial discrimination. Pager sent four young men out to look for an entry-level job in Milwaukee, Wisconsin. All four were 23-year-old college students, but they presented themselves as high school graduates with similar job histories. Two of the men were Black and two were White. One Black applicant and one White applicant claimed to have served 18 months in jail for a felony conviction (possession of cocaine with intent to distribute).

As one might expect, the four men's experiences with 350 potential employers were vastly different. Predictably, the White applicant with a purported prison record received only half as many callbacks as the other White applicant—17 percent compared to 34 percent. But as dramatic as the effect of his criminal record was, the effect of his race was more significant. Despite his prison record, he received slightly more callbacks than the Black applicant *with no criminal record* (17 percent compared to 14 percent). Race, it seems, was more of a concern to potential employers than a criminal background.

The implications of this research are not limited to any one city, such as Milwaukee. Pager and fellow sociologist Bruce Western replicated (that is, repeated) her study in New York City, with similar results. Other studies have confirmed discriminatory handling of job applications in Chicago, San Diego, and Washington, DC. Over time, the cumulative effect of such differential behavior by employers contributes to significant differences in income (Pager 2007; Pager et al. 2009).

MEASURING DISCRIMINATION

Can discrimination be measured in terms of lost income or opportunities? Doing so is a complicated process. Researchers must first confirm that prejudice exists by assessing people's attitudes toward a racial or ethnic group and showing that its members are treated differently from others. Then they must find a way to assign a cost to the discrimination.

Researchers have managed to draw some tentative conclusions, however, by comparing income data for African Americans versus Whites and for men versus women. As Figure 6–3 shows, with a median income of $60,508, White men earned 43 percent more money than Black men in 2015 and nearly one and one-half times what Hispanic women earned. Black women earned significantly less than White women ($35,407 compared to $45,371), indicating that they bore a double burden because of their race and gender. The strong disparity between Black women's and White men's incomes has remained unchanged over more than 70 years. As great as this apparent inequality of income is, studies show that inequality in wealth among racial and ethnic groups is even greater.

These differences are not entirely the result of discrimination in employment, for members of these groups are not equally prepared to obtain high-paying jobs. Past discrimination is a significant factor in the poor educational backgrounds of some groups. Historically, taxpayers, who are predominantly White, have been unwilling to subsidize the public education of African Americans and Hispanics at the same level as that of White pupils. Test results in today's inner-city schools show the continuing effect of such discriminatory spending patterns.

Figure 6–3

U.S. Median Income by Race, Ethnicity, and Gender

NOTE: *Data released in 2016 for income earned in 2015. Median income is from all sources and is limited to year-round, full-time workers at least 25 years old (American Indian data for 16 years or older). Data for White men and women are for non-Hispanics.*

SOURCES: American Community Survey 2016a; American Social and Economic Supplement 2016.

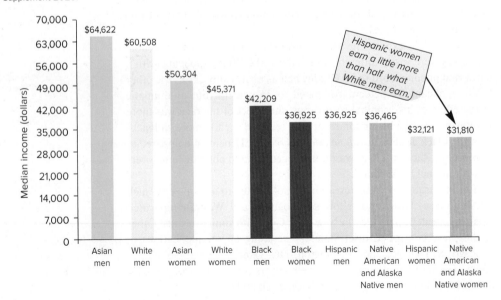

Thinking over the long term, a woman with a bachelor's degree will work full-time for three years to earn $173,000. The typical male will exceed that income in a little more than 29 months. Women, regardless of race, pay at every point. They are often hired at lower starting salaries in jobs comparable to those held by men. Salary increases come more slowly. And by their 30s, their earnings rarely recover from even short maternity leaves.

Note what happens to Asian American households. Asian American families often match similarly educated White families in annual income, but typically this requires more earners per household collectively earning that money than in White households.

The income gap shown in Table 6–4 may not be caused entirely by employment discrimination. The table shows only the level of schooling obtained by workers, not the quality. Though in recent years, efforts have been made to eliminate geographical disparities in school funding, subordinate racial groups are still more likely than Whites to attend inadequately financed schools. Inequality of educational opportunity may also affect women, since educational institutions often shepherd women into low-paid sex-segregated occupations, such as nursing and elementary education.

Table 6–4 Median Income by Race and Sex, Holding Education Constant

Even at the very highest levels of schooling, the income gap between Whites and Blacks remains. Education also has little apparent effect on narrowing the income gap between male and female workers (income values in dollars).

	Race				Sex	
	White Families	Black Families	Asian Families	Hispanic Families	Male	Female
Total	81,531	39,689	91,780	48,359	52,305	41,679
High school						
Nongraduate	36,308	22,211	44,464	34,708	32,143	22,670
Graduate	60,328	36,790	51,687	44,515	41,569	31,249
College						
Associate Degree	79,783	53,183	79,269	68,897	52,072	40,180
Bachelor's degree	105,017	81,455	104,884	88,020	71,385	57,681
Master's degree	122,576	92,344	135,972	104,864	86,738	62,379
Professional degree	164,066	127,250	197,355	122,628	131,189	82,473

NOTE: Data released in 2016 for income earned in 2015. Figures are median income from all sources except capital gains. Included are public-assistance payments, dividends, pensions, and unemployment compensation. Incomes are for all workers 25 years of age and older with earnings. High-school graduates include those with GEDs. Data for Whites are for White non-Hispanics. Family data for Black professional degree-holders' families are author's estimate.

SOURCE: Bureau of Census 2016i: Tables FINC01-4, 6, 8, 9, P-24.

What is the collective effect of discrimination in employment? Economist Andrew Brimmer (1995), citing numerous government studies, estimates that if employers used African Americans' talents and abilities, based on their formal schooling, to the fullest, the nation's gross domestic product (GDP) would be about 3 or 4 percent higher each year. Estimates of the economic cost of discrimination have not changed much since the mid-1960s. The percentage of GDP lost would be even higher, of course, if economists were to include losses from the underutilization of women's and other subordinate groups' talents. The widespread practice of steering women toward low-paid, low-level jobs, even if they are qualified for more challenging and rewarding work, has a hidden cost to society.

Sociology Matters

Sociology matters because it makes us think about why some people in our society are treated better than others.

- Do you hold any prejudices against subordinate racial or ethnic groups? If so, has your reading of this chapter helped you to see those groups from a different perspective? How would your life change if you yourself were a member of one of those groups?

- Are you White? If so, what privileges, perhaps because of your race or citizenship, do you enjoy that you have always taken for granted? Can you think of a way to reduce one or more of those privileges so that others can be more equal—and would you cooperate with such an effort?

Sociology matters because it makes us more aware of prejudice and discrimination against members of certain racial and ethnic groups.

- Are you non-White? If so, what kinds of stereotyping and discrimination have you seen non-Whites experience? Do you think racial discrimination can be reduced through cooperative contact among people of different races?

- Are you or your parents recent immigrants to the United States? If so, what is the primary basis on which others react to you—your ethnic group, race, or country of origin? Do you think you or your children will someday blend into mainstream society in the United States, and if so, what might hasten that process?

Summary

The social dimensions of race and ethnicity are important factors in shaping people's lives. In this chapter, we defined the meaning of race and ethnicity and examined the social construction of those ascribed statuses. We discussed four theoretical perspectives on the unequal treatment of individuals based on their **racial** and **ethnic groups.** We noted some patterns of **prejudice** and **discrimination** against members of those groups, many of whom are recent immigrants. And we studied the economic effects of the unequal treatment of subordinate groups.

1. In the United States, people who are White enjoy numerous rights and immunities simply because they are White. Yet they rarely acknowledge their **White privilege,** to themselves or to people of other races.

2. Race and ethnicity are socially constructed. The meaning people attach to the physical characteristics of certain groups, which are often expressed in **stereotypes,** gives race and ethnicity their social significance.

3. A **racial group** is set apart from others by obvious physical differences, whereas an **ethnic group** is set apart primarily because of national origin or distinctive cultural patterns.

4. Over the last century, the racial and ethnic composition of immigrants to the United States has changed as the major sending nations changed. One hundred years ago, White ethnics from Europe predominated; today's immigrants come mainly from Latin America and Asia.

5. Functionalists point out that to the dominant groups in a society, discrimination against subordinate groups may seem to be functional. But for society as a whole, discrimination can be dysfunctional.

6. Conflict theorists stress the harmful consequences of racial subordination. They see the unequal treatment of subordinate groups as an integral part of capitalism, a view known as **exploitation theory.**

7. Interactionists focus on the micro level of race relations, pointing out the ways in which Whites dominate members of other racial and ethnic groups in everyday social interactions. According to their **contact hypothesis,** racial prejudice and discrimination can be reduced through cooperative contact between the races.

8. **Prejudice** is a negative attitude toward an entire group, often an ethnic or racial minority. Prejudice is often based on **ethnocentrism**—the belief that one's own culture is superior to all others—or on **racism**—the belief that one race is supreme and all others are inferior.

9. Prejudice often leads to **discrimination** against members of certain racial and ethnic groups. In the workplace, members of these groups may encounter a **glass ceiling,** an invisible barrier that blocks their promotion.

10. Discrimination that results from the normal operations of a society is known as **institutional discrimination.** To remedy this kind of discrimination, governments, businesses, and schools have developed **affirmative action** programs.

Key Terms

affirmative action, 181

color-blind racism, 178

contact hypothesis, 176

discrimination, 179

ethnic group, 166

ethnocentrism, 177

exploitation theory, 175

glass ceiling, 179

institutional discrimination, 180

Jim Crow, 179

prejudice, 177

racial formation, 165

racial group, 166

racial profiling, 175

racism, 177

refugees, 172

remittances, 171

stereotype, 166

symbolic ethnicity, 169

White privilege, 163

Inequality by Gender

©Mike Watson Images/Alamy

He works. She works. Both are family practice physicians—a high-status occupation with considerable financial rewards. He makes $140,000. She makes $88,000.

These median earnings for physicians in the United States were released by the Census Bureau. They are typical of the results of the bureau's detailed study of occupations and income. Take air traffic controllers. He makes $67,000; she earns $56,000. Or housekeepers: he makes $19,000; she earns $15,000. What about teacher's assistants? He makes $20,000; she earns $15,000. Statisticians at the bureau looked at the median earnings for no fewer than 821 occupations ranging from dishwasher to chief executive. After adjusting for workers' age, education, and work experience, they came to an unmistakable conclusion: Across the board, there is a substantial gender gap in the median earnings of full-time workers.

Men do not always earn more than women for doing the same work. Researchers at the Census Bureau found 2 occupations out of 821 in which women typically earn about 1 percent more income than men: hazardous materials recovery and telecommunications line installation. These two occupations, however, employed less than 1 out of every 1,000 workers the bureau studied. Forecasting analyses show no convincing evidence that the wage gap is narrowing.

What accounts for these yawning wage gaps between men and women in the same occupation? Scholars at the Census Bureau studied the following characteristics of men and women in the same occupation:

- Age and degree of formal education
- Marital status and the presence of children at home
- Specialization within the occupation (for example, family practice versus surgical practice)
- Years of work experience
- Hours worked per year

Taking all these factors into consideration reduced the pay gap between men and women by only three cents. Women still earned only 82 cents for every dollar earned by men. In sum, the disparity in pay between men and women cannot be explained by pointing to women's career choices (Bureau of Labor Statistics 2017b; Government Accountability Office 2003; Weinberg 2004, 2007).

But women are catching up, and pay equity is around the corner! Well, yes, there has been progress, but at the recent rate of change it will still take White women until 2059 to reach overall wage equity. It will take African American women until 2124 to reach those levels and Latinos until 2248—over 200 more years (Swartz and Jones 2017).

In this chapter we will see how the ascribed characteristic of gender creates privilege for men and discrimination for women. Like differences in race, differences in gender are visible. And like race and ethnicity, gender is socially constructed. Though functionalists, conflict theorists, feminists, and interactionists take different views of this subject, all agree that our society treats women and men unequally. Women may be a majority in terms of their numbers, but they are treated more like a subordinate racial or ethnic group. For some women, the intersection of gender, race, and class creates a degree of discrimination that no other subordinate group faces.

The Social Construction of Gender

How do airline passengers react when the captain's voice belongs to a female? What do we make of a father who announces that he will be late for work because his son has a routine medical checkup? Consciously or unconsciously, we are likely to assume that flying a commercial plane is a *man's* job, and that most parental duties are, in fact, *maternal* duties. Gender is such a routine part of our everyday activities that we typically take it for granted, noticing only when someone deviates from conventional behavior and expectations.

Although a few people begin life with an unclear sexual identity, the overwhelming majority begin with a definite sex and quickly receive societal messages about how to behave. Many societies have established social distinctions between females and males that do not inevitably result from biological differences between the sexes (such as women's reproductive capabilities).

In studying gender, sociologists are interested in the gender-role socialization that leads females and males to behave differently. In Chapter 2, *gender role* was defined as expectations regarding the proper behavior, attitudes, and activities of males or females. The application of traditional gender roles leads to many forms of differentiation between women and men. Both sexes are physically capable of learning to cook and sew, yet most Western societies determine that women should perform these tasks. Both men and women are capable of learning to weld and fly airplanes, but these functions are generally assigned to men.

Gender roles are evident not only in our work and behavior but in how we react to others. We are constantly "doing gender" without realizing it. If the father just mentioned sits in the doctor's office with his son in the middle of a workday, he will probably receive approving glances from the receptionist and from other patients. "Isn't he a wonderful father?" runs through their minds. But if the boy's mother leaves *her* job and sits with the son in the doctor's office, she will not receive such silent applause.

We socially construct our behavior to create or exaggerate male–female differences. For example, men and women come in a variety of heights, sizes, and ages. Yet traditional norms regarding marriage and even casual dating tell us that in heterosexual couples, the man should be older, taller, and wiser than the woman. As we will see throughout this chapter, such social norms help to reinforce and legitimize patterns of male dominance.

In recent decades, women have entered occupations and professions that were once dominated by men. Yet our society still focuses on "masculine" and "feminine" qualities, as if men and women must be evaluated

How does the social construction of gender compare with the social construction of race?

©Kirk Anderson/kirktoons.com

in those terms. Clearly, we continue to "do gender," and the social construction of gender continues to define significantly different expectations for females and males.

GENDER-ROLE SOCIALIZATION

Male babies get blue blankets; females get pink ones. Boys are expected to play with trucks, blocks, and toy soldiers; girls receive dolls and kitchen goods. Boys must be masculine—active, aggressive, tough, daring, and dominant—but girls must be feminine—soft, emotional, sweet, and submissive. These traditional gender-role patterns have been influential in the socialization of children in the United States.

An important element in traditional views of proper "masculine" and "feminine" behavior is *homophobia,* or fear of and prejudice against homosexuality. Homophobia contributes significantly to rigid gender-role socialization, since many people stereotypically associate male homosexuality with femininity and lesbianism with masculinity. Consequently, men and women who deviate from traditional expectations about gender roles are often presumed to be gay. Despite the advances made by the gay liberation movement, the continuing stigma attached to homosexuality in our culture places pressure on all males (whether gay or not) to exhibit only narrow "masculine" behavior and on all females (whether lesbian or not) to exhibit only narrow "feminine" behavior (Lindsey 2005; Seidman 2002).

It is *adults,* of course, who play a critical role in guiding children into those gender roles deemed appropriate by society. Parents are normally the first and most crucial agents of socialization. But other adults, older siblings, the mass media, and religious and educational institutions also exert an important influence on gender-role socialization, in the United States and elsewhere.

It is not hard to test how rigid gender-role socialization can be. Just try transgressing some gender norm—say, by smoking a cigar in public if you are female, or by carrying a purse if you are male. That was exactly the assignment given to sociology students at the University of Colorado and Luther College in Iowa. Professors asked students to behave in ways that they thought violated the norms of how a man or woman should act. The students had no trouble coming up with gender-norm transgressions (see Table 7-1), and they kept careful notes on others' reactions to their behavior, ranging from amusement to disgust (Nielsen et al. 2000).

WOMEN'S AND MEN'S GENDER ROLES

How does a girl come to develop a feminine self-image, while a boy develops one that is masculine? In part, they do so by identifying with females and males in their families and neighborhoods and in the media. If a young girl regularly sees female characters on television working as defense attorneys and judges, she may believe that she herself can become a lawyer.

Table 7–1 An Experiment in Gender Norm Violation by College Students

Norm Violations by Women	Norm Violations by Men
Send men flowers	Wear fingernail polish
Spit in public	Needlepoint in public
Use men's bathroom	Throw Tupperware party
Buy jock strap	Cry in public
Buy/chew tobacco	Have pedicure
Talk knowledgeably about cars	Apply to babysit
Open doors for men	Shave body hair

SOURCE: Adapted from Nielsen et al. 2000:287.

In an experiment testing gender-role stereotypes, sociology students were asked to behave in ways that might be regarded as violations of gender norms, and to keep notes on how others reacted. This is a sample of their choices of behavior over a seven-year period.

Think About It

Do you agree that these behaviors test the boundaries of conventional gender behavior? How have those standards changed since the experiment was completed in 2000?

It will not hurt if the women that she knows—her mother, sister, parents' friends, or neighbors—are lawyers. But if she sees women portrayed in the media only as models, nurses, and secretaries, her identification and self-image will be quite different. Even if she does become a professional, she may secretly regret falling short of the media stereotypes—a shapely, sexy young woman in a bathing suit, or the perfect wife and mother.

And what about men's gender roles? Until recent decades the idea of stay-at-home fathers was unthinkable. Yet in a 2012 nationwide survey, 22 percent of men said they preferred to stay at home and take care of the house and family. That lifestyle preference is much more common among women, however; 44 percent of women said they preferred to stay at home. But while people's conceptions of gender roles are obviously changing, the fact is that men who stay home to care for their children are still an unusual phenomenon. Among couples with a stay-at-home parent, 84 percent have mothers staying home, while 16 percent have fathers staying home (Livingstone 2014a; Saad 2012).

While attitudes toward parenting may be changing, studies show little change in the traditional male gender role. Men's roles are socially constructed in much the same way as women's are. Family, peers, and the media all influence how a boy or man comes to view his appropriate role in society. The male gender role, besides being antifeminine (no "sissy stuff"), includes proving one's masculinity at work and sports—often by using force in dealing with others—as well as initiating and controlling all sexual relations.

Males who do not conform to the socially constructed gender role face constant criticism and even humiliation, both from children when they are boys and from adults as men. It can be agonizing to be treated as a "chicken" or a "sissy" as a youth—particularly if such remarks come from one's father or brothers. And grown men who pursue nontraditional occupations, such as preschool teaching or nursing, must constantly deal with others' misgivings and strange looks. In one study, interviewers found that such men frequently had to alter their behavior in order to minimize others' negative reactions. One 35-year-old nurse reported that he had to claim he was "a carpenter or something like that" when he "went clubbing," because women weren't interested in getting to know a male nurse. The subjects made similar accommodations in casual exchanges with other men (Cross and Bagilhole 2002:215).

At the same time, boys who successfully adapt to prevailing cultural standards of masculinity may grow up to be inexpressive men who cannot share their feelings with others. They remain forceful and tough, but are closed and isolated as a result. In fact, a small but growing body of scholarship suggests that for men as well as women, traditional gender roles may be disadvantageous. In many communities across the nation, girls seem to outdo boys in high school, grabbing a disproportionate share of the leadership positions, from valedictorian to class president to yearbook editor—everything, in short, except captain of the boys' athletic teams. Their advantage continues after high school. In the 1980s, girls in the United States became more likely than boys to go to college. Since then, women have consistently accounted for 54 to 55 percent of first-year students at community colleges and four-year colleges. This trend is projected to continue through at least 2021 (Hussar and Bailey 2013:Table 30).

Aside from these disadvantages, many men find that traditional masculinity does not serve them well in the job market. The growth of a service economy over the past two generations has created a demand for skills, attitudes, and behaviors that are the antithesis of traditional masculinity. Increasingly, this sector is the place where low-skilled men must look for jobs. As a British study showed, many out-of-work men are reluctant to engage in the kind of sensitive, deferential behavior required by service sector jobs (Nixon 2009).

In the past 40 years, inspired in good part by the contemporary feminist movement (examined later in the chapter), increasing numbers of men in the United States have criticized the restrictive aspects of the traditional male gender role. Some men have taken strong public positions in support of women's struggle for full equality, and have even organized voluntary associations for the purpose. However, their actions have been countered by other men who feel they are unfairly penalized by laws related to alimony, child support and custody, family violence, and affirmative action (Kimmel 2008; National Organization for Men Against Sexism 2017).

A CROSS-CULTURAL PERSPECTIVE

To what extent do actual biological differences between the sexes contribute to these cultural differences associated with gender? This question brings us back to the debate over nature versus nurture (see Chapter 2). In assessing the alleged and real differences between men and women, it is useful to examine cross-cultural data.

Around the world, anthropologists have documented highly diverse constructions of gender that do not always conform to our own ideals of masculinity and femininity. Beginning with the path-breaking work of Margaret Mead ([1935] 2001) and continuing through contemporary fieldwork, these scholars have shown that gender roles can vary greatly from one physical environment, economy, and political system to the next.

In any society, gender stratification requires not only individual socialization into traditional gender roles within the family, but also the promotion and support of those traditional roles by other social institutions, such as religion and education. Moreover, even with all major institutions socializing the young into conventional gender roles, every society has women and men who resist and successfully oppose the stereotypes: strong women who become leaders or professionals, gentle men who care for children, and so forth. It seems clear that differences between the sexes are not dictated by biology. Indeed, the maintenance of traditional gender roles requires constant social controls—and those controls are not always effective.

You are living in a society in which there are no gender roles. What is your life like?

We can see the social construction of gender roles in process in societies strained by war and social upheaval. U.S. troops were sent to Afghanistan primarily to quell terrorist operations, but also to improve women's rights in a country where social protections and the rule of law have broken down. In this patriarchal society wracked by poverty and war, Afghani women have never been secure; their appearance in public is especially dangerous. Not only is violence against women common in Afghanistan, it is seldom investigated or prosecuted, even in the most severe cases. Victims of violence risk being charged with adultery if they report the crime to authorities. Thanks to UN intervention on women's behalf, however, Afghanis are beginning to recognize that violence against women is a social problem (Organisation for Economic Co-operation and Development 2012b).

Sociological Perspectives on Gender

THE FUNCTIONALIST PERSPECTIVE

Cross-cultural studies have shown that societies dominated by men are much more common than those in which women play the decisive role. Functionalists maintain that this type of gender differentiation contributes to overall social stability. Sociologists Talcott Parsons and Robert

Bales (1955), for instance, argued that to function most effectively, the family requires adults who will specialize in particular roles. They viewed the traditional arrangement of gender roles as arising out of the need to establish a division of labor between marital partners.

Parsons and Bales contended that women take the expressive, emotionally supportive role and men the instrumental, practical role, with the two complementing each other. *Instrumentality* refers to an emphasis on tasks, a focus on more distant goals, and a concern for the external relationship between one's family and other social institutions. *Expressiveness* denotes a concern for the maintenance of harmony and the internal emotional affairs of the family. According to this theory, women's interest in expressive goals frees men for instrumental tasks, and vice versa. Women become "anchored" in the family as wives, mothers, and household managers; men become anchored in the occupational world outside the home. Of course, Parsons and Bales offered this framework in the 1950s, when many more women were full-time homemakers than is true today. Though they did not explicitly endorse traditional gender roles, they implied that dividing tasks between spouses was functional for the family unit.

Given the typical socialization of women and men in the United States, the functionalist view may seem persuasive. However, it would lead us to expect girls and women with no interest in children to become babysitters and mothers. Similarly, males who love spending time with children might be "programmed" into careers in the business world. Such differentiation might harm the individual who does not fit into prescribed roles, while depriving society of the contributions of many talented people who are confined by gender stereotyping. Moreover, the functionalist approach does not convincingly explain why men should be categorically assigned to the instrumental role and women to the expressive role.

THE CONFLICT PERSPECTIVE

Viewed from a conflict perspective, the functionalist approach to explaining gender distinctions masks the underlying power relations between men and women. Parsons and Bales never explicitly presented the expressive and instrumental tasks as being of unequal value to society, yet their inequality is quite evident. Although social institutions may pay lip service to women's expressive skills, men's instrumental skills are more highly rewarded, whether in terms of money or prestige. Consequently, any division of labor by gender into instrumental and expressive tasks is far from neutral in its impact on women.

Conflict theorists contend that the relationship between females and males has traditionally been one of unequal power, with men occupying the dominant position. Men may originally have become powerful in preindustrial times because their size, physical strength, and freedom from childbearing duties allowed them to dominate women physically. In contemporary societies, such considerations are not so important, yet cultural beliefs about the sexes are long established. Such beliefs support a social structure that places males in controlling positions.

Thus, conflict theorists see gender differences as a reflection of the subjugation of one group (women) by another group (men). If we use an analogy to Marx's analysis of class conflict (see Chapter 5), we can say that males are like the bourgeoisie, or capitalists; they control most of society's wealth, prestige, and power. Females are like the proletariat, or workers; they can acquire valuable resources only by following the dictates of their "bosses." Men's work is uniformly valued; women's work (whether unpaid labor in the home or wage labor outside the home) is devalued.

THE FEMINIST PERSPECTIVE

A significant component of the conflict approach to gender stratification draws on feminist theory. Although use of the term *feminist theory* is comparatively recent, the critique of women's position in society and culture goes back to some of the earliest influences on sociology. Among the most important are Mary Wollstonecraft's *A Vindication of the Rights of Women* (originally published in 1792), John Stuart Mill's *The Subjection of Women* (originally published in 1869), and Friedrich Engels's *The Origin of the Family, Private Property, and the State* (originally published in 1884).

Engels, a close associate of Karl Marx, argued that women's subjugation coincided with the rise of private property during the Industrial Revolution. Only when people moved beyond an agrarian economy could males enjoy the luxury of leisure and withhold rewards and privileges from women. Drawing on the work of Marx and Engels, contemporary feminist theorists often view women's subordination as part of the overall exploitation and injustice they see as inherent in capitalist societies. Some radical feminist theorists, however, view the oppression of women as inevitable in *all* male-dominated societies, whether they are labeled "capitalist," "socialist," or "communist" (Feuer 1959; Tuchman 1992; Tucker 1978:734–759).

Feminist sociologists would find little to disagree with in the conflict theorists' perspective, but they are more likely to embrace a political action agenda. Feminists would also argue that the very discussion of women and society, however well meaning, has been distorted by the exclusion of women from academic thought, including sociology. In Chapter 1 we noted the many accomplishments of Jane Addams and Ida Wells-Barnett, but they generally worked outside the discipline, focusing on what we would now call *applied sociology* and social work. At the time, their efforts, while valued as humanitarian, were seen as unrelated to the research and conclusions being reached in academic circles, which of course were male academic circles (Andersen 2015; J. Howard 1999; Ridgeway 2011).

INTERSECTIONALITY

Race and ethnicity as well as other social identifiers are important in defining relationships of power (or lack of power). Yet they do not exist in isolation. Rather, they coexist with religion, gender, age, disability status, and sexual identity (among other identities). *Intersectionality* refers to the overlapping and interdependent system of advantage and disadvantage that positions people in society on the basis of race, class, gender, and other characteristics (Crenshaw 1989). Awareness of intersectionality grew as female scholars noted that an emphasis on race could result in ignoring other related processes of domination. For example, many women experience social inequality not only because of their gender but also because of their race and ethnicity. These citizens face a double or triple subordinate status based on their intersecting identities. A disproportionate share of this low-status group also is poor. African American feminist Patricia Hill Collins (2000, 2015) views intersectionality as creating a *matrix of domination* (Figure 7-1). Whites dominate non-Whites, men dominate women, and the affluent dominate the poor—race, class, and gender are interconnected.

Gender, race, and social class are not the only systems of oppression, but they do profoundly affect women and people of color in the United States. Other forms of categorization and stigmatization can also be included in this matrix. If we turn to the global stage, we can add citizenship status and being perceived as a "colonial subject" even long after colonialism has ended.

Critics argue that intersectionality is all about people who are obsessed with "identity politics" and who form alliances based on allegedly shared social groupings. Yet intersectionality is not so much about the identities themselves but rather about how society uses and abuses these identities to exclude some people and privilege others. Addressing exclusion and acknowledging privilege are not easy and call for change, as noted in the previous section (Crenshaw 2015).

Feminists have addressed themselves to the needs of minority women, but the oppression of these women because of their sex is overshadowed by the subordinate status that White men and White women impose on them because of their race or ethnicity. The question for the Latina (Hispanic woman), African American woman, Asian American woman, Native American woman, and so on appears to be whether she should unify with her brothers against racism or

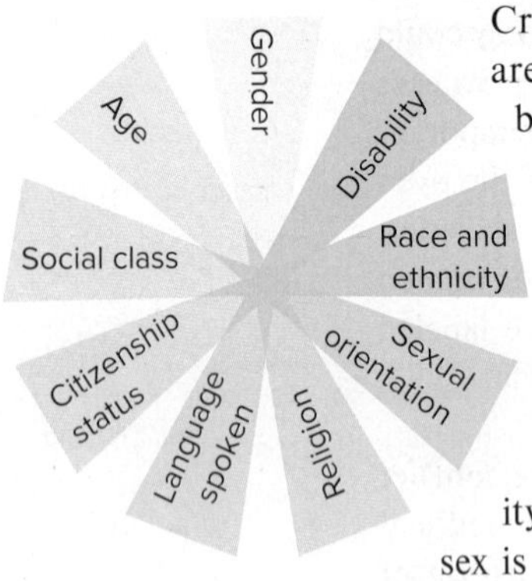

Figure 7–1

Matrix of Domination

Intersectionality illustrates how several social factors—including gender, social class, language spoken, and race and ethnicity—intersect and overlap to create a cumulative impact on a person's social standing.

> **Think About It**
> What are the implications of the matrix of domination for an immigrant woman from Central America? For an immigrant man from Syria?

challenge them for their sexism. The answer is that society cannot afford to let up on the effort to eradicate sexism, racism, and the other forces that create social inequality.

THE INTERACTIONIST PERSPECTIVE

While functionalists and conflict theorists who study gender distinctions typically focus on macro-level social forces and institutions, interactionist researchers tend to examine gender stratification on the micro level of everyday behavior. The key to this approach is the way gender is socially constructed in everyday interactions. We "do gender" by reinforcing traditionally masculine and feminine actions. For example, a man "does masculinity" by opening a door for his girlfriend; she "does femininity" by consenting to his assistance. Obviously, the social construction of gender goes beyond these relatively trivial rituals. Interactionists recognize, too, that people can challenge traditional gender roles. A female golfer who uses the "men's tees" and a man who actively arranges a birthday luncheon at work are redoing gender (Deutsch 2007; West and Zimmerman 1987).

One continuing subject of investigation is the role of gender in cross-sex conversations (sometimes referred to as "crosstalk"), specifically the idea that men interrupt women more than women interrupt men. Interestingly, empirical research does not clearly support this assertion. True, people in positions of authority or status—who are much more likely to be male than female—do dominate interpersonal conversations. That does not necessarily mean that women per se cannot be heard, however. Future research results may deemphasize the cliched advice that women must speak up in favor of a focus on the situational structures that cast men in dominant positions (Tannen 1990; Weatherall 2015).

Table 7-2 summarizes the major sociological perspectives on gender.

Use Your Sociological Imagination

Which elements of the matrix of domination privilege you? Which place you at a disadvantage?

Tracking Perspectives

Table 7-2 Sociological Perspectives on Gender	
Theoretical Perspective	**Emphasis**
Functionalist	Gender differentiation contributes to social stability
Conflict	Gender inequality is rooted in the female–male power relationship
Feminist	Women's subjugation is integral to society and social structure
Interactionist	Gender distinctions and doing gender are reflected in people's everyday behavior

Women: The Oppressed Majority

Many people, both male and female, find it difficult to conceive of women as a subordinate and oppressed group. Yet take a look at the political structure of the United States: women remain noticeably underrepresented. Women in the United States constitute 53 percent of the voting population and 49 percent of the labor force but only 8 percent of those who hold high government positions. As of the beginning of 2017, Congress included only 104 women (out of 435 members) in the House of Representatives and only 21 women (out of 100 members) in the Senate. The number of women serving in Congress has steadily increased. However, only four states—New Mexico, Oklahoma, Oregon, and Rhode Island—had a woman governor at the beginning of 2017.

SEXISM AND SEX DISCRIMINATION

Just as African Americans are victimized by racism, women suffer from sexism in our society. *Sexism* is the ideology that one sex is superior to the other. The term is generally used to refer to male prejudice and discrimination against women. In Chapter 6 we noted that Blacks can suffer from both individual acts of racism and institutional discrimination. *Institutional discrimination* was defined as the denial of opportunities and equal rights to individuals or groups that results from the normal operations of a society. In the same sense, women suffer from both individual acts of sexism (such as sexist remarks or acts of violence) and institutional sexism.

It is not simply that particular men in the United States are biased in their treatment of women. All the major institutions of our society—the government, the armed forces, large corporations, the media, universities, and the medical establishment—are controlled by men. In their "normal," day-to-day operations, these institutions often discriminate against women, perpetuating sexism. For example, if the central office of a nationwide bank sets a policy that single women are a bad risk for loans—regardless of their incomes and investments—the bank will discriminate against women in state after state. It will do so even at branches in which loan officers hold no personal biases concerning women but are merely "following orders."

Our society is run by male-dominated institutions, yet with the power that flows to men come responsibility and stress. Men have higher reported rates of certain types of mental illness than women do and a greater likelihood of death from heart attack or stroke. The pressure on men to succeed, and then to remain on top in the competitive world of work, can be especially intense. That is not to suggest that gender stratification is as damaging to men as it is to women. But the power and privilege men enjoy are no guarantee of personal well-being.

Think of organizations or institutions you belong to whose leadership positions are customarily held by men. What would those organizations be like if they were led by women?

THE STATUS OF WOMEN WORLDWIDE

According to a detailed overview of the status of the world's women, issued by the World Bank in 2012, the lives of girls and women have changed dramatically over the past quarter century. Progress has been limited in some respects, however. In many parts of the world, women still lag far behind men in their earnings and in their ability to speak out politically (World Bank 2015c).

This critique applies to Western as well as non-Western countries. Although Westerners tend to view some societies—for example, Muslim countries—as being particularly harsh toward women, that perception is actually an overgeneralization. Muslim countries are exceedingly varied and complex and do not often fit the stereotypes created by the Western media.

Regardless of culture, however, women everywhere suffer from second-class status. It is estimated that women grow half the world's food, but they rarely own land. They constitute one-third of the world's paid labor force, but are generally found in the lowest-paying jobs. Single-parent households headed by women, which appear to be on the rise in many nations, are typically found in the poorest sections of the population. The feminization of poverty has become a global phenomenon. As in the United States, women around the world are underrepresented politically.

Despite these challenges, women are not responding passively; they are mobilizing, individually and collectively. Given the significant under-representation of women in government offices and national legislatures, however, the task is difficult.

In industrialized countries, women's unequal status can be seen in the division of housework as well as in the jobs they hold and the pay they earn. Sociologist Jan Paul Heisig analyzed gender inequality among the rich (the top 10 percent in income) and the poor (the bottom 10 percent) in 33 industrialized countries. Typically, poor men did more housework than rich men, but rich or poor, men did much less housework than women. The recent economic recession accentuated this unequal division of housework. Obviously, being unemployed leaves both men and women with more time for household chores. However, unemployed women do double the amount of extra housework as unemployed men (Gough and Killewald 2011).

Women in the Workforce of the United States

More than 35 years ago, the Commission on Civil Rights (1976:1) con-cluded that the passage in the Declaration of Independence proclaiming that "all men are created equal" had been taken too literally for too long. That is especially true with respect to opportunities for employment. In this section we will see how gender bias has limited women's opportu-nities for employment outside the home, at the same time that it forces them to carry a disproportionate burden inside the home.

LABOR FORCE PARTICIPATION

Women's participation in the paid labor force of the United States increased steadily throughout the 20th century and into the 21st century. Today, millions of women—married or single, with or without children, pregnant or recently having given birth—are working in the labor force. Overall, 57 percent of adult women in the United States were in the labor force in 2014, compared to 41 percent in 1970. For men, the data were 69 percent in 2015, compared to 76 percent in 1970 (Bureau of Labor Statistics 2015; Bureau of the Census 2011a:377).

Still, women entering the job market find their options restricted in important ways. Women are *underrepresented* in occupations historically defined as "men's jobs," which often carry much greater financial rewards and prestige than women's jobs (see Table 7–3).

Women from all groups and men from minority groups sometimes encounter attitudinal or organizational bias that prevents them from reaching their full potential. As we saw in Chapter 6, the term *glass ceiling* refers to an invisible barrier that blocks the promotion of a qualified individual in a work environment because of the individual's gender, race, or ethnicity. Women are doing better at achieving top management positions than racial minorities are, but they still lag far behind men.

Table 7–3 U.S. Women in Selected Occupations: Women as a Percentage of All Workers in the Occupation

Underrepresented		Overrepresented	
Firefighters	8%	High school teachers	59%
Aircraft pilots and engineers	9	Flight attendants	75
Civil engineers	13	Travel agents	76
Police officers	14	Elementary school teachers	81
Chefs and head cooks	20	Social workers	84
Clergy	21	Bank tellers	82
Dentists	26	Librarians	83
Computer systems analysts	34	Registered nurses	89
Lawyers	35	Receptionists	91
Athletes, coaches, and umpires	36	Word processors	92
Physicians	38	Child care workers	95
Postal service mail carriers	41	Dental hygienists	96

NOTE: Women constituted 47 percent of the labor force age 16 and over.

SOURCE: Data for 2015 reported in Bureau of Labor Statistics 2016a.

Considering the top 500 companies listed on the S&P stock index as of March 1, 2017, women accounted for

- 5.8 percent of all CEOs
- 9.5 percent of top earners
- 44.9 percent of total employees

Among top business leaders, 29 are women. They include the heads of General Motors, Hershey, Mattel, Yahoo!, PepsiCo, and Hewlett-Packard. While that is impressive, it still means 471 of the top corporations are led by men (Catalyst 2017a, 2017b).

When women do gain entry to corporate boards of directors, the response in the financial world is not entirely positive. Despite objective tests showing that gender diversity in leadership is associated with strong financial performance, some investors tend to balk. Research by Frank Dobbin and Jiwook Jung (2011) shows that small investors tend to sell their shares when women become corporate leaders. These investors seem to subscribe to the stereotype that associates males with success. Their sell pattern is not characteristic of large institutional investors, who have long argued that diversification is good for business.

This type of inequality is not unique to the United States. Worldwide, women hold less than 1 percent of corporate managerial positions. In recognition of the underrepresentation of women on boards of directors, the Norwegian legislature established minimum quotas for the number of female board members. As the architects of the plan put it, "instead of assuming what people *can't* do at work, provide opportunities for employees to prove what they can do." The goal was not complete equity for women, but 40 percent representation by 2008. By 2012 the percentage stood at 18 percent (European PWN 2012).

THE SOCIAL CONSEQUENCES OF WOMEN'S EMPLOYMENT

Today, many women face the challenge of trying to juggle work and family. Their situation has many social consequences. For one thing, it puts pressure on child care facilities, public financing of day care, and even the fast-food industry, which provides many of the meals women used to prepare themselves. For another, it raises questions about what responsibility male wage earners have in the household.

Who does the housework when women become productive wage earners? Studies indicate that there is a clear gender gap in the performance of housework, although the differences are narrowing. Women do more housework and spend more time on child care than men, whether on a workday or a nonworkday. Taken together, then, a woman's workday on and off the job is much longer than a man's (Sayer et al. 2004).

Sociologist Arlie Hochschild (1989, 2016) has used the phrase *second shift* to describe the double burden—work outside the home, followed by

Use Your Sociological Imagination

In your opinion, how important is it for a couple to share the housework?

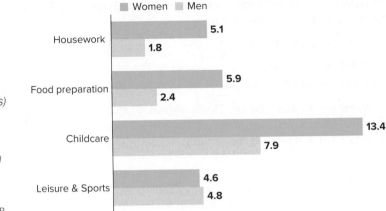

Figure 7–2

Weekly Time (in Hours) Spent on Primary Activities, by Gender

NOTE: *Data for 2015 in households where a child under 6 is present and parents are employed.*

SOURCE: Bureau of Labor Statistics 2016b: Table 8B.

child care and housework—that many women face and few men share equitably. Unfortunately, today's workplace is becoming a 24/7 virtual office thanks to the advent of mobile information technologies. As these devices take over what little personal time employees have left, the physical toll on women becomes even more burdensome.

The second shift persists, and men have not picked up much of the work traditionally performed by women. While fathers have gradually taken on more child care responsibilities, there is still a clear division within the home in how couples divide work and chores. Annually the Department of Labor interviews nearly 12,000 individuals to find out how they spend their time, not only at work but also at home and at leisure. The data are collected for both weekdays and weekends. As Figure 7–2 shows, men and women spend their time differently.

These time use surveys, which have been done since 2003, show that today both men and women spend less time directly on housework and child care than in the past, instead relying more on outside help, both paid and unpaid, for these tasks. Another trend is that while more men today do some child care than they did in the past, the significant gap in number of hours per week that men and women spend caring for children remains (Bureau of Labor Statistics 2004, 2016).

Sociology Matters

Sociology matters because it explains how we come to be feminine or masculine.

- What was your childhood idea of how a person of your gender should behave, and where did you get it? Did you ever feel confined by the gender roles you learned as a child? In what ways?

- Has your concept of your gender role changed over time? If so, who or what influenced you to change your thinking and behavior? Will your children learn the same gender roles as you? Why or why not?

Sociology matters because it raises our awareness of the unequal treatment of women and men.

- Have you and a friend ever been treated differently because one of you was male and the other was female? If so, did you resent the unequal treatment? Can you think of a way to change it?
- Do you believe men and women will ever be equal? Why or why not?

Sociology matters because it highlights the many different social statuses that affect men's and women's lives.

- Have you begun to pay more attention to the ways in which gender, social class, and even citizenship status affect people's lives?
- Which statuses have the biggest effect on those who are closest to you?

CHAPTER RESOURCES

Summary

Like race and ethnicity, gender has an enormous influence on people's lives. In this chapter we explained the cultural basis for gender and examined the ways in which gender defines a person's social roles. We discussed four theoretical perspectives on gender and studied the economic and social effects of prejudice and discrimination on women around the world.

1. Like race, gender is an ascribed status that is socially constructed. **Gender roles** show up in our work and behavior and in how we react to others. Throughout history, these roles have restricted women much more than they have men.

2. In the United States, **homophobia**—fear of and prejudice against homosexuality—contributes to rigid gender-role socialization. Family, peers, and the media reinforce gender-role stereotypes for both sexes.

3. Anthropological research points to the importance of cultural conditioning in defining the social roles of males and females.

4. Functionalists maintain that well-defined gender roles contribute to a society's stability. They stress the **instrumentality,** or emphasis on tasks, of the male role and the **expressiveness,** or emphasis on harmony, of the female role.

5. Conflict theorists stress men's dominance over women. They see women's inequality of income, wealth, prestige, and power as the result of men's deliberate subjugation of women.

6. Like conflict theorists, feminists stress the power struggle between the sexes. More than conflict theorists, they tend to see women's inequality as part of the exploitation inherent in capitalist societies.

7. Race and ethnicity as well as other social identifiers are important in defining relationships of power, but they do not exist in isolation. Rather, they coexist with religion, gender, age, disability status, and sexual identity (among other identities). **Intersectionality** refers to the system of advantage and disadvantage that positions people in society on the basis of these characteristics.

8. Interactionists stress that gender is socially constructed through people's everyday interactions. People "do gender" by reinforcing traditionally masculine and feminine behavior.

9. Women experience a special kind of prejudice known as sexism. They also suffer institutional discrimination in the form of lower pay and restricted opportunities.

10. Worldwide, women are undereducated, underpaid, and overworked. In the United States, women who work in the paid labor force are restricted by a **glass ceiling** that blocks their promotion to higher-paying jobs. These women commonly work a **second shift** when they get home.

Key Terms

expressiveness, 194	homophobia, 190	matrix of domination, 196
gender role, 189	instrumentality, 194	
glass ceiling, 200	intersectionality, 196	second shift, 201
		sexism, 198

Social Institutions: Family and Religion

©fstop123/Getty Images

Among the Nyinba people of Nepal and Tibet, a woman may be married to more than one man at a time, usually brothers. This system allows sons to share the limited amount of good land they may inherit. Among the Betsileo of Madagascar, a man has multiple wives, each one living in a different village where he cultivates rice. Wherever he has the best rice field, that wife is considered his first or senior wife. Among the Yanomami of Brazil and Venezuela, it is considered proper to have sexual relations with your opposite-sex cousins if they are the children of your mother's brother or your father's sister. But if your opposite-sex cousins are the children of your mother's sister or your father's brother, the same practice is considered to be incest. What can we learn from such varied patterns of family life? Though they may seem to defy generalization, sociologists have discovered that the stunning diversity of families around the world masks similarities in their social function (Haviland et al. 2015; Kelly 2012; Kottak 2015).

Similar observations may be made about the diversity of religion around the world. When we in the United States think of religion, a variety of images may spring to mind. We may picture a solemn prayer service in a small New England town, a passionate revival meeting in the Deep South, or a Hare Krishna group chanting on the streets of San Francisco. If we think of worldwide religious observances, we may imagine Islamic travelers on pilgrimage to Mecca, Orthodox Jews praying at Jerusalem's Western Wall, or an African tribe marking the birth of a child through ritual. Around the world, we find an amazing diversity in religion. Yet sociologists would stress the social functions that all religions perform.

Religion and the family are both **social institutions**—organized patterns of beliefs and behavior that are centered on basic social needs, such as replacing personnel (the family) and preserving order (the government). All societies have social institutions; they may be thought of as *cultural universals*—general practices found in every culture, such as sports, cooking, marriage, religious ritual, and sexual restrictions (see Chapter 2). The fact that all societies have these cultural universals is not surprising, for they meet our needs for food, clothing, and shelter as well as for support and reassurance, occupational training, and social order. In this chapter we will begin by considering social institutions from the three major sociological perspectives: functionalist, conflict, and interactionist. Then we will apply those perspectives to two major social institutions, the family and religion. We will also consider human sexuality, which is integral to the family's function of replacing personnel. In Chapter 9 we will extend the analysis to three more social institutions: education, government, and the economy (Murdock 1945).

Sociological Perspectives on Social Institutions

Though social institutions are fundamental to the well-being of any society, not all sociologists see them in the same way. Functionalists, as we will see, stress the basic needs that social institutions fulfill. But conflict theorists see social institutions such as the family and religion as mixed blessings—as sources of inequality and oppression as well as of nurturing and reassurance. Interactionists stress the ways in which social institutions help to define individuals' social roles and statuses.

FUNCTIONALIST PERSPECTIVE

One way to study social institutions is to examine how they fulfill essential functions. To survive, any society or relatively permanent group must accomplish five major tasks, or functional prerequisites (see Table 8–1).

1. *Replacing personnel.* Any group or society must replace personnel when they die, leave, or become incapacitated. This function is accomplished through such means as immigration, annexation of neighboring groups, acquisition of slaves, or sexual reproduction. The Shakers, a religious sect that came to the United States in 1774,

Functional Prerequisite	Related Social Institutions
Replacing personnel	Family Government (immigration)
Teaching new recruits	Family (basic skills) Economy (occupations) Education (schools) Mass media Religion (sacred teachings)
Producing and distributing goods and services	Family (food preparation) Economy Government (regulations regarding labor and commerce) Health care system
Preserving order	Family (childrearing, regulation of sexual behavior) Government Religion (morals)
Providing and maintaining a sense of purpose	Government (patriotism) Religion

Table 8–1 Five Major Functions of Institutions

summing UP

are a conspicuous example of a group that has *failed* to replace personnel. Their religious beliefs commit the Shakers to celibacy; to survive, the group must recruit new members. At first, the Shakers proved quite successful in attracting members, reaching a peak of about 64,000 in the 1840s. As of 2017, however, the only remaining Shaker community was a farm in Maine with two members—a sixty-year-old man and a seventy-eight-year old woman (*The Economist* 2017; Schaefer and Zellner 2015).

2. *Teaching new recruits.* No group or society can survive if many of its members reject the established behavior and responsibilities. Thus, finding or producing new members is not sufficient. The group or society must encourage recruits to learn and accept its values and customs. Such learning can take place formally in schools (where learning is a manifest function) or informally, through interaction and negotiation in peer groups (where learning is a latent function).

3. *Producing and distributing goods and services.* Any relatively permanent group or society must provide and distribute desired goods and services to its members. Each society establishes a set of rules for the allocation of financial and other resources. These rules must satisfy the needs of most members to some extent, or the society will risk the possibility of discontent and ultimately disorder.

4. *Preserving order.* Throughout the world, indigenous and aboriginal peoples have struggled to protect themselves from outside invaders,

with varying degrees of success. Failure to preserve order and defend against conquest leads to the death not only of a people but of a culture as well.

5. *Providing and maintaining a sense of purpose.* In order to fulfill the first four requirements, people must feel motivated to continue as members of a group or society. Patriotism, tribal identities, religious values, or personal moral codes can help people to develop and maintain such a sense of purpose. Whatever the motivator, in any society there remains one common and critical reality: if an individual does not have a sense of purpose, he or she has little reason to contribute to a society's survival.

This list of functional prerequisites does not specify *how* a society and its corresponding social institutions should perform each task. For example, one society may protect itself from external attack by amassing a frightening arsenal of weaponry, while another may make a determined effort to remain neutral in world politics and to promote cooperative relationships with its neighbors. No matter what the strategy, any society or relatively permanent group must attempt to satisfy all these functional prerequisites for survival. If a society fails on even one condition, it runs the risk of extinction (Aberle et al. 1950; Mack and Bradford 1979).

CONFLICT PERSPECTIVE

Conflict theorists do not concur with the functionalist approach to social institutions. Although theorists of both perspectives agree that institutions are organized to meet basic social needs, conflict theorists object to the implication that the outcome is necessarily efficient and desirable.

From a conflict perspective, the present organization of social institutions is no accident. Major institutions, such as education, help to maintain the privileges of the most powerful individuals and groups in a society, while contributing to the powerlessness of others. To give one example, public schools in the United States are financed largely through property taxes, an arrangement that allows people from more affluent areas to provide their children with better-equipped schools and better-paid teachers than people from low-income areas can provide. As a result, children from prosperous communities are better prepared to compete academically than children from impoverished communities. The structure of the nation's educational system permits and even promotes such unequal treatment of schoolchildren.

Conflict theorists argue that social institutions such as education are inherently conservative. Without question, it has been difficult to implement educational reforms that promote equal opportunity—whether bilingual education, school desegregation, or mainstreaming of students with disabilities. From a functionalist perspective, social change can be dysfunctional, since it often leads to instability. But from a conflict view, why should we preserve the existing social structure if it is unfair and discriminatory?

Social institutions also operate in gendered and racist environments, as conflict theorists, as well as feminists and interactionists, have pointed out. In schools, offices, and government institutions, assumptions about what people can do reflect the sexism and racism of the larger society. For instance, many people assume that women cannot make tough decisions—even those in the top echelons of corporate management. Others assume that all Black students at elite colleges represent affirmative action admissions. Inequality based on gender, economic status, race, and ethnicity thrives in such an environment—to which we might add discrimination based on age, physical disability, and sexual orientation. The truth of this assertion can be seen in routine decisions by employers on how to advertise jobs as well as whether to provide fringe benefits such as child care and parental leave.

INTERACTIONIST PERSPECTIVE

Social institutions affect our everyday behavior, whether we are driving down the street or waiting in a long shopping line. Sociologist Mitchell Duneier (1994a, 1994b) studied the social behavior of the word processors, all women, who work in the service center of a large Chicago law firm. Duneier was interested in the informal social norms that emerged in this work environment and the rich social network that the female employees had created.

The Network Center, as it is called, is a single, windowless room in a large office building where the law firm occupies seven floors. The center is staffed by two shifts of word processors, who work either from 4:00 P.M. to midnight or from midnight to 8:00 A.M. Each word processor works in a cubicle with just enough room for her keyboard, terminal, printer, and telephone. Work assignments for the word processors are placed in a central basket and completed according to precise procedures.

At first glance, we might think that these women labor with little social contact, apart from limited work breaks and occasional conversations with their supervisor. However, drawing on the interactionist perspective, Duneier learned that despite working in a large office, these women found private moments to talk (often in the halls or outside the washroom) and share a critical view of the law firm's attorneys and daytime secretaries. Indeed, the word processors routinely suggested that their assignments represented work that the "lazy" secretaries should have completed during the normal workday. One word processor in particular resented the lawyers' superior attitude and pointedly refused to recognize or speak with any attorney who would not address her by name (Duneier 1994b).

Interactionist theorists emphasize that our social behavior is conditioned by the roles and statuses we accept, the groups we belong to,

How would a functionalist, a conflict theorist, and an interactionist view your college as a social institution?

Table 8–2 Sociological Perspectives on Social Institutions

Perspective	Role of Social Institutions	Focus
Functionalist	Meeting basic social needs	Essential functions
Conflict	Meeting basic social needs	Maintenance of privileges and inequality
Interactionist	Fostering everyday behavior	Influence of the roles and statuses we accept

and the institutions within which we function. For example, the social roles associated with being a judge occur within the larger context of the criminal justice system. The status of "judge" stands in relation to other statuses, such as attorney, plaintiff, defendant, and witness, as well as to the social institution of government. Although courts and jails have great symbolic importance, the judicial system derives its continued significance from the roles people carry out in their social interactions (Berger and Luckmann 1966).

Table 8-2 summarizes the three major sociological perspectives on social institutions.

The Family: A Global View

As we saw at the beginning of this chapter, there are many variations in "the family" from one culture to the next. Yet the family as a social institution exists in all cultures. Moreover, certain general principles concerning its composition, kinship patterns, and authority patterns are universal.

COMPOSITION: WHAT IS THE FAMILY?

A *family* may be defined as a set of people who are related by blood, marriage (or some other agreed-upon relationship), or adoption who share the primary responsibility for reproduction and caring for members of society. If we were to take our information on what a family is from what we see on television, we might come up with some strange scenarios. The media don't always present a realistic view of the family. Moreover, many people still think of the family in very narrow terms—as a married couple and their unmarried children living together. However, that is but one type of family, what sociologists refer to as a *nuclear family*. The term *nuclear family* is well chosen, since this type of family serves as the nucleus, or core, on which larger family groups are built.

Most people in the United States see the nuclear family as the preferred family arrangement. Yet as long ago as 2000, only about a third of the nation's family households fit this model. The proportion of households in the United States composed of married couples with children at home has decreased steadily over the last 50 years and is expected to

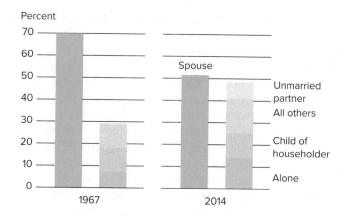

Percent

Figure 8–1

Living Arrangements
of Adults Age 18 and
Over, 2014

NOTE: "All others" includes
adults who live with a parent, roommate, sibling,
foster child, or grandchild.

SOURCE: Bureau of the Census 2015d:Figure AD-3a.

continue shrinking. At the same time, the number of single-parent house-holds has increased (see Figure 8-1).

A family in which relatives—such as grandparents, aunts, or uncles—live in the same home as parents and their children is known as an *extended family.* Although not common, such living arrangements do exist in the United States. The structure of the extended family offers certain advan-tages over that of the nuclear family. Crises such as death, divorce, and ill-ness put less strain on family members, since there are more people who can provide assistance and emotional support. In addition, the extended family constitutes a larger economic unit than the nuclear family. If the family is engaged in a common enterprise—a farm or small business—the additional family members may represent the difference between prosper-ity and failure.

In considering these differing family types, we have limited our-selves to the form of marriage that is characteristic of the United States—monogamy. The term *monogamy* describes a form of marriage in which one woman and one man are married only to each other. Some observers, noting the high rate of divorce in the United States, have suggested that "serial monogamy" is a more accurate description of the form that monogamy takes in the United States. In *serial monog-amy,* a person may have several spouses in his or her life, but only one spouse at a time.

Serial monogamy is certainly more common today than it was a century ago due to a greater incidence and acceptance of divorce. In the United States and many other countries, divorce began to increase in the late 1960s but then leveled off; since the late 1980s, it has declined by 30 percent. This trend is due partly to the aging of the baby boomer popu-lation and the corresponding decline in the proportion of people of mar-riageable age. However, it also indicates an increase in marital stability in recent years (Coontz 2006).

Some cultures allow an individual to have several husbands or wives simultaneously. This form of marriage is known as *polygamy.* In fact,

Use Your
Sociological Imagination

In a society that maximizes the welfare of all family members, how easy should it be for couples to divorce? How easy should it be to get married?

most societies throughout the world, past and present, have preferred polygamy to monogamy. Anthropologist George Murdock (1949, 1957) sampled 565 societies and found that some type of polygamy was the preferred form in more than 80 percent. While polygamy declined steadily through most of the 20th century and into the 21st, in at least five African nations 20 percent or more of the men are still living in polygamous unions (Population Reference Bureau 1996).

There are two basic types of polygamy. According to Murdock, the most common—endorsed by the majority of cultures he sampled—was *polygyny,* in which a husband may have several wives at the same time. The wives are often sisters, who are expected to hold similar values and to have experience sharing a household. In polygynous societies, relatively few men have multiple spouses. Most individuals live in monogamous families; having multiple wives is viewed as a mark of status.

The other principal variation of polygamy is *polyandry,* in which a woman may have several husbands at the same time. Such is the case in Tibet, as we saw in the chapter opening. Polyandry, however, is exceedingly rare. It is accepted in some extremely poor societies that practice female infanticide (the killing of baby girls) and thus have a relatively small number of women. Like many other societies, polyandrous cultures devalue the social worth of women (Zeitzen 2008).

KINSHIP PATTERNS: TO WHOM ARE WE RELATED?

Many of us can trace our roots by looking at a family tree or listening to our elders talk about their lives—and the lives of ancestors who died long before we were born. Yet a person's lineage is more than a personal history; it reflects societal patterns that govern descent. In every culture, children encounter relatives to whom they are expected to show an emotional attachment. This state of being related to others is called *kinship.* Kinship is culturally learned, rather than being totally determined by biological or marital ties. For example, adoption creates a kinship tie that is legally acknowledged and socially accepted.

The family and the kin group are not necessarily one and the same. The family is a household unit, but kin do not always live together or function as a collective body on a daily basis. Kin groups include aunts, uncles, cousins, in-laws, and so forth. In a society such as the United States, the kinship group may come together only rarely, usually for a wedding or funeral. However, kinship ties frequently create obligations and responsibilities. We may feel compelled to assist our kin, and we feel free to call upon relatives for many types of aid, including loans and babysitting.

How do we identify kinship groups? The principle of descent assigns people to kinship groups according to their relationship to their mother or father. There are three primary ways of determining descent. The United States follows the system of *bilateral descent,* in which both sides of a person's family are regarded as equally important. For example, no higher value is given to the brothers of one's father than to the brothers of one's mother.

Most societies—according to George Murdock, 64 percent—favor one side of the family or the other in tracing descent. *Patrilineal* (from Latin *pater,* "father") *descent* favors the father's relatives in terms of property, inheritance, and emotional ties. *Matrilineal* (from Latin *mater,* "mother") *descent* favors the mother's relatives.

New forms of reproductive technology will soon force a new way of looking at kinship. Today, a combination of biological and social processes can "create" a family member, requiring that more distinctions be made about who is related to whom.

In your own family, which relatives do you have a significant relationship with? Which do you hardly ever see? Explain the reasons for the difference in relationships.

AUTHORITY PATTERNS: WHO RULES?

Imagine that you have recently married and must begin to make decisions about the future of your new family. You and your spouse face many questions. Where will you live? How will you furnish your home? Who will do the cooking, the shopping, the cleaning? Whose friends will be invited to dinner? Each time a decision must be made, an issue is raised: Who has the power to make the decision? In simple terms, who rules the family? Conflict theorists examine these questions in the context of traditional gender distinctions, which have given men a dominant position over women.

Societies vary in the way that power is distributed within the family. If a society expects men to dominate in family decision making, it is termed a *patriarchy.* In patriarchal societies such as Iran, the eldest male frequently wields the greatest power, although wives are expected to be treated with respect and kindness. An Iranian woman's status is typically defined by her relationship to a male relative, usually as a wife or daughter. In many patriarchal societies, women find it more difficult to obtain a divorce than a man does. By contrast, in a *matriarchy,* women dominate in family decision making. Matriarchies are rare; they emerged among Native American tribal societies and in nations where men were absent for long periods, for warfare or food gathering expeditions (Farr 1999).

In a third type of authority pattern, the *egalitarian family,* spouses are regarded as equals. This pattern does not mean that each decision is shared, however. Wives may hold authority in some spheres, husbands in others. Many sociologists believe the egalitarian family has begun to replace the patriarchal family as the social norm in the United States.

Clearly, there is great variation in the composition, kinship patterns, and authority patterns of families around the world. Yet as we have seen, the family fulfills certain universal social functions. In the next section we will examine those functions from three different sociological perspectives.

Sociological Perspectives on the Family

Do we really need the family? A century ago, Friedrich Engels ([1884] 1959), a colleague of Karl Marx, described the family as the ultimate source of social inequality because of its role in the transfer of power, property, and privilege. More recently, conflict theorists have argued that the family contributes to societal injustice, denies women opportunities that are extended to men, and limits freedom in sexual expression and mate selection. In contrast, the functionalist perspective focuses on the ways in which the family gratifies the needs of its members and contributes to social stability. The interactionist view considers the intimate, face-to-face relationships that occur in the family. And the feminist approach examines the role of the wife and mother, especially in the absence of an adult male.

FUNCTIONALIST PERSPECTIVE ON THE FAMILY

The family performs six major functions, first outlined nearly 80 years ago by sociologist William F. Ogburn (Ogburn and Tibbits 1934):

1. *Reproduction.* For a society to maintain itself, it must replace dying members. In this sense, the family contributes to human survival through its function of reproduction.

2. *Protection.* Unlike the young of other animal species, human infants need constant care and economic security. In all cultures, the family assumes the ultimate responsibility for the protection and upbringing of children.

3. *Socialization.* Parents and other kin monitor a child's behavior and transmit the norms, values, and language of their culture to the child.

4. *Regulation of sexual behavior.* Sexual norms are subject to change both over time (for instance, in the customs for dating) and across cultures (compare strict Saudi Arabia to the more permissive Denmark). Whatever the period or cultural values of a society, however, standards of sexual behavior are most clearly defined within the family circle.

5. *Affection and companionship.* Ideally, the family provides members with warm and intimate relationships, helping them to feel satisfied and secure. Of course, a family member may find such rewards outside the family—from peers, in school, at work—and may even perceive the home as an unpleasant or abusive setting. Nevertheless, we expect our relatives to understand us, to care for us, and to be there for us when we need them.

6. *Provision of social status.* We inherit a social position because of the family background and reputation of our parents and siblings. The family presents the newborn child with an ascribed status based on

race and ethnicity that helps to determine his or her place within society's stratification system. Moreover, family resources affect children's ability to pursue certain opportunities, such as higher education and special lessons.

Traditionally, the family has fulfilled a number of other functions, such as providing religious training, education, and recreation. But Ogburn argued that other social institutions have gradually assumed many of those functions. Education once took place by the family fireside; now it is the responsibility of professionals working in schools and colleges. Even the family's traditional recreational function has been transferred to outside groups such as Little Leagues, athletic clubs, and Twitter.

CONFLICT PERSPECTIVE ON THE FAMILY

Conflict theorists view the family not as a contributor to social stability but as a reflection of the inequality in wealth and power that is found within the larger society. Feminist and conflict theorists note that the family has traditionally legitimized and perpetuated male dominance. Throughout most of human history—and in a wide range of societies—husbands have exercised overwhelming power and authority in the family. Not until the first wave of contemporary feminism in the United States during the mid-1800s was a substantial challenge made to the historic status of wives and children as the legal property of husbands.

While the egalitarian family has become a more common pattern in the United States in recent decades—owing in good part to the activism of feminists beginning in the late 1960s and early 1970s—male dominance over the family has hardly disappeared. The number of fathers who are at home with their children for any reason has nearly doubled since 1989. It reached its highest point in 2010, just after the official end of the Great Recession. Since that time, the number has fallen slightly. Side by side with this trend is a continuing rapid increase in the number of fathers who do not live with the family, leaving all caretaking to the mother or other caregivers. Sociologists have found that while married men are increasing their involvement in child care, their wives still perform a disproportionate amount of it. Furthermore, for every stay-at-home dad there are five stay-at-home moms. And unfortunately, many husbands reinforce their power and control over wives and children through acts of domestic violence (Livingstone 2014a).

Conflict theorists also view the family as an economic unit that contributes to societal injustice. The family is the basis for transferring power, property, and privilege from one generation to the next. Although the United States is viewed widely as a land of opportunity, social mobility is restricted in important ways. Children inherit the privileged or less-than-privileged social and economic status of their parents (and in some cases, of earlier generations as well). As conflict theorists point out, the social class of parents significantly influences children's socialization experiences and the degree of protection they receive. Thus, the socioeconomic status of a child's family will have a marked influence on his or her nutrition, health care, housing, educational opportunities, and in many respects, life chances as an adult. For this reason, conflict theorists argue that the family helps to maintain inequality.

INTERACTIONIST PERSPECTIVE ON THE FAMILY

Interactionists focus on the micro level of family and other intimate relationships. They are interested in how individuals interact with one another, whether they are cohabiting partners or longtime married couples. For example, in a study of both Black and White two-parent households, researchers found that when fathers are more involved with their children (reading to them, helping them with homework, or restricting their television viewing), children have fewer behavior problems, get along better with others, and are more responsible (Mosley and Thomson 1995).

Another interactionist study might examine the role of the stepparent. The increased number of single parents who remarry has sparked interest in those who are helping to raise other people's children. Studies have found that stepmothers are more likely than stepfathers to accept the blame for bad relations with their stepchildren. Interactionists theorize that stepfathers (like most fathers) may simply be unaccustomed to interacting directly with children when the mother isn't there (Bastaits and Mortelmans 2014).

FEMINIST PERSPECTIVE ON THE FAMILY

Because "women's work" has traditionally focused on family life, feminist sociologists have taken a strong interest in the family as a social institution. As we saw in Chapter 7, research on gender roles in child care and household chores has been extensive. Sociologists have looked particularly closely at how women's work outside the home impacts their child care and housework—duties Arlie Hochschild (1990, 2005, 2012) has referred to as the "second shift." Today, researchers recognize that for many women, the second shift includes the care of aging parents as well.

Feminist theorists have urged social scientists and social agencies to rethink the notion that families in which no adult male is present are automatically a cause for concern, or even dysfunctional. They have also contributed to research on single women, single-parent households, and lesbian couples. In the case of single mothers, researchers have focused on the resiliency of many such households, despite economic stress. According to Velma McBride Murray and her colleagues (2001) at the University of Georgia, such studies show that among African Americans, single mothers draw heavily on kinfolk for material resources, parenting

Table 8–3 Sociological Perspectives on the Family	
Theoretical Perspective	**Emphasis**
Functionalist	The family as a contributor to social stability Roles of family members
Conflict	The family as a perpetuator of inequality Transmission of poverty or wealth across generations
Interactionist	Relationships among family members
Feminist	The family as a perpetuator of gender roles Female-headed households

Tracking Perspectives

Use Your Sociological Imagination

How would functionalist, conflict, interactionist, and feminist theorists explain a polygamous family structure?

advice, and social support. Considering feminist research on the family as a whole, one researcher concluded that the family is the "source of women's strength" (V. Taylor et al. 2009).

Finally, feminists who take the interactionist perspective stress the need to investigate neglected topics in family studies. For instance, in a growing number of dual-income households, the wife earns a higher income than the husband. In 1987, in families where both wives and husbands had earnings, women earned more than men in fewer than 18 percent of the households. That proportion has steadily grown to over 29 percent by 2013 (Bureau of Labor Statistics 2015f).

Table 8–3 summarizes the four major theoretical perspectives on the family.

Labeling and Human Sexuality

Gender roles are a very important part of how we interact in everyday life, but they do not actually define who we are or how we see ourselves. The relationship between gender roles and our self-identity is complex. As we have seen, gender roles involve cultural expectations that we learn through social interaction with other members of society.

GENDER AND HUMAN SEXUALITY

Related but different are gender identity and sexual identity. *Gender identity* refers to how people see themselves: as male or female or something else. This identity can be different from one's biological sex at birth, although most people develop a gender identity that conforms to that biological identity.

Sexual identity, also referred to as sexual orientation, is the self-awareness of being romantically or sexually attracted to a defined group of people. Typically, people become aware of their gender identity at a very young age, but a strong sexual identity may not emerge until well into adolescence.

218

CHAPTER 8: SOCIAL INSTITUTIONS: FAMILY AND RELIGION

What are some consequences for society as a whole of recognizing that sexual identity exists along a continuum?

Society's recognition that gender is not necessarily fixed at birth as either male or female and that individuals are not automatically heterosexual has emerged only in the last generation, perhaps, and even in the last 10 years. Today, online sites routinely include or solicit descriptions of almost any kind of human sexuality. Increasing numbers of jurisdictions around the world accept same-sex marriage on equal footing with traditional heterosexual marriage. In 2014, Facebook offered, instead of the original two choices of self-designation (male or female), 50 designations that users could choose for gender identity.

Despite this recognition in social media of a broadening of sexual identities, society is only just beginning to avoid stigmatizing people who do not conform to the either/or male/female paradigm. Until recently, these individuals have occupied a lower position in the social stratification hierarchy.

LABELING AND IDENTITY

We have seen how society singles out certain groups of people by labeling them in positive or negative ways—as "good kids" or "delinquents," for example. Labeling theorists have also studied how labels are used to sanction certain sexual behaviors as "deviant."

The definition of deviant sexual behavior has varied significantly over time and in different cultures. Until 1973, the American Psychiatric Association considered homosexuality a "sociopathic personality disorder," which in effect meant that homosexuals should seek therapy. Two years later, however, the association removed homosexuality from its list of mental illnesses. Today, the organization publicly proclaims that "being

©Harley Schwadron

gay is just as healthy as being straight." To use Goffman's term, mental health professionals have removed the *stigma* from this form of sexual expression. As a result, in the United States and many other countries, consensual sex between same-sex adults is no longer a crime (American Psychological Association 2008; OutRight Action International 2015).

Despite the change in health professionals' attitudes, however, the social stigma of homosexuality lingers. As a result, many people prefer the more positive terms *gay* and *lesbian*. Others, in defiance of the stigma, have proudly adopted the pejorative term *queer* in a deliberate reaction to the ridicule they have borne because of their sexual identity. Still others maintain that constructing one's sexual identity as either homosexual or heterosexual is too limiting. Indeed, such labels ignore those who are *bisexual*, or sexually attracted to both sexes.

Placing gays and lesbians on equal footing in the stratification system with heterosexuals is just one part of reducing stratification by sex. We are only just beginning to address the disadvantages involved in other sexual identities, such as transgender.

Many people find the male and female categories either too restrictive or inaccurate descriptions of how they identify. In the United States and many other societies, we are moving toward a gender spectrum where, while many people identify themselves as either male or female, many others see themselves as somewhere between these two traditional fixed categories. One such group is *transgender people*, or those whose current gender identity does not match their physical identity at birth. Some transgender people see themselves as both male and female. Others, called *transsexuals*, may take hormones or undergo surgery in an effort to draw physically closer to their chosen gender identity. Transgender people are sometimes confused with *transvestites*, or cross-dressers who wear the clothing of the opposite sex. Transvestites are typically men, either gay or heterosexual, who choose to wear women's clothing.

Transgender people have recently experienced both welcome respect and continuing stigmatization. In 2016, the Pentagon ended its ban of transgender troops in the military and announced that the armed forces would pay for gender-affirming transition surgery in accordance with accepted medical standards. In both the private and public sectors, efforts have been made to allow transgender people to use the bathrooms that correspond with their gender identity, yet some legislators have sought to require people to use bathrooms that match the sex on their original birth certificates, regardless of how they identify themselves.

The use of these terms even in a positive or nonjudgmental way is problematic, since they still imply that human sexuality can be confined in neat, mutually exclusive categories. Moreover, the destigmatization of these labels tends to reflect the influence of the socially privileged—that is, the affluent—who have the resources to overcome the stigma. In contrast, the traditional Native American concept of the *two spirit*, a personality that blends the masculine and the feminine, has been largely ridiculed or ignored (Gilley 2006; Wentling et al. 2008).

What does constitute sexual deviance, then? The broadening of sexual identities beyond the traditional heterosexual categories means that people may more openly express who they are sexually as well as engage in consensual relationships that in the past were considered wrong or even criminal. The answer to the question of what is deviance seems to change with each generation.

Religion as a Social Institution

According to Émile Durkheim ([1912] 2001), *religion* is a unified system of beliefs and practices relative to sacred things. As a cultural universal, religion plays a basic role that includes both manifest and latent social functions. Among its *manifest* (open and stated) functions, religion defines the spiritual world and gives meaning to the divine. Religion also provides an explanation for events that seem difficult to understand, such as what lies beyond the grave. In contrast, the *latent* functions of religion are unintended, covert, or hidden. Even though the manifest function of church services is to offer a forum for religious worship, they might at the same time fulfill a latent function as a meeting ground for unmarried members.

In this section we'll consider four functions that sociologists have stressed in their study of religion. We'll see that religion helps to integrate society and provides people with social support in time of need. We'll discuss Max Weber's view of religion as a source of social change. Finally, we'll examine the conflict perspective on religion as a means of social control. Note that for the most part, religion's impact is best understood from a macro-level viewpoint, oriented toward the larger society. The social support function is an exception: it is best viewed on the micro level, directed toward the individual.

THE INTEGRATIVE FUNCTION OF RELIGION

Émile Durkheim viewed religion as an integrative power in human society—a perspective that is reflected in functionalist thought today. Durkheim sought to answer a perplexing question: "How can human societies be held together when they are composed of individuals and social groups with diverse interests and aspirations?" In his view, religious bonds often transcend these personal and divisive forces. Durkheim acknowledged that religion is not the only integrative force; nationalism or patriotism may serve the same end.

How does religion provide this "societal glue"? Religion, whether it be Buddhism, Islam, Christianity, or Judaism (see Table 8-4), offers people meaning and purpose. It gives them certain ultimate values and ends to hold in common. Although those values and ends are subjective and

summing UP

Table 8–4 Major World Religions

Faith	Current Following, in Millions (and Percent of World Population)	Primary Location of Followers Today	Founder (and Approximate Birth Date)	Important Texts (and Holy Sites)
Buddhism	516 (7.1%)	Southeast Asia, Mongolia, Tibet	Gautama Siddhartha (563 B.C.)	Tripitaka (areas in Nepal)
Christianity	2,390 (33.0%)	Europe, North America, South America	Jesus (6 B.C.)	Bible (Jerusalem, Rome)
Hinduism	975 (13.5%)	India, Indian communities overseas	No specific founder (1500 B.C.)	Sruti and Smriti texts (seven sacred cities, including Varanasi)
Islam	1,674 (23.1%)	Middle East, Central Asia, North Africa, Indonesia	Muhammad (A.D. 570)	Qur'an or Koran (Mecca, Medina, Jerusalem)
Judaism	14 (0.2%)	Israel, United States, France, Russia	Abraham (2000 B.C.)	Torah, Talmud (Jerusalem)

SOURCES: C. Adams 2015 at Britannica Online; Swatos 1998. Data as of mid-2014.

not always fully accepted, they help society to function as an integrated social system. For example, funerals, weddings, bar and bat mitzvahs, and confirmations serve to integrate people into larger communities through shared beliefs and values about the ultimate questions of life.

The integrative power of religion can be seen, too, in the role that churches, synagogues, and mosques have traditionally played and continue to play for immigrant groups in the United States. For example, Roman Catholic immigrants may settle near a parish church that offers services in their native language, such as Polish or Spanish. Similarly, Korean immigrants may join a Presbyterian church with many Korean American members and with religious practices like those of churches in Korea. Like other religious organizations, these Roman Catholic and Presbyterian churches help to integrate immigrants into their new homeland.

RELIGION AND SOCIAL SUPPORT

Most of us find it difficult to accept the stressful events of life—the death of a loved one, a serious injury, bankruptcy, divorce, and so forth. Our difficulty is especially pronounced when something "senseless" happens. How can family and friends come to terms with the death of a talented college student, not even 20 years old?

Use Your Sociological Imagination

What evidence do you see of different religions in the area surrounding your college or university? What about on campus?

Through its emphasis on the divine and the supernatural, religion allows us to "do something" about the calamities we face. In some faiths, adherents can offer sacrifices or pray to a deity in the belief that such acts will change their earthly condition. At a more basic level, religion encourages us to view our personal misfortunes as relatively unimportant in the broader perspective of human history—or even as part of an undisclosed divine purpose. Friends and relatives of the deceased college student may see his death as being "God's will," as having some ultimate benefit that we cannot understand now. This perspective may be much more comforting than the terrifying feeling that any of us can die senselessly at any moment—that there is no divine "answer" to why one person lives a long and full life, while another dies tragically at a relatively early age.

RELIGION AND SOCIAL CHANGE

When a person seems driven to work and succeed, we often attribute his or her ambition to the "Protestant work ethic." The term comes from the writings of Max Weber, who carefully examined the connection between religious allegiance and capitalist development. Weber's findings appeared in his pioneering work *The Protestant Ethic and the Spirit of Capitalism* ([1904] 2009).

Weber noted that in European nations with both Protestant and Catholic citizens, an overwhelming number of business leaders, owners of capital, and skilled workers were Protestant. In his view, this pattern was no mere coincidence. Weber pointed out that the followers of John Calvin (1509–1564), a leader of the Protestant Reformation, emphasized a disciplined work ethic, this-worldly concerns, and a rational orientation to life that he termed the ***Protestant ethic.*** One by-product of the Protestant ethic was a drive to accumulate savings that could be used for future investment. This "spirit of capitalism," to use Weber's phrase, contrasted with the moderate work hours, leisurely work habits, and lack of ambition that he saw as typical of the times.

Few books on the sociology of religion have aroused as much commentary and criticism as Weber's work. It has been hailed as one of the most important theoretical works in the field and an excellent example of macro-level analysis. Like Durkheim, Weber demonstrated that religion is not solely a matter of intimate personal belief. Rather, the collective nature of religion has social consequences for society as a whole. Indeed, a recent analysis of historical economic data shows that the Protestant ethic was an important factor in the growth of capitalism from 1500 through 1870 (Sanderson et al. 2011).

Weber provided a convincing description of the origins of European capitalism. But the capitalist economic system has since been adopted by non-Calvinists in many parts of the world. Contemporary studies done in the United States show little or no difference in achievement orientation between Roman Catholics and Protestants. Apparently, the "spirit of capitalism" has become a generalized cultural trait (Greeley 1989).

Conflict theorists caution that Weber's theory—even if it is accepted—should not be regarded as applicable to mature capitalism, as reflected in the rise of multinational corporations. Marxists would disagree with Weber, not on the origins of capitalism, but on its future. Unlike Marx, Weber believed that capitalism could endure indefinitely as an economic system. He added, however, that the decline of religion as an overriding force in society opened the way for workers to express their discontent more vocally (R. Collins 1980).

RELIGION AND SOCIAL CONTROL: A CONFLICT PERSPECTIVE

Karl Marx ([1844] 1964) thought that religion *impeded* social change by encouraging oppressed people to focus on other worldly concerns rather than on their immediate poverty or exploitation. Marx described religion as an "opiate" that was particularly harmful to oppressed peoples. He felt that religion often drugged the masses into submission by offering a consolation for their harsh lives on earth: the hope of salvation in an ideal afterlife. For example, during the period of slavery in the United States, White masters forbade Blacks to practice native African religions. Instead, they encouraged them to adopt Christianity, which taught that obedience would lead to salvation and eternal happiness. Viewed from a conflict perspective, Christianity may have pacified certain slaves and blunted the rage that often fuels rebellion.

Today, however, people around the world see religion more as a source of support through adversity than a source of oppression. In a combination of public opinion polls taken across 114 nations, 95 percent of those living in the poorest nations felt that religion was important in daily life, compared to only 47 percent of those in the wealthiest countries (Crabtree 2010).

Religion does play an important role in propping up the existing social structure. Religious values, as already noted, reinforce other social institutions and the social order as a whole. From Marx's perspective, however, religion's promotion of social stability only helps to perpetuate patterns of social inequality. According to Marx, the dominant religion reinforces the interests of those in power.

For example, contemporary Christianity reinforces traditional patterns of behavior that call for the subordination of the less powerful. The role of women in the church is an example of uneven distribution of power. Assumptions about gender roles leave women in a subservient position both within Christian churches and at home. In fact, women find it as difficult to achieve leadership positions in many churches as they do in large corporations. A "stained glass ceiling" tends to stunt clergywomen's career development, even in the most liberal denominations.

Use Your Sociological Imagination

The social support that religious groups provide is suddenly withdrawn from your community. How will your life or the lives of others change? What will happen if religious groups stop pushing for social change?

Like Marx, conflict theorists argue that to whatever extent religion actually does influence social behavior, it reinforces existing patterns of dominance and inequality. From a Marxist perspective, religion keeps people from seeing their lives and societal conditions in political terms—for example, by obscuring the overriding significance of conflicting economic interests. Marxists suggest that by inducing a "false consciousness" among the disadvantaged, religion lessens the possibility of collective political action that could end capitalist oppression and transform society.

Religion is not the only social institution whose functions have been the subject of controversy among theorists. Conflict theorists charge that schools, too, discriminate in favor of the powerful and against the disadvantaged, as we will see in Chapter 9.

FEMINIST PERSPECTIVE ON RELIGION

Drawing on the feminist approach, researchers and theorists have stressed the fundamental role women play in religious socialization. Most people develop their allegiance to a particular faith in their childhood, with their mothers playing a critical role in the process. Significantly, nonworshiping mothers tend to influence their children to be highly skeptical of organized religion.

However, women generally take a subordinate role in religious governance. Indeed, most faiths have a long tradition of exclusively male spiritual leadership. Furthermore, because most religions are patriarchal, they tend to reinforce men's dominance in secular as well as spiritual matters. Women do play a vital role as volunteers, staff, and religious educators, but even today, religious decision making and leadership typically fall to the men. Exceptions to this rule, such as the Shakers and Christian Scientists, as well as Hinduism with its long goddess heritage, are rare (Schaefer and Zellner 2015).

In the United States, women are much more likely than men to be affiliated with religion, to pray, to believe in God, to claim that religion is important in their lives, and to attend weekly worship services. Yet organized religion typically does not give them leadership roles. Nationally, women compose 21 percent of U.S. clergy, though they account for 28 percent of students enrolled in theological institutions. Women clerics typically have shorter careers than men, often in related fields that do not involve congregational leadership, such as counseling. In faiths that restrict leadership positions to men, women still serve unofficially. For example, about 4 percent of Roman Catholic congregations are led by women who hold nonordained pastoral positions—a necessity in a church that faces a shortage of male priests (Association of Theological Schools 2015:Table 2-12B; Bureau of Labor Statistics 2016a).

Table 8-5 summarizes the major sociological perspectives on religion.

Table 8–5 Sociological Perspectives on Religion

Theoretical Perspective	Emphasis
Functionalist	Religion as a source of social integration and unification
	Religion as a source of social support for individuals
Conflict	Religion as a potential obstacle to structural social change
Interactionist	Individual religious expression through belief, ritual, and experience
Feminist	Religion as an instrument of women's subordination, except for their role in religious socialization

Components of Religion

All religions have certain elements in common, yet those elements are expressed in the distinctive manner of each faith. These patterns of religious behavior, like other patterns of social behavior, are of great interest to sociologists—especially interactionists—since they underscore the relationship between religion and society.

Religious beliefs, religious rituals, and religious experience all help to define what is sacred and to differentiate the sacred from the profane. Let's examine these three dimensions of religious behavior, as seen through the eyes of interactionists.

BELIEF

Some people believe in life after death, in supreme beings with unlimited powers, or in supernatural forces. *Religious beliefs* are statements to which members of a particular religion adhere. These views can vary dramatically from one religion to another.

In the late 1960s, something rather remarkable took place in the expression of religious beliefs in the United States. Denominations that held to relatively liberal interpretations of religious scripture (such as the Presbyterians, Methodists, and Lutherans) declined in membership, while those that held to more conservative interpretations grew in numbers. Furthermore, in most faiths, those members who held strict views of scripture became more outspoken, questioning those who remained open to a variety of newer interpretations.

This trend toward *fundamentalism* ran counter to the secularization that was evident in the wider society. *Fundamentalism* may be defined as an emphasis on doctrinal conformity and the literal interpretation of sacred texts. The phrase "religious fundamentalism" was first applied to

Protestant believers in the United States who took a literal interpretation of the Bible, but fundamentalism is found worldwide among all major religious groups, including Roman Catholicism, Islam, and Judaism. Even in relatively new faiths, some adherents contend that too much has changed. For followers of many religions, fundamentalists can be as challenging to accommodate as secularists.

Fundamentalists vary immensely in their behavior. Some stress the need to be strict in their own personal faith but take little interest in broad social issues. Others are watchful of societal actions, such as government policies, that they see as conflicting with fundamentalist doctrine.

The Adam and Eve account of creation found in Genesis, the first book of the Old Testament, is an example of a religious belief. Many people in the United States strongly adhere to this biblical explanation of creation and even insist that it be taught in public schools. These people, known as *creationists,* are worried by the secularization of society and oppose teaching that directly or indirectly questions biblical scripture.

In general, spirituality is not as strong in industrialized nations as in developing nations. The United States is an exception to the trend toward secularization, in part because the government encourages religious expression (without explicitly supporting it) by allowing religious groups to claim charitable status and even to receive federal aid for activities such as educational services. And although belief in God is relatively weak in formerly communist states such as Russia, surveys show a growth in spirituality in communist countries over the last 10 years (Mazurczak 2014).

RITUAL

Religious rituals are practices required or expected of members of a faith. Rituals usually honor the divine power (or powers) worshiped by believers; they also remind adherents of their religious duties and responsibilities. Rituals and beliefs can be interdependent; rituals generally affirm beliefs, as in a public or private statement confessing a sin. Like any social institution, religion develops distinctive norms to structure people's behavior. Moreover, sanctions are attached to religious rituals, whether rewards (bar mitzvah gifts) or penalties (expulsion from a religious institution for violation of norms).

In the United States, rituals may be very simple, such as saying grace at a meal or observing a moment of silence to commemorate someone's death. Yet certain rituals, such as the process of canonizing a saint, are quite elaborate. Most religious rituals in our culture focus on services conducted at houses of worship. Attendance at a service, silent and spoken prayers, communion, and singing of spiritual hymns and chants are common forms of ritual behavior that generally take place in group settings. From an interactionist perspective, these rituals serve as important

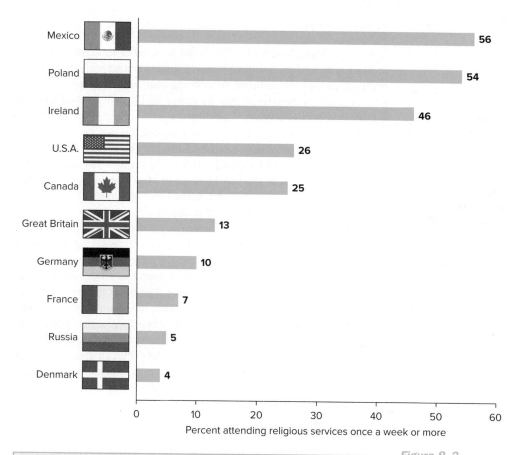

Percent attending religious services once a week or more

Figure 8–2

Religious Participation in Selected Countries, 2006

NOTE: Data are for 2006, except for Canada and Mexico, which are for 2004.

SOURCE OF DATA: Smith, 2009:28,60,72.

(Flags): ©admin_design/ Shutterstock

Think About It
Are you surprised by the variation in religious participation from one nation to another? Why or why not?

face-to-face encounters in which people reinforce their religious beliefs and their commitment to their faith.

For Muslims, a very important ritual is the *hajj,* a pilgrimage to the Grand Mosque in Mecca, Saudi Arabia. Every Muslim who is physically and financially able is expected to make this trip at least once. Each year 2 million pilgrims go to Mecca during the one-week period indicated by the Islamic lunar calendar. Muslims from all over the world make the *hajj,* including those in the United States, where many tours are arranged to facilitate the trip.

In recent decades, participation in religious rituals has tended to hold steady or decline in most countries. Figure 8–2 shows rates of religious participation in selected countries.

Choose a religious
tradition other than
your own. How
would your religious
beliefs, rituals, and
experiences differ if
you had been raised
in that tradition?

EXPERIENCE

In the sociological study of religion, the term *religious experience* refers
to the feeling or perception of being in direct contact with the ultimate
reality, such as a divine being, or of being overcome with religious emotion. A religious experience may be rather slight, such as the feeling of
exaltation a person receives from hearing a choir sing Handel's "Halle-
lujah Chorus." However, many religious experiences are more profound,
such as a Muslim's experience on *hajj*. In his autobiography, the late African American activist Malcolm X (1964:338) wrote of his *hajj* and how
deeply moved he was by the way Muslims in Mecca came together across
race and color lines. For Malcolm X, the color blindness of the Muslim
world "proved to me the power of the One God."

Another profound religious experience, for many Christians, is being
born again—that is, at a turning point in one's life, making a personal
commitment to Jesus. According to a 2014 national survey, 35 percent
of people in the United States claim they have had a born-again Christian experience at some time in their lives. The collective nature of religion, as emphasized by Durkheim, is evident in the way the beliefs and
rituals of a particular faith can create an atmosphere either friendly or
indifferent to this type of religious experience (Pew Research Center
2015b). The beliefs and rituals of a particular faith can create an atmosphere either friendly or indifferent to this type of religious experience.
Thus, a Baptist would be encouraged to come forward and share such
experiences with others, whereas an Episcopalian who claims to have
been born again would receive much less interest (Gallup 2011a; Gallup
Opinion Index 1978).

Table 8–6 summarizes the three elements of religious belief.

Table 8–6 Elements of Religious Belief

Element	Definition	Examples
Belief	Statement to which members of a particular religion adhere	Creation account Sacred characters or people
Ritual	Practice required or expected of members of a faith	Worship Prayer Singing or chanting
Experience	Feeling or perception of being in direct contact with the ultimate reality (such as a divine being) or of being overcome with religious emotion	Born-again experience Communion with Holy Spirit

summing UP

Sociology Matters

Sociology matters because it explains the purposes and functions of our most basic social institutions.

- Do you see the institutions of the family and religion differently now that you have read this chapter? Did anything you learned surprise you?

- The family and religion are two social institutions whose authority has declined over the last century. Why do you think they have lost some of their importance? Do you think our society is weaker or stronger as a result?

Sociology matters because it helps us to look at familiar social institutions from new and different perspectives.

- Which of the four major perspectives on the family strikes you as the most meaningful? Why?

- Which of the four major perspectives would be most helpful to you in studying religion?

CHAPTER RESOURCES

Summary

The **social institutions** of the **family** and **religion** are cultural universals, found in various forms in all human cultures. Functionalists stress the essential tasks social institutions perform, but conflict theorists charge that social institutions strengthen the powerful at the expense of the powerless. This chapter examined **kinship** and the family around the world; four sociological perspectives on the family; the family and human sexuality; the social functions of religion; and three components of religion.

1. To survive, a society must perform five essential functions: it must replace its personnel, teach new recruits, produce and distribute goods and services, preserve order, and provide people with a sense of purpose. **Social institutions** perform these essential functions.

2. The **extended family,** common in the past, offers certain advantages over today's **nuclear family.** Some sociologists think that in the United States, the **egalitarian family** has become the norm, replacing the older **patriarchal family.**

230

CHAPTER 8: SOCIAL INSTITUTIONS: FAMILY AND RELIGION

3. All cultures determine **kinship** in one of three ways: by descent from both parents, a method called **bilateral descent;** by descent from the father only, called **patrilineal descent;** or by descent from the mother only, called **matrilineal descent.**

4. Stratification exists by sexual as well as by gender identity. Not only gays but also transgender people suffer from stigma.

5. William F. Ogburn outlined six basic functions of the **family:** reproduction, protection, socialization, regulation of sexual behavior, companionship, and the provision of social status.

6. Conflict theorists charge that male dominance of the family contributes to social injustice and denies women opportunities that are extended to men. Like feminists, they see the family's role in socializing children as the primary source of sexism.

7. Émile Durkheim stressed the social impact of **religion** in attempting to understand individual religious behavior within the context of the larger society.

8. Religion helps to integrate a diverse society and provides social support in time of need. It can serve as a source of social change and a means of social control.

9. Max Weber saw a connection between religion and capitalism, which he termed the **Protestant ethic.** Karl Marx charged that religion reinforces capitalist oppression.

10. Religious behavior is expressed through **religious belief, ritual,** and **experience.** These three components of religion help to define the sacred and differentiate it from the profane.

Key Terms

bilateral descent, 212

egalitarian family, 213

extended family, 211

family, 210

fundamentalism, 225

gender identity, 217

kinship, 212

matriarchy, 213

matrilineal descent, 213

monogamy, 211

nuclear family, 210

patriarchy, 213

patrilineal descent, 213

polyandry, 212

polygamy, 211

polygyny, 212

Protestant ethic, 222

religion, 220

religious belief, 225

religious experience, 228

religious ritual, 226

serial monogamy, 211

sexual identity, 217

social institution, 206

Social Institutions: Education, Government, and the Economy

©Erica Simone Leeds

On September 11, 2001, the World Trade Center's twin towers, hit by two hijacked commercial airliners, took only minutes to collapse. Today, a memorial to those lost on that horrific day marks the place where the towers once stood. Two huge square footprints, sunk in a reflecting pool surrounded by cascading water, suggest the absence of those massive columns. Along the sides of the reflecting pool, the names of those who died in the attack are chiseled into the bronze walls: friends and co-workers in the buildings; passengers on the two commandeered aircraft; first responders to the scene. Victims of the simultaneous attack on the Pentagon and passengers on the flight headed for a target in Washington, DC, who were struggling to thwart the hijackers when the plane went down in Pennsylvania, are also memorialized. The names of six people killed in a truck bombing at the World Trade Center in 1993 complete the list.

Located close to Wall Street, one of the world's great financial hubs, the World Trade Center was a symbol of globalization. To the terrorists who brought it down, it also stood for capitalism and Western imperialism. In targeting the World Trade Center, they were in essence attacking the global economic system. Through their coordinated strike on the Pentagon and Washington, DC, they tried to

231

topple the U.S. government, command center of the most powerful country in the world.

In the last chapter we learned that a *social institution* is an organized pattern of beliefs and behavior centered on basic social needs. We saw that two institutions, the family and religion, meet our need for support and a sense of purpose, much as the 9/11 memorial does. In this chapter we will concentrate on three more institutions, education, government, and the economy, which are devoted to fulfilling our needs for learning, social order, and the goods and services that sustain life.

We will begin with a discussion of four sociological perspectives on education, followed by a consideration of schools as formal organizations. Then we will examine government as the source of legitimate authority and power. We'll look at three different models of the power structure in the United States, and at the growth of a global power elite based in multinational corporations. Next, we'll compare two major economic systems, capitalism and socialism. The chapter will close with a discussion of the economic transformations our own society and those of developing countries are currently undergoing, spurred by globalization. Those transformations, together with the social change they bring, underlie a great deal of the ferment in the world today, from global terrorism to recent protest movements such as Occupy Wall Street.

Sociological Perspectives on Education

Education is a formal process of learning in which some people consciously teach while others adopt the social role of learner. Besides being a major industry in the United States, education is the social institution that formally socializes members of our society.

FUNCTIONALIST PERSPECTIVE ON EDUCATION

Like other social institutions, education has both manifest (open, stated) and latent (hidden) functions. The most basic *manifest* function of education is the transmission of knowledge. Schools teach students how to read, speak foreign languages, and repair automobiles. Another important manifest function is the bestowal of status. Because many believe this function is performed inequitably, we will consider it later, in the section on the conflict view of education.

In addition to these manifest functions, schools perform a number of *latent* functions: transmitting culture, promoting social and political integration, maintaining social control, and serving as an agent of change.

Transmitting Culture   As a social institution, education performs the function of transmitting the dominant culture. Schooling exposes each generation of young people to the existing beliefs, norms, and values of their culture. In our society, we learn respect for social control and reverence for established institutions, such as religion, the family, and the presidency. Of course, this statement is true of many other cultures as well. While schoolchildren in the United States are hearing about the accomplishments of George Washington and Abraham Lincoln, British children are hearing about the distinctive contributions of Queen Elizabeth I and Sir Winston Churchill.

Sometimes nations may reassess the ways in which they transmit culture. Recently, the Chinese government revised the nation's history curriculum. Students are now taught that the Chinese Communist Party, not the United States, played a central role in defeating Japan in World War II. No mention is made of the estimated 30 million Chinese who died from famine because of party founder Mao Zedong's Great Leap Forward (1958–1962), a failed effort to transform China's agrarian economy into an industrial powerhouse. In the urban, Western-oriented areas of Shanghai, textbooks acknowledge the technological advances made in Western industrial countries but avoid any criticism of past policies of the Chinese government (French 2004; Kahn 2006).

Promoting Social and Political Integration Many institutions require students in their first year or two of college to live on campus, to foster a sense of community among diverse groups. Education serves the latent function of promoting social and political integration by transforming a population composed of diverse racial, ethnic, and religious groups into a society whose members share—to some extent—a common identity. Historically, schools in the United States have played an important role in socializing the children of immigrants into the norms, values, and beliefs of the dominant culture. From a functionalist perspective, the common identity and social integration fostered by education contribute to societal stability and consensus (Touraine 1974).

How do the functions of integration and social control reinforce each other? How do they work against each other?

In the past, the integrative function of education was most obvious in its emphasis on promoting a common language. Immigrant children were expected to learn English. In some instances, they were even forbidden to speak their native language on school grounds. More recently, bilingualism has been defended both for its educational value and as a means of encouraging cultural diversity. However, critics argue that bilingualism undermines the social and political integration that education has traditionally promoted.

Maintaining Social Control In performing the manifest function of transmitting knowledge, schools go far beyond teaching skills like reading, writing, and mathematics. Like other social institutions, such as the family and religion, education prepares young people to lead productive and orderly lives as adults by introducing them to the norms, values, and sanctions of the larger society.

Through the exercise of social control, schools teach various skills and values essential to students' future in the labor force. Students learn punctuality, discipline, scheduling, and responsible work habits, as well as how to negotiate the complexities of a bureaucratic organization. As a social institution, education reflects the interests of both the family and another social institution, the economy. Students are trained for what is ahead, whether it be the assembly line or a physician's office. In effect, then, schools serve as a transitional agent of social control, bridging the gap between parents and employers in the life cycle of most individuals (Bowles and Gintis 1976; Cole 1988).

Serving as an Agent of Change   So far, we have focused on the con-servative functions of education—on its role in transmitting the existing culture, promoting social and political integration, and maintaining social control. Yet education can also stimulate or bring about desired social change. Sex education classes were introduced in public schools in response to a soaring pregnancy rate among teenagers. Affirmative action in admissions—giving priority to females or minorities—has been endorsed as a means of countering racial and sexual discrimination. Project Head Start, an early childhood program that serves more than 1 million children annually, has sought to compensate for the disadvantages in school readiness experienced by children from low-income families.

These educational programs can and have transformed people's lives. For example, continued formal education has had a positive effect on the income people earn; median earnings rise significantly with each step up the educational ladder (see Figure 9-1). Consider the difference that

Figure 9–1
Annual Median Earnings by Educational Level, Workers Aged 25–34

NOTE: *Includes full-time, full-year wages and salaries for 2015.*

SOURCE: Proctor et al. 2016:PINC-03.

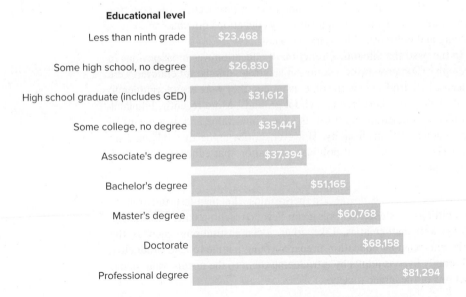

Educational level

Less than ninth grade	$23,468
Some high school, no degree	$26,830
High school graduate (includes GED)	$31,612
Some college, no degree	$35,441
Associate's degree	$37,394
Bachelor's degree	$51,165
Master's degree	$60,768
Doctorate	$68,158
Professional degree	$81,294

these substantial annual increases can make when they are multiplied by the number of years a person works.

CONFLICT PERSPECTIVE ON EDUCATION

Conflict theorists view education as an instrument of elite domination. They point to the sharp inequalities that exist in the educational opportunities available to different racial and ethnic groups. The year 2004 marked the 50th anniversary of the Supreme Court's landmark decision *Brown v. Board of Education,* which declared unconstitutional the segregation of public schools. Yet today, our schools are still characterized by racial isolation. For example, although White students account for just over half the nation's school enrollment, the typical White student attends a school where three-quarters of his or her peers are White. Fully 15 percent of Black students and 14 percent of Latino students attend what have been termed "apartheid schools," where Whites make up less than 1 percent of the enrollment. And despite the dramatic suburbanization of African American and Hispanic families in recent decades, across the nation, 80 percent of Latino students and 74 percent of Black students still attend majority non-White schools—that is, schools that are 50 to 100 percent minority (Orfield et al. 2012).

Conflict theorists also argue that the educational system socializes students into values dictated by the powerful, that schools stifle individualism and creativity in the name of maintaining order, and that the level of change they promote is relatively insignificant. From a conflict perspective, the inhibiting effects of education are particularly apparent in the "hidden curriculum" and the differential way in which status is bestowed on students.

The Hidden Curriculum Schools are highly bureaucratic organizations, as we will see later. Many teachers rely on rules and regulations to maintain order. Unfortunately, the need for control and discipline can take precedence over the learning process. Teachers may focus on obedience to the rules as an end in itself, in which case students and teachers alike become victims of what Philip Jackson (1968) has called the *hidden curriculum.*

In what ways did the high school you attended convey the hidden curriculum of education?

The term ***hidden curriculum*** refers to standards of behavior that are deemed proper by society and are taught subtly in schools. According to this curriculum, children must not speak until the teacher calls on them and must regulate their activities according to the clock or bells. In addition, they are expected to concentrate on their own work rather than assist other students who learn more slowly. A hidden curriculum is evident in schools around the world. For example, Japanese schools offer guidance sessions that seek to improve the classroom experience and develop healthy living skills. In effect, these sessions instill values and encourage behavior useful in the Japanese business world, such as self-discipline and openness to group problem solving and decision making (Okano and Tsuchiya 1999).

Credentialism   Sixty years ago, a high school diploma was the minimum requirement for entry into the paid labor force of the United States. Today, a college diploma is virtually the bare minimum. This change reflects the process of *credentialism*—a term used to describe an increase in the lowest level of education needed to enter a field.

In recent decades, the number of occupations that are viewed as professions has risen. Credentialism is one symptom of this trend. Employers and occupational associations typically contend that such changes are a logical response to the increasing complexity of many jobs. However, in many cases, employers raise the degree requirements for a position simply because all applicants have achieved the existing minimum credential (D. Brown 2001; Hurn 1985).

Conflict theorists observe that credentialism may reinforce social inequality. Applicants from poor and minority backgrounds are especially likely to suffer from the escalation of qualifications, because they lack the financial resources needed to obtain degree after degree. In addition, upgrading of credentials serves the self-interest of the two groups most responsible for this trend. Educational institutions profit from prolonging the investment of time and money that people make by staying in school. Moreover, current jobholders have a stake in raising occupational requirements, since credentialism can increase the status of an occupation and lead to demands for higher pay. Max Weber anticipated this possibility as early as 1916, concluding that the "universal clamor for the creation of educational certificates in all fields makes for the formation of a privileged stratum in businesses and in offices" (Gerth and Mills 1958:240–241).

Bestowal of Status   As noted earlier, an increasing proportion of people in the United States are obtaining high school diplomas, college degrees, and advanced professional degrees. From a functionalist perspective, this widening bestowal of status is beneficial not only to particular recipients but to society as a whole. Conflict theorists are far more critical of the *differential* way in which education bestows status. They stress that schools sort pupils according to their social class backgrounds. Although the educational system helps certain poor children to move into middle-class professional positions, it denies most disadvantaged children the same educational opportunities afforded to children of the affluent. In this way, schools tend to preserve social class inequalities in each new generation. Higher education in particular acts more like a sieve that sorts people out of the educated classes than a social ladder that helps all with ambition to rise (Duncan and Murnane 2014; Giroux 1988; Sacks 2007).

Even a single school can reinforce class differences by putting students in tracks. The term *tracking* refers to the practice of placing students in

How would you react if the job you have or plan to pursue suddenly required a higher-level degree? If suddenly the requirements were lowered?

What are the functions and dysfunctions of tracking in schools? In what ways might tracking have a positive impact on the self-concepts of various students? In what ways might it have a negative impact?

specific curriculum groups on the basis of their test scores and other criteria. Tracking begins very early, often in reading groups during first grade. The practice can reinforce the disadvantages that children from less affluent families may face if they haven't been exposed to reading materials, computers, and other forms of educational stimulation during their early childhood years. To ignore this connection between tracking and students' race and social class is to fundamentally misunderstand how schools perpetuate the existing social structure.

Children placed in academic tracks (with the expectation that they will attend college) typically receive text-based instruction that demands written and verbal displays of knowledge. In contrast, students in nonacademic tracks receive watered-down, slower paced instruction that aims them toward the world of work after high school. Studies of tracking show that children placed in lower tracks tend to come from low-income or one-parent households or from minority groups. The most damaging aspect of tracking is that it can become a caste system: Once students are placed into low-ability groups, they remain there and are seldom promoted to high-ability groups later on (Mehan 2015).

FEMINIST PERSPECTIVE ON EDUCATION

The educational system of the United States, like many other social institutions, has long been characterized by discriminatory treatment of women. In 1833 Oberlin College became the first institution of higher learning to admit female students—some 200 years after the first men's college was established. But Oberlin's administrators believed that women should aspire to become wives and mothers, not lawyers and intellectuals. In addition to attending classes, female students washed men's clothing, cared for their rooms, and served them at meals. In the 1840s, Lucy Stone, then an Oberlin undergraduate and later one of the nation's most outspoken feminist leaders, refused to write a commencement address because it would have been read to the audience by a male student.

Sexism in education showed up in many ways—in textbooks with negative stereotypes of women, counselors' pressure on female students to prepare for "women's work," and unequal funding for women's and men's athletic programs. But perhaps nowhere was educational discrimination more evident than in the employment of teachers. The positions of university professor and college administrator, which hold relatively high status in the United States, were generally filled by men. Public school teachers, who earn much lower salaries, were largely female.

Women have made great strides in one area: the proportion of women who continue their schooling. Women's access to graduate education and to medical, dental, and law schools has increased dramatically in the last few decades as a result of the Education Act of 1972, which forbade discrimination against women in education.

Much has been made of the superior academic achievement of girls and women. Today, researchers are beginning to examine the reasons for their comparatively strong performance in school—or to put it another way, for men's lackluster performance. Some studies suggest that men's aggressiveness, together with the fact that they do better in the workplace than women, even with less schooling, predisposes them to undervalue higher education. While the "absence of men" on many college campuses has captured headlines, it has also created a false crisis in public discourse. Few students realize their potential exclusively through formal education; other factors, such as ambition and personal talent, contribute to their success. And many students, including low-income and immigrant children, face much greater challenges than the so-called gender gap in education (Sutherland 2015).

In cultures in which traditional gender roles remain the social norm, women's education suffers appreciably. Since September 11, 2001, the growing awareness of the Taliban's repression of Afghan women has dramatized the gender disparities in education in developing nations. Research has demonstrated that women are critical to economic development and good governance, and that education is instrumental in preparing them for those roles. Educating women, especially young girls, yields high social returns by lowering birthrates and improving agricultural productivity through better management (World Bank 2016).

INTERACTIONIST PERSPECTIVE ON EDUCATION

The labeling approach suggests that if we treat people in particular ways, they may fulfill our expectations. Children who are labeled as "troublemakers" may come to view themselves as delinquents. Similarly, a dominant group's stereotyping of subordinate racial groups may limit their opportunities to break away from expected roles.

Can the labeling process operate in the classroom? Psychologist Robert Rosenthal and school principal Lenore Jacobson (1968, 1992) documented what they referred to as a *teacher-expectancy effect*—the impact that a teacher's expectations about a student's performance may have on the student's actual achievements. This effect is especially evident in the lower grades (through grade three).

Studies in the United States have revealed that teachers wait longer for an answer from a student they believe to be a high achiever and are more likely to give such children a second chance. In one experiment, teachers' expectations were even shown to have an impact on students' athletic achievements. Teachers obtained better athletic performance—as measured by the number of sit-ups or push-ups performed—from those students of whom they *expected* higher numbers (Babad and Taylor 1992; Brint 1998; Rosenthal and Jacobson 1992: 247–262).

Table 9-1 summarizes the four major theoretical perspectives on education.

What kinds of labels do school authorities apply to students? What is the outcome of those labels?

Table 9–1 Sociological Perspectives on Education

Theoretical Perspective	Emphasis
Functionalist	Transmission of the dominant culture Integration of society Promotion of social norms, values, and sanctions Promotion of desirable social change
Conflict	Domination by the elite through unequal access to schooling Hidden curriculum Credentialism Differential bestowal of status
Feminist	Treatment of female students Role of women's education in economic development
Interactionist	Teacher-expectancy effect

Think About It

Which of the emphases listed in the table have you witnessed in the schools you have attended?

Education: Schools as Formal Organizations

Nineteenth-century educators would be amazed at the scale of schools in the United States as we head into the 21st century. The nation has about 15 million high school students today, compared to 10 million in 1961 and 5 million in 1931 (Bureau of the Census 2011a:161, Table 246; 2012c:Table HS-20).

In many respects, today's schools are similar to factories, hospitals, and business firms when viewed as formal organizations. Like those other organizations, schools do not operate autonomously; they are influenced by the market of potential students. This market orientation is especially true of private schools, but could have broader impact if acceptance of voucher plans and other school choice programs increases. The parallels between schools and other formal organizations will become more apparent as we examine the bureaucratic nature of schools, teaching as an occupational role, and student subcultures (K. Dougherty and Hammack 1992).

BUREAUCRATIZATION OF SCHOOLS

A single teacher simply cannot transmit culture and skills to children of varying ages or prepare them for many diverse occupations. The growing number of students being served by individual schools and school systems, as well as the greater degree of specialization required by a technologically complex society, have combined to bureaucratize schools.

Max Weber noted five basic characteristics of bureaucracy, all of which are evident in the vast majority of schools, whether at the elementary, secondary, or college level.

1. *Division of labor.* Specialized experts teach particular age levels and specific subjects. For example, public elementary and secondary schools now employ instructors whose sole responsibility is to work with children with learning disabilities or physical impairments.

2. *Hierarchy of authority.* Each employee of a school system is responsible to a higher authority. Teachers must report to principals and assistant principals and may also be supervised by department heads. Principals are answerable to a superintendent of schools, and the superintendent is hired and fired by a board of education.

3. *Written rules and regulations.* Teachers and administrators must conform to numerous rules and regulations in the performance of their duties. This bureaucratic requirement can become dysfunctional; the time invested in completing forms could instead be spent on preparing lessons or conferring with students.

4. *Impersonality.* As class sizes have swelled at schools and universities, it has become more difficult for teachers to give personal attention to each student. In fact, bureaucratic norms may actually encourage teachers to treat all students in the same way, despite the fact that students have distinctive personalities and learning needs.

5. *Employment based on technical qualifications.* At least in theory, the hiring of teachers and college professors is based on professional competence and expertise. Promotions are normally dictated by written personnel policies; people who excel may be granted lifelong job security through tenure.

How would you make your school less bureaucratic? What would it be like?

Functionalists take a generally positive view of the bureaucratization of education. Teachers can master the skills needed to work with a specialized clientele, since they no longer are expected to cover a broad range of instruction. The chain of command within schools is clear. Students are presumably treated in an unbiased fashion because of uniformly applied rules. Finally, security of position protects teachers from unjustified dismissal. In general, then, functionalists maintain that bureaucratization of education increases the likelihood that students, teachers, and administrators will be dealt with fairly—that is, on the basis of rational, equitable criteria.

In contrast, conflict theorists argue that the trend toward more centralized education has had harmful consequences for disadvantaged people. The standardization of educational curricula, including textbooks, generally reflects the values, interests, and lifestyles of the most powerful groups in our society and may ignore those of racial and ethnic minorities. In addition, the disadvantaged, more so than the affluent, will find it difficult to sort through complex educational bureaucracies and to organize effective lobbying groups. In the view of conflict theorists, then, low-income and minority parents are likely to have even less influence over citywide and statewide educational administrators than they have over local school officials (Bowles and Gintis 1976; Katz 1971).

Finally, some schools can seem overwhelmingly bureaucratic, with the effect of stifling rather than nourishing intellectual curiosity in students. This problem has led many parents and policy makers to push for school choice programs—that is, allowing parents to choose the school that suits their children's needs, forcing schools to compete for their "customers."

TEACHERS: EMPLOYEES AND INSTRUCTORS

Whether they instruct preschoolers or graduate students, teachers are employees of formal organizations with bureaucratic structures. There is an inherent conflict in serving as a professional within a bureaucracy. The organization follows a hierarchy of authority and expects adherence to its rules, but professionalism demands individual responsibility of the practitioner. This conflict is very real for teachers, who experience all the positive and negative consequences of working in bureaucracies.

A teacher undergoes many perplexing stresses every day. While teachers' academic assignments have become more specialized, the demands on their time remain diverse and contradictory. Conflicts arise from serving as an instructor, a disciplinarian, and an employee of a school district at the same time. In too many schools, discipline means dealing with violence. Burnout is one result of these stresses: between a quarter and a third of new teachers quit within their first three years, and as many as half leave poor urban schools in their first five years (Wallis 2008).

Given these difficulties, does teaching remain an attractive profession in the United States? In 2015, 2.4 percent of first-year college students indicated that they were interested in becoming either elementary or high school teachers. These figures are dramatically lower than the 11 percent of first-year male students and 37 percent of first-year female students who held those occupational aspirations in 1966 (Eagan et al. 2016; Pryor et al. 2007:122, 76).

Undoubtedly, economic considerations enter into students' feelings about the attractiveness of teaching. In 2015 the average salary for all public elementary and secondary school teachers in the United States was reported at $57,379, placing teachers somewhere near the average of all the nation's wage earners. In most other industrial countries, teachers' salaries are higher in relation to the general standard of living. Of course, teachers' salaries vary considerably from state to state, and even from one school district to another. Nevertheless, the economic reward for teaching is miniscule compared to some career options: The CEO of a major corporation makes more money in a day than the average teacher makes in a year (National Education Association 2015).

The status of any job reflects several factors, including the level of education required, financial compensation, and the respect given the

U.S. EDUCATION: RACE To the TOP!

From preschool through high school, teachers face a variety of challenges, including preparing students for standardized tests.

SOURCE: ©*Signe Wilkinson Editorial Cartoon* used with the permission of Signe Wilkinson, the Washington Post Writers Group and the Cartoonist Group. All rights reserved.

occupation by society. The teaching profession is feeling pressure in all three of these areas. First, the level of formal schooling required for teaching remains high, and the public has begun to call for new competency examinations. Second, the statistics just cited demonstrate that teachers' salaries are significantly lower than those of many professionals and skilled workers. Finally, the overall prestige of the teaching profession has declined in the last decade. Many teachers have become disappointed and frustrated and have left the educational world for careers in other professions.

Government: Power and Authority

A society does not exist in a vacuum. Someone or some group makes important decisions about how to use resources and how to allocate goods, whether it be a tribal chief, a parliament, or a dictator. A cultural universal common to all societies, then, is the exercise of authority and power. The struggle for authority and power inevitably involves *politics,* which political scientist Harold Lasswell (1936) tersely defined as "who gets what, when, and how." In their study of politics and government, sociologists are concerned with social interactions among individuals and groups and their impact on the larger political and economic order.

Power lies at the heart of a political system. According to Max Weber, *power* is the ability to exercise one's will over others. To put it another way, whoever can control the behavior of others is exercising power. Power relations can involve large organizations, small groups, or even people in an intimate association.

Because Weber developed his conceptualization of power in the early 1900s, he focused primarily on the nation-state and its sphere of influence. Today scholars recognize that the trend toward globalization has brought new opportunities, and with them new concentrations of power. Power is now exercised on a global as well as a national stage, as countries and multinational corporations vie to control access to resources and manage the distribution of capital (R. Schaefer 2008b; Sernau 2001).

There are three basic sources of power in any political system—force, influence, and authority. *Force* is the actual or threatened use of coercion to impose one's will on others. When leaders imprison or even execute political dissidents, they are applying force; so, too, are terrorists when they seize or bomb an embassy or assassinate a political leader.

In the 21st century, force has taken on new meaning as nations clamp down on use of the Internet to oppose the central government or assert freedom of expression, human rights, and minority or religious views. When a military coup overthrew the democratically elected government of Thailand in September 2006, for example, citizens lost access to websites that criticized the takeover. Censorship of online content is just as much a use of force as closing down a newspaper or arresting dissidents (Deibert et al. 2008; Zittrain and Palfrey 2008).

Influence, on the other hand, refers to the exercise of power through a process of persuasion. A citizen may change his or her position regarding a Supreme Court nominee because of a newspaper editorial, the expert testimony of a law school dean before the Senate Judiciary Committee, or a stirring speech at a rally by a political activist. In each case, sociologists would view such efforts to persuade people as examples of influence. Now let's take a look at the third source of power, *authority*.

TYPES OF AUTHORITY

The term *authority* refers to power that has been institutionalized and is recognized by the people over whom it is exercised. Sociologists commonly use the term in connection with those who hold legitimate power through elected or publicly acknowledged positions. A person's authority is limited by the constraints of a particular social position. Thus, a referee has the authority to decide whether a penalty should be called during a football game but has no authority over the price of tickets to the game.

Max Weber ([1913–1922] 1947) developed a system for classifying authority that has become one of the most useful and frequently cited contributions of early sociology. Weber identified three ideal types of authority: traditional, rational-legal, and charismatic. He did not insist that only one type characterizes a given society or organization. All can be present in a single society, but their relative importance will vary. Sociologists have found Weber's typology valuable in understanding different manifestations of legitimate power.

Traditional Authority   Until the middle of the last century, Japan was ruled by a revered emperor, whose absolute power was passed down from generation to generation. In a political system based on *traditional authority*, legitimate power is conferred by custom and accepted practice. A king or queen is accepted as ruler of a nation simply by virtue of inheriting the crown; a tribal chief rules because that is the accepted practice. The ruler may be loved or hated, competent or destructive; in terms of legitimacy, that does not matter. For the traditional leader, authority rests in custom, not in personal characteristics, technical competence, or even written law. People accept such authority because "this is how things have always been done." Traditional authority is absolute when the ruler has the ability to determine a society's laws and policies.

Rational-Legal Authority   The U.S. Constitution gives Congress and the president the authority to make and enforce laws and policies. Power made legitimate by law—by the written rules and regulations of a political system—is known as *rational-legal authority*. Generally, in societies based on rational-legal authority, leaders are thought to have specific fields of competence and authority but are not thought to be endowed with divine inspiration, as in certain societies with traditional forms of authority.

What would our government be like if it were founded on traditional rather than rational-legal authority? What difference would it make to the average citizen?

Charismatic Authority   Joan of Arc was a simple peasant girl in medieval France, yet she was able to rally the French people and lead them into battle against English invaders. How was this possible? As Weber observed, power can be legitimized by an individual's *charisma*. The term *charismatic authority* refers to power made legitimate by a leader's exceptional personal or emotional appeal to his or her followers.

Charisma lets a person lead or inspire without relying on set rules or traditions. In fact, charismatic authority is derived more from the beliefs of followers than from the actual qualities of leaders. So long as people *perceive* a leader to have qualities that set him or her apart from ordinary citizens, that leader's authority will remain secure and often unquestioned.

Observing from an interactionist perspective, sociologist Carl Couch (1996) points out that the growth of the electronic media has facilitated the development of charismatic authority. During the 1930s and 1940s, the heads of state of the United States, Great Britain, and Germany all used radio to issue direct appeals to citizens. In recent decades, television has allowed leaders to "visit" people's homes and communicate with them. Time and again, Saddam Hussein rallied the Iraqi people through shrewd use of television appearances. In both Taiwan and South Korea in 1996, troubled political leaders facing reelection campaigns spoke frequently to national audiences and exaggerated military threats from neighboring China and North Korea, respectively.

On your campus, what are some examples of the three types of authority?

As we noted earlier, Weber used traditional, rational-legal, and charismatic authority as ideal types. In reality, individual leaders and political systems often combine two or more of these forms. Presidents Franklin D. Roosevelt, John F. Kennedy, and Ronald Reagan wielded power largely through rational-legal authority. At the same time, they were unusually charismatic leaders who commanded the personal loyalty of large numbers of citizens.

WHO RULES IN THE UNITED STATES?

Who really holds power in the United States? Do "we the people" genuinely run the country through our elected representatives? Or is it true that behind the scenes, a small elite controls both our government and our economic system? It is difficult to determine the location of power in a society as complex as the United States. In exploring this critical question, social scientists have developed two basic views of our nation's power structure: the power elite and the pluralist models.

Power Elite Models Karl Marx believed that 19th-century representative democracy was essentially a sham. He argued that industrial societies were dominated by relatively small numbers of people who owned factories and controlled natural resources. In Marx's view, government officials and military leaders were servants of this capitalist class and followed their wishes. Therefore, any key decisions made by politicians inevitably reflected the interests of the dominant bourgeoisie. Like others who hold to an *elite model* of power relations, Marx believed that society is ruled by a small group of individuals who share a common set of political and economic interests.

Mills's Model Sociologist C. Wright Mills took this model a step further in his pioneering work *The Power Elite* ([1956] 2000b). Mills described a small group of military, industrial, and government leaders who controlled the fate of the United States. Power rested in the hands of a few, both inside and outside government, called the *power elite.*

A pyramid illustrates the United States' power structure in Mills's model (see Figure 9–2a). At the top are the corporate rich, leaders of the executive branch of government, and heads of the military (whom Mills called the "warlords"). These are the power elite. Directly below are local opinion leaders, members of the legislative branch of government, and leaders of special interest groups. Mills thought these individuals and groups would basically follow the wishes of the dominant power elite. At the bottom of the pyramid are the unorganized, exploited masses.

This power elite model is similar to the work of Karl Marx in many respects. The most striking difference is that Mills believed that the economically powerful coordinate their maneuvers with the military and political establishments, to serve their common interests. Yet, reminiscent of Marx, Mills argued that the corporate rich were perhaps the most powerful element of the power elite (first among "equals"). And of course, the powerless masses at the bottom of Mills's power elite model certainly bring to mind Marx's portrait of the oppressed workers of the world, who have "nothing to lose but their chains."

Figure 9–2

Power Elite Models

SOURCES: Mills (1956)
2000b; Domhoff, William
G., "Who Rules America?
The Triumph of the
Corporate Rich," McGraw-
Hill Companies 2014.

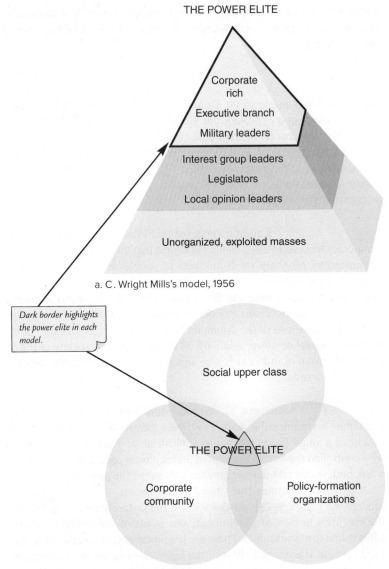

THE POWER ELITE

Corporate rich

Executive branch

Military leaders

Interest group leaders

Legislators

Local opinion leaders

Unorganized, exploited masses

a. C. Wright Mills's model, 1956

Dark border highlights the power elite in each model.

Social upper class

THE POWER ELITE

Corporate community

Policy-formation organizations

b. G. William Domhoff's model, 2010

A fundamental element in Mills's thesis is that the power elite operates as a self-conscious, cohesive unit. Although not necessarily diabolical or ruthless, the elite comprises similar types of people who interact with one another regularly and have essentially the same political and economic interests. Mills's power elite is not a conspiracy, but rather a community of interest and sentiment among a small number of influential people (Hacker 1964).

Admittedly, Mills failed to clarify when the elite opposes protests and when it tolerates them; he also failed to provide detailed case studies to substantiate the interrelationship among members of the power elite. Nevertheless, his challenging theory forced scholars to look more critically at the democratic political system of the United States.

One outgrowth of Mills's power elite model is current research on the presence of a *global power elite*—that is, those business, political, and former military leaders who exercise influence across national borders. Because this avenue of scholarship is relatively new, there is some disagreement on the definition of the term. Must the members of the global power elite demonstrate as much consensus as the members of Mills's power elite? Or can the global power elite include such diverse voices as Wikileaks founder Julian Assange, illegal arms dealer Leonid Minin, and former president Bill Clinton, in his role as head of the Clinton Global Initiative?

Domhoff's Model   Over the past three decades, sociologist G. William Domhoff (2010) has agreed with Mills that a powerful elite runs the United States. He finds that it is still largely White, male, and upper class, as he wrote in his book with Richard L. Zweigenhaft (2006). However, Domhoff stresses the role played both by elites of the corporate community and by leaders of organizations in the policy-planning network, such as chambers of commerce and labor unions. Many of the people in both groups are also members of the social upper class. And he notes the presence of a small number of women and minority men in key positions—groups that were excluded from Mills's top echelon and are still underrepresented today.

Though the three groups in Domhoff's power elite model overlap, as Figure 9–2b shows, they do not necessarily agree on specific policies. Domhoff notes that in the electoral arena, two different coalitions have exercised influence. A *corporate-conservative coalition* has played a large role in both political parties, generating support for particular candidates through direct-mail appeals. A *liberal-labor coalition* is based in unions, local environmental organizations, a segment of the minority group community, liberal churches, and the university and arts communities (Zweigenhaft and Domhoff 2006).

The Pluralist Model   Several social scientists insist that in the United States, power is more widely shared than the elite models indicate. In their view, a *pluralist model* more accurately describes the nation's political system. According to the **pluralist model,** many competing groups within the community have access to government officials, so that no single group is dominant.

The pluralist model suggests that a variety of groups play a significant role in decision making. Typically, pluralists make use of intensive case studies or community studies based on observation research. One of the most famous—an investigation of decision making in New Haven, Connecticut—was reported by Robert Dahl in his book *Who Governs?* (1961).

Dahl found that although the number of people involved in any important decision was rather small, community power was nonetheless diffuse. Few political actors exercised decision-making power on all issues. One individual or group might be influential in a battle over urban renewal but at the same time have little impact on educational policy.

The pluralist model, however, has not escaped serious questioning. Domhoff (1978, 2010) reexamined Dahl's study of decision making in New Haven and argued that Dahl and other pluralists had failed to show that elites prominent in local decision making belonged to a larger national ruling class. In addition, studies of community power, such as Dahl's work in New Haven, can examine decision making only on issues that become part of the political agenda. They fail to address the possible power of elites to keep certain matters that threaten their dominance entirely *out* of the realm of government debate.

The pluralist model, however, has not escaped serious questioning. Domhoff (1978, 2014) reexamined Dahl's study of decision making in New Haven and argued that Dahl and other pluralists had failed to trace how local elites who were prominent in decision making belonged to a larger national ruling class. In addition, studies of community power, such as Dahl's work in New Haven, can examine decision making only on issues that become part of the political agenda. They fail to address the potential power of elites to keep certain matters entirely out of the realm of government debate.

The most significant criticism of the pluralist model is that, as originally proposed, it failed to note that it is largely a pluralism of White Americans from which racial and ethnic minorities are largely absent. Yes, there are important Black, Latino, and Asian decision makers, but their influence is overwhelmingly felt in policy areas where members of racial and ethnic minorities dominate, such as voting rights or immigration reform. Even in those areas Whites continue to play significant roles, while minorities are rarely important actors in political spheres composed primarily of Whites (Berry and Junn 2015; Pinderhughes 1987).

The power struggles that underlie government and politics, no matter what model a social scientist uses to analyze them, have a great deal to do with the distribution of a society's economic resources. In the next sections of this chapter we will study the economy, both in theory and in its practical implications for tomorrow's workforce.

Use Your Sociological Imagination

Which is a better model of the power structure in the United States, the power elite model or the pluralist model? Justify your answer.

Economic Systems

The economy fulfills the basic social function of producing and distributing goods and services (see Table 8-1 on page 207). But how is this seemingly amorphous social institution organized? A society's *economic system* for producing, distributing, and consuming goods and services will depend on both its level of development and its political ideology.

The *Industrial Revolution*—which took place largely in England during the period 1760 to 1830—brought about changes in the social organization of the workplace. People left their homesteads and began working in central locations such as factories. As the Industrial Revolution proceeded, a new form of social structure emerged: the **industrial society,** a society that depends on mechanization to produce its goods and services.

The scope of these large economies is massive, as Figure 9–3 shows. Over the last three centuries, industrialization has greatly increased the

Figure 9–3
World's Largest Economies

Generally, they handle this responsibility.

Source of data: WorldBank 2011: Table 4-10.

(Flags): ©admin_design/ Shutterstock

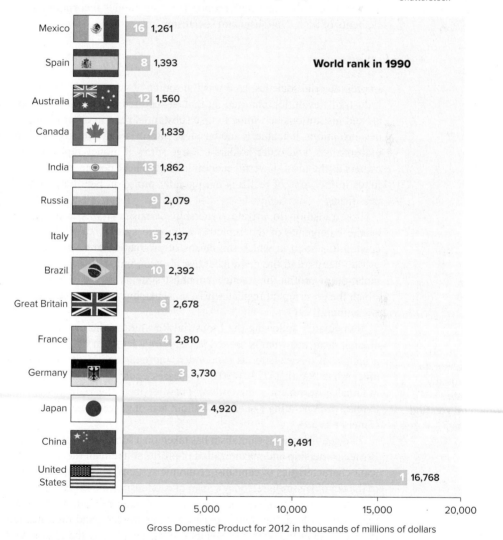

World rank in 1990

Country	Rank	GDP
Mexico	16	1,261
Spain	8	1,393
Australia	12	1,560
Canada	7	1,839
India	13	1,862
Russia	9	2,079
Italy	5	2,137
Brazil	10	2,392
Great Britain	6	2,678
France	4	2,810
Germany	3	3,730
Japan	2	4,920
China	11	9,491
United States	1	16,768

Gross Domestic Product for 2012 in thousands of millions of dollars

Think About It
Note the changes in rank since 1990. What further changes would you expect to see in the next 30 years?

wealth of nations. Since 1990, China, which only began to mechanize its rural areas in the last half of the 20th century, has grown from the eleventh largest economy in the world to the second largest.

In this section we will consider the two basic economic systems associated with contemporary industrial societies: capitalism and socialism. In theory, these two economic systems conform perfectly to certain ideals, such as private or collective ownership. However, real economic systems rarely measure up to the ideal types on which they are based. To a greater or lesser extent, most economic systems today incorporate some elements of both capitalism and socialism.

CAPITALISM

In preindustrial societies, land was the source of virtually all wealth. The Industrial Revolution changed all that. It required that certain individuals and institutions be willing to take substantial risks in order to finance new inventions, machinery, and business enterprises. Eventually, bankers, industrialists, and other holders of large sums of money replaced landowners as the most powerful economic force. These people invested their funds in the hope of realizing even greater profits in factories and business firms.

The transition to private ownership of business was accompanied by the emergence of the capitalist economic system. *Capitalism* is an economic system in which the means of production are held largely in private hands, and the main incentive for economic activity is the accumulation of profits. In practice, capitalist systems vary in the degree to which the government regulates private ownership and economic activity (Rosenberg 1991).

Which aspects of capitalism do you personally appreciate? Which do you find worrisome?

Immediately following the Industrial Revolution, the prevailing form of capitalism was what is termed *laissez-faire* ("let them do"). Under the principle of laissez-faire, as expounded and endorsed by British economist Adam Smith (1723–1790), businesses could compete freely, with minimal government intervention. They retained the right to regulate themselves, operating essentially without fear of government interference (Smelser 1963).

Two centuries later, capitalism has taken on a somewhat different form. Private ownership and maximization of profits still remain the most significant characteristics of capitalist economic systems. However, in contrast to the era of laissez-faire, today's form of capitalism features extensive government regulation of economic relations. Without restrictions, business firms can mislead consumers, endanger their workers, and even defraud investors—all in the pursuit of greater profits. That is why the government of a capitalist nation often monitors prices, sets safety standards for industries, protects the rights of consumers, and regulates collective bargaining between labor unions and management. Yet in a capitalist system, government rarely takes over ownership of an entire industry.

Contemporary capitalism also differs from laissez-faire in another important respect: it tolerates monopolistic practices. A *monopoly* exists when a single business firm controls the market. Domination of an industry allows the firm to effectively control a commodity by dictating pricing, standards of quality, and availability. Buyers have little choice but to yield to the firm's decisions; there is no other place to purchase the product or service. Monopolistic practices violate the ideal of free competition cherished by Adam Smith and other supporters of laissez-faire capitalism.

Some capitalistic nations, such as the United States, attempt to outlaw monopolies through antitrust legislation. Such laws are meant to prevent any business from taking over so much of an industry that it gains control of the market. The U.S. government approves of monopolies only in certain exceptional cases, such as the utility and transportation industries. Even then, regulatory agencies scrutinize these officially approved monopolies to protect the public. The protracted legal battle between the Justice Department and Microsoft, owner of the dominant operating system for personal computers, illustrates the uneasy relationship between government and virtual private monopolies in capitalistic countries.

Conflict theorists point out that although *pure* monopolies are not a basic element of the U.S. economy, competition is much more restricted than one might expect in what is called a *free enterprise system.* In numerous industries, a few companies dominate the field and prevent new enterprises from entering the marketplace.

During the severe economic downturn that began in 2008, the United States moved even further away from the laissez-faire ideal. To keep major financial institutions from going under, the federal government invested hundreds of billions of dollars in distressed banking, investment, and insurance companies. Then in 2009, the government bailed out the failing automobile industry, taking a 60 percent interest in General Motors. The Canadian government took another 12 percent.

SOCIALISM

Socialist theory was refined in the writings of Karl Marx and Friedrich Engels. These European radicals were disturbed by the exploitation of the working class that emerged during the Industrial Revolution. In their view, capitalism forced large numbers of people to exchange their labor for low wages. The owners of industry profited from workers' labor primarily because they paid workers less than the value of the goods produced.

As an ideal type, a socialist economic system attempts to eliminate such economic exploitation. Under *socialism,* the means of production and distribution in a society are collectively rather than privately owned. The basic objective of the economic system is to meet people's needs rather than to maximize profits. Socialists reject the laissez-faire philosophy that free competition benefits the general public. Instead, they believe that the central government, acting on behalf of the people, should make basic economic decisions. Therefore, government ownership of all major industries—including steel production, automobile manufacturing, and agriculture—is a major feature of socialism as an ideal type.

In practice, socialist economic systems vary in the extent to which they tolerate private ownership. For example, in Great Britain, a nation with some aspects of both a socialist and a capitalist economy, passenger airline service was once concentrated in the government-owned corporation British Airways. Even before the airline was privatized in 1987, however, private airlines were allowed to compete with it.

Socialist societies differ from capitalist nations in their commitment to social service programs. For example, the U.S. government provides health care and health insurance to those who are elderly and poor through the Medicare and Medicaid programs. In contrast, socialist countries typically offer government-financed medical care to *all* citizens. In theory, the wealth of the people as a collectivity is used to provide health care, housing, education, and other key services to each individual and family.

Marx believed that the socialist state would eventually "wither away" and evolve into a *communist* society. As an ideal type, **communism** refers to an economic system in which all property is communally owned and no social distinctions are made on the basis of people's ability to produce. In recent decades, the Soviet Union, the People's Republic of China, Vietnam, Cuba, and the nations of Eastern Europe were popularly thought of as communist economic systems. However, this viewpoint represents an incorrect usage of a term with sensitive political connotations. All nations known as communist actually fall far short of the ideal type (Walder and Nguyen 2008).

By the early 1990s, Communist parties were no longer ruling the nations of Eastern Europe. Just two decades later, in 2015, Moscow had no fewer than 78 billionaires—the same as New York (78) and more than London (46). That same year, traditionally communist China had 45 billionaires in its capital city, Beijing, plus 64 in Hong Kong, 25 in Shenzhen, and 2 in Shanghai. Also in 2015 the Shanghai Stock Exchange, with market capitalization of over $2.7 trillion, was the world's fifth largest stock exchange. Obviously capitalism has found a place in countries politically ruled by Communist parties (Chen 2015).

As we have seen, capitalism and socialism serve as ideal types. In reality, the economy of each industrial society—including the United States, the European Union, and Japan—contains certain elements of both capitalism and socialism (see Table 9-2). Whatever the differences—whether a country more closely fits the ideal type of capitalism or socialism—all industrial societies rely chiefly on mechanization in the production of goods and services. And all economies, whether capitalist or socialist, change as a result of social and technological advances.

Use Your Sociological Imagination

The U.S. economy has become predominantly socialistic rather than capitalistic. What do you as a worker have now that you did not have before? What do you lack?

Table 9–2 Characteristics of the Three Major Economic Systems

Economic System	Characteristics	Contemporary Examples
Capitalism	Private ownership of the means of production Accumulation of profits the main incentive	Canada Mexico United States
Socialism	Collective ownership of the means of production Meeting people's needs the basic objective	Russia Sweden
Communism	Communal ownership of all property No social distinctions made on basis of people's ability to produce	Cuba North Korea

NOTE: Countries listed in column 3 are typical of one of the three economic systems, but not perfectly so. In practice, the economies of most countries include a mix of elements from the three major systems.

The Informal Economy

In many countries, one aspect of the economy defies description as either capitalist or socialist. In the *informal economy,* transfers of money, goods, or services take place but are not reported to the government. Examples of the informal economy include trading services with someone—say, a haircut for a computer lesson; selling goods on the street; and engaging in illegal transactions, such as gambling or drug deals. The informal economy also includes off-the-books work in landscaping, child care, and housecleaning. Participants in this type of economy avoid taxes and government regulations.

In the United States, the informal economy accounts for about 8 percent of total economic activity. In other industrialized nations it varies, from 11 percent in Great Britain to 20 percent in Spain and Portugal and 25 percent in Greece. In developing nations, the informal economy represents a much larger (40 to 60 percent) and often unmeasured part of total economic activity. Yet because this sector of the economy depends to a large extent on the labor of women, work in the informal economy is undervalued or even unrecognized the world over (T. Barnes 2009; F. Schneider 2010).

Functionalists contend that bureaucratic regulations sometimes contribute to the rise of an informal, or underground, economy. In the developing world, governments often set up burdensome business regulations that overworked bureaucrats must administer. When requests for licenses and permits pile up, delaying business projects, legitimate entrepreneurs find they need to go underground to get anything done. Despite its apparent efficiency, this type of informal economy is dysfunctional for a country's overall political and economic well-being. Since informal firms typically operate in remote locations to avoid detection, they cannot easily expand when they become profitable. And given the limited protection for their property and contractual rights,

Use Your Sociological Imagination

In the United States, what factors might encourage the growth of the informal economy? Are those factors related to the country's economic system?

participants in the informal economy are less likely than others to save and invest their income.

Whatever the functions an informal economy may serve, it is in some respects dysfunctional for workers. Working conditions in these illegal businesses are often unsafe or dangerous, and the jobs rarely provide any benefits to those who become ill or cannot continue to work. Perhaps more significant, the longer a worker remains in the informal economy, the less likely that person is to make the transition to the formal economy. No matter how efficient or productive a worker, employers expect to see experience in the formal economy on a job application. Experience as a successful street vendor or self-employed cleaning person does not carry much weight with interviewers (Venkatesh 2006; WIEGO 2016).

Changing Economies

As advocates of the power elite model point out, the trend in capitalist societies has been toward concentration of ownership by giant corporations, especially multinational ones. The U.S. economy is changing in important ways, in part because it is increasingly intertwined with and dependent on the global economy. In the following sections we will examine three outgrowths of this trend in the United States: the changing face of the workforce, deindustrialization, the sharing economy, and the temporary workforce. As these trends show, any change in the economy has social and political implications.

THE CHANGING FACE OF THE WORKFORCE

The workforce in the United States is constantly changing. During World War II, when men were mobilized to fight abroad, women entered the workforce in large numbers. And with the rise of the civil rights movement in the 1960s, minorities found numerous job opportunities opening to them.

What evidence of deindustrialization or downsizing do you see, specifically, in your community? What broad economic shifts brought about those changes?

Although predictions are not always reliable, sociologists and labor specialists foresee a workforce increasingly composed of women and racial and ethnic minorities. In 1960 there were twice as many men in the labor force as women. From 1988 to 2018, however, 52 percent of new workers are expected to be women. The dynamics for minority group workers are even more dramatic, as the number of Black, Latino, and Asian American workers continues to increase at a faster rate than the number of White workers (Toossi 2009).

More and more, then, the workforce reflects the diversity of the population, as ethnic minorities enter the labor force and immigrants and their children move from marginal jobs or employment in the informal economy to positions of greater visibility and responsibility (see Figure 9–4).

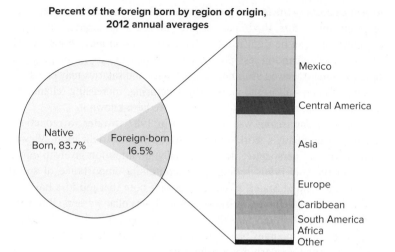

Percent of the foreign born by region of origin, 2012 annual averages

Native Born, 83.7%

Foreign-born 16.5%

Mexico

Central America

Asia

Europe

Caribbean
South America
Africa
Other

Figure 9–4
Foreign-Born Workers in the United States, by World Region
SOURCE: U.S. Bureau of Labor Statistics

The impact of this changing labor force is not merely statistical. A more diverse workforce means that relationships between workers are more likely to cross gender, racial, and ethnic lines. Interactionists note that people will soon find themselves supervising and being supervised by people very different from themselves.

DEINDUSTRIALIZATION

What happens when a company decides it is more profitable to move its operations out of a long-established community to another part of the country, or out of the country altogether? People lose jobs; stores lose customers; the local government's tax base declines and it cuts services. This devastating process has occurred again and again in the past decade or so.

The term *deindustrialization* refers to the systematic, widespread withdrawal of investment in basic aspects of productivity, such as factories and plants. Giant corporations that deindustrialize are not necessarily refusing to invest in new economic opportunities. Rather, the targets and locations of investment change, and the need for labor decreases as advances in technology continue to automate production. First, companies may move their plants from the nation's central cities to the suburbs. The next step may be relocation from suburban areas of the Northeast and Midwest to the South, where labor laws place more restrictions on unions. Finally, a corporation may simply relocate outside the United States to a country with a lower rate of prevailing wages. General Motors, for example, decided to build a multi-billion-dollar plant in China rather than in Kansas City or even in Mexico (Lynn 2003).

Although deindustrialization often involves relocation, in some instances it takes the form of corporate restructuring, as companies seek to reduce costs in the face of growing worldwide competition. When such restructuring occurs, the impact on the bureaucratic hierarchy of formal organizations can be significant. A large corporation may choose to sell off or entirely abandon less productive divisions and to eliminate layers of management viewed as unnecessary. Wages and salaries may be frozen and benefits cut—all in the name of restructuring. Increasing reliance on automation also spells the end of work as we have known it.

The term *downsizing* was introduced in 1987 to refer to reductions taken in a company's workforce as part of deindustrialization. Viewed from a conflict perspective, the unprecedented attention given to downsizing in the mid-1990s reflected the continuing importance of social class in the United States. Conflict theorists note that job loss has long been a feature of deindustrialization among blue-collar workers. But when large numbers of middle-class managers and other white-collar employees with substantial incomes began to be laid off, suddenly the media began expressing great concern over downsizing.

The extended economic downturn that began in 2008 accelerated the processes of deindustrialization and downsizing. As the recession deepened, many plants shut down either temporarily or permanently, leaving more and more workers without jobs. With those jobs and shuttered plants went the hope of restoring or expanding heavy industry, including automobile manufacturing. The bankruptcy of Chrysler and General Motors hit the Midwestern states particularly hard.

The social costs of deindustrialization and downsizing cannot be overemphasized. Plant closings lead to substantial unemployment in a community, which has a devastating impact on both the micro and macro levels. On the micro level, the unemployed person and his or her family must adjust to a loss of spending power. Painting or re-siding the house, buying health insurance or saving for retirement, even thinking about having another child must be put aside. Both marital happiness and family cohesion may suffer as a result. Although many dismissed workers eventually reenter the paid labor force, they must often accept less desirable positions with lower salaries and fewer benefits. Unemployment and underemployment are tied to many of the social problems discussed throughout this textbook, among them the need for child care and the controversy over welfare.

THE SHARING ECONOMY

Why pay a high retail price for a product or service, in a store or online, when you can buy or rent it more cheaply from a stranger? This is the principle behind a range of online services that enable people to share cars (such as Uber and Lyft), accommodations (Airbnb), pet care, bicycles, household appliances and other items. *Sharing economy* refers to connecting owners of underused assets with others willing to pay to use them.

Critics argue that the sharing economy is just an extension of the temporary workforce and that most of sharing economy entrepreneurs would prefer to work for a firm with better wages, legal protection, guaranteed minimum weekly hours, and fringe benefits. They argue that it is not a coincidence that many peer-to-peer rental firms were founded between 2008 and 2010, in the midst of the Great Recession, when conventional employment opportunities tanked. Others argue that the sharing economy serves to commodify services that might otherwise have been given away for free such as offering rides or places to sleep to friends or acquaintances.

Consumers of the sharing economy are attracted to the notion that they may be saving money, and workers like the income and flexible work. However, established businesses question the quality of the services rendered. For example, taxi companies and hotel chains question the nature of their competition in this emerging online marketplace. In addition, governments are beginning to regulate such services, especially when the taxes that competing businesses would pay for their income are not being paid in the sharing economy (DuPuis and Rainwater 2014; *The Week* 2014; White 2015).

THE TEMPORARY WORKFORCE

Over the last four decades, U.S. employers have been relying more and more on the part-time workforce. The recent economic downturn and the slow recovery that followed only accelerated the trend, which began in 1970. In 2015, about 26 million of the 149 million people employed in the United States were working part time, many of them at more than one job (Bureau of Labor Statistics 2015g).

This pattern of expanding part-time work is slowly reshaping the U.S. workforce. Traditionally, businesses employed workers through good times and bad, protecting them from economic ups and downs. In numerous industries, however, that is no longer the case. Today, many part-time employees—those who work 1 to 34 hours a week—are actually temporary or seasonal employees, who work part time for part of the year. These workers typically do not enjoy benefits like health insurance, paid sick-leave, or even unemployment compensation. Certainly some workers seek out part-time jobs, welcoming the flexibility they offer. For example, students taking college classes may prefer part-time work. For most workers, however, part-time employment is not a first choice. In response to the trend away from traditional fulltime jobs, more and more workers are adopting a "free agent mentality," actively seeking work wherever and whenever they can find it instead of expecting to be hired full time. This change in attitude is related to an increase in what has been termed *precarious work*—employment that is poorly paid, and from the worker's perspective, insecure and unprotected (P. Davidson 2012).

Sociology Matters

Sociology matters because it prompts us to look critically at the social institutions that shape our lives.

- What was the hidden curriculum in the primary and secondary schools you attended? Were students assigned to tracks? Do you think the teachers' expectations had an effect on students' academic achievement?

- Do you know anyone who has lost a job because a factory closed, an office was downsized, or jobs were sent to a foreign country? Do the cost savings U.S. consumers get when jobs are sent overseas make up for the losses to U.S. workers?

Sociology matters because it highlights the struggle between the powerful and the powerless.

- Analyze your school or workplace in terms of power and authority. Who governs it, and by what kind of authority? Which model (power elite or pluralist) better fits its power structure?

- Do you consider the division of power and authority in the United States to be fair and just? If not, which social institution do you think is most in need of reform? How would you work to change it?

CHAPTER RESOURCES

Summary

Like the family and religion, the social institutions of **education,** government, and the economy are cultural universals, found in various forms in all human cultures. This chapter examined four sociological perspectives on education; schools as formal organizations; forms of **authority** and **power** in government; two basic **economic systems;** and several trends that are transforming the U.S. and world economies.

1. Functionalists stress that schools perform *latent* as well as *manifest functions.* Their latent (hidden) functions include the transmission of culture, the promotion of social and political integration, the maintenance of social control, and the advancement of social change.

2. Conflict theorists note that schools have a **hidden curriculum** that supports conventional social standards. They charge that schools *track* students according to their social class and perpetuate the unequal treatment of women.

3. Interactionists have noted a **teacher-expectancy effect,** in which teachers' assumptions about students' abilities may affect students' academic performance.

4. Today, most schools in the United States are organized in a bureaucratic fashion. Max Weber's five basic characteristics of bureaucracy are all evident in schools.

5. Schools are complex social organizations. Teachers suffer from the stress of role conflict—that of being both an educator and a disciplinarian—that is inherent in their job.

6. There are three basic sources of **power** in any political system: **force, influence,** and **authority.** Max Weber identified three ideal types of authority: **traditional, rational-legal,** and **charismatic.**

7. Advocates of the **elite model** of the nation's power structure see the United States as being ruled by a small group of individuals, called the **power elite,** who share common political and economic interests. Advocates of the **pluralist model** believe that power is shared more widely among conflicting groups.

8. Though capitalist **economic systems** vary in the degree to which government regulates economic activity, all emphasize the two fundamental principles of **capitalism,** private ownership and the profit motive.

9. Socialist economic systems, in contrast, aim to eliminate economic exploitation and meet people's needs through government regulation and even ownership. Marx believed that **communism** would evolve naturally out of **socialism.**

10. In developing nations, the informal economy represents a significant part of total economic activity. Yet because this sector depends largely on women's work, it is undervalued.

11. The world's economies are changing, both in the United States and abroad. In the United States, workers are coping with **deindustrialization,** the **sharing economy,** and temporary work, and employers are training an increasingly diverse workforce.

Key Terms

Population, Community, Health, and the Environment

Source: U.S. Coast Guard photo by Petty Officer 3rd Class Patrick Kelley

In mid-July 2010, three months after the Gulf Coast oil spill began, the National Commission on the BP Deepwater Horizon Oil Spill and Offshore Drilling held its first meeting in New Orleans. Although presidential commissions are nothing new, the circumstances of this particular meeting were unusual. Events were still unfolding in the Gulf of Mexico and the surrounding communities even as commission members began to deliberate. On shore, small business owners and workers in the fishing and tourist industries were grappling with the spill's implications for their own livelihoods, as well as for the region as a whole. Workers in the oil industry, still reeling from a government-ordered moratorium on oil drilling throughout the Gulf, were wondering whether they had a future in oil. All were struggling to put food on the table and pay their bills.

In the committee room, there was much disagreement about both the scope of the problem and the spill's consequences. Estimates of the amount of oil that was gushing from the well varied widely. It was obvious, however, that the extent of the contamination dwarfed that of the *Exxon Valdez* spill off the coast of Alaska 20 years earlier. The environmental catastrophe had begun in April with a spectacular explosion on one of BP's drilling platforms, which was followed by a devastating fire. Eleven workers had died in the blast. Since then, Americans had watched helplessly as BP made one unsuccessful attempt after another to cap the damaged well. Although the spill was located far off the coast in extremely deep water, oil slicks soon began to wash up on the shores of Alabama, Louisiana, Mississippi, Florida, and Texas. Photos of oil-soaked birds and dirty beaches filled the news.

What had caused this disastrous accident? What would its impact be on the environment and on the well-being of Gulf Coast communities—on people's health, on the economy, on the population? In the months to come, members of the national commission would debate these and other questions, which are not easily answered. We'll see that a region's communities, population, and health depend in many ways on the environment, and that the reverse is also true: a healthy environment depends on the people and communities who live in it.

This chapter begins with the debate about the threat of overpopulation, a subject that has occupied some of the world's best minds since the end of the 18th century. To better understand this debate, we will learn some basic concepts that researchers have developed in their study of population. Then we will look at communities, health, and the environment from a sociological perspective, noting their interdependence and their connection to population issues.

Demography: The Study of Population

Population issues engage the attention of both natural and social scientists. The biologist explores the nature of reproduction and factors that affect *fertility,* the level of reproduction in a society. The medical pathologist examines and analyzes trends in the causes of death. Geographers, historians, and psychologists also have distinctive contributions to make to our understanding of population. Sociologists, more than these other researchers, focus on the *social* factors that influence population rates and trends.

Sociologists are keenly aware that the norms, values, and social patterns of a society profoundly affect various elements of population, such as fertility and *mortality* (the death rate). Fertility is influenced by people's age of entry into sexual unions and by their use of contraception—both of which, in turn, reflect the social and religious values that guide a particular culture. Mortality is shaped by a nation's level of nutrition, acceptance of immunization, and provisions for sanitation, as well as its general commitment to health care and health education. Migration from one country to another can depend on marital and kinship ties, the relative degree of racial and religious tolerance in various societies, and people's evaluation of their employment opportunities.

The formal term for the scientific study of population is *demography.* Demographers draw on several components of population, including size, composition, and territorial distribution, to understand the social consequences of population change. They study geographical variations and historical trends in their effort to develop population forecasts. They also analyze the structure of a population—the age, gender, race, and ethnicity of its members. This type of analysis was popularized by Thomas Malthus.

MALTHUS'S THESIS AND MARX'S RESPONSE

The Reverend Thomas Robert Malthus (1766-1834) was educated at Cambridge University and spent his life teaching history and political economy. He strongly criticized two major institutions of his time—the church and slavery—yet his most significant legacy for contemporary scholars is his still-controversial *Essays on the Principle of Population,* published in 1798.

Essentially, Malthus held that the world's population was growing more rapidly than the available food supply. He argued that food supply increases in an arithmetic progression (1, 2, 3, 4, and so on), whereas population expands by a geometric progression (1, 2, 4, 8, and so on). According to his analysis, the gap between food supply and population will continue to grow over time. Even though the food supply will increase, it will not increase nearly enough to meet the needs of an expanding world population.

Malthus advocated population control to close the gap between rising population and food supply, yet he explicitly denounced artificial means of birth control because they were not sanctioned by religion. For Malthus, one appropriate way to control population was to postpone marriage. He argued that couples must take responsibility for the number of children they choose to bear; without such restraint, the world would face widespread hunger, poverty, and misery (Malthus et al. [1824] 1960; Mayhew 2014).

Karl Marx strongly criticized Malthus's views on population. Marx pointed to the nature of economic relations in Europe's industrial societies as the central problem. He could not accept the Malthusian notion that rising world population, rather than capitalism, was the cause of social ills. In Marx's opinion, there was no special relationship between world population and the supply of resources (including food). If society is well ordered, he reasoned, increases in population should lead to greater wealth, not to hunger and misery.

Of course, Marx did not believe that capitalism operated under these ideal conditions. He maintained that capitalism devoted resources to the financing of buildings and tools rather than to more equitable distribution of food, housing, and other necessities of life. Marx's work is important to the study of population because he linked overpopulation to the unequal

You are living in a country that is so heavily populated, basic resources such as food, water, and living space are running short. What will you do? How will you respond to the crisis if you are a government social planner? A politician?

distribution of resources. His concern with the writings of Malthus also testifies to the importance of population in political and economic affairs.

The insights of Malthus and Marx regarding population issues have since been incorporated in what is termed the *neo-Malthusian view.* Paul Ehrlich (1968; Ehrlich and Ehrlich 1990), author of *The Population Bomb,* and other neo-Malthusians agree with Malthus that world population growth is outstretching natural resources. However, in contrast to the British theorist, they insist that birth control measures are needed to regulate population increases. Their condemnation of developed nations, which despite their low birthrates consume a disproportionately large share of world resources, is founded on Marxist thought. While they are rather pessimistic about the future, these theorists stress that birth control and sensible use of resources are essential responses to rising world population (Tierney 1990; Weeks 2012).

STUDYING POPULATION TODAY

The relative balance of births and deaths is no less important today than it was during the lifetime of Malthus and Marx. The suffering that Malthus spoke of is certainly a reality for many people of the world. Malnutrition accounts for 45 percent of the 6 million annual children deaths in developing countries. Warfare and large-scale migration intensify problems of population and food supply. For example, recent strife in Syria, Afghanistan, the Congo, and Iraq has caused maldistribution of food supplies, leading to regional health concerns. Combating world hunger may require reducing human births, dramatically increasing the world's food supply, or perhaps both. The study of population-related issues, then, seems to be essential (World Health Organization Media Centre 2014).

In the United States and most other countries, the census is the primary mechanism for collecting population information. A *census* is an enumeration, or counting, of a population. The Constitution of the United States requires that a census be held every 10 years to determine congressional representation. This periodic investigation is supplemented by *vital statistics,* or records of births, deaths, marriages, and divorces that are gathered through a registration system maintained by governmental units. In addition, other governmental surveys provide up-to-date information on commercial developments, educational trends, industrial expansion, agricultural practices, and the status of such groups as children, aged people, racial minorities, and single parents.

In administering a nationwide census and conducting other types of research, demographers employ many of the skills and techniques described in Chapter 1, including questionnaires, interviews, and sampling. The precision of population projections depends on the accuracy of a series of estimates that demographers must make. First, they must determine past population trends and establish a base population as of the date for which the forecast begins. Next, birthrates and death rates must be established, along with estimates of future fluctuations. In projecting a nation's population trends, demographers must consider migration as well, since a significant number of individuals may enter and leave a country.

ELEMENTS OF DEMOGRAPHY

Demographers communicate population facts with a language derived from the basic elements of human life—birth and death. The **birthrate** (or more specifically, the *crude birthrate*) is the number of live births per 1,000 population in a given year. In 2015, for example, there were 13 live births per 1,000 people in the United States. The birthrate provides information on the actual reproductive patterns of a society.

One way demographers can project future growth in a society is to make use of the ***total fertility rate (TFR).*** The TFR is the average number of children born alive to any woman, assuming that she conforms to current fertility rates. The TFR reported for the United States in 2015 was 1.0 live births per woman—not high compared to over 8 births per woman in a developing country like Niger.

Mortality, like fertility, is measured in several different ways. The ***death rate*** (also known as the *crude death rate*) is the number of deaths per 1,000 population in a given year. In 2015, the United States had a death rate of 6.0 per 1,000 population. The ***infant mortality rate*** is the number of deaths of infants under one year of age per 1,000 live births in a given year. This particular measure serves as an important indicator of a society's level of health care; it reflects prenatal nutrition, delivery procedures, and infant screening measures. The infant mortality rate also functions as a useful indicator of future population growth, since those infants who survive to adulthood will contribute to further population increases. Figure 10-1 compares the infant mortality rates in selected countries.

Another general measure of health used by demographers is ***life expectancy,*** or the median number of years a person can be expected to live under current mortality conditions. This figure is usually reported as life expectancy *at birth*. At present, Japan reports a life expectancy at birth of 83 years—slightly higher than the United States' figure of 79 years. By contrast, life expectancy at birth is as low as 49 in the African nation of Lesotho.

The ***growth rate*** of a society is the difference between births and deaths, plus the difference between *immigrants* (those who enter a country to establish permanent residence) and *emigrants* (those who leave a country permanently) per 1,000 population. For the world as a whole, the growth rate is simply the difference between births and deaths per 1,000 population, since worldwide immigration and emigration must of necessity be equal. In 2012, the United States had a growth rate of 0.8 percent (Kaneda and Bietsch 2015).

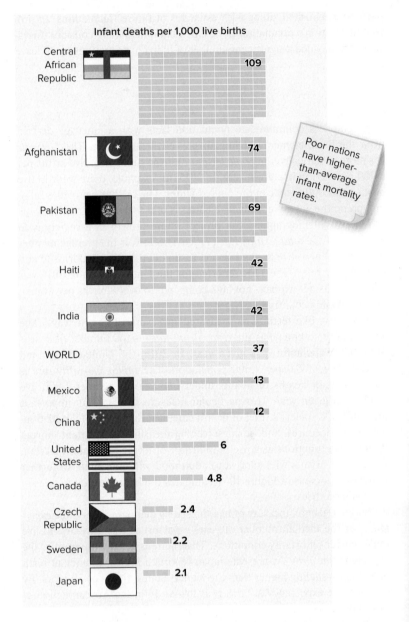

Figure 10-1

Infant mortality rates in selected countries

SOURCE of data: Kaneda and Bietsch 2015.

(Flags): ©admin_design/ Shutterstock

Infant deaths per 1,000 live births

Central African Republic	109
Afghanistan	74
Pakistan	69
Haiti	42
India	42
WORLD	37
Mexico	13
China	12
United States	6
Canada	4.8
Czech Republic	2.4
Sweden	2.2
Japan	2.1

Poor nations have higher-than-average infant mortality rates.

Think About It
Why do you think the United States has a relatively high infant mortality rate for a rich country?

What do these growth rates suggest about the world's future? Was Malthus right when he wrote that the world's population will inevitably outstrip our ability to feed ourselves? Before we attempt to answer this question, let's take a look at how agricultural production has changed over time. The next section will present a brief history of communities, including their methods of production, from the early days of civilization to the present.

How Did Communities Originate?

EARLY COMMUNITIES

A *community* is a unit of social organization, either spatial or political, that gives people a sense of belonging. How did this social arrangement come into being? For most of human history, people used very basic tools and knowledge to survive. They satisfied their need for an adequate food supply through hunting, foraging for fruits and vegetables, fishing, and herding. In comparison with later industrial societies, early civilizations were much more dependent on the physical environment and much less able to alter that environment to their advantage. Perhaps that is why early peoples banded together in nomadic groups in the first known communities.

The emergence of horticultural societies, in which people actually cultivated food rather than merely gathering fruits and vegetables, led to many dramatic changes in human social organization. It was no longer necessary to move from place to place in search of food. Because people had to remain in specific locations to cultivate crops, more stable and enduring communities began to develop. As agricultural techniques became more and more sophisticated, a cooperative division of labor involving both family members and others developed. Gradually it became possible for people to produce more food than they actually needed for themselves. They could give food, perhaps as part of an exchange, to others who might be involved in nonagricultural labor.

This transition from subsistence to surplus represented a critical step in the emergence of cities. Eventually, people produced enough goods to cover both their own needs and those of people not engaged in agricultural tasks. The surplus was limited to agricultural products at first, but slowly evolved to include all types of goods and services. Residents of a city came to rely on community members who provided craft products and means of transportation, gathered information, and so forth (Nolan and Lenski 2015).

With these social changes came an even more elaborate division of labor, as well as greater opportunity for differential rewards and privileges. So long as everyone was engaged in the same tasks, stratification was limited to such factors as gender, age, and perhaps the ability to perform the task (a skillful hunter could win unusual respect from the community). However, the surplus allowed for expansion of goods and services, leading to greater differentiation, a hierarchy of occupations, and social inequality. Therefore, surplus was a precondition not only for the establishment of cities but for the division of members of a community into social classes (see Chapter 5). The ability to produce goods for other communities, then, marked a fundamental shift in human social organization.

PREINDUSTRIAL CITIES

It is estimated that beginning about 10,000 B.C., permanent settlements free from dependence on crop cultivation emerged. By today's standards, these early communities would barely qualify as cities. The *preindustrial city*, as it is termed, generally had only a few thousand people living within its borders, and was characterized by a relatively closed class system and limited mobility. In these early cities, status was usually based on ascribed characteristics such as family background, and education was limited to members of the elite. All the residents relied on perhaps 100,000 farmers and their own part-time farming to provide the needed agricultural surplus. The Mesopotamian city of Ur had a population of about 10,000 and was limited to roughly 220 acres of land, including the canals, the temple, and the harbor.

Why were these early cities so small and relatively few in number? Several key factors restricted urbanization:

- *Reliance on animal power (both humans and beasts of burden) as a source of energy for economic production.* This factor limited the ability of humans to make use of and alter the physical environment.

- *Modest levels of surplus produced by the agricultural sector.* Between 50 and 90 farmers may have been required to support one city resident (K. Davis [1949] 1995).

- *Problems in transportation and the storage of food and other goods.* Even an excellent crop could easily be lost as a result of such difficulties.

- *Hardships of migration to the city.* For many peasants, migration was both physically and economically impossible. A few weeks of travel was out of the question without more sophisticated food storage techniques.

- *Dangers of city life.* Concentrating a society's population in a small area left it open to attack from outsiders, as well as more susceptible to extreme damage from plagues and fires.

A sophisticated social organization was also an essential precondition for urban existence. Specialized social roles were important because cities brought people together in new ways through the exchange of goods and services. A well-developed social organization ensured that these relationships were clearly defined and acceptable to all.

INDUSTRIAL AND POSTINDUSTRIAL CITIES

Advances in agricultural technology led to dramatic changes in community life, but so did the process of industrialization. The *Industrial Revolution,* which began in the middle of the 18th century, focused on the application of nonanimal sources of power to labor tasks. Industrialization had a wide range of effects on people's lifestyles, as well as on the structure of communities. Emerging urban settlements became centers not only of industry but of banking, finance, and industrial management.

The factory system that developed during the Industrial Revolution led to a much more refined division of labor than existed in early preindustrial cities. In turn, the many new jobs it created produced a complex set of relationships among workers. Thus, the *industrial city* was not merely more populous than its preindustrial predecessors; it was based on very different principles of social organization (see Table 10–1).

In comparison with preindustrial cities, industrial cities had a more open class system and more mobility. After initiatives in industrial cities by women's rights groups, labor unions, and other political activists, formal education gradually became available to children from poor and working-class families. While ascribed characteristics such as gender, race, and ethnicity remained important, a talented or skilled individual

Table 10–1 Comparing Types of Cities

Preindustrial Cities (through 18th century)	Industrial Cities (18th through mid-20th century)	Postindustrial Cities (beginning late 20th century)
Closed class system—pervasive influence of social class at birth	Open class system—mobility based on achieved characteristics	Wealth based on ability to obtain and use information
Economic realm controlled by guilds and a few families	Relatively open competition	Corporate power dominates
Beginnings of division of labor in creation of goods	Elaborate specialization in manufacturing of goods	Sense of place fades, transnational networks emerge
Pervasive influence of religion on social norms	Influence of religion limited to certain areas as society becomes more secularized	Religion becomes more fragmented; greater openness to new religious faiths
Little standardization of prices, weights, and measures	Standardization enforced by custom and law	Conflicting views of prevailing standards
Population largely illiterate, communication by word of mouth	Emergence of communication through posters, bulletins, and newspapers	Emergence of extended electronic networks
Schools limited to elites and designed to perpetuate their privileged status	Formal schooling open to the masses and viewed as a means of advancing the social order	Professional, scientific, and technical personnel become increasingly important

SOURCES: E. Phillips 1996:132–135; Sjoberg 1960:323–328.

had more opportunity to better his or her social position than in the past. In these and other respects, the industrial city was genuinely a different world from the preindustrial urban community.

In the latter part of the 20th century, a new type of urban community emerged. The *postindustrial city* is a city in which global finance and the electronic flow of information dominate the economy. Production is decentralized and often takes place outside urban centers, but control is centralized in multinational corporations whose influence transcends urban and even national boundaries. Social change is a constant feature of the postindustrial city. Economic and spatial restructuring seems to occur each decade, if not more frequently. In the postindustrial world, cities are forced into increasing competition with one another for economic opportunities, which deepens the plight of the urban poor (E. Phillips 1996; D. Smith and Timberlake 1993).

Sociologist Louis Wirth (1928, 1938) argued that a relatively large and permanent settlement leads to distinctive patterns of social behavior, which he called *urbanism.* He identified three critical factors that contribute to urbanism: the size of the population, population density, and the heterogeneity (variety) of the population. A frequent result of urbanism, according to Wirth, is that residents become insensitive to events around them and restrict their attention to the primary groups to which they are emotionally attached.

In most parts of the world today, populations are concentrating more and more in urban areas. What are the effects of urbanization on the people who congregate in cities? In the following section we will see how urbanization shapes both the neighborhoods Americans live or do not live in and the economic well-being of people in developing countries.

What would the ideal city of the future look like? Describe its architecture, public transportation, neighborhoods, schools, and workplaces. What kinds of people would live and work there?

Urbanization and Its Consequences

The 1990 census was the first to demonstrate that more than half the U.S. population lives in urban areas of 1 million or more residents. In only four states (Maine, Mississippi, Vermont, and West Virginia) do more than half the residents live in rural areas. Clearly, urbanization has become a central aspect of life in the United States (Bureau of the Census 2009a).

Urbanization can be seen throughout the rest of the world, too. In 1900 only 10 percent of the world's people lived in urban areas, but by 2005 that proportion had risen to around 50 percent. By the year 2025, the number of city dwellers could reach 5 billion (Koolhaas et al. 2001:3; United Nations Population Division 2004b).

During the 19th and early 20th centuries, rapid urbanization occurred primarily in European and North American cities. Since World War II, however, an urban "explosion" has hit the world's developing countries. Such rapid growth is evident in the rising number of "squatter settlements," outlying areas occupied by the very poor.

The trend toward urbanization is so important, some sociologists have devoted their careers to the study of its effects. In the following sections we will examine two contrasting perspectives on urbanization, a functionalist view called *urban ecology* and a conflict view called the *new urban sociology.*

FUNCTIONALIST PERSPECTIVE: URBAN ECOLOGY

Human ecology is an area of study that is concerned with the interrelationships between people and their spatial setting and physical environment. Human ecologists have long been interested in how the physical environment shapes people's lives (for example, rivers can serve as a barrier to residential expansion) as well as in how people influence the surrounding environment (for example, air-conditioning has accelerated the growth of major metropolitan areas in the Southwest). *Urban ecology* focuses on such relationships as they emerge in urban areas. Although the urban ecological approach examines social change in cities, it is nevertheless functionalist in its orientation because it emphasizes that different elements in urban areas contribute to social stability.

Early urban ecologists such as Robert Park (1916, 1936) and Ernest Burgess (1925) concentrated on city life but drew on the approaches used by ecologists in studying plant and animal communities. With few exceptions, today's urban ecologists trace their work back to the *concentric-zone theory* Burgess devised in the 1920s (see Figure 10–2a). Using Chicago as an example, Burgess proposed a theory for describing land use in industrial cities. At the center, or nucleus, of such a city is the central business district. Large department stores, hotels, theaters, and financial institutions occupy this highly valued land. Surrounding this urban center are zones devoted to other types of land use. According to this theory, the city grows over time by spreading outward from the center.

Consider the spatial arrangements in your everyday life from the point of view of urban ecology. How do artificial constructions and barriers affect your travel patterns?

Figure 10–2
Ecological Theories of Urban Growth

SOURCE: Harris and Ullman 1945:13.

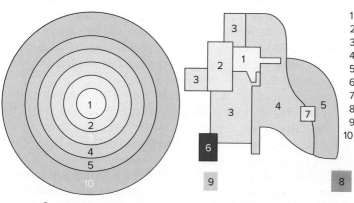

1. Central business district
2. Wholesale light manufacturing
3. Low-class residential
4. Medium-class residential
5. High-class residential
6. Heavy manufacturing
7. Outlying business district
8. Residential suburb
9. Industrial suburb
10. Commuters' zone

a. Concentric-zone theory   b. Multiple-nuclei theory

Note that the creation of zones is a *social* process, not the result of nature alone. Families and business firms compete for the most valuable land; those possessing the most wealth and power generally win. Thus, the concentric-zone theory is a dynamic model of urban growth. As urban growth proceeds, each zone moves even farther from the central business district.

Because of its functionalist orientation and its emphasis on stability, the concentric-zone theory tended to understate or ignore certain tensions apparent in metropolitan areas. For example, urban ecologists viewed uncritically the growing use by the affluent of land in a city's peripheral areas. Some described the arrival of African Americans in White neighborhoods in the 1930s with terms such as "invasion" and "succession." Moreover, urban ecologists gave little thought to gender inequities, such as the establishment of men's softball and golf leagues in city parks without any programs for women. Consequently, the urban ecological approach has been criticized for its failure to address issues of gender, race, and class.

By the middle of the 20th century, urban populations had spread beyond traditional city limits. No longer could urban ecologists focus exclusively on growth in the central city, for large numbers of urban residents were abandoning the cities to live in suburban areas. In response to the emergence of more than one focal point in some metropolitan areas, Chauncy D. Harris and Edward Ullman (1945) presented the ***multiple-nuclei theory*** (see Figure 10–2b). In their view, all urban growth does not radiate outward from a central business district. Instead, a metropolitan area may have many centers of development, each of which reflects a particular urban need or activity. Thus, a city may have a financial district, a manufacturing zone, a waterfront area, an entertainment center, and so forth. Certain types of business firms and certain types of housing will naturally cluster around each distinctive nucleus (Squires 2002).

The rise of suburban shopping malls is a vivid example of the phenomenon of multiple nuclei within metropolitan areas. Initially, all major retailing was located in the city's central business district. Each residential neighborhood had its own grocers, bakers, and butchers, but people traveled to the center of the city to make major purchases at department stores. However, as metropolitan areas expanded and the suburbs became more populous, an increasing number of people began to shop nearer their homes. Today, the suburban mall is a significant retailing and social center in communities across the United States.

In a refinement of the multiple-nuclei theory, contemporary urban ecologists have begun to study what journalist Joel Garreau (1991) has called "edge cities." These communities, which have grown up on the outskirts of major metropolitan areas, are economic and social centers with identities of their own. By any standard of measurement—height of buildings, amount of office space, presence of medical or leisure-time facilities, or of course, population—edge cities qualify as independent cities rather than as large suburbs.

Use Your Sociological Imagination

You have fast-forwarded to a future in which there are no central cities—just sprawling suburbs and isolated rural communities. What are the economic and social effects of the disappearance of the downtown area?

Whether metropolitan areas include edge cities or multiple nuclei, more and more of them are characterized by spread-out development and unchecked growth. The social consequences of such rapid growth are equally dramatic, from a shortage of affordable housing and an inadequate number of food pantries to an overstretched water supply, poor health care delivery, and impossible traffic. Today's cities are very different from the preindustrial cities of a thousand years ago.

CONFLICT PERSPECTIVE: NEW URBAN SOCIOLOGY

Contemporary sociologists point out that metropolitan growth is not governed by waterways and rail lines, as a purely ecological interpretation might suggest. From a conflict perspective, communities are human creations that reflect people's needs, choices, and decisions—though some people have more influence than others over those decisions. Drawing on conflict theory, proponents of an approach that has come to be called the *new urban sociology* consider the interplay of local, national, and worldwide forces and their effect on local space, with special emphasis on the impact of global economic activity (Gottdiener et al. 2015).

New urban sociologists note that urban ecologists typically have avoided examining the social forces, largely economic in nature, that have guided urban growth. For example, central business districts may be upgraded or abandoned, depending on whether urban policy makers grant substantial tax exemptions to developers. The suburban boom in the post–World War II era was fueled by federal housing policies that channeled investment capital into the construction of single-family homes rather than affordable rental housing in the cities. Similarly, while some observers suggest that the growth of sun-belt cities is due to a "good business climate," new urban sociologists counter that the term is actually a euphemism for hefty state and local government subsidies and antilabor policies intended to draw manufacturers. In addition, rapid growth has carried with it significant environmental costs that are only beginning to be measured (Gottdiener and Feagin 1988; Gottdiener et al. 2015; M. Smith 1988).

The new urban sociology draws generally on the conflict perspective and more specifically on sociologist Immanuel Wallerstein's *world systems analysis* (see Chapter 5). Wallerstein argues that certain industrialized nations (among them the United States, Japan, and Germany) hold a dominant position at the *core* of the global economic system. The poor developing countries of Asia, Africa, and Latin America occupy the *periphery* of the global economy, where they are controlled and exploited by core industrialized nations.

Using world systems analysis, new urban sociologists consider urbanization from a global perspective. They view cities not as independent and autonomous entities but rather as the outcome of decision-making processes directed or influenced by a society's dominant classes and by

Table 10–2 Sociological Perspectives on Urbanization

	Urban Ecology	New Urban Sociology
Theoretical Perspective	Functionalist	Conflict
Primary Focus	Relationship of urban areas to their spatial setting and physical environment	Relationship of urban areas to global, national, and local forces
Key Source of Change	Technological innovations such as new methods of transportation	Economic competition and monopolization of power
Initiator of Actions	Individuals, neighborhoods, communities	Real estate developers, banks and other financial institutions, and multinational corporations
Allied Disciplines	Geography, architecture	Political science, economics

core industrialized nations. New urban sociologists note that the rapidly growing cities of the world's developing countries were shaped first by colonialism and then by a global economy controlled by core nations and multinational corporations (Gottdiener and Feagin 1988; D. Smith 1995).

As we have seen throughout this textbook, in studying such varied issues as deviance, race, and ethnicity, no single theoretical approach necessarily offers the only valuable perspective. As Table 10-2 shows, urban ecology and the new urban sociology offer significantly different ways of viewing urbanization, both of which enrich our understanding of this complex phenomenon. Clearly, however, urbanization does affect the well-being of those who live in our cities, including their health and quality of life. In the following two sections we will discuss the concepts of health and illness from a sociological perspective, as well as the distribution of health care and the relative health of different social groups.

Health and Illness: Sociological Perspectives

In the preamble to its 1946 constitution, the World Health Organization defined *health* as a "state of complete physical, mental, and social well-being, and not merely the absence of disease and infirmity" (Leavell and Clark 1965:14). Imagine a continuum with health on one end and death on the other. In this definition, the "healthy" end of our continuum represents an ideal rather than a precise condition. Along the continuum, people define themselves as "healthy" or "sick" on the basis of criteria established by themselves, relatives, friends, co workers, and medical practitioners. Health and illness, in other words, are socially constructed. They are rooted in culture and are defined by claims makers—people who describe themselves as healthy or ill—as well as by a broad range of interested parties, including health care providers, pharmaceutical firms, and even food providers (Conrad and Barker 2010). Because health is socially constructed, we can consider how it varies in different situations or cultures. Who controls definitions of health and illness in our society, and for what ends? Why is it that you may consider yourself sick or well when others do not agree? What are the consequences of viewing yourself (or of being viewed) as ill or disabled? In this section, by drawing on four sociological perspectives—functionalism, conflict theory, interactionism, and labeling theory—we will gain insight into the social context that shapes definitions of health and the treatment of illness.

FUNCTIONALIST PERSPECTIVE ON HEALTH AND ILLNESS

Illness entails breaks in our social interactions both at work and at home. From a functionalist perspective, then, "being sick" must be controlled so that not too many people are released from their societal responsibilities at any one time. Functionalists contend that an overly broad definition of illness would disrupt the workings of a society.

"Sickness" requires that one take on a social role, even if temporarily. The *sick role* refers to societal expectations about the attitudes and behavior of a person viewed as being ill. Sociologist Talcott Parsons (1951, 1975), well known for his contributions to functionalist theory, has outlined the behavior required of people considered "sick." They are exempted from their normal, day-to-day responsibilities and generally do not suffer blame for their condition. Yet they are obligated to try to get well, which includes seeking competent professional care. This obligation arises from the common view that illness is dysfunctional, because it can undermine social stability. Attempting to get well is particularly important in the world's developing countries. Modern, automated industrial societies can absorb a greater degree of illness or disability than horticultural or agrarian societies, where the availability of workers is far more critical (Conrad and Leiter 2013).

According to Parsons's theory, physicians function as "gatekeepers" for the sick role. They either verify a patient's condition as "illness" or designate the patient as "recovered." The ill person becomes dependent on the doctor, who can control valuable rewards (not only treatment of illness but excused absences from work and school). Parsons suggests that the doctor–patient relationship is somewhat like that between parent and child. Like a parent, the physician helps the patient to enter society as a full and functioning adult (Frank 2015).

The concept of the sick role is not without criticism. First, patients' judgments regarding their own state of health may be related to their gender, age, social class, and ethnic group. For example, younger people may fail to detect warning signs of a dangerous illness, while older people may focus too much on the slightest physical malady. Second, the sick role may be more applicable to people experiencing short-term illnesses than to those with recurring, long-term illnesses. Finally, even simple factors, such as whether or not a person is employed, seem to affect the willingness

Describe some situations you have witnessed that illustrate different definitions of the "sick role."

to assume the sick role—as does the impact of socialization into a particular occupation or activity. For example, beginning in childhood, athletes learn to define certain ailments as "sports injuries" and therefore do not regard themselves as "sick." Nonetheless, sociologists continue to rely on Parsons's model for functionalist analysis of the relationship between illness and societal expectations of the sick (Curry 1993).

CONFLICT PERSPECTIVE ON HEALTH AND ILLNESS

Conflict theorists observe that the medical profession has assumed a preeminence that extends well beyond whether to excuse a student from school or an employee from work. Sociologist Eliot Freidson (1970:5) has likened the position of medicine today to that of state religions yesterday—it has an officially approved monopoly of the right to define health and illness and to treat illness. Conflict theorists use the term *medicalization of society* to refer to the growing role of medicine as a major institution of social control.

The Medicalization of Society   Social control involves techniques and strategies for regulating behavior in order to enforce the distinctive norms and values of a culture. Typically, we think of informal social control as occurring within families and peer groups, and of formal social control as being carried out by authorized agents such as police officers, judges, school administrators, and employers. However, viewed from a conflict perspective, medicine is not simply a "healing profession"; it is a regulating mechanism as well.

How does medicine manifest its social control? First, the field has greatly expanded its domain of expertise in recent decades. Physicians now examine a wide range of issues, among them sexuality (including homosexuality), old age, anxiety, obesity, child development, alcoholism, and drug addiction. Society tolerates such expansion of the boundaries of medicine in the hope that these experts can bring new "miracle cures" to complex human problems, just as they have to the control of certain infectious diseases.

The social significance of this expanding medicalization is that once a problem is viewed using a *medical model*—once medical experts become influential in proposing and assessing relevant public policies—it becomes more difficult for "common people" to join the discussion and exert influence on decision making. It also becomes more difficult to view these issues as being shaped by social, cultural, or psychological factors rather than simply by physical or medical factors (Caplan 1989; Conrad 2009).

Second, medicine serves as an agent of social control by retaining absolute jurisdiction over many health care procedures. It has even attempted to guard its jurisdiction by placing health care professionals such as chiropractors and nurse-midwives outside the realm of acceptable medicine. Despite the fact that midwives first brought professionalism to child delivery, they have been portrayed as having invaded the "legitimate" field of obstetrics in both the United States and Mexico. Nurse-midwives have sought licensing as a way to achieve professional respectability, but physicians continue to exert power to ensure that midwifery remains a subordinate occupation (Scharnberg 2007).

Inequities in Health Care   The medicalization of society is but one concern of conflict theorists. As we have seen throughout this textbook, when analyzing any issue, conflict theorists seek to determine who benefits, who suffers, and who dominates at the expense of others. From a conflict perspective, glaring inequities exist in health care delivery in the United States. For example, poor and rural areas tend to be underserved, because medical services concentrate where people are wealthy.

Similarly, from a global perspective, we can see obvious inequities in health care delivery. Today, the United States has about 25 times the number of physicians per 1,000 people that most African and Asian nations have. This situation is only worsened by the **brain drain**—the immigration to the United States and other industrialized nations of skilled workers, professionals, and technicians who are desperately needed in their home countries. As part of the brain drain, physicians, nurses, and other health care professionals have come to the United States from developing countries such as India, Pakistan, and various African states. Conflict theorists view such emigration out of the Third World as yet another way in which the world's core industrialized nations enhance their quality of life at the expense of developing countries. One way that developing countries suffer is in lower life expectancy. In Africa and much of Latin America and Asia, life expectancy is far lower than in industrialized nations (Migration Policy Institute).

From a sociological point of view, what might be the greatest challenge to reducing inequities in health care?

Conflict theorists emphasize that inequities in health care have clear life-and-death consequences. From a conflict perspective, the dramatic differences in infant mortality rates around the world (see Figure 10–1) reflect, at least in part, unequal distribution of health care resources based on the wealth or poverty of various nations. This measure is an important indicator of a society's level of health care; it reflects prenatal nutrition, delivery procedures, and infant screening measures. Still, despite the wealth of the United States, at least 49 nations have *lower* infant mortality rates. Conflict theorists point out that unlike the United States, these countries offer some form of government-supported health care for all citizens, which typically leads to greater availability and use of prenatal care.

INTERACTIONIST PERSPECTIVE ON HEALTH AND ILLNESS

From an interactionist point of view, patients are not passive; often, they actively seek the services of a health care practitioner. In examining health, illness, and medicine as a social institution, then, interactionists

engage in micro-level study of the roles played by health care professionals and patients. Interactionists are particularly interested in how physicians learn to play their occupational role. According to Brenda L.
Beagan (2001), the technical language students learn in medical school
becomes the basis for the script they follow as novice physicians. The
familiar white coat is their costume—one that helps them to appear confi-
dent and professional at the same time that it identifies them as doctors
to patients and other staff members. Beagan found that many medical
students struggle to project the appearance of competence they think
their role demands.

Sometimes patients play an active role in health care by *failing* to follow a physician's advice. For example, some patients stop taking medications long before they should. Some take an incorrect dosage on purpose,
and others never even fill their prescriptions. Such noncompliance results
in part from the prevalence of self-medication in our society; many people
are accustomed to self-diagnosis and self-treatment. On the other hand,
patients' active involvement in their health care can sometimes have very
positive consequences. Some patients read books about preventive health
care techniques, attempt to maintain a healthful and nutritious diet, carefully monitor any side effects of medication, and adjust the dosage based
on perceived side effects.

LABELING PERSPECTIVE ON HEALTH AND ILLNESS

Labeling theory helps us to understand why certain people are *viewed* as
deviants, "bad kids," or criminals, whereas others whose behavior is similar are not. Labeling theorists also suggest that the designation "healthy"
or "ill" generally involves social definition by others. Just as police officers,
judges, and other regulators of social control have the power to define certain people as criminals, health care professionals (especially physicians)
have the power to define certain people as "sick." Moreover, like labels
that suggest nonconformity or criminality, labels associated with illness
commonly reshape how others treat us and how we see ourselves.

A historical example illustrates perhaps the ultimate extreme in labeling social behavior as a sickness. In the 19th century, as enslavement
of Africans in the United States came under increasing attack, medical
authorities provided new rationalizations for the oppressive practice.
Noted physicians published articles stating that the skin color of Africans
deviated from "healthy" white skin coloring because Africans suffered
from congenital leprosy. Moreover, the continuing efforts of enslaved
Africans to escape from their White masters were classified as an example of the "disease" of drapetomania (or "crazy runaways"). The prestigious *New Orleans Medical and Surgical Journal* suggested that the remedy
for this "disease" was to treat slaves kindly, as one might treat children.
Apparently, medical authorities would not entertain the view that it was
healthy and sane to flee slavery or join in a slave revolt (T. Szasz 2010).

Table 10–3 Sociological Perspectives on Health and Illness				
	Functionalist	**Conflict**	**Interactionist**	**Labeling**
Major Emphasis	Control of the number of people who are considered sick	Overmedicalization Gross inequities in health care	Doctor–patient relationship Interaction of medical staff	Definition of illness and health
Controlling Factors	Physician as gatekeeper	Medical profession Social inequities	Medical profession	Medical profession
Proponents	Talcott Parsons	Thomas Szasz Irving Zola	Howard Becker	Thomas Szasz

According to labeling theorists, we can view a variety of life experiences as illnesses or not. Recently, premenstrual syndrome, posttraumatic disorders, and hyperactivity have been "labeled" medically recognized disorders. In addition, disagreements have arisen in the medical community over whether chronic fatigue syndrome constitutes a medical illness.

A new concern about how illness can be stigmatized grows out of the dependence on electronic health records. As more and more medical records are digitized to facilitate access by medical professionals, concerns have increased over how a person's medical history may be viewed or misinterpreted if the records are improperly shared. There are a host of medical labels, from cancer survivor to diabetic, that could result in discrimination, despite laws prohibiting such practices (Stablen et al. 2015).

Describe an occasion on which people you know disagreed about a socially applied medical label. What was the label, and why did people disagree?

Probably the most noteworthy medical example of labeling is the case of homosexuality. For years, psychiatrists classified being gay or lesbian not as a lifestyle but as a mental disorder subject to treatment. This official sanction became an early target of the growing gay and lesbian rights movement in the United States. In 1974, members of the American Psychiatric Association finally voted to drop homosexuality from the standard manual on mental disorders (Conrad 2009).

Table 10-3 summarizes the four sociological approaches to health and illness just described. They share certain common themes. First, any person's health or illness is more than an organic condition, since it is subject to the interpretation of others. The impact of culture, family and friends, and the medical profession means that health and illness are not purely biological occurrences but sociological occurrences as well. Second, since members of a society (especially industrial societies) share the same health care delivery system, health is a group and societal concern. Although health may be defined as the complete well-being of an individual, it is also the result of the social environment, as the next section will show (Cockerham 2012).

Social Epidemiology

Social epidemiology is the study of the distribution of disease, impairment, and general health status across a population. The first epidemiologists concentrated on the scientific study of epidemics, focusing on how the diseases started and spread. Contemporary social epidemiology is much broader in scope, concerned not only with epidemics but with nonepidemic diseases, injuries, drug addiction and alcoholism, suicide, and mental illness. Epidemiologists have taken on the new role of tracking bioterrorism. In 2001, they mobilized to trace the anthrax outbreak and prepare for any terrorist use of smallpox or other lethal microbes. Epidemiologists draw on the work of a wide variety of scientists and researchers, among them physicians, sociologists, public health officials, biologists, veterinarians, demographers, anthropologists, psychologists, and meteorologists.

Researchers in social epidemiology commonly use two concepts: *incidence* and *prevalence*. *Incidence* refers to the number of new cases of a specific disorder occurring within a given population during a stated period, usually a year. For example, the incidence of AIDS in the United States in 2010 was 48,079 cases. In contrast, *prevalence* refers to the total number of cases of a specific disorder that exist at a given time. The prevalence of HIV/AIDS in the United States through 2010 was about 800,000 cases.

When incidence figures are presented as rates, or as the number of reports of a disorder per 100,000 people, they are called *morbidity rates.* The term *mortality rate* refers to the incidence of *death* in a given population. Sociologists find morbidity rates useful because they reveal that a specific disease occurs more frequently among one segment of a population than another. As we shall see, social class, race, ethnicity, gender, and age can all affect a population's morbidity rates.

SOCIAL CLASS

Social class is clearly associated with differences in morbidity and mortality rates. Studies in the United States and other countries have consistently shown that people in the lower classes have higher rates of mortality and disability than others.

Why is class linked to health? Crowded living conditions, substandard housing, poor diet, and stress all contribute to the ill health of many low-income people in the United States. In certain instances, poor education may lead to a lack of awareness of measures necessary to maintain good health. Financial strains are certainly a major factor in the health problems of less affluent people.

What is particularly troubling about social class differences is that they appear to be cumulative. Little or no health care in childhood or young adulthood is likely to mean more illness later in life. The longer that low income presents a barrier to adequate health care, the more chronic and difficult to treat illness becomes.

Another reason for the link between class and health is that the poor—many of whom belong to racial and ethnic minorities—are less able than others to afford quality medical care. The affluent are more likely than others to have health insurance, either because they can afford it or because they have jobs that provide it. Pharmacists report that people purchase only those medications they "need the most," or buy in small quantities, such as four pills at a time. Between 2008 and 2013, the uninsured rate ranged from 14.5 percent to 15.5 percent. The percentage of the population who were uninsured dropped between 2013 and 2014 to 11.7, marking the largest decline in the uninsured rate during this period. While health insurance coverage has improved, children in households earning less than $25,000 are still half as likely to have access to any kind of insurance plan than the more affluent.

Finally, in the view of Karl Marx and contemporary conflict theorists, capitalist societies such as the United States care more about maximizing profits than they do about the health and safety of industrial workers. As a result, government agencies do not take forceful action to regulate conditions in the workplace, and workers suffer many preventable job-related injuries and illnesses. As we will see later in this chapter, research also shows that the lower classes are more vulnerable to environmental pollution than are the affluent, not only where they work but where they live.

In what ways do the costs of health care affect the way you receive medical services?

RACE AND ETHNICITY

Health profiles of many racial and ethnic minorities reflect the social inequality evident in the United States. Research shows that the lower classes and members of racial and ethnic minorities are more vulnerable than affluent citizens to environmental pollution. Class plays a role, but race is more oppressive: though upwardly mobile Whites can generally escape from pollution centers, even well-off Blacks tend to be restricted in their residential mobility. The poor economic and environmental conditions of groups such as African Americans, Hispanics, and Native Americans are manifested in high morbidity and mortality rates. It is true that some afflictions, such as sickle-cell anemia among Blacks, have a clear genetic basis, but in most instances, environmental factors contribute to the differential rates of disease and death.

As noted earlier, infant mortality is regarded as a primary indicator of the level of health care. There is a significant gap in the United States between the infant mortality rates of African Americans and Whites. Generally, the rate of infant death is more than twice as high among Blacks. African Americans account for 15 percent of all live births in the nation but 29 percent of infant deaths. Puerto Ricans and Native Americans have infant mortality rates that are lower than African Americans' but higher than Whites' (MacDorman et al. 2005; MacDorman and Mathews 2009).

The medical establishment is not exempt from racism. Unfortunately, the media often focus on obvious forms of racism, such as hate crimes, while overlooking more insidious forms in social institutions like the medical establishment. Minorities receive inferior medical care even when they are insured. Despite having access to care, Blacks, Latinos, and Native Americans are treated unequally as a result of racial prejudice and differences in the quality of various health care plans. Furthermore, national clinical studies have shown that even allowing for differences in income and insurance coverage, racial and ethnic minorities are less likely than other groups to receive both standard health care and life-saving treatment for conditions such as HIV infection (Centers for Disease Control and Prevention 2013; Phelan and Link 2015).

Drawing on the conflict perspective, sociologist Howard Waitzkin (1986) suggests that racial tensions contribute to the medical problems of Blacks. In his view, the stress resulting from racial prejudice and discrimination helps to explain the higher rates of hypertension found among African Americans (and Hispanics) compared with Whites. Hypertension, which affects over 41 percent of Blacks but fewer than 29 percent of non-Hispanic Whites, is believed to be a critical factor in high mortality rates from heart disease, kidney disease, and stroke found among African Americans (Gillespie and Hurvitz 2013).

Some Mexican Americans, as well as many other Latinos, adhere to cultural beliefs that make them less likely to use the established medical system. They may interpret their illnesses according to traditional Latino folk practices, or *curanderismo*—a form of holistic health care and healing. *Curanderismo* influences how one approaches health care and even how one defines illness. Most Hispanics probably use *curanderos,* or folk healers, infrequently, but perhaps 20 percent rely on home remedies. Some define illnesses according to folk beliefs, such as *susto* (fright sickness) and *atague* (or fighting attack). Because these complaints often have biological bases, sensitive medical practitioners need to deal with them carefully and diagnose and treat illnesses accurately. Moreover, it would be a mistake to blame the poor health care that Latinos receive on cultural differences. Latinos are much more likely to seek treatment for pressing medical problems at clinics and emergency rooms than they are to receive regular preventive care through a family physician (Centers for Disease Control and Prevention 2013; Hendrickson 2015).

GENDER

A large body of research indicates that in comparison with men, women experience a higher prevalence of many illnesses, though they tend to live longer. There are variations—for example, men are more likely to have parasitic diseases, whereas women are more likely to become diabetic—but as a group, women appear to be in poorer health than men.

The apparent inconsistency between the ill health of women and their greater longevity deserves an explanation, and researchers have advanced a theory. Women's lower rate of cigarette smoking (reducing their risk of heart disease, lung cancer, and emphysema), lower consumption of alcohol (reducing their risk of auto accidents and cirrhosis of the liver), and lower rate of employment in dangerous occupations explain about one-third of their greater longevity. Moreover, some clinical studies suggest that the differences in morbidity may actually be less pronounced than the data show. Researchers argue that women are much more likely than men to seek treatment, to be diagnosed as having a disease, and thus to have their illness reflected in the data examined by epidemiologists.

From a conflict perspective, women have been particularly vulnerable to the medicalization of society, with everything from birth to beauty being treated in an increasingly medical context. Such medicalization may contribute to women's higher morbidity rates compared to those of men. Ironically, even though women have been especially affected by medicalization, medical researchers have often excluded women from clinical studies. Female physicians and researchers charge that sexism lies at the heart of such research practices and insist there is a desperate need for studies of female subjects (Centers for Disease Control and Prevention 2013; Gengler and Jarrell 2015).

Which is a more important factor in the adequate delivery of health care, race or gender?

AGE

Health is the overriding concern of older people. In the United States, most older people report having at least one chronic illness, but only some of those conditions are potentially life threatening or require medical care. At the same time, health problems can affect the quality of life of older people in important ways. Almost half of older people in the United States are troubled by arthritis, and many have visual or hearing impairments that can interfere with the performance of everyday tasks.

Older people are also especially vulnerable to certain types of mental health problems. Alzheimer's disease, the leading cause of dementia in the United States, afflicts an estimated 5.1 million older people—that is, 11 percent of that segment of the population. While some individuals with Alzheimer's exhibit only mild symptoms, the risk of severe problems resulting from the disease rises substantially with age (Alzheimer's Association 2016).

Not surprisingly, older people in the United States (aged 75 and older) are five times more likely to use health services than younger people (aged 15–24). The disproportionate use of the U.S. health care system by older people is a critical factor in all discussions about the cost of health care and possible reforms of the health care system.

In sum, to achieve greater access and reduce health disparities, federal health officials must overcome inequities that are rooted not just in age, but in social class, race and ethnicity, and gender. If that were not enough, they must also deal with a geographical disparity in health care resources.

The disparity in resources that exists from one place to another, both within the United States and throughout the globe, is only one way in which our environment can affect our well-being. Our quality of life, whether in the cities, the suburbs, or rural areas, is closely related to the environment. In the final section of this chapter we will see how burgeoning population levels and consumption patterns can have a negative effect on our natural surroundings and on the health of whole communities.

The Environment: The World and Our Place in It

Urban sprawl has been encroaching on the fields and forests that surround U.S. cities, replacing them with residential developments and malls. The new construction disturbs wildlife and threatens the water supply, and the cars residents drive to work every day choke the highways, contributing to air pollution and global warming.

In recent years, public attention has turned increasingly to global warming, manifested in the shrinking of the polar ice caps and the increasing ferociousness of tropical storms as they cross warmer-than-normal ocean waters. Human activities have contributed to the documented warming of the planet over the last half-century, through the altered chemical composition of the atmosphere and the buildup of greenhouse gases such as carbon dioxide, methane, and nitrous oxide. While environmental problems may be easy to identify scientifically, devising socially and politically acceptable solutions is much more difficult. In the following sections we will survey some identifiable environmental issues and see what sociologists have to say about them.

ENVIRONMENTAL ISSUES

Around the world, people are recognizing the need to address the challenges to our environment. Yet in the United States, survey respondents do not see environmental issues as the most pressing of problems, and they often balk at proposed solutions. Unfortunately, framing environmental issues as "problems" may prevent people from seeing environmental deterioration as the by-product of both institutional practices and their own behavior. Thus, in a 2015 global study, only 45 percent of the people in the United States felt that climate change was a very serious problem, compared to 61 percent of people in Africa and 74 percent in Latin America (Stokes et al. 2015).

We will discuss the enormous challenge of global warming later in this section. First, we will discuss air and water pollution, which are thought to contribute to global warming. We will close the section with a discussion of the impact of globalization.

Air Pollution   Worldwide, more than 1 billion people are exposed to potentially health-damaging levels of air pollution. Unfortunately, in cities around the world, residents have come to accept smog and polluted air as normal. Urban air pollution is caused primarily by emissions from automobiles and secondarily by emissions from electric power plants and heavy industries. Smog not only limits visibility; it can lead to health problems as uncomfortable as eye irritation and as deadly as lung cancer. Such problems are especially severe in developing countries.

Although people are capable of changing their behavior, they are unwilling to make such changes permanent. During the 1984 Olympics in Los Angeles, residents were asked to carpool and stagger their work hours to relieve traffic congestion and improve the quality of the air athletes would breathe. These changes resulted in a remarkable 12 percent drop in ozone levels. But when the Olympians left, people reverted to their normal behavior and the ozone levels climbed back up. Similarly, in the 2008 Olympics, China took drastic action to ensure that Beijing's high levels of air pollution did not mar the games. Construction work in the city ceased, polluting factories and power plants closed down, and roads were swept and sprayed with water several times a day. However, this temporary solution hardly solved China's ongoing problem (A. Jacobs 2010).

On an everyday basis—that is, when cities are not holding down their emissions because of global sports events—air pollution remains a serious issue. Today, half of all people live in countries where they are exposed to dangerously high levels of air pollution, either short-term or year-round. Solutions range from community efforts to clean up power plants and enforce or strengthen air quality standards to individual actions, like driving less often or using less electricity (American Lung Association 2015).

Water Pollution   Throughout the United States, dumping of waste materials by industries and local governments has polluted streams, rivers, and lakes. Consequently, many bodies of water have become unsafe for drinking, fishing, and swimming. Around the world, pollution of the oceans is an issue of growing concern. Such pollution results regularly from waste dumping and is made worse by fuel leaks from shipping and occasional oil spills. When the oil tanker *Exxon Valdez* ran aground in Prince William Sound, Alaska, in 1989, its cargo of 11 million gallons of crude oil spilled into the sound and washed onto the shore, contaminating 1,285 miles of shoreline. All together, about 11,000 people joined in a massive cleanup effort that cost over $2 billion. Globally, oil tanker spills occur regularly. BP's Deepwater Horizon oil spill in the Gulf of Mexico (see the opening to this chapter) was estimated at *16 times or more* the size of the *Exxon Valdez* spill (ITOPF 2006; Shapley 2010).

Less dramatic than large-scale accidents or disasters, but more common in many parts of the world, are problems with the basic water supply. The situation is worsened by heavy, widespread pollution of surface and groundwater by towns, industries, agriculture, and mining operations.

Which issue is more significant in your local community, air or water pollution? Why?

In Egypt, a typical example, agricultural and industrial waste pours into the Nile. Every year about 17,000 Egyptian children die from diarrhea and dehydration after contact with the river's polluted water (Hengeveld 2012).

As you think about all the issues facing our society, how often do you consider climate change? How often do your friends give it much thought?

Climate Change   *Climate change* is an observable alteration of the global atmosphere that affects natural weather patterns over several decades or longer. Periods of climate change occurred well before humans walked the earth. Recently, climate change has included rapid global warming.

The term *global warming* refers to the significant rise in the earth's surface temperatures that occurs when industrial gases like carbon dioxide turn the planet's atmosphere into a virtual greenhouse. These so-called *greenhouse gas emissions,* which also include methane, nitrous oxide, and ozone, trap heat in the lower atmosphere. Even one additional degree of warmth in the globe's average surface temperature can increase the likelihood of wildfires, shrinkage of rivers and lakes, expansion of deserts, and torrential downpours, including typhoons and hurricanes (Giddens 2011; Lynas 2008).

"The End of Snow?" asked a newspaper headline during the 2014 Winter Olympics. Although snow will not disappear from the earth, climatologists predict that finding suitable sites for the snow-dependent international competition will become increasingly difficult. Of the 19 cities that have hosted the Winter Olympics in the past, as few as 10 might be cold enough to do so in 2050, and just 6 in 2100. For people digging out from the record snowfalls of 2014–2015, that prediction might have seemed laughable, but the global trend is toward reduced snowfall. Decline in the snowpack is now jeopardizing half of all ski resorts in the northeastern United States; if it continues, they may not be viable 30 years from now. Similar trends are threatening ski resorts in the western United States. More important, snowpack is not just for skiers; the spring runoff from melting snow is critical to maintaining water supplies (Fox 2014).

Although scientific concern over global warming has heated up, climate change remains low on policy makers' list of concerns. The problem seems abstract, and in many countries, officials think that the real impact of any action they may take depends on decisive action by other nations. The Kyoto Protocol was intended to reduce global emissions of heat-trapped gases, which can contribute to global warming and climate change. To date, 192 countries have signed the accord, but the United States has failed to ratify it. Opponents of the protocol argue that doing so would place the nation at a disadvantage in the global marketplace.

In writing about the global environment, activists often assert, "We're all in this together." Though we are all in this together, the reality is that globally, the most vulnerable countries tend to be the poorest. Developing nations are more likely than others to have economies that are built on limited resources or on a small number of crops vulnerable to

"Two can live as carbon-neutral as one."

To combat global warming, increasing numbers of people are seeking to achieve net-zero carbon emissions, both by avoiding emissions when possible—for example, by walking rather than driving—and through offsets (such as planting trees).

©Joseph Farris Cartoons/ josephfarris.com

drought, flood, and fluctuations in worldwide demand (Nordhaus and Shellenberger 2007; Revkin 2007).

We can view global warming from the point of view of world systems analysis. Historically, core nations have been the major emitters of greenhouse gases. Today, however, manufacturing has moved to semiperiphery and periphery nations, where greenhouse gas emissions are escalating. Ironically, many of the forces that are now calling for a reduction in the human activity that contributes to global warming are located in core nations, which have contributed disproportionately to the problem. We want our hamburgers, but we decry the destruction of the rain forests to create grazing land for cattle. We want inexpensive clothes and toys, but we condemn developing countries for depending on coal-fired power plants.

What are the causes of this global environmental crisis? Some observers, such as Paul Ehrlich and Anne Ehrlich, see the pressure of world population growth as the central factor in environmental deterioration. They argue that population control is essential in preventing widespread starvation and environmental decay. Table 10–4 shows the dramatic escalation of population growth over the last two centuries.

Barry Commoner, a biologist, counters that the primary cause of environmental ills is the increasing use of technological innovations that are destructive to the environment—among them plastics, detergents, synthetic fibers, pesticides, herbicides, and chemical fertilizers. Conflict

Table 10–4 Estimated Time for Each Successive Increase of 1 Billion People in World Population

Population Level	Time Taken to Reach New Population Level	Year of Attainment
First billion	Human history before 1800	1804
Second billion	123 years	1927
Third billion	32 years	1959
Fourth billion	15 years	1974
Fifth billion	13 years	1987
Sixth billion	12 years	1999
Seventh billion	12 years	2011
Eighth billion	15 years	2026
Ninth billion	16 years	2042

SOURCES: Bureau of the Census 2013b; Kunzig 2011:40.

theorists see the despoliation of the environment through the lens of world systems analysis. And interactionists stress efforts by informed individuals and groups to reduce their carbon footprint—that is, their daily or even lifetime production of greenhouse gases—through careful selection of the goods they consume (Carbon Trust 2015; Commoner 1990, 2007; Ehrlich and Ellison 2002).

The Impact of Globalization   Globalization can be both good and bad for the environment. On the negative side, it can create a race to the bottom, as polluting companies relocate to countries with less stringent environmental standards. Similarly, globalization allows multinationals to reap the resources of developing countries for short-term profit. From Mexico to China, the industrialization that often accompanies globalization has increased pollution of all types.

Yet globalization can have a positive impact, as well. As barriers to the international movement of goods, services, and people fall, multinational corporations have an incentive to carefully consider the cost of natural resources. Overusing or wasting resources makes little sense, especially when they are in danger of depletion (Gallagher 2009; Kwong 2005).

One reflection of the interplay between globalization and the environment is the emergence of so-called *environmental refugees*. Europe in particular is beginning to see an influx of such immigrants from developing nations. According to a European Union report, global warming can be viewed as a "threat multiplier" that exacerbates prolonged droughts and a shortage of arable land, and along with them, poverty, poor health, and poor living conditions. Viewed through the lens of world systems analysis, periphery countries may become overburdened by environmental problems, precipitating migrations to industrial nations or conflicts that cause mass displacements of their populations. "Europe must expect substantially increased migratory pressure" from these environmental refugees, the report concludes (L. Brown 2011).

Against these potentially negative effects of globalization we must note the potential for new jobs in what are called green industries. Installing solar panels, weatherizing homes, brewing biofuels, building hybrid cars, growing organic foods, manufacturing organic garments, and erecting giant wind turbines are all classified as *green-collar jobs.* However, skeptics question how many such jobs will be created, and to what degree they will offset job losses in pollution-prone industries like oil, gas, and coal mining (S. Greenhouse 2008b; R. Pinderhughes 2008).

HUMAN ECOLOGY

Earlier, we noted that human ecology is concerned with interrelationships between people and their environment. As Barry Commoner (1971:39) has stated, "Everything is connected to everything else." Human ecologists focus both on how the physical environment shapes people's lives and on how people influence the surrounding environment.

There is no shortage of illustrations of the interconnectedness of people and their environment. For example, scientific research has linked pollutants in the physical environment to people's health and behavior. The increasing prevalence of asthma, lead poisoning, and cancer has been tied to human alterations to the environment. Similarly, the rise in melanoma (skin cancer) diagnoses has been linked to global warming. And ecological changes in our food and diet have been related to early obesity and diabetes.

With its view that "everything is connected to everything else," human ecology stresses the trade-offs inherent in every decision that alters the environment. In facing the environmental challenges of the 21st century, government policy makers and environmentalists must determine how they can fulfill humans' pressing needs for food, clothing, and shelter while preserving the environment.

A CONFLICT PERSPECTIVE ON ENVIRONMENTAL ISSUES

in Chapter 5 we drew on world systems analysis to show how a growing share of the human and natural resources of developing countries is being redistributed to the core industrialized nations. This process only intensifies the destruction of natural resources in poorer regions of the world. From a conflict perspective, less affluent nations are being forced to exploit their mineral deposits, forests, and fisheries in order to meet their debt obligations to industrialized nations. The poor turn to the only means of survival available to them: They plow mountain slopes, burn tropical forests, and overgraze grasslands (World Bank 2010b).

Brazil exemplifies this interplay between economic troubles and environmental destruction. Each year more than 5.7 million acres of forest are cleared for crops and livestock. The elimination of the rain forest affects worldwide weather patterns, heightening the gradual warming of the earth. These socioeconomic patterns, with their harmful environmental consequences, are evident not only in Latin America but in many regions of Africa and Asia as well.

Conflict theorists are well aware of the environmental implications of land use policies in the Third World, but they contend that focusing on the developing countries is ethnocentric. Who, they ask, is more to blame for environmental deterioration: the poverty-stricken and "food-hungry" populations of the world or the "energy-hungry" industrialized nations? These theorists point out that the industrialized nations of North America and Europe account for only 12 percent of the world's population but are responsible for 60 percent of worldwide consumption. The money their residents spend on ocean cruises each year could provide clean drinking water for everyone on the planet. Ice cream expenditures in Europe alone could be used to immunize every child in the world. Thus, conflict theorists charge, the most serious threat to the environment comes from the global consumer class (Pellow and Brehm 2013).

Allan Schnaiberg (1994) further refines this analysis by shifting the focus from affluent consumers as the cause of environmental troubles. In his view, a capitalist system creates a "treadmill of production" because of its inherent need to build ever-expanding profits. This treadmill necessitates creating an increasing demand for products, obtaining natural resources at minimal cost, and manufacturing products as quickly and cheaply as possible—no matter what the long-term environmental consequences.

ECOLOGICAL MODERNIZATION

Critics of the human ecological and conflict models argue that they are too rooted in the past. People who take these approaches, they charge, have become bogged down in addressing existing practices. Instead, proponents of *ecological modernization,* an approach that emerged in the 1980s, focus on the alignment of environmentally favorable practices with economic self-interest through constant adaptation and restructuring (Gould and Lewis 2015).

Ecological modernization can occur on both the macro and micro levels. On a macro level, adaptation and restructuring can mean reintegrating industrial waste back into the production process. On a micro level, it can mean reshaping individual lifestyles, including the consumption patterns described at the start of this section. In a sense, those who practice ecological modernization seek to refute the oft-expressed notion that being environmentally conscious means "going back to nature" or "living off the grid." Even modest changes in production and consumption patterns, they believe, can increase environmental sustainability (York et al. 2010).

ENVIRONMENTAL JUSTICE

In autumn 1982, nearly 500 African Americans participated in a six-week protest against a hazardous waste landfill in North Carolina. Their protests and legal actions against the dangerous cancer-causing chemicals continued until 2002, when decontamination of the site finally began. This 20-year battle could be seen as yet another "not in my backyard" (NIMBY) event. But today, the Warren County struggle is viewed as a transformative moment in contemporary environmentalism: the beginning of the environmental justice movement (Bullard 1993; McGurty 2000; North Carolina Department of Environment and Natural Resources 2008).

Environmental justice is a legal strategy based on claims that racial minorities and the lower classes are subjected disproportionately to environmental hazards. Some observers have heralded environmental justice as the "new civil rights of the 21st century" (Kokmen 2008:42). Since the start of the environmental justice movement, activists and scholars have discovered other environmental disparities that break along racial and social class lines. In general, poor people and people of color are much more likely than others to be victimized by the everyday consequences of our built environment, including the air pollution from expressways and incinerators.

Some people cannot safely drink their tap water even after boiling it. No, this situation did not occur in a developing nation but in Flint, Michigan, a city of over 100,000 people. In what was described as a case of environmental racism by some candidates in the 2016 general election, the city of Flint, faced with huge budget problems, decided in 2014 to save money by obtaining its water from the industrially polluted Flint River. As a result, water polluted with unsafe levels of lead and other toxic chemicals entered people's homes. The people of Flint,

Use Your Sociological Imagination

How are the physical and human environments connected in your neighborhood or community?

who are overwhelmingly Black and disproportionately poor, found their early concerns ignored or discounted as "grandstanding" by government officials.

Regrettably, Flint is not a unique case of environmental injustice (Eligon 2016). African Americans making $50,000 to $60,000 per year are much more likely to live in a polluted environment than White families making just $10,000. An analysis of over 600 hazardous waste treatment, storage, and disposal facilities in the United States found that non-Whites and Latinos make up 43 percent of the people who live within one mile of these dangerous sites. Skeptics often argue that minorities move near such sites because of low housing prices. However, two recent longitudinal (long-term) research studies, done over 30- and 50-year periods, found that toxic facilities tend to be located in minority communities (Ellison 2015; Mohai and Saha 2007; Mohai et al. 2009:413).

The environmental justice movement has become globalized, for several reasons. In many nations, activists have noticed similar patterns in the location of hazardous waste sites. These groups have begun to network across international borders, to share their tactics and remedies. Their unified approach is wise, because the offending corporations are often multinational entities (see Chapter 5); influencing their actions, much less prosecuting them, is difficult. As we have noted before, the global warming debate often focuses criticism on developing nations like China and India, rather than on established industrial giants with a long history of greenhouse gas emissions (Pellow and Brehm 2013).

Sociologists, then, have emphasized both the interconnectedness of humans and the environment and the divisiveness of race and social class in their work on humans and their alteration of the environment. Scientists, too, have taken different approaches, disagreeing sharply on the likely outcomes of environmental change. When these disagreements threaten to affect government policy and economic regulations, they become highly politicized.

Sociology Matters

Sociology matters because it explains the connection between population patterns and the community in which you live.

- What kind of community—urban, suburban, or rural—do you live in? Is your community growing, or has its population been declining? What is responsible for the growth or decline of your community?

- Examine the city nearest you from the point of view of an urban sociologist. Is its economy industrial or postindustrial? Which theory describes its growth better, the concentric-zone theory or the multiple-nuclei theory? Does the city have any global economic ties?

Sociology matters because it highlights the relationship between your race, ethnicity, and social class and your quality of life.

- Evaluate the health of the people in your community: Do you think it is better than average, average, or worse than average? How many people in your community have low incomes or are members of minority groups? How many lack health care or health insurance?

- Describe your community's environment. Does it present any health hazards? If so, could some of the health problems in your community be related to those hazards?

CHAPTER RESOURCES

Summary

The size, composition, and distribution of the world's population have an important influence on our **communities,** our **health,** and our environment. This chapter introduced **demography,** the scientific study of population. We followed the growth of communities from prehistory through the present and considered urbanization from both the functionalist and conflict perspectives. We studied the relationship between people's health, their geographic distribution, and the social groups to which they belong. And we acknowledged the connection between our health and the environment.

1. Thomas Robert Malthus suggested that the world's population was growing more rapidly than the available food supply and that the gap between the two would increase over time. But Karl Marx saw capitalism, rather than rising population, as the main cause of the world's social ills.

2. The primary tool for obtaining **vital statistics** on the population of the United States and most other countries is the **census.**

3. Stable **communities** first developed when humans became farmers, and their surplus production allowed others to live in **preindustrial cities.** Thousands of years later, the mechanization of production

ushered in the era of the **industrial city,** a large population center dominated by factories. In the 20th century, globalization and the electronic flow of information gave rise to the **postindustrial city,** characterized by corporate offices rather than factories.

4. **Urban ecology** is a functionalist view of urbanization that focuses on the interrelationships between city dwellers and their environment. Urban ecologists developed two theories of urban growth, the **concentric-zone theory** and the **multiple-nuclei theory.**

5. **New urban sociology,** a conflict view of urbanization, focuses on the interplay of local, national, and global economic forces and their effect on cities throughout the world. This school of thought draws on Immanuel Wallerstein's **world systems analysis.**

6. Functionalists, conflict theorists, and labeling theorists all see medicine as an institution of social definition and control. Functionalists see doctors as gatekeepers to the **sick role;** conflict theorists see them as proponents of the medicalization of society.

7. **Social epidemiology** is the study of the distribution of disease, disability, and **health** across a population. Epidemiological studies have shown that lower-class people have higher rates of **mortality** and disability than upper-class people. Similarly, racial and ethnic minorities have higher rates of **morbidity** and mortality than Whites.

8. Conflict theorists charge that the most serious threat to the environment comes from Western industrialized nations, which consume a disproportionate amount of the world's resources.

9. To reduce this threat to the environment, proponents of **ecological modernization** recommend the alignment of economic self-interest with environmentally favorable practices through a process of constant adaptation and restructuring.

10. Racial minorities and the lower classes tend to be exposed more than other groups to environmental hazards, a social pattern that has prompted calls for **environmental justice.**

Key Terms

birthrate, 265

brain drain, 277

census, 264

climate change, 286

community, 267

concentric-zone
    theory, 271

curanderismo, 282

death rate, 265

demography, 263

ecological modern-
    ization, 290

environmental
    justice, 291

fertility, 262

global warming, 286

growth rate, 265

health, 274

human ecology, 271

incidence, 280

industrial city, 269

infant mortality
    rate, 265

life expectancy, 265

Social Movements, Social Change, and Technology

©Dave Moyer

Social Movements

Theories of Social Change

Resistance to Social Change

Technology and the Future

Who runs the United States now, and who will run it in the future? Is it the elite—the top 1 percent of the population—or everyone else, the so-called 99 percent?

In 2011–2012, during a deep and lengthy recession, this question became the central issue of Occupy Wall Street. The movement began in Vancouver, Canada, after the editors of *Adbusters* magazine suggested a protest against "corporate rule" in lower Manhattan. Their call to action, reflecting the latest technology, went out in a tweet ending with the link "#occupywallstreet."

On September 17, 2011, the first day of the movement, 2,000 protesters gathered in New York City. Claiming to speak for the vast majority of Americans, they said they had come to represent "the 99 percent": those Americans who had lost their jobs, their homes, or their retirement savings when the stock market collapsed. In the next few weeks, the movement would spread across the United States to Honolulu and throughout the world, where millions more were suffering from the global financial crisis (Peralta 2011; M. Scherer 2011).

What did Americans make of this new movement? Opinions ran the gamut, from former New York City mayor Rudy Giuliani's sarcastic "How about you occupy a job?" to sociologist Craig Calhoun's comparison to student protests in China. The New York City Police response to Occupy

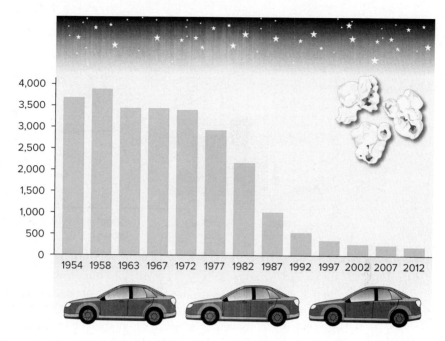

4,000
3,500
3,000
2,500
2,000
1,500
1,000
500
0

1954 1958 1963 1967 1972 1977 1982 1987 1992 1997 2002 2007 2012

Wall Street, Calhoun wrote, was "reminiscent of the Chinese govern-ment ousting protesters from Tiananmen." Native Americans observed that their land had been occupied for over five centuries without much notice from White protesters. And homeless people marveled at the sudden concern over people (protesters) sleeping in city parks (Cal-houn 2011; Lawler 2011).

Figure 11–1
Declining Drive-Ins,
1954–2012
SOURCE: Bureau of the Census 2015i.

More than anything, Occupy Wall Street protesters were seeking change. To get their message out, they relied on social networking sites. As we have seen before, when new technologies are introduced, society experiences *social change*.

Social change may be defined as significant alteration over time in behavior patterns and culture (Moore 1967). Eventually, the existence of social networking sites may greatly influence the way people behave, but this is not the only way in which social change happens.

Consider two changes to which you probably have not given much thought. First is the decline of drive-in movie theaters in the United States (Figure 11–1). You may have never been to a drive-in, but half a century ago they were a major entertainment destination. Now we go to a multiplex or stream movies rather than go to a drive-in. A second example of social change is walking to work (Figure 11–2). Who does that anymore in the United States? Not many. In certain urban areas it is a bit more common—10 percent of people in New York City walk to work, 12 percent in Washington, D.C., and 15 per-cent in Boston, but almost anywhere else, it just does not happen (McKenzie 2014).

Figure 11–2
*Walking to Work,
1980 To 2012*

Source: Bureau of the
Census 2014d.

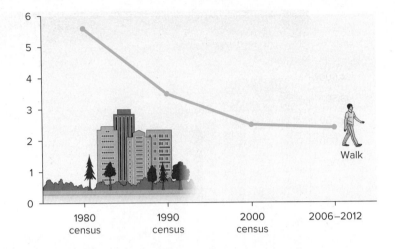

In this chapter, we will examine the process of social change, with special emphasis on the impact of technological advances. We will begin with social movements, which often spearhead social change. Then we will consider different sociological perspectives on change and note how vested interests attempt to block it. Finally, we will look at the role of technology in spurring social change, from Web surfing and the offshoring of service jobs to censorship and genetic engineering.

Social Movements

Social movements are the most powerful source of social change. Although such factors as the physical environment, population, technology, and social inequality also serve as sources of change, it is the *collective* effort of individuals organized into social movements that ultimately leads to change.

Sociologists use the term *social movement* to refer to an organized collective activity to bring about or resist fundamental change in an existing group or society (Benford 1992). Herbert Blumer (1955:19) recognized the special importance of social movements when he defined them as "collective enterprises to establish a new order of life."

In many nations, including the United States, social movements have had a dramatic impact on the course of history and the evolution of social structure. Consider the actions of abolitionists, suffragists, civil rights workers, and activists opposed to the war in Vietnam. Members of each social movement stepped outside traditional channels for bringing about social change and yet had a noticeable influence on public policy. In Eastern Europe, equally dramatic collective efforts helped to topple

Communist regimes in a largely peaceful manner, in nations that many observers had felt were "immune" to such change (Ramet 1991).

Though social movements imply the existence of conflict, we can also analyze their activities from a functionalist perspective. Even when unsuccessful, social movements contribute to the formation of public opinion. Initially, the ideas of Margaret Sanger and other early advocates of birth control were viewed as "radical," yet contraceptives are now widely available in the United States.

Because social movements know no borders, even nationalistic movements are deeply influenced by global events. Increasingly, social movements are taking on an international dimension from the start. Global enterprises, in particular, lend themselves to targeting through international mobilization, whether they are corporations like McDonald's or governmental bodies like the World Trade Organization. Global activism is not new, however; it began with the writing of Karl Marx, who sought to mobilize oppressed peoples in other industrialized countries. Today, activist networking is facilitated by the Internet. Participation in transnational activism is much more widespread now than in the past, and passions are quicker to ignite.

How and why do social movements emerge? Obviously, people are often discontented with current conditions. But what causes them to organize at a particular moment in a collective effort to work for change? In this section we will examine two different explanations for why people mobilize: the relative deprivation approach and the resource mobilization approach. We will also acknowledge the often underestimated role of gender in social movements and study recent changes in the character of social movements.

What social movements are most visible on your campus? In the community where you live? What do you think these groups need to do to be effective?

THE RELATIVE DEPRIVATION APPROACH

Those members of a society who feel most frustrated and disgruntled by the social and economic conditions of their lives are not necessarily "worst off" in an objective sense. Social scientists have long recognized that what is most significant is how people *perceive* their situation. Karl Marx pointed out that although the misery of the workers was important to their perception of their oppressed state, so was their position *relative* to the capitalist ruling class (Marx and Engels [1847] 1955).

The term ***relative deprivation*** is defined as the conscious feeling of a negative discrepancy between legitimate expectations and present actualities (J. Wilson 1973). In other words, life isn't as good as you hoped it would be. Such a state may be characterized by scarcity rather than complete lack of necessities (as we saw in the distinction between absolute and relative poverty in Chapter 5). A relatively deprived person is dissatisfied because he or she feels downtrodden relative to some appropriate reference group. Thus, blue-collar workers who live in two-family houses with little lawn space—though they are hardly at the bottom of the economic ladder—may nevertheless feel deprived in comparison with corporate managers and professionals who live in lavish and exclusive suburbs.

In addition to the feeling of relative deprivation, two other elements must be present before discontent will be channeled into a social movement. First, people must feel that they have a *right* to their goals, that they deserve better than what they have. Sociologists at Oxford University gathered data on 404 militant extremists from 31 nations. Among them the researchers found many highly educated individuals, including engineers and other high-level achievers. Yet these relatively fortunate people still felt disadvantaged by what they perceived as corrupt or misguided governments. Second, the disadvantaged people must perceive that they cannot attain their goals through conventional means. This belief may or may not be correct. Whichever is the case, the group will not mobilize into a social movement unless members share the perception that they can end their relative deprivation *only* through collective action (*The Atlantic* 2008; Gambetta and Hertog 2007).

Critics of this approach have noted that an increase in feelings of deprivation is not always necessary before people are moved to act. In addition, this approach fails to explain why certain feelings of deprivation are transformed into social movements, whereas in other similar situations, no collective effort is made to reshape society. Consequently, in recent years, sociologists have given increasing attention to the forces needed to bring about the emergence of social movements (G. Martin 2015).

Why might well-off people feel deprived?

THE RESOURCE MOBILIZATION APPROACH

It takes more than desire to start a social movement. Money, political influence, access to the media, and personnel all help. The term *resource mobilization* refers to the ways in which a social movement utilizes such resources. The success of a movement for change will depend in good part on what resources it has and how effectively it mobilizes them. In other words, recruiting adherents and marshaling resources is critical to the growth and success of social movements (D. Miller 2014).

Leadership is a central factor in the mobilization of the discontented into social movements. Often, a movement will be led by a charismatic figure, such as Dr. Martin Luther King Jr. As Max Weber described it in 1904, *charisma* is that quality of an individual that sets him or her apart from ordinary people. Of course, charisma can fade abruptly, which accounts for the fragility of certain social movements (Morris 2000).

Many social movements are mobilized by institutional insiders. During the nationwide debate of the Obama administration's plan for health care reform in 2009, for example, health insurance companies encouraged their employees to attend the forums arranged by the White House. Managers distributed "Town Hall Tips" that included a list of concerns employees could raise and suggestions on how to make their comments as personal as possible, by talking about their own health issues (Walker 2010).

Why do certain individuals join a social movement, whereas others in similar situations do not? Some people are recruited to join. Karl Marx recognized the importance of recruitment when he called on workers to become *aware* of their oppressed status and develop a shared class consciousness. Marx held that the development of a social movement (specifically, the revolt of the proletariat) would require leaders to sharpen the awareness of the oppressed. They would need to help workers to overcome *false consciousness,* or attitudes that did not reflect workers' objective position, in order to organize a revolutionary movement. Similarly, sociologists who take the resource mobilization approach point out that one of the challenges women's liberation activists of the late 1960s and early 1970s faced was to convince women that they were being deprived of their rights and of socially valued resources.

GENDER AND SOCIAL MOVEMENTS

Sociologists point out that gender and sexual identities are important elements in understanding social movements. Our society has traditionally been dominated by male leaders and policy makers, and day-to-day life tends to assume that relationships are heterosexual. Further, traditional examination of the sociopolitical system tends to focus on such male-dominated corridors of power as legislatures and corporate boardrooms, to the neglect of more female-dominated domains such as households, community-based groups, and faith-based networks. While the feminist approach is changing that bias, many scholars still consider social movements only through a framing that entirely overlooks same-sex relationships.

Scholars of social movements now realize that gender can affect even the way we view organized efforts to bring about or resist change. For example, an emphasis on using rationality and cold logic to achieve goals helps to obscure the importance of passion and emotion in successful social movements. Calls for a more serious study of the role of emotion are frequently seen as applying only to the women's movement, because emotion is traditionally thought of as feminine. It would be difficult to find any movement, from labor battles to voting rights to animal rights, in which passion was not part of the consensus-building force. Yet calls for a more serious study of the role of emotion are frequently seen as applying only to the women's movement, because emotion is traditionally thought of as being feminine (Hurwitz and Taylor 2012).

What aspects of traditional gender roles explain the roles that women and men typically play in social movements?

NEW SOCIAL MOVEMENTS

Beginning in the late 1960s, European social scientists observed a change in both the composition and the targets of emerging social movements. In the past, traditional social movements had focused on economic issues, often led by labor unions or by people who shared the same occupation. However, many social movements that have become active in recent decades—including the contemporary women's movement, the peace movement, and the environmental movement—do not have the social class roots typical of the labor protests in the United States and Europe over the past century (Tilly 1993, 2004).

The term *new social movement* refers to an organized collective activity that addresses values and social identities as well as improvements in the quality of life. These movements may be involved in developing collective identities. Many have complex agendas that go beyond a single issue and even cross national boundaries. Educated, middle-class people are significantly represented in some of these new social movements, such as the women's movement and the movement for lesbian and gay rights.

New social movements generally do not view government as their ally in the struggle for a better society. While they typically do not seek to overthrow the government, they may criticize, protest, or harass public officials. Researchers have found that members of new social movements show little inclination to accept established authority, even scientific or technical authority. This characteristic is especially evident in the environmental and anti-nuclear power movements, whose activists present their own experts to counter those of government or big business (Garner 1996; Polletta and Jasper 2001; A. Scott 1990).

The environmental movement is one of many new movements that have adopted a worldwide focus. In their efforts to reduce air and water pollution, curtail global warming, and protect endangered animal species, environmental activists have realized that establishing strong regulatory measures within a single country is not sufficient. Similarly, labor union leaders and human rights advocates cannot adequately address exploitative sweatshop conditions in a developing country if a multinational corporation can simply move the factory to another country where workers are paid even less. Whereas traditional social movements tend to emphasize resource mobilization on a local level, new social movements take a broader, global perspective on social and political activism.

Table 11-1 summarizes the three sociological approaches that have contributed to social movement theory. Each approach has added to our

Try to imagine a society without any social movements. Under what conditions could such a society exist? Would you want to live in it?

Table 11–1 Contributions to Social Movement Theory

summing UP

Approach	Emphasis
Relative deprivation approach	Social movements are especially likely to arise when rising expectations are frustrated.
Resource mobilization approach	The success of social movements depends on which resources are available and how effectively they are used.
New social movement theory	Social movements arise when people are motivated by value issues and social identity questions.

understanding of the development of social movements. But in a larger sense, what causes social change? In the next section we will see how sociologists have used some of the major theoretical perspectives to analyze and interpret the process of social change.

Theories of Social Change

We have defined *social change* as a significant alteration over time in behavior patterns and culture. Social change can occur so slowly as to be almost undetectable to those it affects, but it can also happen with breathtaking rapidity. As Figure 11-3 shows, the U.S. economy has grown through rapid change in just the beginning of the 21st century. For example, we can see the rapid growth in health and social assistance jobs to the point where these are now the leading sector of employment. Meanwhile, manufacturing continues the decline it began in the last century.

Explanations of social change are clearly a challenge in the diverse and complex world we inhabit today. Nevertheless, theorists from several disciplines have sought to analyze social change. In some instances, they have examined historical events to arrive at a better understanding of contemporary changes. We will review three theoretical approaches to change—evolutionary, functionalist, and conflict theory—and then take a look at global social change.

EVOLUTIONARY THEORY

The pioneering work of Charles Darwin (1809–1882) in biological evolution contributed to 19th-century theories of social change. Darwin's approach stresses a continuing progression of successive life forms. For example, human beings came at a later stage of evolution than reptiles and represent a more complex form of life. Social theorists seeking an analogy to this biological model originated *evolutionary theory,* in which society is viewed as moving in a definite direction. Early evolutionary theorists generally agreed that society was progressing inevitably to a higher state. As might be expected, they concluded in ethnocentric fashion that their own behavior and culture were more advanced than those of earlier civilizations.

Auguste Comte (1798–1857), a founder of sociology, was an evolutionary theorist of social change. He saw human societies as moving forward in their thinking from mythology to the scientific method. Similarly, Émile Durkheim ([1893] 1933) maintained that society progressed from simple to more complex forms of social organization.

Today, evolutionary theory influences sociologists in a variety of ways. For example, it has encouraged sociobiologists to investigate the behavioral links between humans and other animals. It has also influenced human ecology, the study of the interaction between communities and their environment (Maryanski 2004).

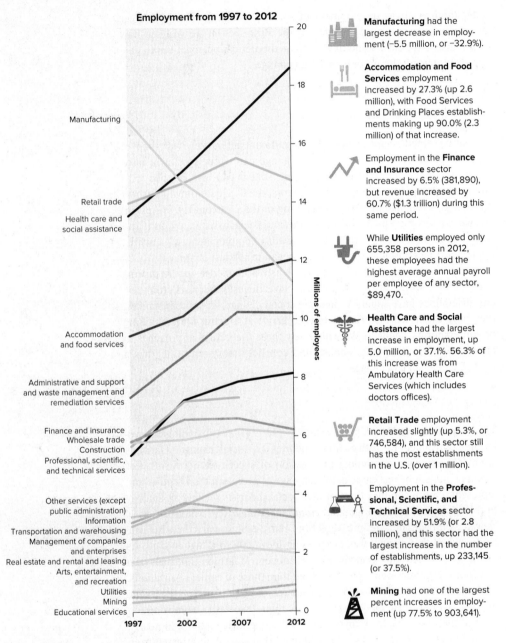

Employment from 1997 to 2012

Manufacturing had the largest decrease in employment (−5.5 million, or −32.9%).

Accommodation and Food Services employment increased by 27.3% (up 2.6 million), with Food Services and Drinking Places establishments making up 90.0% (2.3 million) of that increase.

Employment in the **Finance and Insurance** sector increased by 6.5% (381,890), but revenue increased by 60.7% ($1.3 trillion) during this same period.

While **Utilities** employed only 655,358 persons in 2012, these employees had the highest average annual payroll per employee of any sector, $89,470.

Health Care and Social Assistance had the largest increase in employment, up 5.0 million, or 37.1%. 56.3% of this increase was from Ambulatory Health Care Services (which includes doctors offices).

Retail Trade employment increased slightly (up 5.3%, or 746,584), and this sector still has the most establishments in the U.S. (over 1 million).

Employment in the **Professional, Scientific, and Technical Services** sector increased by 51.9% (or 2.8 million), and this sector had the largest increase in the number of establishments, up 233,145 (or 37.5%).

Mining had one of the largest percent increases in employment (up 77.5% to 903,641).

Figure 11–3

The Changing U.S. Economy, 1997–2012

SOURCE: Bureau of the Census 2014e.

FUNCTIONALIST PERSPECTIVE

Functionalist sociologists focus on what *maintains* a system, not on what changes it. This statement might seem to suggest that functionalists can offer little of value to the study of social change. Yet as the work of sociologist Talcott Parsons demonstrates, functionalists have made a distinctive contribution to this area of sociological investigation.

Parsons (1902–1979), a leading proponent of functionalist theory, viewed society as being in a natural state of equilibrium. By "equilibrium," he meant that society tends toward a state of stability or balance. Parsons would view even prolonged labor strikes or civilian riots as temporary disruptions in the status quo rather than as significant alterations in social structure. Therefore, according to his **equilibrium model,** as changes occur in one part of society, adjustments must be made in other parts. If adjustments are not made, society's equilibrium will be threatened.

Taking an evolutionary approach, Parsons (1966) maintained that four processes of social change are inevitable. The first, *differentiation,* refers to the increasing complexity of social organization. The change from "medicine man" to physician, nurse, and pharmacist is an illustration of differentiation in the field of health care. This process is accompanied by *adaptive upgrading,* through which social institutions become more specialized. The division of physicians into obstetricians, internists, surgeons, and so forth is an example of adaptive upgrading.

The third process identified by Parsons is the *inclusion* into society of groups that were once excluded because of such factors as gender, race, and social class background. Medical schools have practiced inclusion by admitting increasing numbers of women and African Americans. Finally, Parsons suggested that societies experience *value generalization,* the development of new values that tolerate and legitimate a greater range of activities. The acceptance of preventive and alternative medicine is an example of value generalization: our society has broadened its view of health care. All four processes identified by Parsons stress consensus— societal agreement on the nature of social organization and values (B. Johnson 1975; Wallace and Wolf 1980).

Though Parsons's approach explicitly incorporates the evolutionary notion of continuing progress, the dominant theme in his model is balance and stability. Society may change, but it remains stable through new forms of integration. For example, in place of the kinship ties that provided social cohesion in the past, society develops laws, judicial processes, and new values and belief systems.

CONFLICT PERSPECTIVE

The functionalist perspective minimizes the significance of change. It emphasizes the persistence of social life and sees change as a means of maintaining social equilibrium (or balance). In contrast, conflict theorists contend that social institutions and practices persist because powerful groups have the ability to maintain the status quo. Change has crucial significance, since it is needed to correct social injustices and inequalities.

Karl Marx accepted the evolutionary argument that societies develop along a particular path. However, unlike Comte and Spencer, he did not view each successive stage as an inevitable improvement over the previous one. Society, according to Marx, proceeds through a series of stages,

Table 11–2 Sociological Perspectives on Social Change

Evolutionary	Social change moves society in a definite direction, frequently from simple to more complex.
Functionalist	Social change must contribute to society's stability. Modest adjustments must be made to accommodate social change.
Conflict	Social change can correct social injustices and inequalities.

each of which exploits a class of people. Ancient society exploited slaves; the estate system, or feudalism, exploited serfs; modern capitalist society exploits the working class. Ultimately, through a socialist revolution led by the proletariat, human society will move toward the final stage of development: a classless communist society, or "community of free individuals," as Marx described it in *Das Kapital* in 1867 (see Bottomore and Rubel 1956:250).

As we have seen, Marx had an important influence on the development of sociology. His thinking offered insights into such institutions as the economy, the family, religion, and government. The Marxist view of social change is appealing because it does not restrict people to a passive role in responding to inevitable cycles or changes in material culture. Rather, Marxist theory offers a tool to those who wish to seize control of the historical process and gain their freedom from injustice. In contrast to functionalists' emphasis on stability, Marx argues that conflict is a normal and desirable aspect of social change. In fact, change must be encouraged as a means of eliminating social inequality.

Table 11–2 summarizes the differences between the three major theories of social change.

GLOBAL SOCIAL CHANGE

We are living at a truly dramatic time in history to consider global social change. Maureen Hallinan (1997), in her presidential address to the American Sociological Association, asked those present to consider just a few of the recent political events: the collapse of communism; terrorist attacks in various parts of the world, including the United States; the dismantling of the welfare system in the United States; revolution and famine in Africa and Eastern Europe; the spread of AIDS; and the computer revolution. Just a few months after her remarks came the first verification of the cloning of a complex animal, Dolly the sheep.

In this era of massive social, political, and economic change, is it possible to predict change? Some technological changes seem obvious, but the collapse of Communist governments in the former Soviet Union and Eastern Europe in the early 1990s took people by surprise. Prior to the Soviet collapse, however, sociologist Randall Collins (1986, 1995), a conflict theorist, had observed a crucial sequence of events that most observers had missed.

In seminars as far back as 1980, and in a book published in 1986, Collins had argued that Soviet expansionism had resulted in an overextension of resources, including disproportionate spending on military forces. Such an overextension will strain a regime's stability. Moreover, geopolitical theory suggests that nations in the middle of a geographic region, such as the Soviet Union, tend to fragment into smaller units over time. Collins predicted that the coincidence of social crises on several frontiers would precipitate the collapse of the Soviet Union.

Which theory of social change do you find most convincing? Why?

And that is just what happened. In 1979 the success of the Iranian revolution had led to an upsurge of Islamic fundamentalism in nearby Afghanistan, as well as in Soviet republics with substantial Muslim populations. At the same time, resistance to Communist rule was growing, both throughout Eastern Europe and within the Soviet Union itself. Collins had predicted that the rise of a dissident form of communism within the Soviet Union might facilitate the breakdown of the regime. Beginning in the late 1980s, Soviet leader Mikhail Gorbachev chose not to use military power and other types of repression to crush dissidents in Eastern Europe. Gorbachev offered plans for democratization and social reform of Soviet society, and seemed willing to reshape the Soviet Union into a loose federation of somewhat autonomous states. But in 1991, six republics on the western periphery declared their independence, and within months the entire Soviet Union had formally disintegrated into Russia and a number of other independent nations.

In her presidential address to the American Sociological Association, Maureen Hallinan (1997) cautioned that we need to move beyond restrictive models of social change—both the linear view of evolutionary theory and the assumptions about equilibrium within functionalist theory. She and other sociologists have looked to the "chaos theory" advanced by mathematicians to see erratic events as an integral part of change. Hallinan noted that upheavals and major chaotic shifts do occur, and that sociologists must learn to predict their occurrence, as Collins did with the collapse of the Soviet Union. Imagine, for instance, the dramatic nonlinear social change that will result from major innovations in communications and biotechnology, a topic we will discuss later in this chapter.

Resistance to Social Change

Efforts to promote social change are likely to meet with resistance. In the midst of rapid scientific and technological innovation, many people become frightened. Moreover, certain individuals and groups have a stake in maintaining the status quo. Social economist Thorstein Veblen

(1857–1929) coined the term *vested interests* to refer to those people or groups who will suffer in the event of social change. For example, efforts to regulate, restrict, or ban a product or service typically encounter stiff opposition from those who provide those goods and services. Recent history has witnessed major lobbying efforts to resist regulation by such industries as tobacco, alcohol, and firearms. More recently, policy makers and health professionals have advocated increased restriction if not an outright ban of tanning salons, to prevent unnecessary exposure to ultraviolet light, a proven cause of skin cancer. In 2003, Brazil became the first country to ban tanning beds for people under 18; in 2009 the ban was extended to cover all use for solely aesthetic purposes. Not surprisingly, a variety of organizations have sprung up in the United States to fight against similar restrictions and to discredit research that shows tanning devices to be carcinogenic to humans.

ECONOMIC AND CULTURAL FACTORS

Economic factors play an important role in resistance to social change. For example, meeting high standards for the safety of products and workers can be expensive for manufacturers. Conflict theorists argue that in a capitalist economic system, many firms are not willing to pay the price of meeting strict safety standards. They may resist social change by cutting corners or by pressuring the government to ease regulations.

Communities, too, protect their vested interests, often in the name of "protecting property values." The cry "not in my backyard" is often heard when people protest landfills, prisons, nuclear power facilities, and even bike trails and group homes for people with developmental disabilities. The targeted community may not challenge the need for the facility but may simply insist that it be located elsewhere. The "not in my backyard" attitude has become so common that it is almost impossible for policy makers to find acceptable locations for such facilities as hazardous waste dumps (Jasper 1997).

On the world stage, what amounts to a "not on planet Earth" campaign has emerged. Members of this movement stress many issues, from profiteering to nuclear proliferation, from labor rights to the eradication of poverty and disease. Essentially an antiglobalization movement, it manifests itself at international summit meetings.

Like economic factors, cultural factors frequently shape resistance to change. William F. Ogburn (1922) distinguished between material and nonmaterial aspects of culture. *Material culture* includes inventions, artifacts, and technology; *nonmaterial culture* encompasses ideas, norms, communications, and social organization. In music, for instance, the instruments musicians play and the music they record are aspects of material culture; their style of playing, such as rap, and the rules of pitch and rhythm they follow are aspects of nonmaterial culture. Ogburn pointed out that one cannot devise methods for controlling and utilizing a new technology before its introduction. Thus, nonmaterial culture typically must respond to changes in material culture. Ogburn introduced the term *culture lag* to refer to the period of maladjustment when the nonmaterial culture is still struggling to adapt to new material conditions. One example of culture lag is the questions that have been raised by the rapid, uncontrolled growth of the Internet—whether to regulate it, and if so, to what degree.

In certain cases, changes in material culture can strain the relationships between social institutions. For example, new means of birth control have been developed in recent decades. Large families are no longer economically necessary, nor are they commonly endorsed by social norms. But certain religious faiths, among them Roman Catholicism, continue to extol large families and to disapprove most methods of limiting family size, such as contraception and abortion. This gap in values represents a lag between aspects of material culture (technology) and nonmaterial culture (religious beliefs). Conflicts may emerge between religion and other social institutions, such as government and the educational system, over the dissemination of birth control and family-planning information (Riley et al. 1994a, 1994b).

What kind of change do you find the hardest to accept? The easiest?

RESISTANCE TO TECHNOLOGY

Technological innovations are examples of changes in material culture that have often provoked resistance. The *Industrial Revolution,* which took place largely in England during the period 1760 to 1830, was a scientific revolution focused on the application of nonanimal sources of power to labor tasks. As the revolution proceeded, societies relied more and more on new inventions that facilitated agricultural and industrial production, and on new sources of energy such as steam. In some industries, the introduction of power-driven machinery reduced the need for factory workers and made it easier for factory owners to cut wages.

Strong resistance to the Industrial Revolution emerged in some countries. In England, beginning in 1811, masked craft workers took extreme measures: They raided factories and destroyed some of the new machinery. The government hunted these rebels, known as *Luddites,* and banished or hung them. In a similar effort in France, angry workers threw their wooden shoes (*sabots*) into factory machinery to destroy it, giving rise to the term *sabotage.* While the resistance of the Luddites and the French workers was short-lived and unsuccessful, they have come to symbolize resistance to technology over the last two centuries.

Are we now in the midst of a second Industrial Revolution, with a contemporary group of Luddites resisting? Many sociologists believe that we are living in a *postindustrial society.* When this era began is difficult to pinpoint exactly. Generally, it is viewed as having begun in the 1950s, when for the first time the majority of workers in industrial societies became involved in services rather than in the actual manufacturing of goods.

Just as the Luddites resisted the Industrial Revolution, people in many countries have resisted postindustrial technological changes. The term *neo-Luddites* refers to those who are wary of technological innovations and who question the incessant expansion of industrialization, the increasing destruction of the natural and agrarian world, and the "throw-it-away" mentality of contemporary capitalism, with its resulting pollution of the environment (Volti 2010).

A new slang term, *urban amish,* refers specifically to those who resist technological devices that have become part of our daily lives, such as cell phones. These people insist that whatever the presumed benefits of industrial and postindustrial technology, such technology has distinctive social costs and may represent a danger to the future of the human species.

Other people will resist a new technology because they find it difficult to use or because they suspect that it will complicate their lives. Both these objections are especially true of new information and media technologies. Whether it is the iPhone or the latest digital camera, many consumers are leery of these so-called must-have items.

Typically, younger people embrace technological change more than older people, who tend either to be indifferent toward new technologies or to find them annoying. Such concerns are worth remembering as we turn to our technological future and its possible impact on social change.

Technology and the Future

Technology is cultural information about the ways in which the material resources of the environment may be used to satisfy human needs and desires. Technological advances—the airplane, the automobile, the television, the atomic bomb, and more recently the computer, the fax machine, and the cellular phone—have brought striking changes in our cultures, our patterns of socialization, our social institutions, and our day-to-day social interactions. Technological innovations are, in fact, emerging and being accepted with remarkable speed.

In the past generation alone, industrial countries have seen a major shift in consumer technologies. No longer do we buy electronic devices to last for even 10 years. Increasingly, we buy them with the expectation that within as little as 3 years, we will need to upgrade to an entirely new technology, whether it be a handheld device or a home computer.

In the following sections we will examine various aspects of our technological future and consider their overall impact on social change, including the strains they will bring. We will focus in particular on recent developments in computer technology—especially their effects on global offshoring and censorship—and biotechnology.

COMPUTER TECHNOLOGY

The last decade witnessed an explosion of computer technology in the United States and around the world. Its effects were particularly noteworthy with regard to the Internet, the world's largest computer network. In 2015 the Internet reached 3.3 billion users, compared to just 50 million in 1996 (Internet World Stats 2015).

The Internet evolved from a computer system built in 1962 by the U.S. Defense Department to enable scholars and military researchers to continue their government work even if part of the nation's communications system were destroyed by a nuclear attack. A generation ago, it was difficult to gain access to the Internet without holding a position at a university or a government research laboratory. Today, however, virtually anyone can reach the Internet with a cell phone. People buy and sell cars, trade stocks, auction off items, research new medical remedies, vote, and track down long-lost friends online—to mention just a few of the thousands of possibilities. Earlier in this book we discussed the impact of the Internet on social interaction (see Chapter 3).

Unfortunately, not everyone can get onto the information highway, especially not the less affluent. Moreover, this pattern of inequality is global. The core nations that Immanuel Wallerstein described in his world systems analysis have a virtual monopoly on information technology; the peripheral nations of Asia, Africa, and Latin America depend on the core nations both for technology and for the information it provides. For example, North America, Europe, and a few industrialized nations in other regions possess almost all the world's *Internet hosts*—computers that are connected directly to the worldwide network.

Recently, however, some developing nations have begun to benefit from the ease with which information—particularly business information—can be transferred around the world instantaneously, as we will see in the next section.

Global Offshoring   In semiperiphery countries like India, where a growing segment of the workforce speaks English and is computer literate, multinational corporations have been opening new offices, creating well-paid service and professional jobs that boost the local economy. This business approach is not new; U.S. firms have been *outsourcing* certain types of work for generations. For example, moderate-sized businesses such as furniture stores and commercial laundries have long relied on outside trucking firms to make deliveries to their customers. The new trend toward **offshoring** carries this practice one step further, by transferring other types of work to foreign contractors.

Now, even large companies are turning to overseas firms, many of them located in developing countries. Offshoring has become the latest tactic in the time-worn business strategy of raising profits by reducing costs. Significantly, the transfer of work from one country to another

Table 11–3 Occupations Most Vulnerable to Offshoring

Rank	Occupation
1	Computer programming
2	Data entry
3	Electrical and electronics drafting
4	Mechanical drafting
5	Computer and information science, research
6	Actuarial science
7	Mathematics
8	Statistics
9	Mathematical science (all other)
10	Film and video editing

SOURCES: Bureau of Labor Statistics data cited in Hira 2008; Moncarz et al. 2008.

is no longer limited to manufacturing. Office and professional jobs are being exported, too, thanks to advanced telecommunications. Table 11–3 lists those occupations most likely to be offshored.

In 2012, complaints about working conditions in Apple's factories in China called attention to the fact that the company's financial success had been built on outsourced labor. At one time, Apple manufactured its computers in the United States. Today the company still employs about 43,000 full-time workers in the United States, and another 20,000 full-time workers abroad. However, Apple contracts on a short-term basis with an additional 700,000 workers who both engineer and build its products overseas. As complaints grew about Apple's offshoring, economists released estimates that in the next four years, another 375,000 well-paid jobs in information technology, human resources, and finance and merchandising would be lost to overseas competition (China Labor Watch 2015; Duhigg and Bradsher 2012; P. Davidson 2012).

Because offshoring, like outsourcing in general, tends to improve the efficiency of business operations, it can be viewed as functional to society. Offshoring also increases economic interdependence in the production of goods and services, both in enterprises located just across town and in those located around the globe. Still, conflict theorists charge that this aspect of globalization furthers social inequality. Although moving high-tech work to developing countries does help to lower a company's costs, the impact on technical and service workers at home is clearly devastating. Certainly middle-class workers are alarmed by the trend. Because offshoring increases efficiency, economists oppose efforts to block the practice, and instead recommend assistance to displaced workers.

There is a downside to offshoring for foreigners, as well. Although outsourcing is a significant source of employment for the upper-middle class

Do you know anyone whose job has been transferred to a foreign country? If so, was the person able to find a comparable job in the same town, or did he or she have to relocate? How long was the person unemployed?

in developing countries, hundreds of millions of other foreign workers have seen little to no positive impact from the trend. Thus the long-term impact of offshoring on developing nations is difficult to predict.

Privacy and Censorship in a Global Village   Today, new technologies like robots, cars that can park themselves, and smartphones are bringing about sweeping social change. While much of that change is beneficial, there are some negative effects.

Recent advances in computer technology have made it increasingly easy for business firms, government agencies, and even criminals to retrieve and store information about everything from our buying habits to our web-surfing patterns. In public places, at work, and on the Internet, surveillance devices now track our every move, be it a keystroke or an ATM withdrawal. The ever-present cell phone enables the most pervasive and sophisticated attacks on people's privacy and anonymity. In response, some people are beginning to advocate for the creation of a new agency that would respond to electronic viruses the way the CDC (Centers for Disease Control and Prevention) responds to biological threats. However, the trade-off for ensuring total privacy is to restrict the ability of law enforcement to search electronic communications for messages that reveal potential threats, whether those are theft or terrorism (Lucas 2015; Rosen 2015).

From a sociological point of view, the complex issues of privacy and censorship can be considered illustrations of culture lag. As usual, the material culture (technology) is changing faster than the nonmaterial culture (norms for controlling the use of technology). Too often, the result is an anything-goes approach to the use of new technologies.

Legislation regarding the surveillance of electronic communications has not always upheld citizens' right to privacy. In 1986, the federal government passed the Electronic Communications Privacy Act, which outlawed the surveillance of telephone calls except with the permission of both the U.S. attorney general and a federal judge. Telegrams, faxes, and e-mail did not receive the same degree of protection, however. Then in 2001, one month after the terrorist attacks of September 11, Congress passed the USA PATRIOT Act, which relaxed existing legal checks on surveillance by law enforcement officers. Federal agencies are now freer to gather data electronically, including credit card receipts and banking records. In 2005, Americans learned that the National Security Agency was covertly monitoring phone calls with the cooperation of major U.S. telecommunications companies. Four years later, a federal court ruled that wiretapping without warrants is legal (ACLU 2015b).

Sociologists' views on the use and abuse of new technologies differ depending on their theoretical perspective. Functionalists take a generally positive view of the Internet, pointing to its manifest function of facilitating communication. From their perspective, the Internet performs the latent function of empowering those with few resources—from

Though the USA PATRIOT Act was intended to protect citizens from terrorism, in practice it has raised concerns about the potential violation of their privacy.

©Harley Schwadron

Do you hold strong views regarding the privacy of your electronic communications? If your safety were in jeopardy, would you be willing to sacrifice your privacy?

hate groups to special interest organizations—to communicate with the masses. Conflict theorists, in contrast, stress the danger that the most powerful groups in a society will use technology to violate the privacy of the less powerful. Indeed, officials in the People's Republic of China have attempted to censor online discussion groups and Web postings that are critical of the government. The same abuses can occur in the United States, civil liberties advocates remind us, if citizens are not vigilant in protecting their right to privacy (Magnier 2004).

If anything, people seem to be less vigilant today about maintaining their privacy than they were before the information age. Young people who have grown up browsing the Internet seem to accept the existence of the "cookies" and "spyware" they may pick up while surfing. They have become accustomed to adult surveillance of their conversation in electronic chat rooms. Many see no risk in providing personal information about themselves to the strangers they meet online. Little wonder that college professors find their students do not appreciate the political significance of their right to privacy (Turkle 2004).

BIOTECHNOLOGY AND THE GENE POOL

Another field in which technological advances have spurred global social change is biotechnology. Sex selection of fetuses, genetically engineered organisms, cloning of sheep and cows—these have been among the significant yet controversial scientific advances in the field of biotechnology in recent years. George Ritzer's (2015) concept of McDonaldization applies to the entire area of biotechnology. Just as the fast-food concept has permeated society, no phase of life now seems exempt from therapeutic or medical intervention. In fact, sociologists view many aspects of biotechnology as an extension of the recent trend toward the medicalization of society, discussed in Chapter 10. Through genetic manipulation, the medical profession is expanding its turf still further (Clarke et al. 2003; Human Genome Project 2015).

One notable success of biotechnology—an unintended consequence of modern warfare—has been progress in the treatment of traumatic injuries. In response to the massive numbers of soldiers who survived serious injury in Iraq and Afghanistan, military doctors and therapists have come up with electronically controlled prosthetic devices. Their innovations include artificial limbs that respond to thought-generated nerve impulses, allowing amputees to move legs, arms, and even individual fingers. These applications of computer science to the rehabilitation of the injured will no doubt be extended to civilians.

One startling biotechnological advance is the possibility of altering human behavior or physical traits through genetic engineering. Fish and plant genes have already been mixed to create frost-resistant potato and tomato crops. More recently, human genes have been implanted in pigs to provide humanlike kidneys for organ transplant. William F. Ogburn probably could not have anticipated such scientific developments when he wrote of culture lag over 80 years earlier. However, advances like these or even the successful cloning of sheep illustrate again how quickly material culture can change, and how nonmaterial culture moves more slowly in absorbing such changes.

Although today's biotechnology holds itself out as totally beneficial to human beings, it is in constant need of monitoring. Biotechnological advances have raised many difficult ethical and political questions, among them the desirability of tinkering with the gene pool, which could alter our environment in unexpected and unwanted ways. In particular, controversy has been growing concerning genetically modified (GM) food, an issue that arose in Europe but has since spread to other parts of the world, including the United States. The idea behind the technology is to increase food production and make agriculture more economical. But critics use the term *Frankenfood* (as in "Frankenstein") to refer to everything from breakfast cereals made from genetically engineered grains to fresh GM tomatoes. Members of the antibiotech movement object to tampering with nature, and are concerned about the possible health effects of GM food. Supporters of genetically modified food include not just biotech companies, but those who see the technology as a way to help feed the burgeoning populations of Africa and Asia (Shuttleworth 2015).

In contrast, less expensive and controversial technologies can further agriculture where it is needed more, in the developing world. Consider cell phones. Unlike most new technologies, the majority of the world's cell phones are used in *less* developed countries. Relatively cheap and

Try to imagine the world 100 years from now. On balance, is it a world in which technology contributes to or threatens people's well-being? In what ways?

not as dependent as computers on expensive communications infrastructure, cell phones are common in the world's poorest areas. In Uganda, farmers use them to check weather forecasts and commodity prices. In South Africa, laborers use them to look for work. Researchers at the London Business School have found that in developing countries, a 10 percent increase in cell phone use is correlated with a 0.6 percent rise in GDP (Bures 2011).

Sociology Matters

Sociology matters because it helps you to understand the social change you encounter.

- Have you had any experience working in a social movement? If so, what kind of social change were you hoping to support? What resources did the movement try to mobilize? Who were the vested interests who opposed the movement?
- Have you yourself experienced culture lag, or have you observed it in others? If so, what kind of change caused the lag—was it a new technology, or some other kind of change? Did you notice a generational difference in the way people responded to the change? Did you see any open resistance to it?
- Have new technologies helped you in any significant way, and if so, how? On balance, do you see new technologies as a benefit or a threat to society? Explain.

CHAPTER RESOURCES

Summary

Social movements are a form of collective behavior that promotes **social change,** or a significant alteration over time in behavior patterns and culture. This chapter examined social movements, sociological theories of social change, resistance to social change, and the impact of **technology** on social change.

1. A group will not mobilize into a **social movement** unless its members believe they can end their **relative deprivation** only through collective action.

2. The success of a social movement depends in good part on effective **resource mobilization.** Increasingly, social movements are using **technology**—including the Internet—to mobilize their resources.

3. Early advocates of the **evolutionary theory** of social change believed that society was progressing steadily and inevitably toward a higher state.

4. Talcott Parsons, a leading advocate of functionalist theory, thought that **social change** would always return society to a natural state of equilibrium, or balance. Conflict theorists see change more as a necessity in correcting social injustices and inequities.

5. In general, those with a disproportionate share of society's wealth, status, and power, called **vested interests,** will resist social change and attempt to preserve the status quo.

6. A period of maladjustment, called **culture lag,** occurs when a non-material culture strains to adapt to new material conditions.

7. The Internet, the world's largest computer network, has revolutionized communications and commercial activity around the world.

8. Though developing nations typically have little access to new technologies, some semiperiphery nations have begun to benefit from the **offshoring** of service and professional jobs once done in core nations.

9. New computer, video, and GPS technologies have compromised our privacy and facilitated government censorship.

10. Advances in biotechnology have both benefited humans and raised difficult ethical questions about genetic engineering.

Key Terms

culture lag, 309

equilibrium model, 305

evolutionary theory, 303

false consciousness, 301

Luddites, 309

new social movement, 302

offshoring, 311

relative deprivation, 299

resource mobilization, 300

social change, 303

social movement, 298

technology, 310

vested interests, 308

For the last two decades, the number of U.S. college students who have graduated with a degree in sociology has risen steadily. In this appendix we'll consider some of the options these students have after completing their undergraduate education.

How do students first learn about the sociological perspective on society? Some may take a sociology course in high school. Others may study sociology at community college, where 40 percent of all college students in the United States are enrolled. Indeed, many future sociology majors first develop their sociological imaginations at a community college.

An undergraduate degree in sociology doesn't just serve as excellent preparation for future graduate work in sociology. It also provides a strong liberal arts background for entry-level positions in business, social services, foundations, community organizations, not-for-profit groups, law enforcement, and many government jobs. A number of fields—among them marketing, public relations, and broadcasting—now require investigative skills and an understanding of the diverse groups found in today's multiethnic and multinational environment. Moreover, a sociology degree requires accomplishment in oral and written communication, interpersonal skills, problem solving, and critical thinking—all job-related skills that may give sociology graduates an advantage over those who pursue more technical degrees. Consequently, while few occupations specifically require an undergraduate degree in sociology, such academic training can be an important asset in entering a wide range of occupations.

Figure 1 summarizes the occupations of college graduates with BA or BS degrees in sociology. It shows that fields including nonprofit organizations, education, business, and government offer major career opportunities for sociology graduates. Undergraduates who know where their career interests lie are well advised to enroll in sociology courses and specialties best suited to those interests. For example, students hoping to become health planners would take a class in medical sociology; students seeking employment as social science research assistants would focus on courses in statistics and methods. Internships, such as placements at city planning agencies and survey research organizations, afford another way for sociology students to prepare for careers. Studies show that students who choose an internship placement have less trouble finding jobs, obtain better jobs, and enjoy greater job satisfaction than students without internship placements. Finally, students should expect to change fields during their first five years of employment after graduation—for example, from sales and marketing to management (American Sociological Association 2013; Salem and Grabarek 1986).

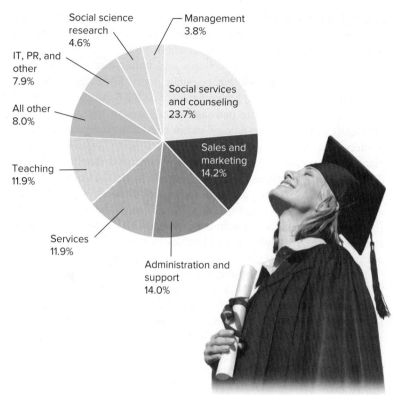

Social science research 4.6%

Management 3.8%

IT, PR, and other 7.9%

Social services and counseling 23.7%

All other 8.0%

Sales and marketing 14.2%

Teaching 11.9%

Services 11.9%

Administration and support 14.0%

Figure 1
Occupations of Graduating Sociology Majors

NOTE: *Based on a national survey of current occupation in 2013 of 759 graduates with a sociology major in the Class of 2012.*

SOURCE: Spalter-Roth et al. 2013:Table 2. Photo: © Stockbyte/PunchStock RF.

Many college students view social work as the field most closely associated with sociology. Traditionally, social workers received their undergraduate training in sociology and allied fields such as psychology and counseling. After some practical experience, social workers would generally seek a master's degree in social work (MSW) to be considered for supervisory or administrative positions. Today, however, some students choose (where it is available) to pursue a bachelor's degree in social work (BSW). This degree prepares graduates for direct service positions, such as caseworker or group worker.

Many students continue their sociological training beyond the bachelor's degree. More than 250 universities in the United States have graduate programs in sociology that offer PhD and/or master's degrees. These programs differ greatly in their areas of specialization, course requirements, costs, and the research and teaching opportunities available to graduate students. About 71 percent of the graduates are women (American Sociological Association 2005; National Center for Educational Statistics 2012).

Higher education is an important source of employment for sociologists with graduate degrees. About 83 percent of recent PhD recipients in sociology seek employment in colleges and universities. These

Did you know that as a student at Princeton University, Michelle Obama majored in sociology? She used that degree as a stepping-stone to Harvard law school. Read her senior thesis at www. politico.com.

sociologists teach not only majors committed to the discipline but also students hoping to become doctors, nurses, lawyers, police officers, and so forth (American Sociological Association 2005).

Sociologists who teach in colleges and universities may use their knowledge and training to influence public policy. For example, sociologist Andrew Cherlin (2003) has commented on the debate over proposed federal funding to promote marriage among welfare recipients. Citing the results of two of his studies, Cherlin questioned the potential effectiveness of such a policy in strengthening low-income families. Because many single mothers choose to marry someone other than the father of their children—sometimes for good reason—their children often grow up in stepfamilies. Cherlin's research shows that children who are raised in stepfamilies are no better off than those in single-parent families. He sees government efforts to promote marriage as a politically motivated attempt to foster traditional social values in a society that has become increasingly diverse.

For sociology graduates interested in academic careers, the road to a PhD (or doctorate) can be long and difficult. This degree symbolizes competence in original research; each candidate must prepare a book-length study known as a dissertation. Typically, a doctoral student in sociology will engage in four to seven years of intensive work, including the time required to complete the dissertation. Yet even this effort is no guarantee of a job as a sociology professor.

The good news is that over the next 10 years, the demand for instructors is expected to increase because of high rates of retirement among faculty from the baby-boom generation, as well as the anticipated slow but steady growth in the college student population in the United States. Nonetheless, anyone who launches an academic career must be prepared for considerable uncertainty and competition in the college job market (American Sociological Association 2013).

Of course, not all people working as sociologists teach or hold doctoral degrees. Take government, for example. The Census Bureau relies on people with sociological training to interpret data for other government agencies and the general public. Virtually every agency depends on survey research—a field in which sociology students can specialize—in order to assess everything from community needs to the morale of the agency's own workers. In addition, people with sociological training can put their academic knowledge to effective use in probation and parole, health sciences, community development, and recreational services. Some people working in government or private industry have a master's degree (MA or MS) in sociology; others have a bachelor's degree (BA or BS).

Currently, about 15 percent of the members of the American Sociological Association use their sociological skills outside the academic world, whether in social service agencies or in marketing positions for business firms. Increasing numbers of sociologists with graduate degrees are employed by businesses, industry, hospitals, and nonprofit organizations. Studies show that many sociology graduates are making career changes from social service areas to business and commerce. For an undergraduate major, sociology is excellent preparation for employment in many parts of the business world (Spalter-Roth et al. 2013).

Whether you take a few courses in sociology or actually complete a degree, you will benefit from the critical thinking skills developed in this discipline. Sociologists emphasize the value of being able to analyze, interpret, and function within a variety of working situations—an asset in virtually any career. Moreover, given rapid technological change and the expanding global economy, all of us will need to adapt to substantial social change, even in our own careers. Sociology provides a rich conceptual framework that can serve as a foundation for flexible career development and assist you in taking advantage of new employment opportunities.

Glossary

Numbers following the definitions indicate pages where the terms were identified. Consult the index for further page references.

Absolute poverty: A standard of poverty based on a minimum level of subsistence that no family should be expected to live below. (143)

Achieved status: A social position attained by a person largely through his or her own efforts. (76, 126)

Affirmative action: Positive efforts to recruit members of subordinate groups or women for jobs, promotions, and educational opportunities. (181)

Agrarian society: The most technologically advanced form of preindustrial society, in which members are engaged primarily in the production of food but increase their crop yields through technological innovations such as the plow. (86)

Anomie: Émile Durkheim's term for the loss of direction felt in a society when social control of individual behavior has become ineffective. (105)

Anomie theory of deviance: A theory developed by Robert Merton that explains deviance as an adaptation either of socially prescribed goals or of the norms governing their attainment, or both. (106)

Anticipatory socialization: Processes of socialization in which a person "rehearses" for future positions, occupations, and social relationships. (68)

Applied sociology: The use of the discipline of sociology with the specific intent of yielding practical applications for human behavior and organizations. (32)

Argot: Specialized language used by members of a subculture. (44)

Ascribed status: A social position that is assigned to a person by society without regard for the person's unique talents or characteristics. (75, 126)

Authority: Power that has been institutionalized and is recognized by the people over whom it is exercised. (243)

Basic sociology: Sociological inquiry conducted with the objective of gaining a more profound knowledge of the fundamental aspects of social phenomena. Also called *pure sociology.* (33)

Bilateral descent: A kinship system in which both sides of a person's family are regarded as equally important. (212)

Birthrate: The number of live births per 1,000 population in a given year. Also known as the *crude birthrate.* (265)

Bourgeoisie: Karl Marx's term for the capitalist class, or the owners of the means of production. (131)

Brain drain: The immigration to the United States and other industrialized nations of skilled workers, professionals, and technicians who are desperately needed in their home countries. (277)

Bureaucracy: A component of formal organization in which rules and hierarchical ranking are used to achieve efficiency. (89)

Capitalism: An economic system in which the means of production are held largely in private hands, and the main incentive for economic activity is the accumulation of profits. (131, 250)

Caste: A hereditary system of rank, usually religiously dictated, that tends to be fixed and immobile. (128)

Causal logic: The relationship between a condition or variable and a particular consequence, with one event leading to the other. (23)

Census: An enumeration, or counting, of a population. (264)

Charismatic authority: Max Weber's term for power made legitimate by a leader's exceptional personal or emotional appeal to his or her followers. (244)

Class: A term used by Max Weber to refer to a group of people who have a similar level of wealth and income. (133)

Class consciousness: In Karl Marx's view, a subjective awareness of common vested interests and the need for collective political action to bring about social change. (132)

Class system: A social ranking based primarily on economic position in which achieved characteristics can influence social mobility. (129)

Classical theory: An approach to the study of formal organizations in which workers are viewed as being motivated almost entirely by economic rewards. (92)

Climate change: An observable alteration of the global atmosphere that affects natural weather patterns over several decades or longer. (286)

Clinical sociology: The use of the discipline of sociology with the specific intent of altering social relationships or restructuring social institutions. (33)

Closed system: A social system in which there is little or no possibility of individual mobility. (147)

Code of ethics: The standards of acceptable behavior developed by and for members of a profession. (31)

Cognitive theory of development: Jean Piaget's theory that children's thought progresses through four stages of development. (60)

Colonialism: The maintenance of political, social, economic, and cultural domination over a people by a foreign power for an extended period. (152)

Color-blind racism: The use of the principle of race neutrality to defend a racially unequal status quo. (178)

Communism: As an ideal type, an economic system in which all property is communally owned and no social distinctions are made on the basis of people's ability to produce. (252)

Community: A spatial or political unit of social organization that gives people a sense of belonging. (267)

Concentric-zone theory: A theory of urban growth devised by Ernest Burgess that sees growth in terms of a series of rings radiating from the central business district. (271)

Conflict perspective: A sociological approach that assumes that social behavior is best understood in terms of tension between groups over power

or the allocation of resources, including housing, money, access to services, and political representation. (16)

Conformity: Going along with peers—individuals of our own status, who have no special right to direct our behavior. (99)

Contact hypothesis: An interactionist perspective that states that interracial contact between people of equal status engaged in a cooperative task will reduce prejudice. (176)

Content analysis: The systematic coding and objective recording of data, guided by some rationale. (30)

Control group: Subjects in an experiment who are not introduced to the independent variable by the researcher. (29)

Control variable: A factor held constant to test the relative impact of an independent variable. (26)

Correlation: A relationship between two variables in which a change in one coincides with a change in the other. (24)

Counterculture: A subculture that conspicuously and deliberately opposes certain aspects of the larger culture. (45)

Credentialism: An increase in the lowest level of education needed to enter a field. (236)

Crime: A violation of criminal law for which some governmental authority applies formal penalties. (113)

Cultural capital: Noneconomic goods such as family background and education, which are reflected in a knowledge of language and the arts. (14)

Cultural relativism: The evaluation of a people's behavior from the perspective of their own culture. (41)

Cultural transmission: A school of criminology that argues that criminal behavior is learned through social interactions. (108)

Cultural universal: A general practice found in every culture. (40)

Culture: The totality of learned, socially transmitted customs, knowledge, material objects, and behavior. (38)

Culture industry: The worldwide media industry that standardizes the goods and services demanded by consumers. (39)

Culture lag: William F. Ogburn's term for the period of maladjustment when the nonmaterial culture is still struggling to adapt to new material conditions. (43, 309)

Culture shock: The feeling of surprise and disorientation that people experience when they witness cultural practices different from their own. (45)

Culture war: The polarization of society over controversial elements of culture. (51)

Curanderismo: Traditional Latino folk practices for holistic health care and healing. (282)

Cybercrime: Illegal activity primarily conducted through the use of computer hardware or software. (115)

Death rate: The number of deaths per 1,000 population in a given year. Also known as the *crude death rate.* (265)

Degradation ceremony: An aspect of the resocialization process within total institutions, in which people are subjected to humiliating rituals. (69)

Deindustrialization: The systematic, widespread withdrawal of investment in basic aspects of productivity, such as factories and plants. (255)

Demography: The scientific study of population. (263)

Dependency theory: An approach to global stratification that contends that industrialized nations exploit developing countries for their own gain. (153)

Dependent variable: The variable in a causal relationship that is subject to the influence of another variable. (23)

Deviance: Behavior that violates the standards of conduct or expectations of a group or society. (102)

Differential association: A theory of deviance proposed by Edwin Sutherland that holds that violation of rules results from exposure to attitudes favorable to criminal acts. (108)

Differential justice: Differences in the way social control is exercised over different groups. (111)

Diffusion: The process by which a cultural item spreads from group to group or society to society. (42)

Discovery: The process of making known or sharing the existence of some aspect of reality. (42)

Discrimination: The denial of opportunities and equal rights to individuals and groups based on some type of arbitrary bias. (179)

Dominant ideology: A set of cultural beliefs and practices that help to maintain powerful social, economic, and political interests. (52, 136)

Double consciousness: The division of an individual's identity into two or more social realities. (11)

Downsizing: Reductions taken in a company's workforce as part of deindustrialization. (256)

Dramaturgical approach: A view of social interaction popularized by Erving Goffman that examines people as if they were theatrical performers. (59)

Dysfunction: An element or process of a society that may actually disrupt the social system or reduce its stability. (16)

Ecological modernization: The alignment of environmentally favorable practices with economic self-interest through constant adaptation and restructuring. (290)

Economic system: The social institution through which goods and services are produced, distributed, and consumed. (248)

Education: A formal process of learning in which some people consciously teach while others adopt the social role of learner. (232)

Egalitarian family: An authority pattern in which spouses are regarded as equals. (213)

Elite model: A view of society as being ruled by a small group of individuals who share a common set of political and economic interests. (249)

Environmental justice: A legal strategy based on claims that racial minorities and the lower classes are subjected disproportionately to environmental hazards. (291)

Equilibrium model: Talcott Parsons's functionalist view of society as tending toward a state of stability or balance. (305)

Estate system: A system of stratification under which peasants were required to work land leased to them by nobles in exchange for military protection and other services. Also known as *feudalism.* (129)

Esteem: The reputation that a specific person has earned within an occupation. (138)

Ethnic group: A group that is set apart from others primarily because of its national origin or distinctive cultural patterns. (166)

Ethnocentrism: The tendency to assume that one's own culture and way of life represent the norm or are superior to all others. (40, 177)

Ethnography: The study of an entire social setting through extended systematic observation. (28)

Evolutionary theory: A theory of social change that holds that society is moving in a definite direction. (303)

Experiment: An artificially created situation that allows the researcher to manipulate variables. (29)

Experimental group: Subjects in an experiment who are exposed to an independent variable introduced by a researcher. (29)

Exploitation theory: A Marxist theory that views racial subordination in the United States as a manifestation of the class system inherent in capitalism. (175)

Expressiveness: A concern for the maintenance of harmony and the internal emotional affairs of the family. (194)

Extended family: A family in which relatives—such as grandparents, aunts, or uncles—live in the same home as parents and their children. (211)

False consciousness: A term used by Karl Marx to describe an attitude held by members of a class that does not accurately reflect its objective position. (132, 301)

Family: A set of people related by blood, marriage (or some other agreed-upon relationship), or adoption who share the primary responsibility for reproduction and caring for members of society. (210)

Feminist perspective: A sociological approach that views inequity in gender as central to all behavior and organization. (17)

Feminization of poverty: A trend in which women constitute an increasing proportion of the poor people of the United States. (145)

Fertility: The level of reproduction in a society. (262)

Folkway: A norm governing everyday behavior whose violation raises comparatively little concern. (48)

Force: The actual or threatened use of coercion to impose one's will on others. (243)

Formal norm: A norm that generally has been written down and specifies strict punishment of violators. (48)

Formal organization: A group designed for a special purpose and structured for maximum efficiency. (88)

Formal social control: Control carried out by authorized agents, such as police officers, physicians, school administrators, employers, military officers, and managers of movie theaters. (101)

Functionalist perspective: A sociological approach that emphasizes the way that the parts of a society are structured to maintain its stability. (14)

Fundamentalism: An emphasis on doctrinal conformity and the literal interpretation of sacred texts. (225)

Gemeinschaft: A term used by Ferdinand Tönnies to describe a small, close-knit community, often found in a rural area, in which strong personal bonds unite members. (83)

Gender identity: How people see themselves: as male or female or something else. This identity can be different from one's biological sex at birth, although most people develop a gender identity that conforms to that biological identity. (217)

Gender role: Expectations regarding the proper behavior, attitudes, and activities of males or females. (63, 189)

Generalized other: A term used by George Herbert Mead to refer to the attitudes, viewpoints, and expectations of society as a whole that a child takes into account in his or her behavior. (58)

Gesellschaft: A term used by Ferdinand Tönnies to describe a community, often urban, that is large and impersonal, with little commitment to the group or consensus on values. (84)

Glass ceiling: An invisible barrier that blocks the promotion of a qualified individual in a work environment because of the individual's gender, race, or ethnicity. (179, 204)

Global warming: The significant rise in the earth's surface temperatures that occurs when industrial gases like carbon dioxide turn the planet's atmosphere into a virtual greenhouse. (286)

Globalization: The worldwide integration of government policies, cultures, social movements, and financial markets through trade and the exchange of ideas. (42, 154)

Goal displacement: Within a bureaucracy, overzealous conformity to official regulations. (91)

Group: Any number of people with similar norms, values, and expectations who interact with one another on a regular basis. (79)

Growth rate: The difference between births and deaths, plus the difference between immigrants and emigrants, per 1,000 population. (265)

Hate crime: A criminal offense committed because of the offender's bias against a race, religion, ethnic group, national origin, or sexual orientation. (117)

Hawthorne effect: The unintended influence of observers or experiments on subjects of research. (29)

Health: As defined by the World Health Organization, a state of complete physical, mental, and social well-being, and not merely the absence of disease and infirmity. (274)

Hidden curriculum: Standards of behavior that are deemed proper by society and are taught subtly in schools. (235)

Homophobia: Fear of and prejudice against homosexuality. (190)

Horizontal mobility: The movement of an individual from one social position to another of the same rank. (148)

Horticultural society: A preindustrial society in which people plant seeds and crops rather than merely subsist on available foods. (86)

Human ecology: An area of study that is concerned with the interrelationships between people and their spatial setting and physical environment. (271)

Human relations approach: An approach to the study of formal organizations that emphasizes the role of people, communication, and participation within a bureaucracy and tends to focus on informal groups. (93)

Hunting-and-gathering society: A preindustrial society in which people rely on whatever foods and fibers are readily available in order to survive. (85)

Hypothesis: A speculative statement about the relationship between two or more variables. (23)

Ideal type: A construct or model that serves as a measuring rod against which actual cases can be evaluated. (10, 89)

Impression management: A term used by Erving Goffman to refer to the altering of the presentation of the self in order to create distinctive appearances and satisfy particular audiences. (59)

Incidence: The number of new cases of a specific disorder occurring within a given population during a stated period, usually a year. (280)

Income: Salaries and wages. (126)

Independent variable: The variable in a causal relationship that, when altered, causes or influences a change in a second variable. (23)

Index crimes: The eight types of crime reported annually by the FBI in the *Uniform Crime Reports:* murder, rape, robbery, assault, burglary, theft, motor vehicle theft, and arson. (118)

Industrial city: A city characterized by relatively large size, open competition, an open class system, and elaborate specialization in the manufacturing of goods. (269)

Industrial society: A society that depends on mechanization to produce its goods and services. (86)

Infant mortality rate: The number of deaths of infants under one year of age per 1,000 live births in a given year. (265)

Influence: The exercise of power through a process of persuasion. (243)

Informal economy: An economy in which transfers of money, goods, or services take place but are not reported to the government. (253)

Informal norm: A norm that generally is understood but is not precisely recorded. (48)

Informal social control: Control that people use casually to enforce norms. (101)

In-group: Any group or category to which people feel they belong. (80)

Innovation: The process of introducing a new idea or object to a culture through discovery or invention. (42)

Institutional discrimination: The denial of opportunities and equal rights to individuals and groups that results from the normal operations of a society. (180)

Instrumentality: An emphasis on tasks, a focus on more distant goals, and a concern for the external relationship between one's family and other social institutions. (194)

Interactionist perspective: A sociological approach that generalizes about everyday forms of social interaction. (19)

Intergenerational mobility: Changes in the social position of children relative to their parents. (148)

Intersectionality: The overlapping and interdependent system of advantage and disadvantage that positions people in society on the basis of race, class, gender, and other characteristics.(196)

Interview: A face-to-face or telephone questioning of a respondent to obtain desired information. (27)

Intragenerational mobility: Changes in a person's social position within his or her adult life. (148)

Invention: The combination of existing cultural items into a form that did not exist before. (42)

Jim Crow: Southern laws that kept African Americans in a subordinate position. (179)

Kinship: The state of being related to others. (212)

Labeling theory: A theory that attempts to explain why certain people are viewed as deviants. (110)

Laissez-faire: A form of capitalism in which businesses compete freely, with minimal government intervention in the economy. (250)

Language: An abstract system of word meanings and symbols for all aspects of culture; includes gestures and other nonverbal communication. (46)

Latent function: An unconscious or unintended function; hidden purpose. (16)

Law: Governmental social control. (48, 102)

Life chances: Max Weber's term for people's opportunities to provide themselves with material goods, positive living conditions, and favorable life experiences. (146)

Life expectancy: The median number of years a person can be expected to live under current mortality conditions. (265)

Life-course approach: A research orientation in which sociologists and other social scientists look closely at the social factors that influence people throughout their lives, from birth to death. (68)

Looking-glass self: A concept used by Charles Horton Cooley to emphasize that the self is the product of our social interactions with other people. (57)

Luddites: Rebellious craft workers in 19th-century England who destroyed new factory machinery as part of their resistance to the Industrial Revolution. (309)

Macrosociology: Sociological investigation that concentrates on large-scale phenomena or entire civilizations. (13)

Manifest function: An open, stated, and conscious function. (16)

Master status: A status that dominates others and thereby determines a person's general position within society. (76)

Material culture: The physical or technological aspects of our daily lives. (43)

Matriarchy: A society in which women dominate in family decision making. (213)

Matrilineal descent: A kinship system that favors the mother's relatives. (213)

Matrix of domination: The cumulative impact of oppression because of race, gender, and class, as well as religion, sexual orientation, disability, and age. (196)

McDonaldization: The process through which the principles of the fast-food restaurant have come to dominate certain sectors of society, both in the United States and throughout the world. (42)

Mechanical solidarity: A collective consciousness that emphasizes group solidarity, characteristic of societies with minimal division of labor. (83)

Microsociology: Sociological investigation that stresses the study of small groups, often through experimental means. (13)

Modernization: The far-reaching process through which developing nations move from traditional or less developed institutions to those characteristic of more developed societies. (157)

Modernization theory: The functionalist view that modernization and development will gradually improve the lives of people in developing nations. (158)

Monogamy: A form of marriage in which one woman and one man are married only to each other. (211)

Monopoly: Control of a market by a single business firm. (251)

Morbidity rate: The incidence of disease in a given population. (280)

Mores: Norms deemed highly necessary to the welfare of a society. (48)

Mortality rate: The incidence of death in a given population. (280)

Multinational corporation: A commercial organization that is headquartered in one country but does business throughout the world. (155)

Multiple-nuclei theory: A theory of urban growth developed by Chauncey D. Harris and Edward Ullman that views growth as emerging from many centers of development, each of which reflects a particular urban need or activity. (272)

Natural science: The study of the physical features of nature and the ways in which they interact and change. (4)

Neocolonialism: Continuing dependence of former colonies on foreign countries. (152)

New social movement: An organized collective activity that addresses values and social identities as well as improvements in the quality of life. (302)

New urban sociology: An approach to urbanization that considers the interplay of local, national, and worldwide forces and their effect on local space, with special emphasis on the impact of global economic activity. (273)

Nonmaterial culture: Customs, beliefs, philosophies, governments, and patterns of communication, as well as ways of using material objects. (43)

Nonverbal communication: The sending of messages through the use of posture, facial expressions, and gestures. (20)

Norm: An established standard of behavior maintained by a society. (47)

Nuclear family: A married couple and their unmarried children living together. (210)

Obedience: Compliance with higher authorities in a hierarchical structure. (99)

Objective method: A technique for measuring social class that assigns individuals to classes on the basis of criteria such as occupation, education, income, and place of residence. (138)

Observation: A research technique in which an investigator collects information through direct participation, by closely watching a group or community. (28)

Offshoring: The transfer of work to foreign contractors. (311)

Open system: A social system in which the position of each individual is influenced by his or her achieved status. (147)

Operational definition: An explanation of an abstract concept that is specific enough to allow a researcher to assess the concept. (22)

Organic solidarity: A collective consciousness that rests on mutual interdependence, characteristic of societies with a complex division of labor. (83)

Organized crime: The work of a group that regulates relations between various criminal enterprises involved in various illegal activities. (114)

Out-group: A group or category to which people feel they do not belong. (80)

Patriarchy: A society in which men dominate in family decision making. (213)

Patrilineal descent: A kinship system that favors the father's relatives. (230)

Personality: The individual characteristics, attitudes, needs, and behaviors that set one person apart from another. (38)

Peter Principle: A principle of organizational life originated by Laurence J. Peter, according to which every employee within a hierarchy tends to rise to his or her level of incompetence. (92)

Pluralist model: A view of society in which many competing groups within the community have access to government officials, so that no single group is dominant. (247)

Politics: In Harold D. Lasswell's words, "who gets what, when, and how." (242)

Polyandry: A form of polygamy in which a woman may have several husbands at the same time. (212)

Polygamy: A form of marriage in which an individual may have several husbands or wives simultaneously. (211)

Polygyny: A form of polygamy in which a husband may have several wives at the same time. (212)

Postindustrial city: A city in which global finance and the electronic flow of information dominate the economy. (270)

Postindustrial society: A society whose economic system is engaged primarily in the processing and control of information. (87)

Postmodern society: A technologically sophisticated society that is preoccupied with consumer goods and media images. (87)

Power: The ability to exercise one's will over others. (133, 242)

Power elite: A term used by C. Wright Mills for a small group of military, industrial, and government leaders who control the fate of the United States. (245)

precarious work: Work that is poorly paid, and from the worker's perspective, insecure and unprotected. (257)

Preindustrial city: A city with only a few thousand residents that is characterized by a relatively closed class system and limited social mobility. (268)

Prejudice: A negative attitude toward an entire category of people, often an ethnic or racial group. (177)

Prestige: The respect and admiration that an occupation holds in a society. (138)

Prevalence: The total number of cases of a specific disorder that exist at a given time. (280)

Primary group: A small group characterized by intimate, face-to-face association and cooperation. (79)

Professional criminal: A person who pursues crime as a day-to-day occupation. (114)

Proletariat: Karl Marx's term for the working class in a capitalist society. (131)

Protestant ethic: Max Weber's term for the disciplined work ethic, this-worldly concerns, and rational orientation to life emphasized by John Calvin and his followers. (222)

Qualitative research: Research that relies more on what scientists see in the field or in naturalistic settings than on statistical data. (27)

Quantitative research: Research that collects and reports data primarily in numerical form. (27)

Queer theory: The study of society from the perspective of a broad spectrum of sexual identities, including heterosexuality, homosexuality, and bisexuality. (18)

Questionnaire: A printed or written form used to obtain information from a respondent. (27)

Racial formation: A sociohistorical process in which racial categories are created, inhibited, transformed, and destroyed. (165)

Racial group: A group that is set apart from others because of obvious physical differences. (166)

Racial profiling: Any arbitrary action initiated by an authority based on race, ethnicity, or national origin rather than on a person's behavior. (175)

Racism: The belief that one race is supreme and all others are innately inferior. (177)

Random sample: A sample for which every member of the entire population has the same chance of being selected. (24)

Rational-legal authority: Max Weber's term for power made legitimate by law. (244)

Reference group: Any group that individuals use as a standard in evaluating themselves and their own behavior. (80)

Refugees: People who live outside their country of citizenship for fear of political or religious persecution. (172)

Relative deprivation: The conscious feeling of a negative discrepancy between legitimate expectations and present actualities. (299)

Relative poverty: A floating standard of deprivation by which people at the bottom of a society, whatever their lifestyles, are judged to be disadvantaged in comparison with the nation as a whole. (143)

Reliability: The extent to which a measure produces consistent results. (25)

Religion: According to Émile Durkheim, a unified system of beliefs and practices relative to sacred things. (220)

Religious belief: A statement to which members of a particular religion adhere. (225)

Religious experience: The feeling or perception of being in direct contact with the ultimate reality, such as a divine being, or of being overcome with religious emotion. (228)

Religious ritual: A practice required or expected of members of a faith. (226)

Remittances: The monies that immigrants send home to their countries of origin. (171)

Research design: A detailed plan or method for obtaining data scientifically. (26)

Resocialization: The process of discarding former behavior patterns and accepting new ones as part of a transition in one's life. (68)

Resource mobilization: The ways in which a social movement utilizes such resources as money, political influence, access to the media, and personnel. (300)

Rite of passage: A ritual marking the symbolic transition from one social position to another. (67)

Role conflict: The situation that occurs when incompatible expectations arise from two or more social positions held by the same person. (77)

Role exit: The process of disengagement from a role that is central to one's self-identity in order to establish a new role and identity. (78)

Role strain: The situation that occurs when the same social position imposes conflicting demands and expectations. (78)

Role taking: The process of mentally assuming the perspective of another in order to respond from that imagined viewpoint. (57)

Sample: A selection from a larger population that is statistically representative of that population. (24)

Sanction: A penalty or reward for conduct concerning a social norm. (49, 98)

Science: The body of knowledge obtained by methods based on systematic observation. (4)

Scientific management approach: Another name for the *classical theory* of formal organizations. (92)

Scientific method: A systematic, organized series of steps that ensures maximum objectivity and consistency in researching a problem. (21)

Second shift: The double burden—work outside the home, followed by child care and housework—that many women face and few men share equitably. (201)

Secondary analysis: A variety of research techniques that make use of previously collected and publicly accessible information and data. (29)

Secondary group: A formal, impersonal group in which there is little social intimacy or mutual understanding. (79)

Self: According to George Herbert Mead, a distinct identity that sets one apart from others. (56)

Serial monogamy: A form of marriage in which a person may have several spouses in his or her life, but only one spouse at a time. (211)

Sexism: The ideology that one sex is superior to the other. (198)

Sexual identity: (also called sexual orientation). The self-awareness of being romantically or sexually attracted to a defined group of people. (217)

Sharing economy: Refers to connecting owners of underused assets with others willing to pay to use them. (256)

Sick role: Societal expectations about the attitudes and behavior of a person viewed as being ill. (275)

Significant other: A term used by George Herbert Mead to refer to those individuals who are most important in the development of the self, such as parents, friends, and teachers. (59)

Slavery: A system of enforced servitude in which some people are legally owned by other people. (127)

Social capital: The collective benefit of social networks, which are built on reciprocal trust. (14)

Social change: Significant alteration over time in behavior patterns and culture. (303)

Social control: Techniques and strategies for preventing deviant behavior in any society. (97)

Social disorganization theory: The theory that increases in crime and deviance can be attributed to the absence or breakdown of communal relationships and social institutions, such as the family, school, church, and local government. (109)

Social epidemiology: The study of the distribution of disease, impairment, and general health status across a population. (280)

Social inequality: A condition in which members of a society enjoy different amounts of wealth, prestige, or power. (126)

Social institution: An organized pattern of beliefs and behavior centered on basic social needs. (82, 206)

Social interaction: The ways in which people respond to one another. (73)

Social mobility: The movement of individuals or groups from one position in a society's stratification system to another. (147)

Social movement: An organized collective activity to bring about or resist fundamental change in an existing group or society. (298)

Social network: A series of social relationships that links a person directly to others, and through them, indirectly to still more people. (81)

Social role: A set of expectations for people who occupy a given social position or status. (77)

Social science: The study of various aspects of human society. (4)

Social structure: The way in which a society is organized into predictable relationships. (73)

Socialism: An economic system in which the means of production and distribution are collectively rather than privately owned. (251)

Socialization: The process through which people learn the attitudes, values, and behaviors appropriate for members of a particular culture. (38)

Societal-reaction approach: Another name for *labeling theory.* (110)

Society: A fairly large number of people who live in the same territory, are relatively independent of people outside it, and participate in a common culture. (39)

Sociobiology: The systematic study of how biology affects human social behavior. (54)

Sociocultural evolution: Long-term social trends resulting from the interplay of continuity, innovation, and selection. (85)

Socioeconomic status (SES): A measure of social class that is based on income, education, and occupation. (140)

Sociological imagination: An awareness of the relationship between an individual and the wider society, both today and in the past. (3)

Sociology: The scientific study of social behavior and human groups. (2)

Status: A term used by sociologists to refer to any of the full range of socially defined positions within a large group or society. (75)

Status group: A term used by Max Weber to refer to people who have the same prestige or lifestyle, independent of their class positions. (133)

Stereotype: An unreliable generalization about all members of a group that does not recognize individual differences within the group. (166)

Stigma: A label society uses to devalue members of a certain social group. (103)

Stratification: The structured ranking of entire groups of people that perpetuates unequal economic rewards and power in a society. (126)

Subculture: A segment of society that shares a distinctive pattern of customs, rules, and traditions that differs from the pattern of the larger society. (44)

Survey: A study, generally in the form of an interview or questionnaire, that provides researchers with information about how people think and act. (27)

Symbol: A gesture, object, or language that forms the basis of human communication. (57)

Symbolic ethnicity: An emphasis on such concerns as ethnic food or political issues rather than on deeper ties to one's ethnic heritage. (169)

Teacher-expectancy effect: The impact that a teacher's expectations about a student's performance may have on the student's actual achievements. (238)

Technology: Cultural information about the ways in which the material resources of the environment may be used to satisfy human needs and desires. (43, 85, 310)

Theory: In sociology, a set of statements that seeks to explain problems, actions, or behavior. (6)

Total fertility rate (TFR): The average number of children born alive to any woman, assuming that she conforms to current fertility rates. (265)

Total institution: A term coined by Erving Goffman to refer to institutions that regulate all aspects of a person's life under a single authority, such as prisons, the military, mental hospitals, and convents. (68)

Tracking: The practice of placing students in specific curriculum groups on the basis of their test scores and other criteria. (236)

Traditional authority: Legitimate power conferred by custom and accepted practice. (244)

Trained incapacity: The tendency of workers in a bureaucracy to become so specialized that they develop blind spots and fail to notice obvious problems. (90)

Transnational crime: Crime that occurs across multiple national borders. (117)

Urban ecology: An area of study that focuses on the interrelationships between urban residents and their environment. (271)

Urbanism: A term used by Louis Wirth to describe distinctive patterns of social behavior evident among city residents. (270)

Validity: The degree to which a measure or scale truly reflects the phenomenon under study. (25)

Value: A collective conception of what is considered good, desirable, and proper—or bad, undesirable, and improper—in a culture. (50)

Variable: A measurable trait or characteristic that is subject to change under different conditions. (23)

Verstehen: The German word for "understanding" or "insight"; used by Max Weber to stress the need for sociologists to take into account the subjective meanings people attach to their actions. (10)

Vertical mobility: The movement of a person from one social position to another of a different rank. (148)

Vested interests: Thorstein Veblen's term for those people or groups who will suffer in the event of social change, and who have a stake in maintaining the status quo. (308)

Victimization survey: Questioning of ordinary people, not police officers, to determine whether they have been victims of crime. (120)

Victimless crime: The willing exchange among adults of widely desired but illegal goods and services. (113)

Vital statistics: Records of births, deaths, marriages, and divorces that are gathered through a registration system maintained by governmental units. (264)

Wealth: An inclusive term encompassing all a person's material assets, including land, stocks, and other property. (126)

White-collar crime: Illegal acts committed in the course of business activities. (115)

White privilege: Rights or immunities granted to people as a particular benefit or favor simply because they are White. (163)

World systems analysis: The global economy as an interdependent system of economically and politically unequal nations. (152, 273)

References

Abercrombie, Nicholas, Stephen Hill, and Bryan Turner. 1980. *The Dominant Ideology Thesis.* London: George Allen Unwin.

——, Bryan S. Turner, and Stephen Hill, eds. 1990. *Dominant Ideologies.* Cambridge, MA: Unwin Hyman.

Aberle, David E., A. K. Cohen, A. K. Davis, M. J. Leng, Jr., and F. N. Sutton. 1950. "The Functionalist Prerequisites of a Society." *Ethics* 60 (January):100–111.

Abolition Now. 2016. "About Us." Accessed February 22 (www.abolitionnow.com).

ACLU. 2015b. "NSA Surveillance." Accessible at www.aclu.org.

Adams, Charles Joseph. 2015. "Classification of Religions." *Britannica Online.* May 1. Accessible at www.britannica.com.

Addams, Jane. 1910. *Twenty Years at Hull-House.* New York: Macmillan.

——. 1930. *The Second Twenty Years at Hull-House.* New York: Macmillan.

Adler, Patricia A., and Peter Adler. 2007. "The Demedicalization of Self-Injury: From Psychopathology to Sociological Deviance." *Journal of Contemporary Ethnography* 36 (October):537–570.

——, and ——. 2008b. "The Cyber Worlds of Self-Injurers: Deviant Communities, Relationships, and Selves." *Symbolic Interaction* 31 (1):33–56.

——, and ——. 2011. *The Tender Cut: Inside the Hidden World of Self-Injury.* New York: New York University Press.

——, ——, and John M. Johnson. 1992. "Street Corner Society Revisited." *Journal of Contemporary Ethnography* 21 (April):3–10.

Adorno, Theodor. [1971] 1991. *The Culture Industry.* London: Routledge.

Aguillar, Julián, and Alex Ura. 2016. "Border Communities Have Lower Crime Rates." *The Texas Tribune* (February 23).

Alba, Richard D. 1990. *Ethnic Identity: The Transformation of White America.* New Haven, CT: Yale University Press.

Allen, Bem P. 1978. *Social Behavior: Fact and Falsehood.* Chicago: Nelson-Hall.

Allen, Samantha. 2015. "Marital Rape Is Semi-legal in 8 States." June 9. *The Daily Beast.* Accessible at the dailybeast.com.

Allport, Gordon W. 1979. *The Nature of Prejudice.* 25th Anniv. ed. Reading, MA: Addison-Wesley.

Alvaredo, Facundo. 2011. "Inequality over the Past Century." *Finance & Development* 48 (3):29.

Alzheimer's Association. 2016. "2015 Alzheimer's Disease Facts and Figures." Accessible at www.alz.org.

The Atlantic. 2008. "Engineers for Osama." 301 (January/February):26.

American Community Survey. 2011. "2010 American Community Survey." Accessible at www.census.gov/acs/www/.

American Community Survey. 2016. "2015 American Community Survey 1-Year Estimates. Accessible at www.census.gov.

American Lung Association. 2015. "State of the Air 2015." Accessible at www.stateoftheair.org.

American Community Survey. 2016a. *2015 ACS 1-Year Estimates*. Accessible at www.census.gov.

American Community Survey. 2016b. 2015 American Community Survey 5-Year Estimates. Accessible at www.census.gov.

———. 2016r. *2015 American Community Survey 1-year Estimates*. Accessible at www.census.gov.

American Psychological Association. 2008. "Being Gay Is Just as Healthy as Being Straight." Accessible at www.apa.org.

American Sociological Association. 2005. "Need Today's Data Yesterday." Accessible at www.asanet.org.

———. 2010a. *2010 Guide to Graduate Departments of Sociology.* Washington, DC: ASA.

———. 2013. *21st Century Careers with an Undergraduate Degree in Sociology.* Washington, DC: ASA.

American Social and Economic Supplement. 2016. *Current Population Survey (CPS) 2015 Annual Social and Economic (ASEC) Supplement*. Accessible at www.census.gov.

Ansell, Amy E. 2008. "Color Blindness." Pp. 320–321, in *Encyclopedia of Race, Ethnicity, and Society,* vol. 1, edited by Richard T. Schaefer. Thousand Oaks, CA: Sage.

Apuzzo, Matt, and Joseph Goldstein. 2014. "New York Drops Unit That Spied Among Muslims." *New York Times*, April 16, pp. A1, A3.

Armer, J. Michael, and John Katsillis. 1992."Modernization Theory." Pp. 1299–1304 in *Encyclopedia of Sociology,* vol. 4, edited by Edgar F. Borgatta and Marie L. Borgatta. New York: Macmillan.

Asadullah, Niaz, and Zaki Wahhaj. 2016. "Minimum Wage Attracts Girls to Factories." *New York Times* (March 1).

Association of Theological Schools. 2015. "ATS Data Tables 2014–2015." Accessible at www. ats.edu.

Azumi, Koya, and Jerald Hage. 1972. *Organizational Systems.* Lexington, MA: Heath.

Babad, Elisha Y., and P. J. Taylor. 1992. "Transparency of Teacher Expectancies Across Language, Cultural Boundaries." *Journal of Educational Research* 86:120–125.

Barnes, Taylor. 2009. "Rise of the Shadow Economy." *Christian Science Monitor,* November 8, pp. 30–31.

Bastaits, Kim, and Dimitri Mortelmans. 2014. "Does the Parenting of Divorced Mothers and Fathers Affect Children's Well-Being in the Same Way?" *Child Indicators Research 7* (No. 2):351–367.

Bauman, Kurt J. 1999. "Extended Measures of Well-Being: Meeting Basic Needs." *Current Population Reports,* ser. P-70, no. 67. Washington, DC: U.S. Government Printing Office.

Beagan, Brenda L. 2001. "'Even If I Don't Know What I'm Doing I Can Make It Look Like I Know What I'm Doing': Becoming a Doctor in the 1990s." *Canadian Review of Sociology and Anthropology* 38:275–292.

Bearman, Peter S., James Moody, and Katherine Stovel. 2004. "Chains of Affection: The Structure of Adolescent Romantic and Sexual Networks." *American Journal of Sociology* 110 (July):44–91.

Beaubien, Jason, and Rebecca Davis. 2015. "A Teen Who Fled Syria Had High Hopes of Life in Lebanon." October 25. Accessible at npr.org.

Becker, Howard S., ed. 1964. *The Other Side: Perspectives on Deviance.* New York: Free Press.

Becker, Howard S. [1953] 2015. *Becoming a Marijuana User.* Chicago: University of Chicago Press.

Bell, Daniel. 1953. "Crime as an American Way of Life." *Antioch Review* 13 (Summer):131–154.

——. [1973] 1999. *The Coming of Post-Industrial Society.* Special Anniv. ed. New York: Basic Books.

Bell, Wendell. 1981."Modernization." Pp. 186–187 in *Encyclopedia of Sociology.* Guilford, CT: DPG Publishing.

Beller, Emily. 2009. "Bringing Intergenerational Social Mobility Research into the Twenty-First Century: Why Mothers Matter." *America Sociological Review* 74 (August):507–528.

Benford, Robert D. 1992. "Social Movements." Pp. 1880–1887 in *Encyclopedia of Sociology,* vol. 4, edited by Edgar F. Borgatta and Marie Borgatta. New York: Macmillan.

Berger, Peter, and Thomas Luckmann. 1966. *The Social Construction of Reality.* New York: Doubleday.

Berman, Paul. 2003. *Terror and Liberalism.* New York: W.W. Norton.

Berry, Justin A., and Jane Junn. 2015. "Silent Citizenship among Asian Americans and Latinos: Opting Out or Left Out?" *Citizenship Studies* 19 (5):570–590.

Best, Joel. 2004. *Deviance: Career of a Concept.* Belmont, CA: Wadsworth Thomson.

Bhagat, Chetan. 2007. *One Night at the Call Centre.* London: Black Swan.

Bialik, Carol. 2010. "Seven Careers in a Lifetime? Think Twice, Researchers Say." *Wall Street Journal,* September 4, p. A6.

Billitteri, Thomas, J. 2009. "Middle-Class Squeeze." *CQ Researcher* 19 (March 6):201–224.

Black, Donald. 1995. "The Epistemology of Pure Sociology." *Law and Social Inquiry* 20 (Summer):829–870.

Blank, Rebecca M. 2011. *Changing Inequality.* Berkeley: University of California Press.

Blau, Peter M., and Otis Dudley Duncan. 1967. *The American Occupational Structure.* New York: Wiley.

Blauner, Robert. 1972. *Racial Oppression in America.* New York: Harper and Row.

Blumer, Herbert. 1955. "Collective Behavior." Pp. 165–198 in *Principles of Sociology,* 2nd ed., edited by Alfred McClung Lee. New York: Barnes and Noble.

Bonilla-Silva, Eduardo. 2004. "From Bi-Racial to Tri-Racial: Towards a New System of Racial Stratification in the USA." *Ethics and Racial Studies* 27 (November):931–950.

——. 2006. *Racism Without Racists.* Lanham, MD: Rowman and Littlefield.

Bonilla-Silva, Eduardo. 2014. *Racism without Racists.* 4th ed. New York: Rowman and Littlefield.

Bottomore, Tom, and Maximilien Rubel, eds. 1956. *Karl Marx: Selected Writings in Sociology and Social Philosophy.* New York: McGraw-Hill.

Bourdieu, Pierre, and Jean-Claude Passerson. 1990. *Reproduction in Education, Society and Culture,* 2nd ed. London: Sage. Originally published as *La reproduction.*

Bowles, Samuel, and Herbert Gintis. 1976. *Schooling in Capitalistic America: Educational Reforms and the Contradictions of Economic Life.* New York: Basic Books.

Brannigan, Augustine. 1992. "Postmodernism." Pp. 1522–1525 in *Encyclopedia of Sociology,* vol. 3, edited by Edgar F. Borgatta and Marie L. Borgatta. New York: Macmillan.

Brennan Center. 2006. *Citizens Without Proof.* New York: Brennan Center for Justice, New York University School of Law.

Brewer, Rose M., and Nancy A. Heitzeg. 2008. "The Racialization of Criminal Punishment." *American Behavioral Scientist* 51 (January):625–644.

Brimmer, Andrew F. 1995. "The Economic Cost of Discrimination against Black Americans." Pp. 9–29 in *Economic Perspectives in Affirmative Action,* edited by Margaret C. Simms. Washington, DC: Joint Center for Political and Economic Studies.

Brint, Steven. 1998. *Schools and Societies.* Thousand Oaks, CA: Pine Forge Press.

Brown, David K. 2001. "The Social Sources of Educational Credentialism: Status Cultures, Labor Markets, and Organizations." *Sociology of Education* 74 (Extra Issue):19–34.

Brown, Lester R. 2011. *World on the Edge: How to Prevent Environmental and Economic Collapse.* New York: W.W. Norton.

Bullard, Robert, D. 1993. *Dumping in Dixie: Race, Class, and Environmentalist Quality.* 2nd ed. Boulder, CO: Westin Press.

Burawoy, Michael. 2005. "For Public Sociology." *American Sociological Review* 70 (February):4–28.

Burch, Audra D. S. 2012. "After Trayvon Martin, Hoodie Goes from Fashion Statement to Socio-Political One." *Miami Herald,* March 26. Accessed at http://miamiherald.com/2012/03/24/2712545/after-trayvon-martin-hoodie-goes.html.

Bureau of the Census. 2004a. *Statistical Abstract of the United States, 2004-2005.* Washington, DC: U.S. Government Printing Office.

——2009a. *Statistical Abstract of the United States 2010.* Washington, DC: U.S. Government Printing Office.

Bureau of the Census. 2010b. "America's Families and Living Arrangements: 2010." Released January. Accessed at www.census.gov/population/www/socdemo/hh-fam/cps2010.html.

——. 2011d. *Current Population Survey, Annual Social and Economic Supplements.* Washington, DC: U.S. Government Printing Office.

——. 2012a. *Statistical Abstract of the United States 2013.* Accessible at www.census.gov/.

——. 2012c. "Graphs on Historical Voting Trends." February 15. Accessed at www.census.gov/newsroom/releases/archives/voting/cb12-tps08.html.

——. 2012d. "Census Bureau Releases Estimates of Undercount and Overcount in the 2010 Census." News Release CB12-95, May 22. Accessed at www.census.gov/newroom/ releases/archives/2010_census/cb12-95.html.

——. 2013b. "Estimated Median Age at First Marriage, by Sex: 1890 to the Present." Accessible at www.census.gov.

——. 2014d. "Walking to Work." May 13. *Visualizations and Infographics.* Accessible at www.census.gov.

——. 2015d. *Annual Social and Economic Supplement: 2014 Poverty Table of Contents.* POV46: Poverty Status by State, Below 100% of Poverty—All Ages. Accessible at www.census.gov.

——. 2015i. "Drive-Ins." February 10. *Visualizations and Infographics.* Accessible at www.census.gov.

——. 2016i. *CPS Income Tables.* Accessible at www.census.gov.

Bureau of Labor Statistics. 2004. "Time-Use Survey—First Results Announced by BLS." September 13. Accessible at www.bls.gov.

——. 2015. Women in the Labor Force: A Databook. December. BLS Report 1059. Accessible at www.bls.gov.

——. 2015a. "Number of Jobs Held, Labor Market Activity, and Earnings Growth Among the Youngest Baby Boomers: Results from a Longitudinal Survey Summary." March 31. Accessible at http://www.bls.gov/ news.release/nlsoy.nr0.htm.

——. 2015f. "Wives Who Earn More Than Their Husbands, 1987–2013." June 9. Accessible at www.bls.gov.

——. 2016a. "Employment Status of the Civilian Population by Race, Sex, and Age." Accessible at www.bls.gov.

——. 2016a. "Labor Force Statistics from the Current Population Reports." Accessible at www.bls.gov.

——. 2016b. "Time-Use Survey—2015 Results." June 24. Accessible at www.bls.gov.

——. 2017b. "Household Data, Annual Averages, Table 39." Last updated February 18. Accessible at www.bls.gov.

Bures, Frank. 2011. "Can You Hear Us Now?" *Utne Reader* (March–April): 8–9, 11.

Burger, Jerry M. 2009. "Replicating Milgram: Would People Still Obey Today?" *American Psychologist* 64 (January):1–11.

Burgess, Ernest W. 1925. "The Growth of the City." Pp. 47–62 in *The City,* edited by Robert E. Park, Ernest W. Burgess, and Roderick D. McKenzie. Chicago: University of Chicago Press.

Burns, Melinda. 2010. "Workfare and the Low-Wage Woman." *Miller-McClune* (November/December):76–81.

Butler, Daniel Allen. 1998. *"Unsinkable": The Full Story.* Mechanicsburg, PA: Stackpole Books.

Calhoun, Craig. 2011. "Evicting the Public." Possible Futures: A Project of the Social Science Research Project. November 19. Accessed January 26, 2012 (www.possiblefutures.org/2011/11/19/evicting-the-public-why-has-occupying-public-spaces-brought-such-heavy-handed-repression).

Caplan, Ronald L. 1989. "The Commodification of American Health Care." *Social Science and Medicine* 28 (11):1139–1148.

Carbon Trust. 2015. "About the Carbon Trust." Accessible at www.carbontrust.co.uk.

Catalyst. 2017a. *Pyramid Women in S&P 500 Companies.* March 1. New York: Catalyst.

——. 2017b. *Women CEOs of the S&P 500.* March 1. New York: Catalyst.

Center for Community Initiatives. 2012. "Magnolia Project 2011 Reports." Accessed November 2 (www.unf.edu/coas/cci/magnilia/2011 _Reports.aspx).

———. 2012. "Magnolia Grant Objectives 2012." Accessed April 11 (http:// aries.unfcsd.unf.edu/Magnolia/2012/objectives2012.php).

Centers for Disease Control and Prevention. 2013. "CDC Health Disparities and Inequalities Report-United States, 2013." *Morbidity and Mortality Report* 62 (November 22).

Chambliss, William. 1973. "The Saints and the Roughnecks." *Society* 11 (November/December):24-31.

Chase-Dunn, Christopher, and Peter Grimes. 1995. "World-Systems Analysis." Pp. 387-417 in *Annual Review of Sociology,* 1995, edited by John Hagan. Palo Alto, CA: Annual Reviews.

———, Yukio Kawano, and Benjamin D. Brewer. 2000. "Trade Globalization Since 1795: Waves of Integration in the World System." *American Sociological Review* 65 (February):77-95.

Chen, Liyan. 2015. "New York to Hong Kong with the Most Billionaires in 2015." March 4. Forbes/Lists. Accessible at www.forbes.com.

Chin, Ko-lin. 1996. *Chinatown Gangs: Extortion, Enterprise, and Ethnicity.* New York: Oxford University Press.

China Labor Watch. 2015. "Analyzing Labor Conditions of Pegatron and Foxconn: Apple's Low-cost Reality." February 11. Accessible at www. chinalaborwatch.com.

Christakis, Nicholas A., and James Fowler. 2009. *Connected: The Amazing Power of Social Networks and How They Shape Our Lives.* New York: Harper.

Chung, Esther K., Leny Mathew, Amy C. Rothkopt, Irma T. Elo, James C. Cayne, and Jennifer F. Culhane. 2009. "Parenting Attitudes and Infant Spanking: The Influence of Childhood Experiences." *Pediatrics* 124 (August):278-286.

Clarke, Adele E., Janet K. Shim, Laura Maro, Jennifer Ruth Fusket, and Jennifer R. Fishman. 2003. "Bio Medicalization: Technoscientific Transformations of Health, Illness, and U.S. Biomedicine." *American Sociological Review* 68 (April):161-194.

Cockerham, William C. 2012. *Medical Sociology.* 12th ed. Upper Saddle River, NJ: Prentice Hall.

Colby, Sandra L., and Jennifer M. Ortman. "Projections of the Size and Composition of the U.S. Population: 2014 to 2060." March. *Current Population Reports P25-1143.* Washington, DC: U.S. Government Printing Office.

Cole, Mike. 1988. *Bowles and Gintis Revisited: Correspondence and Contradiction in Educational Theory.* Philadelphia: Falmer.

Coleman, James William. 2006. *The Criminal Elite: Understanding White-Collar Crime.* 6th ed. New York: Worth.

Collins, Patricia Hill. 2000. *Black Feminist Thought: Knowledge, Consciousness, and the Politics of Empowerment.* Revised 10th Anniv. 2nd ed. New York: Routledge.

Collins, Patricia Hill. 2015. "Intersectionality's Definitional Dilemmas." *Annual Review of Sociology* 41:1-20.

Collins, Randall. 1975. *Conflict Sociology: Toward an Explanatory Sociology.* New York: Academic.

——. 1980. "Weber's Last Theory of Capitalism: A Systematization." *American Sociological Review* 45 (December):925–942.

——. 1986. *Weberian Sociological Theory.* New York: Cambridge University Press.

——. 1995. "Prediction in Macrosociology: The Case of the Soviet Collapse." *American Journal of Sociology* 100 (May):1552–1593.

Collura, Heather. 2007. "Roommate Concerns Fed by Facebook." *USA Today,* August 8, p. 6D.

Commission on Civil Rights. 1976. *A Guide to Federal Laws and Regulations Prohibiting Sex Discrimination.* Washington, DC: U.S. Government Printing Office.

——. 1981. *Affirmative Action in the 1980s: Dismantling the Process of Discrimination.* Washington, DC: U.S. Government Printing Office.

Common Sense Media. 2015. The Common Sense Census: Uses by Tweens and Teens. Accessible at www.commonsensemedia.org.

Commoner, Barry. 1971. *The Closing Circle.* New York: Knopf.

——. 1990. *Making Peace with the Planet.* New York: Pantheon.

——. 2007. "At 90, an Environmentalist from the 70's Still Has Hope." *New York Times,* June 19, p. D2.

Connor, Phillip. 2016. "Migrant Remittances Worldwide Drop in 2015 for First Time Since Great Recession." August 31. Accessible at www.pewresearch.org.

Conrad, Peter, ed. 2009. *The Medicalization of Society: On the Transformation of Human Conditions into Treatable Disorders.* 11th ed. Baltimore: Johns Hopkins University.

Conrad, Peter, and Kristin K. Barker. 2010. "The Social Construction of Illness: Key Insights and Policy Implications." *Journal of Health and Social Behavior* 51 (No. 5):567–579.

——, and Valerie Leiter. 2013. *The Sociology of Health and Illness: Critical Perspectives.* 9th ed. New York: Worth.

Contee, Cheryl. 2012. "A Tale of Two Hoodies." May 23. Accessed at http://thegrio.com/2012/05/23/a-tale-of-two-hoodies-mark-zuckerberg-vs-trayvon-martin/.

Cooky, Cheryl, Michael Messner, and Michele Mustro. 2015. "It's Dude Time! A Quarter Century of Excluding Women's Sports in Televised News and Highlight Shows." *Communication and Sport* 3 (September):261–287.

Cooley, Charles. H. 1902. *Human Nature and the Social Order.* New York: Scribner.

Coontz, Stephanie. 2006. "A Pop Quiz on Marriage." *New York Times,* February 19, p. 12.

Cooper, Richard T. 1998. "Jobs Outside High School Can Be Costly, Report Finds." *Los Angeles Times,* November 6, p. A1.

Coser, Lewis A. 1977. *Masters of Sociological Thought: Ideas in Historical and Social Context.* 2nd ed. New York: Harcourt Brace Jovanovich.

Couch, Carl. 1996. *Information Technologies and Social Orders.* Edited with an introduction by David R. Maines and Shing-Ling Chien. New York: Aldine de Gruyter.

Cox, Oliver C. 1948. *Caste, Class, and Race: A Study in Social Dynamics.* Detroit: Wayne State University Press.

Crabtree, Steve. 2010. "Religiosity Highest in World's Poorest Nations." August 31. Accessible at www.gallup.com.

Crenshaw, Kimberlé. 1989. "Demarginalizing the Intersection of Race and Sex: A Black Feminist Critique of Antidiscrimination Doctrine, Feminist Theory, and Antiracist Politics." University of Chicago Legal Foundation.

———. 2015. "Why Intersectionality Can't Wait." *The Washington Post* (December 24). Accessible at www.washingtonpost.com.

Crouse, Kelly. 1999. "Sociology of the Titanic." Teaching Sociology Listserv. May 24.

Cuff, E. C., W. W. Sharrock, and D.W. Francis, eds. 1990. *Perspectives in Sociology.* 3rd ed. Boston: Unwin Hyman.

Currie, Elliot. 1985. *Confronting Crime: An American Challenge.* New York: Pantheon.

———. 1998. *Crime and Punishment in America.* New York: Metropolitan Books.

Curry, Timothy Jon. 1993. "A Little Pain Never Hurt Anyone: Athletic Career Socialization and the Normalization of Sports Injury." *Symbolic Interaction* 26 (Fall):273–290.

Dade, Corey. 2012. "The Fight Over Voter ID Laws Goes to the United Nations." March 9. Accessible at www.npr.org.

Dahl, Robert A. 1961. *Who Governs?* New Haven, CT: Yale University Press.

Darwin, Charles. 1859. *On the Origin of Species.* London: John Murray.

Davidson, James D., and Ralph E. Pyle. 2011. *Ranking Faiths: Religious Stratification in America.* Lanham, MD: Rowman and Littlefield.

Davidson, Paul. 2012. "More U.S. Service Jobs Go Overseas." *USA Today,* December 7, p. B1.

Davies, Christie. 1989. "Goffman's Concept of the Total Institution: Criticisms and Revisions." *Human Studies* 12 (June):77–95.

Davis, Kingsley. 1940. "Extreme Social Isolation of a Child." *American Journal of Sociology* 45 (January):554–565.

———. 1947. "A Final Note on a Case of Extreme Isolation." *American Journal of Sociology* 52 (March):432–437.

———. [1949] 1995. *Human Society.* Reprint, New York: Macmillan.

———, and Wilbert E. Moore. 1945. "Some Principles of Stratification." *American Sociological Review* 10 (April):242–249.

Death Penalty Information Center. 2017. "Number of Executions by State and Region Since 1976." November 9. Accessible at www.dpic.org.

Deegan, Mary Jo, ed. 1991. *Women in Sociology: A Bio-Bibliographical Sourcebook.* Westport, CT: Greenwood.

———. 2003. "Textbooks, the History of Sociology, and the Sociological Stock of Knowledge." *Sociological Theory* 21 (November):298–305.

Deibert, Ronald J., John Palfrey, Rafal Rohozinski, and Jonathan Zittrain. 2008. *Access Denied: The Practice and Policy of Global Internet Filtering.* Cambridge, MA: MIT Press.

DeNavas-Walt, Carmen, and Bernadette D. Proctor. 2015. "Income and Poverty in the United States: 2014." Accessible at census.gov.

DeNavas-Walt, Carmen, Bernadette D. Proctor, and Jessica C. Smith. 2011. *Income, Poverty, and Health Insurance Coverage in the United States: 2010.* Washington, DC: U.S. Government Printing Office.

Department of Justice. 2008. "Hate Crime Statistics, 2007." Accessible at www.Fbi.gov/ucr/ucr.htm.

——. 2011a. "Crime in the United States, 2010." Accessed January 23, 2012 (www.fbi.gov/about-us/cjis/ucr/crime-in-the-u.s/2010/crime-in-the-u.s.-2010).

Department of Justice. 2014. "Crime in the United States, 2014." Accessible at www.fbi.gov.

Department of State. 2017. "Summary of Refugee Admissions as of 31 January 2017." Accessible at www.state.gov.

Deutsch, Francine M. 2007. "Undoing Gender." *Gender and Society* 21 (February):106–127.

Dickler, Jessica. 2011. "Dig Deep to Buy Titanic Visit." *Chicago Tribune,* June 3, p. 25.

Dinovitzer, Ronit, Nancy Reichman, and Joyce Sterling. 2009. "The Differential Valuation of Women's Work: A New Look at the Gender Gap in Lawyers' Incomes." *Social Forces* 88(2):819–864.

Dobbin, Frank, and Jiwook Jung. 2011. "Corporate Board Gender Diversity and Stock Performance: The Competence Gap or Institutional Investor Bias?" *North Carolina Law Review* 89 (No. 3):809–838.

Domhoff, G. William. 1978. *Who Really Rules? New Haven and Community Power Reexamined.* New Brunswick, NJ: Transaction.

——. 2010. *Who Rules America?* 6th ed. New York: McGraw-Hill.

Domhoff, Willian G. 2014. *Who Rules America? The Triumph of the Corporate Rich,* 7th ed. New York: McGraw-Hill.

Dougherty, Kevin, and Floyd M. Hammack. 1992. "Education Organizations." Pp. 525, 541 in *Encyclopedia of Sociology,* vol. 2, edited by Edgar F. Borgatta and Marie L. Borgatta. New York: Macmillan.

DuBois, W. E. B. [1900] 1969. "To the Nations of the World." Pp. 19–23 in *An ABC of Color,* edited by W. E. B. DuBois. Reprint, New York: International Publishers.

——. [1899] 1995. *The Philadelphia Negro: A Social Study.* Reprint, Philadelphia: University of Pennsylvania Press.

——. [1903] 1961. *The Souls of Black Folks: Essays and Sketches.* Reprint, New York: Fawcett.

——. [1903] 2003. *The Negro Church.* Reprint, Walnut Creek, CA: Alta Mira Press.

——. [1935] 1962. *Black Reconstruction in America 1860–1880.* Reprint, New York: Athenaeum.

Duhigg, Charles, and Keith Bradsher. 2012. "How U.S. Lost Out on iPhone Work." *New York Times,* January 22, p. A1.

Duncan, Greg J. and Richard J. Murnane. 2014. "Growing Income Inequality Threatens American Education." March 28. *Phi Delta Kappan.* Accessible at www.edweek.org.

Duneier, Mitchell. 1994a. "On the Job, but Behind the Scenes." *Chicago Tribune,* December 26, pp. 1, 24.

——. 1994b. "Battling for Control." *Chicago Tribune,* December 28, pp. 1, 8.

DuPuis, Nicole, and Brooks Rainwater. 2014. *The Sharing Economy: An Analysis of Current Sentiment Surrounding Homesharing and Ridesharing.* Washington, DC: National League of Cities. Accessible at www.nlc.org.

Durkheim, Émile. [1893] 1933. *Division of Labor in Society.* Translated by George Simpson. Reprint, New York: Free Press.

——. [1895] 1964. *The Rules of Sociological Method.* Translated by Sarah A. Solovay and John H. Mueller. Reprint, New York: Free Press.

——. [1897] 1951. *Suicide.* Translated by John A. Spaulding and George Simpson. Reprint, New York: Free Press.

——. [1912] 2001. *The Elementary Forms of Religious Life.* A new translation by Carol Cosman. Reprint, New York: Oxford University Press.

Eagan, Kevin, Ellen Bara Stolzenberg, Abigail K. Bates, Melissa C. Aragon, Maria Ramirez Suchard, and Cecilia Rios-Arguilar. 2016. *The American Freshman: National Norms Fall 2015.* Los Angeles: Higher Education Research Institute.

Ebaugh, Helen Rose Fuchs. 1988. *Becoming an Ex: The Process of Role Exit.* Chicago: University of Chicago Press.

Economic Mobility Project. 2009. *Findings from a National Survey and Focus Groups on Economic Mobility.* Washington, DC: Pew Charitable Trusts.

The Economist. 2010b. "Plus One Country." (September 4):46.

——. 2017. "Shakers: Not Too Shaken." (January 14):24.

Ehrenreich, Barbara. 2001. *Nickel and Dimed: On (Not) Getting By in America.* New York: Metropolitan.

Ehrlich, Paul R. 1968. *The Population Bomb.* New York: Ballantine.

——, and Anne H. Ehrlich. 1990. *The Population Explosion.* New York: Simon & Schuster.

——, and Katherine Ellison. 2002. "A Looming Threat We Won't Face." *Los Angeles Times,* January 20, p. M6.

El Nasser, Haya, and Paul Overberg. 2011. "Recession Reshapes Life in the USA." *USA Today,* September 12, p. 3A.

Eligon, John. 2016. "A Question of Environmental Racism in Flint." *New York Times,* January 22, pp. A1, A16.

Ellison, Charles D. 2015. "Racism in the Air You Breathe: When Where You Live Determines How Fast You Die." August 17. Accessible at www .theroot.com.

Engels, Friedrich. [1884] 1959. "The Origin of the Family, Private Property, and the State." Pp. 392–394, excerpted in *Marx and Engels: Basic Writings on Politics and Philosophy,* edited by Lewis Feuer. Reprint, Garden City, NY: Anchor.

Ennis, Sharon R., Merarys Rios-Vargas, and Nora G. Albert. 2011. "The Hispanic Population: 2010." C2010BR-404. Accessed at www.census.gov /prod/cen2010/briefs/c2010br-04.pdf.

Etzioni, Amitai. 1964. *Modern Organization.* Englewood Cliffs, NJ: Prentice Hall.

European PWN. 2012. "Women on Boards: The Inside Story on Norway's 40% Target." Accessed February 22(www.europeanpwn.net/index .php?article_id=150).

Farley, Melissa, and Victor Malarek. 2008. "The Myth of the Victimless Crime." *New York Times,* March 12, p. A27.

Farr, Grant M. 1999. *Modern Iran.* New York: McGraw-Hill.

Featherman, David L., and Robert M. Hauser. 1978. *Opportunity and Change.* New York: Aeodus.

Federal Bureau of Investigation. 2015. "Bias Breakdown." November 6. News Release. Accessible at www.fbi.gov.

Ferber, Abby L., and Michael S. Kimmel. 2008. "The Gendered Face of Terrorism." *Sociology Compass* 2:870–887.

Feuer, Lewis S., ed. 1959. *Karl Marx and Friedrich Engels: Basic Writings on Politics and Philosophy.* Garden City, NY: Doubleday.

Fine, Gary C. 2008. " Robbers Cave." Pp. 1163–1164, vol. 3, in *Encyclopedia of Race, Ethnicity, and Society,* edited by Richard T. Schaefer. Thousand Oaks, CA: Sage.

Fitzgerald, Kathleen J. 2008. "White Privilege." Pp. 1403–1405, vol. 3, in *Encyclopedia of Race, Ethnicity, and Society,* edited by Richard T. Schaefer. Thousand Oaks, CA: Sage.

Fitzpatrick, Maureen J., and Barbara J. McPherson. 2010. "Coloring within the Lines: Gender Stereotypes in Contemporary Coloring Books." *Sex Roles* 62:127–137.

Flacks, Richard. 1971. *Youth and Social Change.* Chicago: Markham.

Fletcher, Connie. 1995. "On the Line: Women Cops Speak Out." *Chicago Tribune Magazine,* February 19, pp. 14–19.

Forbes. 2017. "The World's Billionaires." Real-time ranking as of March 13. Accessible at www.forbes.com.

Fonseca, Felicia. 2008. "Dine College on Quest to Rename Navajo Cancer Terms." *News from Indian Country* 22 (January 7):11.

Fox, Porter. 2014. "The End of Snow?" *New York Times,* February 9 (Section SR), pp. 1, 6.

Frank, Arthur W. 2015. "From Sick Role to Narrative Subject: An Analytic Memoir." *Health* (London). Nov 18. pii: 1363459315615395. [Epub ahead of print].

Franke, Richard Herbert, and James D. Kaul. 1978. "The Hawthorne Experiments: First Statistical Interpretation." *American Sociological Review* 43 (October):623–643.

Freese, Jeremy. 2008. "Genetics and the Social Science Explanation of Individual Outcomes." *American Journal of Sociology* 114 (Suppl.): S1–S35.

Freidson, Eliot. 1970. *Profession of Medicine.* New York: Dodd, Mead.

French, Howard W. 2004. "China's Textbooks Twist and Omit History." *New York Times,* December 6, p. A10.

Fridlund, Alan J., Paul Erkman, and Harriet Oster. 1987. "Facial Expressions of Emotion: Review of Literature 1970–1983." Pp. 143–224 in *Nonverbal Behavior and Communication,* 2nd ed., edited by Aron W. Seigman and Stanley Feldstein. Hillsdale, NJ: Lawrence Erlbaum Associates.

Galea, Sandro *[sic],* Melissa Tracy, Katherine J. Hoggatt, Charles DiMaggio, and Adam Karpati. 2011. "Estimated Deaths Attributed to Social Factors in the United States." *American Journal of Public Health* 101 (August):1456–1465.

Gallagher, Kevin P. 2009. "Economic Globalization and the Environment." *Annual Review of Environmental Resources* 34:279–304.

Gallup. 2011a. "Religion." Accessed March 27 (www.gallup.com).

Gallup Opinion Index. 1978. "Religion in America, 1977–1978." 145 (January).

Gambetta, Diego, and Steffen Hertog. 2007. "Engineers of Jihad." Sociology Working Papers (University of Oxford) 2007–10. Accessed June 2008 (www.sociology.ox.ac.uk/swp.html).

Gans, Herbert J. 1995. *The War against the Poor: The Underclass and Antipoverty Policy.* New York: Basic Books.

Garfinkel, Harold. 1956. "Conditions of Successful Degradation Ceremonies." *American Journal of Sociology* 61 (March):420–424.

Garner, Roberta. 1996. *Contemporary Movements and Ideologies.* New York: McGraw-Hill.

Garreau, Joel. 1991. *Edge City: Life on the New Frontier.* New York: Doubleday.

Gates, Gary J. 2012. "LGBT VOTE 2012." Los Angeles: The Williams Institute. Accessible at www.law.ucla.edu/williamsinstitute.

Gecas, Viktor. 2004. "Socialization, Sociology of." Pp. 14525–14530 in *International Encyclopedia of the Social and Behavioral Sciences,* edited by Neil J. Smelser and Paul B. Baltes. Cambridge, MA: Elsevier.

Gengler, Amanda M., and Megan V. Jarrell. 2015. "What Difference Does Difference Make? The Persistence of Inequalities in Healthcare Delivery." *Sociology Compass* 10:718–730.

Gentleman, Amelia. 2006. "Bollywood Captivated by the Call Centre Culture." *Guardian Weekly,* June 2, p. 17.

Gerth, H. H., and C. Wright Mills. 1958. *From Max Weber: Essays in Sociology.* New York: Galaxy.

Giddens, Anthony. 2011. *The Politics of Climate Change.* 2nd ed. Cambridge, UK: Polity.

Giddings, Paul J. 2008. *Ida: A Sword among Lions.* New York: Amistad.

Gillespie, C., and K. Hurvitz. 2013. "Prevalence of Hypertension and Controlled Hypertension – United States, 2007–2010." *Morbidity and Mortality Weekly Report (MMWR)* 62(03):144–148.

Gilley, Brian Joseph. 2006. *Becoming Two-Spirit: Gay Identity and Social Acceptance in Indian Country.* Lincoln: University of Nebraska Press.

Giordano, Peggy C. 2003. "Relationships in Adolescence." Pp. 257–281 in *Annual Review of Sociology, 2003,* edited by Karen S. Cook and John Hagan. Palo Alto, CA: Annual Reviews.

Giroux, Henry A. 1988. *Schooling and the Struggle for Public Life: Critical Pedagogy in the Modern Age.* Minneapolis: University of Minnesota Press.

Goffman, Erving. 1959. *The Presentation of Self in Everyday Life.* New York: Doubleday.

——. 1961. *Asylums: Essays on the Social Situation of Mental Patients and Other Inmates.* Garden City, NY: Doubleday.

——. 1963. *Stigma: Notes on Management of Spoiled Identity.* Englewood Cliffs, NJ: Prentice Hall.

Gottdiener, Mark, and Joe R. Feagin. 1988. "The Paradigm Shift in Urban Sociology." *Urban Affairs Quarterly* 24 (December):163–187.

Gottdiener, Mark, Joe R. Feagin, Ray Hutchison, and Mikael T. Ryan. 2015. *The New Urban Sociology.* 5th ed. Boulder, CO: Westview Press.

Gough, Margaret, and Alexandra Killewald. 2011. "Unemployment in Families: The Case of Housework." *Journal of Marriage and Family* 73 (October):1085–1100.

Gould, Kenneth A., and Tammy L. Lewis, eds. 2015. *Twenty Lessons in Environmental Sociology.* 2nd ed. New York: Oxford University Press.

Gould, Larry A. 2002. "Indigenous People Policing Indigenous People: The Potential Psychological and Cultural Costs." *Social Science Journal* 39:171-188.

Government Accountability Office. 2003. "Women's Earnings: Work Patterns Partially Explain Difference Between Men's and Women's Earnings." Washington, DC: U.S. Government Printing Office.

Gramsci, Antonio. 1929. *Selections from the Prison Notebooks.* Antonio Gramsci. Edited and translated by Quintin Hoare and Geoffrey Nowell Smith. London: Lawrence and Wishort.

Grattet, Ryken. 2011. "Societal Reactions to Deviance." *Annual Review of Sociology* 37:185-204.

Greeley, Andrew M. 1989. "Protestant and Catholic: Is the Analogical Imagination Extinct?" *American Sociological Review* 54 (August):485-502.

Greenhouse, Steven. 2008b. "Millions of Jobs of a Different Collar." *New York Times,* March 26.

Greenstone, Michael, Adam Looney, Jeremy Patashnik, and Muxin Yu. 2013. "Thirteen Economic Facts about Social Mobility and the Role of Education." June. Accessible at www. brookings.edu.

Groza, Victor, Daniela F. Ileana, and Ivor Irwin. 1999. *A Peacock or a Crow: Stories, Interviews, and Commentaries on Romanian Adoptions.* Euclid, OH: Williams Custom Publishing.

Guo, Guang, Michael E. Roettger, and Tianji Cai. 2008. "The Integration of Genetic Propensities into Social-Control Models of Delinquency and Violence among Male Youths." *American Sociological Review* 73 (August):543-568.

Hacker, Andrew. 1964. "Power to Do What?" Pp. 134-146 in *The New Sociology,* edited by Irving Louis Horowitz. New York: Oxford University Press.

Hallinan, Maureen T. 1997. "The Sociological Study of Social Change." *American Sociological Review* 62 (February):1-11.

Hamm, Steve. 2007. "Children of the Web." *BusinessWeek,* July 2, pp. 50-56, 58.

Harding, David J. 2009. "Violence, Older Peers, and the Socialization of Adolescent Boys in Disadvantaged Neighborhoods." *American Sociological Review* 74 (June):445-464.

Harrell, Erika. 2015. *Victims of Identity Theft, 2014.* September 27. Washington, DC: U.S. Government Printing Office.

Harris, Chauncey D., and Edward Ullman. 1945. "The Nature of Cities." *Annals of the American Academy of Political and Social Science* 242 (November):7-17.

Haub, Carl, and Mary Mederius Kent. 2010. *2010 World Population Data Sheet.* Washington, DC: Population Reference Bureau.

Haviland, William A., Harald E. L. Prins, Dana Walrath, and Bunny McBride. 2008. *Cultural Anthropology—The Human Challenge.* 12th ed. Belmont, CA: Wadsworth.

Haviland, William A., Harald E. L. Prins, Dana Walrath, and Bunny McBride. 2015. *Cultural Anthropology: The Human Challenge.* 14th ed. Boston: Cengage.

Heckert, Druann, and Amy Best. 1997. "Ugly Duckling to Swan: Labeling Theory and the Stigmatization of Red Hair." *Symbolic Interaction* 20 (4):365–384.

Hedley, R. Alan. 1992. "Industrialization in Less Developed Countries." Pp. 914–920 in *Encyclopedia of Sociology,* vol. 2, edited by Edgar F. Borgatta and Marie L. Borgatta. New York: Macmillan.

Heilman, Madeline E. 2001. "Description and Prescription: How Gender Stereotypes Prevent Women's Ascent up the Organizational Ladder." *Journal of Social Issues* 57 (4):657–674.

Hendrickson, Brett. 2015. "Neo-shamans, *Curanderismo*, and Scholars." *Nova Religio: The Journal of Alternative and Emergent Religions* 19 (No. 1):25–44.

Hengeveld, Rob. 2012. *Wasted World: How Our Consumption Challenge the Planet.* Chicago: University of Chicago Press.

Hewlett, Sylvia Ann, and Carolyn Buck Luce. 2005. "Off-Ramps and On-Ramps: Keeping Talented Women on the Road to Success." *Harvard Business Review* (March):43–53.

Hill, Michael R., and Susan Hoecker-Drysdale, eds. 2001. *Harriet Martineau: Theoretical and Methodological Perspectives.* New York: Routledge.

Hira, Ron. 2008. "An Overview of the Offshoring of U.S. Jobs." Pp. 14–15 in Marlene A. Lee and Mark Mather, "U.S. Labor Force Trends," *Population Bulletin* 63 (June).

Hitlin, Steven, and Jane Allyn Piliavin. 2004. "Values: Reviving a Dormant Concept." Pp. 359–393 in *Annual Review of Sociology, 2004,* edited by Karen S. Cook and John Hagan. Palo Alto, CA: Annual Reviews.

Hochschild, Arlie. 2016. The Right vs. The Family. *Dissent* 63(1):42–47.

——, with Anne Machung. 1989. *The Second Shift: Working Parents and the Revolution at Home.* New York: Viking Penguin.

Hoeffel, Elizabeth M., Sonya Rastogi, Myoung Ouk Kim, and Hasan Shahid. 2012. *The Asian Population: 2010.* C2010BR-11. Washington, DC: U.S. Government Printing Office.

Homans, George C. 1979. "Nature versus Nurture: A False Dichotomy." *Contemporary Sociology* 8 (May):345–348.

hooks, bell. 1994. "Black Students Who Reject Feminism." *The Chronicle of Higher Education,* 60 (July 13): A44.

Horkheimer, Max, and Theodor Adorno. [1944] 2002. *Dialectic of Enlightenment.* Reprint, Palo Alto, CA: Sanford University Press.

Howard, Judith A. 1999. "Border Crossings between Women's Studies and Sociology." *Contemporary Sociology* 28 (September):525–528.

Howard, Michael C. 1989. *Contemporary Cultural Anthropology.* 3rd ed. Glenview, IL: Scott, Foresman.

Hughes, Everett. 1945. "Dilemmas and Contradictions of Status." *American Journal of Sociology* 50 (March):353–359.

Hughlett, Mike. 2008. "Sitting Pretty." *Chicago Tribune,* September 14, sec. 5, pp. 1, 7.

Human Genome Project. 2015. "All About the Human Genome Project (HGP)." Accessible at www.genome.gov.

Hunter, Herbert M., ed. 2000. *The Sociology of Oliver C. Cox: New Perspectives: Research in Race and Ethnic Relations,* vol. 2. Stamford, CT: JAI Press.

Hunter, James Davison. 1991. *Culture Wars: The Struggle to Define America.* New York: Basic Books.

Huntington, Samuel P. 1993. "The Clash of Civilizations?" *Foreign Affairs* 72 (Summer):22–49.

Hurn, Christopher J. 1985. *The Limits and Possibilities of Schooling.* 2nd ed. Boston: Allyn and Bacon.

Hurwitz, Heather McKee, and Verta Taylor. 2012. "Women's Cultures and Social Movements in Global Context." *Sociology Compass* 6 (October): 808–822.

Hussar, William J., and Tabitha M. Bailey. 2013. "Projection of Education Statistics to 2021." Washington, DC: U.S. Government Printing Office. Accessible at http://nces.ed.gov.

Igo, Sarah E. 2007. *The Average American: Surveys, Citizens, and the Making of a Mass Public.* Cambridge, MA: Harvard University Press.

Inglehart, Ronald, and Wayne E. Baker. 2000. "Modernization, Cultural Change, and the Persistence of Traditional Values." *American Sociological Review* 65 (February):19–51.

Institute for Policy Studies. 2015. "Wealth Inequality." Accessed October 30 (inequality.org).

Internet World Stats. 2015. "Usage and Population Statistics" and "Internet World Users by Language." Updated March 29. Accessible at www .internetworldstats.com.

Isaacs, Julia B. 2007b. *Economic Mobility of Men and Women.* Washington, DC: Economic Mobility Project.

ITOPF. 2006. "Statistics: International Tanker Owners Pollution Federation Limited." Accessed May 2 (www.itopf.com/stats.html).

Jackson, Philip W. 1968. *Life in Classrooms.* New York: Holt.

Jacobe, Dennis. 2008. "Half of Public Favors the Environment over Growth." Accessed April 9 (www.gallup.com).

Jacobs, Andres. 2010. "As China's Economy Grows, Pollution Worsens Despite New Efforts to Control It." *New York Times,* July 29, p. A4.

Jain, Saranga, and Kathleen Kurz. 2007. *New Insights on Preventing Child Marriage: A Global Analysis of Factors and Programs.* Washington, DC: International Center for Research on Women.

Jäntti, Markus. 2009. "Mobility in the United States in Comparative Perspectives." *Focus* 26 (Fall).

Japan Aisaika Organization. 2012. "Aisaika Organization Prospectus." Accessed January 15 (www.aisaika.org/en/prospectus.html).

Jardina, Ashley, and Nancy Burns. 2016. "Advances and Ambivalence: The Consequences of Women's Educational and Workforce Changes for Women's Political Participation in the United States, 1952 to 2012." *The Russell Sage Foundation Journal of the Social Sciences* 2(4):272–301.

Jasper, James M. 1997. *The Art of Moral Protest: Culture, Biography, and Creativity in Social Movements.* Chicago: University of Chicago Press.

Jefferys, Kelly. 2006. *Refugees and Asylees: 2005.* June. Washington, DC: Department of Homeland Security. Accessible at www.dhs.gov.

Jenkins, Richard. 1991. "Disability and Social Stratification." *British Journal of Sociology* 42 (December):557–580.

Jensen, Gary F. 2003. "Social Disorganization Theory in R. A. Wright." *Encyclopedia of Criminology.* New York: Fitzroy Dearborn.

Joas, Hans, and Wolfgang Knöbl. 2009. *Social Theory: Twenty Introductory Lectures.* Cambridge, UK: Cambridge University Press.

Johnson, Benton. 1975. *Functionalism in Modern Sociology: Understanding Talcott Parsons.* Morristown, NJ: General Learning.

Johnson, Kevin, and Alan Gomez. 2012. "Violent Crime Drop Overall in U.S. Border Cities." *USA Today* (November 4).

Johnson, Will. 2009. "Genie: The Wild Child." Accessed August 4, 2010 (http://knol.google.com/k/genie-the-wild-child-chapter-2#).

Juniper Research. 2015. *Cybercrime and the Internet of Threats.* Basingstoke, England: Juniper Research.

Kahn, Joseph. 2006. "Where's Mao? Chinese Revise History Books." *New York Times,* September 1, pp. A1, A6.

Kambayashi, Takehiko. 2008. "Japanese Men Shout the Oft-Unsaid 'I Love You.'" *Christian Science Monitor,* February 13.

Kaneda, Toshiko, and Kristin Bietsch. 2015. *2015 World Population Data Sheet.* Washington, DC: Population Reference Bureau.

Katovich, Michael A. 1987. Correspondence. June 1.

Katz, Michael. 1971. *Class, Bureaucracy, and the Schools: The Illusion of Educational Change in America.* New York: Praeger.

Kelly, Thomas. 2012. "Thomas Kelly on the Nyinba People of Nepal." Accessible at http://www.attenbergspaceforphotography.org.

Kennickell, Arthur B. 2009. *Ponds and Streams: Wealth and Income in the U.S., 1989 to 2007.* Washington, DC: Federal Reserve Board.

Kerbo, Harold R. 2006. *World Poverty: The Roots of Global Inequality and the Modern World System.* New York: McGraw-Hill.

——. 2012. *Social Stratification and Inequality.* 8th ed. New York: McGraw-Hill.

Kimmel, Michael. 2008. *The Gendered Society.* 3rd ed. New York: State University of New York at Stony Brook.

Kitchener, Richard F. 1991. "Jean Piaget: The Unknown Sociologist." *British Journal of Sociology* 42 (September):421–442.

Kleiner, Art. 2003. "Are You In with the In Crowd?" *Harvard Business Review* 81 (July):86–92.

Kleinknecht, William. 1996. *The New Ethnic Mobs: The Changing Face of Organized Crime in America.* New York: Free Press.

Knudsen, Morten. 2010. "Surprised by Method—Functional Method and System Theory." *Forum: Qualitative Social Research* 11 (September): article 12.

Kochhar, Rakesh, Richard Fry, and Paul Taylor. 2011. "Wealth Gaps Rise to Record Highs between Whites, Blacks, and Hispanics." July 26. Accessible at www.pewsocialtrends.org.

Kohut, Andrew, et al. 2005. *American Character Gets Mixed Reviews: 16-Nation Pew Global Attitudes Survey.* Washington, DC: Pew Global Project Attitudes.

——. 2007. *Global Unease with Major World Powers: Rising Environmental Concern in 47-Nation Survey.* Washington, DC: Pew Global Project Attitudes.

Kokmen, Leyla. 2008. "Environmental Justice for All." *Utne Reader* (March–April):42–46.

Koolhaas, Rem, et al. 2001. *Mutations.* Barcelona, Spain: Actar.

Kottak, Conrad. 2015. *Anthropology: Appreciating Human Diversity.* 17th ed. New York: McGraw-Hill.

Krogstad, Jens Manuel. 2016. "5 Facts about Illegal Immigration in the U.S." September 3. Accessible at www.pewresearch.org.

Kunzig, Robert. 2011. "Seven Billion." *National Geographic* (January): 40–69.

Kwong, Jo. 2005. "Globalization's Effects on the Environment." *Society* 42 (January/February):21–28.

LaFraniere, Sharon, and Andrew W. Lehren. 2015. "The Disproportionate Risk of Driving While Black." *New York Times* (October 25):A1, A22–23.

Landtman, Gunnar. [1938] 1968. *The Origin of Inequality of the Social Class.* New York: Greenwood (original edition 1938, Chicago: University of Chicago Press).

Lasswell, Harold D. 1936. *Politics: Who Gets What, When, How.* New York: McGraw-Hill.

Lauer, Robert H. 1982. *Perspectives on Social Change.* 3rd ed. Boston: Allyn and Bacon.

Lawler, Kristen. 2011. "Fear of a Slacker Revolution Futures: A Project of the Social Science Research Project." December 1. Accessed January 26, 2012 (www.possible-futures.org/2011/12/01/fear-slacker-revolution-occupy-wall-street-cultural-politics-class-struggle/).

Leavell, Hugh R., and E. Gurney Clark. 1965. *Preventive Medicine for the Doctor in His Community: An Epidemiologic Approach.* 3rd ed. New York: McGraw-Hill.

Lengermann, Patricia Madoo, and Jill Niebrugge-Brantley. 1998. *The Women Founders: Sociology and Social Theory, 1830–1930.* Boston: McGraw-Hill.

Lenski, Gerhard. 1966. *Power and Privilege: A Theory of Social Stratification.* New York: McGraw-Hill.

Lindsey, Linda L. 2005. *Gender Roles: A Sociological Perspective.* Upper Saddle River, NJ: Prentice Hall.

Linn, Susan, and Alvin F. Poussaint. 1999. "Watching Television: What Are Children Learning about Race and Ethnicity?" *Child Care Information Exchange* 128 (July):50–52.

Lipson, Karen. 1994. "'Nell' Not Alone in the Wilds." *Los Angeles Times,* December 19, pp. F1, F6.

Livingstone, Gretchen. 2014a. "Growing Number of Dads Home with the Kids." June 5. Accessible at www.pewsocialtrends.com.

Loughran, Thomas A., Holly Nguyen, Alex R. Piquero, and Jeffrey Fagan. 2013. "The Returns to Criminal Capital." *American Sociological Review* 78 (6):925–948.

Luhnow, David. 2014. "Most Violent Region in the World: Latin America." *Wall Street Journal* (April 12): A9.

Lucas, Edward. 2015. *Cyberphobia.* London: Bloomsbury.

Lukacs, Georg. 1923. *History and Class Consciousness.* London: Merlin.

Lynas, Mark. 2008. *Six Degrees: Our Future on a Hotter Planet.* Washington, DC: National Geographic.

Lynn, Barry C. 2003. "Trading with a Low-Wage Tiger." *The American Prospect* 14 (February):10–12.

MacDorman, Marian F., and T. J. Mathews. 2009. "Behind International Rankings of Infant Mortality: How the United States Compares with Europe." *NCHS Date Brief* (No. 23, November).

MacDorman, Marian, et al. 2005. "Explaining the 2001–2002 Infant Mortality Increase: Data from the Linked Death/Infant Death Data Set." *National Vital Statistics Reports* 53 (January 24).

Machalek, Richard, and Michael W. Martin. 2010. "Evolution, Biology and Society: A Conversation for the 21st-Century Sociology Classroom." *Teaching Sociology* 38 (1):35–45.

Mack, Raymond W., and Calvin P. Bradford. 1979. *Transforming America: Patterns of Social Change.* 2nd ed. New York: Random House.

Magnier, Mark. 2004. "China Clamps Down on Web News Discussion." *Los Angeles Times,* February 26, p. A4.

Malcolm X, with Alex Haley. 1964. *The Autobiography of Malcolm X.* New York: Grove.

——, with ——. [1964] 1999. *The Autobiography of Malcolm X.* Revised with epilogue by Alex Haley and afterword by Ossie Davis. New York: One World, Ballantine Books.

Males, Mike, and Meda-Chesney Lind. 2010. "The Myth of Mean Girls." *New York Times,* April 2, p. A21.

Malthus, Thomas Robert, Julian Huxley, and Frederick Osborn. [1824] 1960. *Three Essays on Population.* Reprint, New York: New American Library.

Mandel, Hadas. 2016. "The Role of Occupational Attributes in Gender Earnings Inequality, 1970–2010." *Social Science Research* 55 (January):122–138.

Marable, Manning. 2011. *Malcolm X: A Life of Reinvention.* New York: Viking.

Martin, Daniel C., and James E. Yankay. 2013. *Refugees and Asylees: 2012.* Washington, DC: Office of Immigration Statistics.

Martin, Greg. 2015. *Understanding Social Movements.* New York: Palgrave.

Martin, Karin A. 2009. "Normalizing Heterosexuality: Mothers' Assumptions, Talk, and Strategies with Young Children." *American Sociological Review* 74 (April):190–207.

Martin, Susan E. 1994. "Outsider Within the Station House: The Impact of Race and Gender on Black Women Politics." *Social Problems* 41 (August):383–400.

Martineau, Harriet. [1837] 1962. *Society in America.* Edited, abridged, with an introductory essay by Seymour Martin Lipset. Reprint, Garden City, NY: Doubleday.

——. [1838] 1989. *How to Observe Morals and Manners.* Philadelphia: Leal and Blanchard. Sesquentennial edition, edited by M. R. Hill, Transaction Books.

Marx, Karl. [1844] 1964. "Contribution to the Critique of Hegel's Philosophy of Right." In *On Religion,* Karl Marx and Friedrich Engels. Reprint, New York: Schockern Books.

——, and Engels, Friedrich. [1847] 1955. *Selected Work in Two Volumes.* Reprint, Moscow: Foreign Languages Publishing House.

Maryanski, Alexandra R. 2004. "Evaluation Theory." Pp. 257–263 in *Encyclopedia of Social Theory,* edited by George Ritzer. Thousand Oaks, CA: Sage.

Masuda, Takahiko, Phoebe C. Ellsworth, Batja Mesquita, Janxin Leu, Shigehito Tanida, and Ellen Van de Veerdonk. 2008. "Attitudes and Social Cognition—Placing the Face in Context: Cultural Differences in the Perception of Facial Emotion." *Journal of Personality and Social Psychology* 94 (No. 3):365–381.

Matsushita, Yoshiko. 1999. "Japanese Kids Call for a Sympathetic Ear." *Christian Science Monitor,* January 20, p. 15.

Mayhew, Robert J. 2014. *Malthus: The Life and Legacies of an Untimely Prophet.* Cambridge, MA: Harvard University Press.

Mazurczak, Filip. 2014. "Eastern Europe's Christian Awakening." *First Things* (January 17). Accessible at www.firsthtings.com.

McCall, Leslie. 2008. "What Does Class Inequality Among Women Look Like? A Comparison with Men and Families, 1970–2000." Pp. 293–325 in *Social Class, How Does It Work?* edited by Annette Lareau and Dalton Conley. New York: Russell Sage Foundation.

McCarthy, Justin. 2014. "Seven in 10 Americans Back Euthanasia." June 18. Accessible at www. gallup.com.

McGurty, Eileen Maura. 2000. "Warren County, NC, and the Emergence of the Environmental Justice Movement: Unlikely Coalitions and Shared Meanings in Local Collective Action." *Society and Natural Resources* 13:373–387.

McIntosh, Peggy. 1988. "White Privilege and Male Privilege: A Personal Account of Coming to See Correspondence Through Work and Women's Studies." Working Paper No. 189, Wellesley College Center for Research on Women, Wellesley, MA.

McKenzie, Brian. 2014. "Modes Less Traveled: Bicycling and Walking to Work in the United States: 2008–2012." May. *American Community Survey Reports ACS-25.* Accessible at www. census.gov.

McNeil, Donald G. 2004. "Plan to Battle AIDS Worldwide Is Falling Short." *New York Times,* March 28, pp. 1, 14.

Mead, George H. 1934. In *Mind, Self and Society,* edited by Charles W. Morris. Chicago: University of Chicago Press.

——. 1964a. In *On Social Psychology,* edited by Anselm Strauss. Chicago: University of Chicago Press.

——. 1964b. "The Genesis of the Self and Social Control." Pp. 267–293 in *Selected Writings: George Herbert Mead,* edited by Andrew J. Reck. Indianapolis: Bobbs-Merrill.

Mead, Margaret. [1935] 2001. *Sex and Temperament in Three Primitive Societies.* Reprint, New York: Perennial, HarperCollins.

Mehan, Hugh. 2015. "Detracking: A Promising Strategy to Increase Social Mobility for Underserved Youth." Pp. 75–82 in *Opening the Doors to Opportunity for All: Setting a Research Agenda for the Future.* Washington, DC: American Institutes for Research

Mehl, Matthias R., Simine Vazire, Naïrán Ramírez-Esparza, Richard B. Slatcher, and James W. Pennebacker. 2007. "Are Women Really More Talkative Than Men?" *Science* 317 (July 6):82.

Merton, Robert. 1968. *Social Theory and Social Structure.* New York: Free Press.

——, and Alice S. Kitt. 1950. "Contributions to the Theory of Reference Group Behavior." Pp. 40–105 in *Continuities in Social Research: Studies in the Scope and Methods of the American Soldier,* edited by Robert K. Merton and Paul L. Lazarsfeld. New York: Free Press.

Migration Policy Institute. 2016. "Brain Drain and Brain Gain." Accessible at www.migration policy.org.

Milgram, Stanley. 1963. "Behavioral Study of Obedience." *Journal of Abnormal and Social Psychology* 67 (October):371–378.

——. 1975. *Obedience to Authority: An Experimental View.* New York: Harper and Row.

Miller, David L. 2014. *Introduction to Collective Behavior and Collective Action.* 3rd ed. Long Grove, IL: Waveland Press.

Mills, C. Wright. [1959] 2000a. *The Sociological Imagination.* 40th Anniv. Ed. New afterword by Todd Gitlin. New York: Oxford University Press.

——. [1956] 2000b. *The Power Elite.* New edition. Afterword by Alan Wolfe. New York: Oxford University Press.

Mohai, Paul, David Pellow, and J. Timmons Roberts. 2009. "Environmental Justice." *Annual Review of Environmental Research* 34:405–430.

——, and Robin Saha. 2007. "Racial Inequality in the Distribution of Hazardous Waste: A National-Level Reassessment." *Social Problems* 54 (3):343–370.

Moncarz, Roger J., Michael G. Wolf, and Benjamin Wright. 2008. "Service-Providing Occupations, Offshoring, and the Labor Market." *Monthly Labor Review* (December):71–86.

Moore, Wilbert E. 1967. *Order and Change: Essays in Comparative Sociology.* New York: Wiley.

Morris, Aldon. 2000. "Reflections on Social Movement Theory: Criticisms and Proposals." *Contemporary Sociology* 29 (May):445–454.

Morse, Arthur D. 1967. *While Six Million Died: A Chronicle of American Apathy.* New York: Ace.

Mosley, J., and E. Thomson. 1995. Pp. 148–165 in *Fatherhood: Contemporary Theory, Research and Social Policy,* edited by W. Marsiglo. Thousand Oaks, CA: Sage.

Mossaad, Nadwa. 2016. *Refugees and Asylees: 2015.* November. Washington, DC: Department of Homeland Security. Accessible at www.dhs.gov.

Mueller, G. O. 2001. "Transnational Crime: Definitions and Concepts." Pp. 13–21 in *Combating Transnational Crime: Concepts, Activities, and Responses,* edited by P. Williams and D. Vlassis. London: Franklin Cass.

Murdock, George P. 1945. "The Common Denominator of Cultures." Pp. 123–142 in *The Science of Man in the World Crisis,* edited by Ralph Linton. New York: Columbia University Press.

——. 1949. *Social Structure.* New York: Macmillan.

——. 1957. "World Ethnographic Sample." *American Anthropologist* 59 (August):664–687.

Murray, Velma McBride, Amanda Willert, and Diane P. Stephens. 2001. "The Half-Full Glass: Resilient African American Single Mothers and Their Children." *Family Focus,* June, pp. F4–F5.

Nagin, Daniel S. and John V. Pepper (Editors). 2012. *Deterrence and the Death Penalty.* Washington, DC: National Research Council; Division of Behavioral and Social Sciences and Education; Committee on Law and Justice; Committee on Deterrence and the Death Penalty.

Nakao, Keiko, and Judith Treas. 1994. "Updating Occupational Prestige and Socioeconomic Scores: How the New Measures Measure Up." *Sociological Methodology* 24:1–72.

Nash, Manning. 1962. "Race and the Ideology of Race." *Current Anthropology* 3 (June):285–288.

National Advisory Commission on Criminal Justice. 1976. *Organized Crime.* Washington, DC: U.S. Government Printing Office.

National Center for Education Statistics. 2011. "Average Undergraduate Tuition and Fees." Accessed March 29 (http://nces.ed.gov/ programs/ digest/d09/tables/dt09_335.asp).

National Center for Education Statistics. 2012. *Digest of Education Statistics, 2011.* Washington, DC: NCCES.

National Education Association. 2015. *Rankings and Estimates. Rankings of the States 2014 and Estimates of School Statistics 2015.* Accessible at www.nea.org.

National Organization for Men Against Sexism. 2017. 42 Years of NOMAS. Accessible at www.nomas.org.

Navarro, Mirey. 2005. "When You Contain Multitudes." *New York Times,* April 24, pp. 1, 2.

Neuman, Lawrence W. 2009. *Understanding Research.* Boston: Allyn and Bacon.

Newport, Frank. 2017. "About Half of Americans Say Trump Moving Too Fast." February 2. Accessible on www.gallup.com.

Nicklett, Emily J., and Sarah Burgard. 2009. "Downward Social Mobility and Major Depressive Episodes among Latino and Asian-American Immigrants to the United States." *American Journal of Epidemiology,* 170(6):793–801.

Nielsen, Joyce McCarl, Glenda Walden, and Charlotte A. Kunkel. 2000. "Gendered Heteronormativity: Empirical Illustrations in Everyday Life." *Sociological Quarterly* 41 (No. 2):283–296.

Nixon, Darren. 2009. " 'I Can't Put a Smiley Face On': Working-Class Masculinity, Emotional Labor and Service Work in the 'New Economy.' " *Gender, Work and Organization* 16 (No. 3):300–322.

Nolan, Patrick D., and Gerhard Lenski. 2015. *Human Societies: An Introduction to Macrosociology.* 12th ed. New York: Oxford University Press.

Nordhaus, Ted, and Michael Shellenberger. 2007. *Break Through: From the Death of Environmentalism to the Politics of Possibility.* Boston: Houghton Mifflin.

North Carolina Department of Environment and Natural Resources. 2008. "Warren County PCB Landfill Fact Sheet." Accessed April 9 (www.wastenotnc.org/WarrenCo_Fact_Sheet.htm).

Nossiter, Adam. 2012. "Late for School After a Long Journey for a Drop to Drink." *New York Times,* May 22, p. A10.

Office of Immigration Statistics. 2016. *Yearbook of Immigration Statistics 2015 and Data Tables.* Accessible at www.dhs.gov.

Ogburn, William F. 1922. *Social Change with Respect to Culture and Original Nature.* New York: Huebsch (reprinted 1966, New York: Dell).

——, and Clark Tibbits. 1934. "The Family and Its Functions." Pp. 661–708 in *Recent Social Trends in the United States,* edited by Research Committee on Social Trends. New York: McGraw-Hill.

Ogunwole, Stella V. 2006. *We the People: American Indians and Alaska Natives in the United States.* Censr-28. Washington, DC: U.S. Government Printing Office.

Okano, Kaori, and Motonori Tsuchiya. 1999. *Education in Contemporary Japan: Inequality and Diversity.* Cambridge, UK: Cambridge University Press.

Oliver, Melvin L., and Thomas M. Shapiro. 2006. *Black Wealth/White Wealth: New Perspectives on Racial Inequality.* 2nd ed. New York: Routledge.

Omi, Michael, and Howard Winant. 1994. *Racial Formation in the United States.* 2nd ed. New York: Routledge.

Orfield, Gary, John Kucsera, and Genevieve Siegel-Hawley. 2012. "E Pluribus . . . Separation: Deepening Double Segregation for More Students." September 19. Accessible at www.civilrightsproject.ucla.edu.

Organisation for Economic Co-operation and Development. 2012b. "Gender Equality and Social Institutions in Afghanistan." Accessed February 22 (http://genderindex.org/country/Afghanistan).

OutRight Action International. 2016. Home page. Accessible at www.outrightinternational.org.

Pager, Devah. 2003. "The Mark of a Criminal Record." *American Journal of Sociology* 108 (March):937–975.

——. 2007. *Marked: Race, Crime, and Finding Work in an Era of Mass Incarceration.* Chicago: University of Chicago Press.

——, Bruce Weston, and Bart Bonikowski. 2009. "Discrimination in a Low-Wage Labor Market: A Field Experiment." *American Sociological Review* 74 (October):777–799.

Park, Robert E. 1916. "The City: Suggestions for the Investigation of Human Behavior in the Urban Environment." *American Journal of Sociology* 20 (March):577–612.

——. 1936. "Succession, an Ecological Concept." *American Sociological Review* 1 (April):171–179.

Parsons, Talcott. 1951. *The Social System.* New York: Free Press.

——. 1966. *Societies: Evolutionary and Comparative Perspectives.* Englewood Cliffs, NJ: Prentice Hall.

——. 1975. "The Sick Role and the Role of the Physician Reconsidered." *Milbank Medical Fund Quarterly Health and Society* 53 (Summer):257–278.

——, and Robert Bales. 1955. *Family: Socialization and Interaction Process.* Glencoe, IL: Free Press.

Passero, Kathy. 2002. "Global Travel Expert Roger Axtell Explains Why." *Biography,* July, pp. 70–73, 97–98.

Patel, Reena. 2010. *Working the Night Shift: Women in India's Call Center Industry.* Stanford, CA: Stanford University Press.

Pattillo-McCoy, Mary. 1999. *Black Picket Fences: Privilege and Peril among the Black Middle Class.* Chicago: University of Chicago Press.

Pellow, David N., and Hollie Nyseth Brehm. 2013. "An Environmental Sociology for the Twenty-First Century." *Annual Review of Sociology* 39:229–250.

Peralta, Eyder. 2011. "Who Are the 1 Percent? Gallup Finds They're a Lot Like the 99 Percent." December 5. Accessed December 12 (www.wbur .org/npr/143143332/who-are-the-1-percent-gallup-finds-theyre-a-lot-like -the-99-percent).

Peter, Laurence J., and Raymond Hull. 1969. *The Peter Principle.* New York: Morrow.

Pew Charitable Trust. 2012. "Pursuing the American Dream: Economic Mobility Across Generations." July. Accessible at www .economicmobility.org.

Phelan, Jo. C., and Bruce G. 2015. "Is Racism a Fundamental Cause of Inequalities in Health?" *Annual Review of Sociology* 41: 311–330.

Pew Research Center. 2013. "Second-Generation Americans: A Portrait of the Adult Children of Immigrants." February 7. Accessible at www .persocialtrends.org.

Phillips, E. Barbara. 1996. *City Lights: Urban–Suburban Life in the Global Society.* New York: Oxford University Press.

Phillips, Susan A. 1999. *Wallbangin': Graffiti and Gangs in L.A.* Chicago: University of Chicago Press.

Piaget, Jean. 1954. *The Construction of Reality in the Child.* Translated by Margaret Cook. New York: Basic Books.

Picca, Leslie Houts, and Joe Feagin. 2007. *Two Faces of Reason: Frontstage and Backstage.* New York: Routledge.

Pinderhughes, Dianne. 1987. *Race and Ethnicity in Chicago Politics: A Reexamination of Pluralist Theory.* Urbana: University of Illinois Press.

Pinderhughes, Raquel. 2008. "Green Collar Jobs." Accessed June 29 (www .urbanhabitat.org/node/528).

Polletta, Francesca, and James M. Jasper. 2001. "Collective Identity and Social Movements." Pp. 283–305 in *Annual Review of Sociology, 2001,* edited by Karen S. Cook and Leslie Hogan. Palo Alto, CA: Annual Reviews.

Population Reference Bureau. 1996. "Speaking Graphically." *Population Today* 24 (June/July).

Proctor, Bernadette D., Jessica J. Smerga, and Melissa A. Kollar. 2016. "Income and Poverty in the United States 2015." September. Accessible at www.census.gov.

Pryor, John H., Linda DeAngelo, Laura Palucki Blake, Sylvia Hurtado, and Serge Tran. 2011. *The American Freshman: National Norms Fall 2011.* Los Angeles: Higher Education Research Institute, UCLA.

——. Sylvia Hurtado, Victor B. Saenz, José Luis Santos, and William S. Korn. 2007. *The American Freshman: Forty Year Trends.* Los Angeles: Higher Education Research Institute, UCLA.

Putnam, Robert. 1995. *Bowling Along: America's Declining Social Capital.* New York: Simon and Schuster.

Quinney, Richard. 1970. *The Social Reality of Crime.* Boston: Little, Brown.

——. 1974. *Criminal Justice in America.* Boston: Little, Brown.

——. 1979. *Criminology.* 2nd ed. Boston: Little, Brown.

——. 1980. *Class, State and Crime.* 2nd ed. New York: Longman.

Ramet, Sabrina. 1991. *Social Currents in Eastern Europe: The Source and Meaning of the Great Transformation.* Durham, NC: Duke University Press.

Ratnesar, Romesh. 2011. "The Menace Within." *Stanford Magazine* (July/August). Accessible at www.stanfordalumni.org.

Reeves, Richard V., and Joanna Venator. 2014. "Social Mobility Data: How Much Can the Past Teach Us About the Present?" April 25. Brookings Social Mobility Memos. Accessible at www.brookings.edu.

Revkin, Andrew C. 2007. "Wealth and Poverty, Drought and Flood: Report from Four Fronts in the War on Warming." *New York Times,* April 3, pp. D4–D5.

Ridgeway, Cecilia L. 2011. *Framed by Gender: How Gender Inequality Persists in the Modern World.* New York: Oxford University Press.

Riding, Alan. 1998. "Why 'Titanic' Conquered the World." *New York Times,* April 26, sec. 2, pp. 1, 28, 29.

Riley, Matilda White, Robert L. Kahn, and Anne Foner. 1994a. *Age and Structural Lag.* New York: Wiley InterScience.

——, Robert L. Kahn, and Anne Foner, in association with Karin A. Mock. 1994b. "Introduction: The Mismatch between People and Structures." Pp. 1–36 in *Age and Structural Lag,* edited by Matilda White Riley, Robert L. Kahn, and Anne Foner. New York: Wiley InterScience.

Ritzer, George. 2002. *McDonaldization: The Reader.* Thousand Oaks, CA: Pine Forge Press.

Ritzer, George. 2015. The *McDonaldization of Society,* 7th ed. Thousand Oaks, CA: Sage.

Robertson, Roland. 1988. "The Sociological Significance of Culture: Some General Considerations." *Theory, Culture, and Society* 5 (February):3–23.

Rose, Arnold. 1951. *The Roots of Prejudice.* Paris: UNESCO.

Rose, Peter I., Myron Glazer, and Penina Migdal Glazer. 1979. "In Controlled Environments: Four Cases of Intense Resocialization." Pp. 320–338 in *Socialization and the Life Cycle,* edited by Peter I. Rose. New York: St. Martin's Press.

Rosen, Christine. 2015. "They're Out to Get You." *Wall Street Journal,* December 20, p. C7.

Rosenberg, Douglas H. 1991. "Capitalism." Pp. 33–34 in *Encyclopedic Dictionary of Sociology,* 4th ed., edited by Dushkin Publishing Group. Guilford, CT: Dushkin.

Rosenfeld, Richard, and Lenore Jacobson. 1968. *Pygmalion in the Classroom.* New York: Holt.

——, and ——. 1992. *Pygmalion in the Classroom: Teacher Expectations and Pupils' Intellectual Development.* Newly expanded edition. Bancy Felin, UK: Crown House.

Rossides, Daniel W. 1997. *Social Stratification: The Interplay of Class, Race, and Gender.* 2nd ed. Upper Saddle River, NJ: Prentice Hall.

Roszak, Theodore. 1969. *The Making of a Counter-Culture.* Garden City, NY: Doubleday.

Rowe, AimeeCarrillo, Sheena Malhotra, and Kimberlee Pérez. 2013. *Answer the Call: Virtual Migration in Indian Call Centers.* Minneapolis: University of Minnesota Press.

Ryan, William. 1976. *Blaming the Victim.* Rev. ed. New York: Random House.

Sabol, William J., Heather C. West, and Matthew Cooper. 2009. "Prisoners in 2008." *Bureau of Justice Statistics Bulletin* (December).

Sacks, Peter. 2007. *Tearing Down the Gates: Confronting the Class Divide in American Education.* Berkeley: University of California Press.

Said, Edward W. 2001. "The Clash of Ignorance." *The Nation* (October 22).

Salem, Richard, and Stanislaus Grabarek. 1986. "Sociology B.A.s in a Corporate Setting: How Can They Get There and of What Value Are They?" *Teaching Sociology* 14 (October):273–275.

Sampson, Robert J., and W. Byron Groves. 1989. "Community Structure and Crime: Testing Social-Disorganization Theory." *American Journal of Sociology* 94 (January):774–802.

Samuelson, Paul A., and William D. Nordhaus. 2010. *Economics.* 19th ed. New York: McGraw-Hill.

Sanchanta, Mariko. 2010. "Starbucks Plans Major China Expansion." *Wall Street Journal,* April 13.

Sandberg, Sheryl. 2015. *Lean In: Women, Work, and the Will to Lead.* New York: Knopf.

Sandefur, Rebecca L. 2008. "Access to Civil Justice and Race, Class, and Gender Inequality." *Annual Review of Sociology* 34:339–358.

Sanders, Edmund. 2004. "Coming of Age in Iraq." *Los Angeles Times,* August 14, pp. A1, A5.

Sanderson, Stephen K., Seth A. Abrutyn, and Kristopher R. Proctor. 2011. "Testing the Protestant Ethic Thesis with Quantitative Historical Data: A Research Note." *Social Forces* 89 (March):905–912.

Sawhill, Isabel, and Ron Haskins. 2009. "If You Can Make It Here . . ." *Washington Post National Weekly Edition,* November 9, p. 27.

Schaefer, Richard T. 2008b. "'Power' and 'Power Elite.'" In *Encyclopedia of Social Problems,* edited by Vincent Parrillo. Thousand Oaks, CA: Sage.

——. 2012. *Racial and Ethnic Groups.* 13th ed. Upper Saddle River, NJ: Pearson.

Schaefer, Richard, and William Zellner. 2015. *Extraordinary Groups.* 9th ed. Long Grove, IL: Waveland Press.

Scharnberg, Kirsten. 2007. "Black Market for Midwives Defies Bans." *Chicago Tribune,* November 25, pp. 1, 10.

Scherer, Michael. 2011. "Introduction: Taking It to the Streets." Pp. 5–12 in *Occupy: What Is Occupy?* New York: Time Books.

Schlesinger, Traci. 2011. "The Failure of Race-Neutral Policies: How Mandatory Terms and Sentencing Enhancements Increased Racial Disparities in Prison Admission Rates." *Crime & Delinquency* 57 (January):56–81. Published online 2008 (http://cad.sagepub.com/pap.dtl).

Schnaiberg, Allan. 1994. *Environment and Society: The Enduring Conflict.* New York: St. Martin's Press.

Schneider, Friedrich. 2010. "Dues and Don'ts." *The Economist* (August 14):62.

Schulman, Gary I. 1974. "Race, Sex, and Violence: A Laboratory Test of the Sexual Threat of the Black Male Hypothesis." *American Journal of Sociology* 79 (March):1260–1272.

Schur, Edwin M. 1965. *Crimes without Victims: Deviant Behavior and Public Policy.* Englewood Cliffs, NJ: Prentice Hall.

——. 1968. *Law and Society: A Sociological View.* New York: Random House.

——. 1985. "'Crimes without Victims': A 20 Year Reassessment." Paper presented at the annual meeting of the Society for the Study of Social Problems.

Schwartz, Shalom H., and Anat Bardi. 2001. "Value Hierarchies Cultures: Taking a Similarities Perspective." *Journal of Cross-Cultural Perspective* 32 (May):268–290.

Scott, Alan. 1990. *Ideology and the New Social Movements.* London: Unwin Hyman.

Scott, Gregory. 2001. "Broken Windows behind Bars: Eradicating Prison Gangs through Ecological Hardening and Symbolic Cleansing." *Corrections Management Quarterly* 5 (Winter):23–36.

Scott, W. Richard, and Gerald F. Davis. 2007. *Organizations and Organizing: Rational, Natural and Open Systems Perspectives.* New York: Pearson.

Seidman, Steven. 2002. *Beyond the Closet: The Transformation of Gay and Lesbian Life.* New York: Routledge.

Sedgwick, Eve Kosofsky. 1990. *Epistemology of the Closet.* Berkeley: University of California Press.

Sernau, Scott. 2001. *Worlds Apart: Social Inequalities in a New Century.* Thousand Oaks, CA: Pine Forge Press.

Shapley, Dan. 2010. "So How Big Was the BP Oil Spill?" *The Daily Green,* May 28. Accessed August 2 (www.thedailygreen.com).

Shaw, Claude, and Henry D. McKay. 1942. *Juvenile Delinquency and Urban Areas.* Chicago: University of Chicago Press.

Shea, Andrea. 2013. "Facebook Envy: How the Social Work Affects Our Self-Esteem." February 20. Accessible at www.wbur.org.

Sherman, Arloc. 2007. *Income Inequality Hits Record Levels, New CBO Data Show.* Washington, DC: Center on Budget and Policy Priorities.

Short, Kathleen. 2015. *The Research Supplemental: Poverty Measure 2014.* Current Population Reports. P60–254. Washington, DC: U.S. Government Printing Office.

Shuttleworth, Jay. 2015. "Teaching the Social Issues of a Sustainable Food Supply." *The Social Studies* 106 (4):159–169.

Sjoberg, Gideon. 1960. *The Preindustrial City: Past and Present.* Glencoe, IL: Free Press.

Slavin, Barbara. 2007. "Child Marriage Rife in Nations Getting U.S. Aid." *USA Today,* July 17, p. 6A.

Sloan, Allan. 2009. "What's Still Wrong with Wall Street." *Time,* November 9, pp. 24–29.

Slug-Lines.com. 2011. "What's New." Accessed November 10 (www.slug -lines.com).

Smelser, Neil. 1963. *The Sociology of Economic Life.* Englewood Cliffs, NJ: Prentice Hall.

Smith, Craig S. 2006. "Romania's Orphans Face Widespread Abuse, Group Says." *New York Times,* May 10, p. A3.

Smith, David A. 1995. "The New Urban Sociology Meets the Old: Rereading Some Classical Human Ecology." *Urban Affairs Review* 20 (January):432–457.

——, and Michael Timberlake. 1993. "World Cities: A Political Economy/ Global Network Approach." Pp. 181–207 in *Urban Sociology in Transition,* edited by Ray Hutchison. Greenwich, CT: JAI Press.

Smith, Michael Peter. 1988. *City, State, and Market.* New York: Basil Blackwell.

Smith, Stacy L., Marc Choueiti, Katherine Pieper, Traci Gillig, Carmen Lee, and Dylan DeLuca. 2015. *Inequality in 700 Popular Films: Examining Portrayals of Gender, Race, and LGBT Status from 2007 to 2014.* University of Southern California: Annenberg Center.

Smith, Tom W. 2009. *Religious Change around the World.* Chicago: NORC/ University of Chicago.

Sorokin, Pitirim A. [1927] 1959. *Social and Cultural Mobility.* Reprint, New York: Free Press.

Spalter-Roth, Roberta, Nicole Van Vooren, and Mary S. Senter. 2013. "Using the Bachelor's and Beyond Project to Help Launch Students in Careers." Accessible at www.asanet.org.

Spitzer, Steven. 1975. "Toward a Marxian Theory of Deviance." *Social Problems* 22 (June):641–651.

Squires, Gregory D., ed. 2002. *Urban Sprawl: Causes, Consequences and Policy Responses.* Washington, DC: Urban Institute.

Stablen, Timothy, Joseph Lorenzo Hall, Chauna Pervis, and Denise L. Anthony. 2015. "Negotiating Stigma in Health Care: Disclosure and the Role of Electronic Health Records." *Health Sociology Review* 24 (Issue 3).

Steinhardt Social Research Institute. 2016. *American Jewish Population Project.* Accessible at http://ajpp.brandeis.edu/publications.php#section3.

Stokes, Bruce, Richard Wilke, and Jill Carle. 2015. "Global Concern about Climate Change, Broad Support for Limiting Emissions: U.S., China Less Worried; Partisan Divides in Key Countries." December 5. Accessible at www. pewglobal.com.

Stone, Zara. 2016. "What's Behind the Hidden Meanings Behind Mark Zuckerberg's T-shirts?" *Forbes* (July 26). Accessible at www.forbes.com.

Sugimoto, Yoshio. 1997. *An Introduction to Japanese Society.* Cambridge, UK: Cambridge University Press.

Sullivan, Harry Stack. [1953] 1968. *The Interpersonal Theory of Psychiatry.* Edited by Helen Swick Perry and Mary Ladd Gawel. Reprint, New York: W.W. Norton.

Sullivan, Kevin. 2006. "Bridging the Digital Divide." *Washington Post National Weekly Edition* 25 (July 17):11–12.

Sumner, William G. 1906. *Folkways.* New York: Ginn.

Sutch, Richard, and Susan B. Carter. 2006. *Historical Statutes of the U.S.: Earliest Time to the Present.* Cambridge, UK: Cambridge University Press.

Sutherland, Anna. 2015. "What's Behind the Reversal of the Gender Gap in Higher Education?" October 12. Accessible at www.family-studies.org.

Sutherland, Edwin H. 1937. *The Professional Thief.* Chicago: University of Chicago Press.

——. 1940. "White-Collar Criminality." *American Sociological Review* 5 (February):1–11.

——. 1949. *White Collar Crime.* New York: Dryden.

——. 1983. *White Collar Crime: The Uncut Version.* New Haven, CT: Yale University Press.

——, Donald R. Cressey, and David F. Luckenbill. 1992. *Principles of Criminology.* 11th ed. New York: Rowman and Littlefield.

Swartz, Jon, and Charisse Jones. 2017. "Sometime in the 23rd Century." *USA Today* (March 16): 1B, 2B.

Swatos, William H., Jr., ed. 1998. *Encyclopedia of Religion and Society.* Lanham, MD: Alta Mira.

Swidler, Ann. 1986. "Culture in Action: Symbols and Strategies." *American Sociological Review* 51 (April):273–286.

Szasz, Thomas S. 2010. *The Myth of Mental Illness: Foundations of a Theory of Personal Conduct.* New York: HarperCollins.

Tannen, Deborah. 1990. *You Just Don't Understand: Women and Men in Conversation.* New York: Ballantine.

Taylor, Verta. Leila J. Rupp, and Nancy Whittier. 2009. *Feminist Frontiers.* 8th ed. New York: McGraw-Hill.

The Week. 2014. "A New Way of Doing Business." September 4:11.

Thomas, Gordon, and Max Morgan Witts. 1974. *Voyage of the Damned.* Greenwich, CT: Fawcett Crest.

Thomas, William I. 1923. *The Unadjusted Girl.* Boston: Little, Brown.

Tierney, John. 1990. "Betting the Planet." *New York Times Magazine,* December 2, pp. 52–53, 71, 74, 76, 78, 80–81.

Tilly, Charles. 1993. *Popular Contention in Great Britain 1758–1834.* Cambridge, MA: Harvard University Press.

———. 2004. *Social Movements, 1768–2004.* Boulder, CO: Paradigm.

Toossi, Mitra. 2009. "Employment Outlook: 2008–2018." *Monthly Labor Review* (November):30–51.

Tonry, Michael (ed.). 2014. "Why Crime Rates Fall and Why They Don't." Special Issue of *Crime and Justice* 43 (No.1).

Touraine, Alain. 1974. *The Academic System in American Society.* New York: McGraw-Hill.

Transactional Records Access Clearinghouse. 2015. "Justice Department Data Reveal 29 Percent Drop in Criminal Prosecutions of Corporations." October 13. Accessible at www.trac.syr.edu.

Trimble, Lindsey B., and Julie A. Kmec. 2011. "The Role of Social Networks in Getting a Job." *Sociology Compass* 5 (No. 2):165–178.

Truman, Jennifer L. 2011. "Criminal Victimization Survey." *Bureau of Justice Statistics Bulletin* (September).

Truman, Jennifer L., and Lynn Langton. 2015. *Criminal Victimization, 2014.* August, revised September. Accessible at bjs.gov.

Tuchman, Gaye. 1992. "Feminist Theory." Pp. 695–704 in *Encyclopedia of Sociology,* vol. 2, edited by Edgar F. Borgatta and Marie L. Borgatta. New York: Macmillan.

Tucker, Robert C., ed. 1978. *The Marx-Engels Reader.* 2nd ed. New York: W.W. Norton.

Turkle, Sherry. 2004. "How Computers Change the Way We Think." *Chronicle of Higher Education* 50 (January 30):B26–B28.

Tönnies, Ferdinand. [1887] 1988. *Community and Society.* Reprint, Rutgers, NJ: Transaction.

UN Office for the Coordination of Humanitarian Affairs. 2006. "In-Depth: Running Dry: The Humanitarian Impact of the Global Water Crisis." Accessed May 27, 2012 (www.irinnews.org/InDepthMain.aspx?InDepthId=13&ReportId=60537).

UNICEF. 2011. "At a Glance: Niger." Accessed May 27, 2012 (www.unicef.org/infobycountry/niger_57677.html).

United Nations High Commission on Refugees. 2015. "Figures at a Glance." Accessible at www.unchr.org.

United Nations Office on Drugs and Crime. 2012. *The Globalization of Crime: A Transnational Organized Crime Threat Assessment.* New York: UNODO.

United Nations Office on Drugs and Crime. 2015b. *Crime and Criminal Justice Statistics.* Accessible at unodc.org.

United Nations Population Division. 2004b. "Population Division Homepage: World Percentage Urban." Accessed October 4 (http://esa.un.org/unpp/p2kOdata.asp).

van den Berghe, Pierre. 1978. *Race and Racism: A Comparative Perspective.* 2nd ed. New York: Wiley.

Van Gennep, Arnold. [1909] 1960. *The Rites of Passage.* Translated by Monika B. Vizedom and Gabrielle L. Caffee. Reprint, Chicago: University of Chicago Press.

Vaughan, R. M. 2007. "Cairo's Man Show." *Utne Reader* (March/April):94–95.

Veblen, Thorstein. [1899] 1964. *Theory of the Leisure Class.* Reprint, New York: Macmillan. New York: Penguin.

Venkatesh, Sudhir Alladi. 2006. *Off the Books: The Underground Economy of the Urban Poor.* Cambridge, MA: Harvard University Press.

Volti, Rudi. 2010. *Society and Technological Change.* 6th ed. New York: Worth.

Walder, Andrew G, and Giang Hoang Nguyen. 2008. "Ownership, Organization, and Income Inequality: Market Transition in Rural Vietnam." *American Sociological Review* 73 (April):251–269.

Walker, Edward. 2010. "Activism Industry-Driven." *Contexts* (Spring):43–49.

Wallace, Ruth A., and Alison Wolf. 1980. *Contemporary Sociological Theory.* Englewood Cliffs, NJ: Prentice Hall.

Wallerstein, Immanuel. 1974. *The Modern World System.* New York: Academic Press.

——. 1979a. *Capitalist World Economy.* Cambridge, UK: Cambridge University Press.

——. 1979b. *The End of the World as We Know It: Social Science for the Twenty-First Century.* Minneapolis: University of Minnesota Press.

——. 2000. *The Essential Wallerstein.* New York: New Press.

——. 2004. *World-Systems Analysis: An Introduction.* Durham, NC: Duke University Press.

——. 2012. "Reflections on an Intellectual Adventure." *Contemporary Sociology* 41 (1):6–12.

Wallis, Claudia. 2008. "How to Make Great Teachers." *Time* 171 (February 25):28–34.

Walsh, Anthony. 2000. "Behavior Genetics and Anomie/Strain Theory." *Criminology* (November):1075–1107.

Weatherall, Ann. 2015. "Sexism in Language and Talk-in-Interaction." *Journal of Language and Social Psychology* 34(4).

Weber, Max. [1913–1922] 1947. *The Theory of Social and Economic Organization.* Translated by A. Henderson and T. Parsons. Reprint New York: Free Press.

———. [1904] 2009. *The Protestant Ethic and the Spirit of Capitalism.* 4th ed. Translation by Stephen Kalberg. Reprint New York: Oxford University Press.

Weeks, John R. 2012. *Population: An Introduction to Concepts and Issues.* 11th ed. Belmont, CA: Cengage.

Weinberg, Daniel H. 2004. *Evidence from Census 2000 About Earnings by Detailed Occupation for Men and Women.* CENSR-15. Washington, DC: U.S. Government Printing Office.

———. 2007. "Earnings by Gender: Evidence from Census 2000." *Monthly Labor Review* (July/August):26–34.

Wells-Barnett, Ida B. 1970. *Crusade for Justice: The Autobiography of Ida B. Wells.* Edited by Alfreda M. Duster. Chicago: University of Chicago Press.

Wentling, Tre, Elroi Windsor, Kristin Schilt, and Betsy Lucal. 2008. "Teaching Transgender." *Teaching Sociology* 36 (January):49–57.

West, Candace, and Don H. Zimmerman. 1987. "Doing Gender." *Gender and Society* 1 (June):125–151.

White, Gillian. 2015. "In the Sharing Economy, No One's an Employee." *The Atlantic.* June 15. Accessible at www.theatlantic.com.

White House. 2012. "Remarks by the President on the Nomination of Dr. Jim Kim for World Bank President." March 23. Accessible at www.whitehouse.gov/photos-and-video/video/2012/03/23/president -obama-nominated-jim-yong-kim-world-bank-president#transcript.

Whyte, William Foote. 1981. *Street Corner Society: Social Structure of an Italian Slum.* 3rd ed. Chicago: University of Chicago Press.

WIEGO. 2016. "About the Informal Economy." Women in Informal Employment: Globalizing and Organizing. Accessed February 26 (www.wiego.org).

Wilford, John Noble. 1997. "New Clues Show Where People Made the Great Leap to Agriculture." *New York Times,* November 18, pp. B9, B12.

Wilson, Edward O. 1975. *Sociobiology: The New Synthesis.* Cambridge, MA: Harvard University Press.

———. 1978. *On Human Nature.* Cambridge, MA: Harvard University Press.

———. 2000. *Sociobiology: The New Synthesis.* Cambridge, MA: Belknap Press, Harvard University Press.

Wilson, John. 1973. *Introduction to Social Movements.* New York: Basic Books.

Wilson, William J. 1996. *When Work Disappears: The World of the New Urban Poor.* New York: Knopf.

———. 1999. *The Bridge over the Racial Divide: Rising Inequality and Coalition Politics.* Berkeley: University of California Press.

Wimer, Christopher, Barbara Bergmann, David Betson, John Coder, and David B. Grusky. 2011. "The Future of U.S. Poverty Measurement." *Pathways* (Fall):20–25.

Winter, J. Allen. 2008. "Symbolic Ethnicity." Pp. 1288–1290, vol. 3, in *Encyclopedia of Race, Ethnicity, and Society,* edited by Richard T. Schaefer. Thousand Oaks, CA: Sage.

Wirth, Louis. 1928. *The Ghetto.* Chicago: University of Chicago Press.

———. 1931. "Clinical Sociology." *American Journal of Sociology* 37 (July):49-60.

———. 1938. "Urbanism as a Way of Life." *American Journal of Sociology* 44 (July):1-24.

Wolf, Naomi. 1992. *The Beauty Myth: How Images of Beauty Are Used Against Women.* New York: Anchor.

World Bank. 2007. *World Development Indicators 2007.* Washington, DC: World Bank.

———. 2009. "Biotechnology (GM Foods)." Accessed May 11 (www.who.int/foodsafety/biotech/en/).

——— 2010b. *World Development Report 2010: Development and Climate Change.* Washington, DC: World Bank.

———. 2010. "Suicide Prevention." Accessed July 10 (www.who.int/mental_health/prevention/en/).

World Bank 2015c. *World Bank Indicators 2015.* Accessible at www.world-bank.org.

World Bank. 2017. *Databank World Development Indicators.* Accessible at www.databank.worldbank.com.

World Bank Group. 2016. *Migration and Remittance Factbook 2016.* 3rd ed. Washington, DC: World Bank Group.

World Bank. 2016. "Education." Accessed February 25 (www.worldbank .org).

World Health Organization Media Centre. 2014. "Children: Reducing Mortality." Fact Sheet 178. Updated September 2014. Accessible at www .who.int.

Wortham, Robert A. 2008. "DuBois, William Edward Burghardt." Pp. 423-427, vol. 1, in *Encyclopedia of Race, Ethnicity, and Society,* edited by Richard T. Schaefer. Thousand Oaks, CA: Sage.

Wray, Matt, Matthew Miller, Jill Gurvey, Joanna Carroll, and Ichiro Kawachi. 2008. "Leaving Las Vegas: Exposure to Las Vegas and Risk of Suicide." *Social Science and Medicine* 67:1882-1888.

———, Cynthia Colen, and Bernice Pescosolido. 2011. "The Sociology of Suicide." *Annual Review of Sociology* 37:505-528.

Wright, Erik Olin O. 2011. "The Classical Marxist Theory of the History of Capitalism's Future." October 3. Accessed January 20, 2012 (www.ssc .wisc.edu/~wright/621-2011/lecture%208%202011%20-%20Classical%20 Theory%20of%20Capitalisms%20future.pdf).

———, David Hachen, Cynthia Costello, and Joy Sprague. 1982. "The American Class Structure." *American Sociological Review* 47 (December):709-726.

Yamagata, Hisashi, Kuang S. Yeh, Shelby Stewman, and Hiroko Dodge. 1997. "Sex Segregation and Glass Ceilings: A Comparative Statistics Model of Women's Career Opportunities in the Federal Government over a Quarter Century." *American Journal of Sociology* 103 (November):566-632.

Zeitzen, Miriam Koktvedgaard. 2008. *Polygamy: A Cross-Cultural Analysis.* Oxford, UK: Berg.

Zellner, William M. 1995. *Counter Cultures: A Sociological Analysis.* New York: St. Martin's Press.

Zimbardo, Philip G. 2007. "Revisiting the Stanford Prison Experiment: A Lesson in the Power of the Situation." *Chronicle of Higher Education* 53 (March 20):B6, B7.

———. 2015. "Philip Zimbardo Thinks We All Can Be Evil." Interview by Jon Ronson. *New York Times Magazine* (July 19), 58.

———, Robert L. Johnson, and Vivian McCann. 2009. *Psychology: Core Concepts.* 6th ed. Boston: Allyn and Bacon.

Zittrain, Jonathan, and John Palfrey. 2008. "Reluctant Gatekeepers: Corporate Ethics on a Filtered Internet." Pp. 103–122 in *Access Denied,* edited by Ronald Deibert, John Palfrey, Rafal Rohozinski, and Jonathan Zittrain. Cambridge, MA: MIT Press.

Zweigenhaft, Richard L., and G. William Domhoff. 2006. *Diversity in the Power Elite: How It Happened, Why It Matters.* 3rd ed. New York: Rowman and Littlefield.

Index

Note: The letters 't' and 'f' followed by the numbers indicate 'tables' and 'figures' respectively.